Refugees and Rescue

Refugees and Rescue

THE DIARIES AND PAPERS of
James G. McDonald
1935–1945

EDITED BY

Richard Breitman,
Barbara McDonald Stewart,
and Severin Hochberg

INDIANA UNIVERSITY PRESS
BLOOMINGTON AND INDIANAPOLIS

PUBLISHED IN ASSOCIATION WITH THE
UNITED STATES HOLOCAUST MEMORIAL MUSEUM
WASHINGTON, D.C.

This book is a publication of

Indiana University Press
601 North Morton Street
Bloomington, IN 47404-3797 USA

http://iupress.indiana.edu

Telephone orders   800-842-6796
Fax orders   812-855-7931
Orders by e-mail   iuporder@indiana.edu

The paper used in this publication meets the minimum requirements of American National Standard for Information Sciences—Permanence of Paper for Printed Library Materials, ANSI Z39.48-1984.

Manufactured in the United States of America

Library of Congress Cataloging-in-Publication Data

McDonald, James G. (James Grover), 1886–1964.
    Refugees and rescue : the diaries and papers of James G. McDonald, 1935–1945 / edited by Richard Breitman, Barbara McDonald Stewart, and Severin Hochberg.
        p. cm.
    Continues: Advocate for the doomed, the diaries and papers of James G. McDonald, 1932–1935.
    Includes bibliographical references and index.
    ISBN 978-0-253-35307-8 (cloth : alk. paper)   1. McDonald, James G. (James Grover), 1886–1964—Diaries.   2. Diplomats—United States—Diaries.   3. High Commission for Refugees (Jewish and Other) Coming from Germany—Biography.   4. World War, 1939–1945—Refugees—Sources.   5. Germany—History—1933–1945—Sources.   6. National socialism—Germany—History—20th century—Sources.   7. Antisemitism—History—20th century—Sources
I. Breitman, Richard, date   II. Stewart, Barbara McDonald, date
III. Hochberg, Severin.   IV. McDonald, James G. (James Grover), 1886–1964. Advocate for the doomed.   V. Title.
    E748.M1475A3 2009
    940.540092—dc22

                                                2008037080

1 2 3 4 5 14 13 12 11 10 09

To Walter Laqueur

CONTENTS

ACKNOWLEDGMENTS

Even with three active co-editors, a project this big and this complicated needed the assistance of many other brains, hands, and eyes. None of those who helped us is responsible for errors or remaining difficulties, but they certainly deserve much of the credit for the positive elements.

Stephen Mize made this diary materialize in potentially publishable form. Having tracked down its component parts and, just as important, brought the McDonald families into the effort, he did not relinquish his role. He served as an essential member of our research group, showing discernment about what would or would not work well. He also took particular responsibility for photographs. We could not have managed without him. Benton Arnovitz, director of Academic Publications at the United States Holocaust Memorial Museum (hereafter USHMM), steered this effort from the stage of idea all the way to publication, offering judicious advice, nuggets from his experience, and occasional editing along the way. Janet Rabinowitch at Indiana University Press expressed enthusiasm for this volume from the beginning.

Janet McDonald Barrett, Vail Barrett, Halsey V. Barrett, and Patricia Sugrue Ketchum provided invaluable information resolving many historical mysteries culminating in the donation of the McDonald diaries and papers to the USHMM.

Sara Bloomfield, director of the USHMM, had the vision to see the importance of James G. McDonald to the USHMM, and she made these documents a museum priority. Paul Shapiro, director of the Center for Advanced Holocaust Studies, arranged for resources for this project and gave us valuable advice. Amanda Rothey and Anne Rush each served as research assistants for a time and helped us immeasurably.

We received excellent cooperation from L. Rebecca Johnson Melvin, librarian at the University of Delaware (Special Collections); from Director Cynthia Koch, Robert Clark, and Robert Parks at the Franklin D. Roosevelt Presidential Library; from the director and staff of the Houghton Library, Harvard University; from Mary Osielski at the M. E. Grenander Department of Special Collections and Archives at SUNY Albany; from Rabbi Moshe Kolodny, archivist at the Agudath Israel Archives; from Misha Mitsel and Sherry Hyman, at the American Jewish Joint Distribution Committee Archives; from Miriam Intrator at the Leo Baeck Institute (New York); from Director Carl Rheins and archivist Gunnar Berg at the YIVO Institute for Jewish Research; from Judith Cohen at the photo archives of the USHMM; from Vincent Slatt, Ron Coleman, and Mark Ziomek at the library of the USHMM; from Michlean Amir, archivist at the USHMM; and from Jeffrey M. Flannery at the Library of Congress Manuscript Division.

Allan J. Lichtman and Paul Vincent read the entire manuscript and made valuable suggestions for sharpening the focus. Max Paul Friedman passed along useful sources drawn from his own research about Latin America and helped us check proofs. David Bankier helped us obtain some sources in Israel. William S. Levine again generously supported the work that went into this volume, as he had done with *Advocate for the Doomed*. We could not have managed this work in reasonable time without his assistance.

Refugees and Rescue

Introduction

In January 1931 James G. McDonald wrote in his diary:
[Henry] Ford entertained me with some interpretations of world events.
He said, "Do you know, Mr. McDonald, that the world war was caused simply
by the desire of the Jews to get control of everything in Germany?" He said the
situation was quite clear. The same way it is perfectly certain that the Bolshevik
revolution was carried through by the Jews. "I have the documents to prove it.
A Russian made a special investigation for me and gave me the documents,
including photographs of people shot, bullets, etc. The evidence is overwhelming. I have it in my vault. The man who gave me the material, to whom I paid
$10,000 for it, said, 'This has cost me much more than that, but I wanted to
put it in your hands.'"[1]

Like other members of the American establishment in the 1930s, Ford spoke
frankly to McDonald.[2] The premier American carmaker revealed to McDonald some of the entrenched prejudices he soon faced in seeking humanitarian
responses across Europe and parts of South America, as well as in the United
States, to Nazi Germany's persecution of Jews.

Readers of the predecessor to this volume, *Advocate for the Doomed: The
Diaries and Papers of James G. McDonald, 1932–1935*, will find many other continuing themes and threads here. From the time he went to Germany in the
spring of 1933 and met privately with Adolf Hitler, James G. McDonald had a
clear sense of impending catastrophe—and a conviction that once it came, it
would take in German Jews and others. His problem was getting others outside
Germany to share the urgency of his concern and to respond constructively. In
late 1935 and beyond, he was still trying.

This second volume of McDonald's diaries and papers can also stand alone
as a narrative and a new source on nearly a decade of Nazi persecution, Jewish
catastrophe, debates within the League of Nations and later within the American government, and rescue efforts ranging as far as Bolivia. It is a compelling,
mostly tragic story, centered around a Midwesterner who blended the qualities
of political insider and outsider.

1. See chapter 6, insert into entry of February 9, 1936, which includes the diary entry of
January 9, 1931.
2. Ford's comment is particularly interesting since it followed a public apology in 1927 for
the anti-Semitism of his publication the *Dearborn Independent*.

1

James Grover McDonald was born in 1886 in Coldwater, a small town in western Ohio, the third of five boys. He grew up in Albany, Indiana, where his parents ran a small hotel, maybe twenty rooms in all. After the oldest boy had gone to work as a telegraph operator and the next ones were ready for college, the whole family moved to Bloomington, Indiana, so that all of the boys could go to Indiana University, live at home, and work their way through school.

His father, Kenneth, had been born in Glengarry, Ontario, Canada, and had moved to the United States to find a job. Kenneth married a woman named Anna Diederick, born of immigrant German parents. Both of McDonald's parents were Catholic. Grover, as McDonald was called, courted Ruth Stafford, who also grew up in Albany in a strict Methodist family. Grover went to Indiana University, Ruth to Depauw College. After a long engagement the two married in 1915.

Grover had studied history and political science. His academic work, first at Indiana, then at Harvard, had landed him teaching positions along the way, ending with one at Indiana, but he had yet to write his dissertation. In the middle of World War I he and his wife went to Spain to study an obscure sect of Spanish monks. He later explained that he never finished his Ph.D. because he came to realize that no one, including himself, was interested in those friars.

In 1917 a baby daughter, Janet, arrived. The budget at Indiana was tight; Grover could not get a raise, so he accepted a job with the National Civil Service Reform League in New York, taking leave of absence from the university. In January 1919 he was named chairman of the League of Free Nations Association, which campaigned heavily and unsuccessfully for the United States to join the League of Nations, championed by President Wilson to secure the peace. Afterward, McDonald's organization became known as the Foreign Policy Association. Grover stayed as president and chairman until 1933, when he resigned to become High Commissioner for Refugees.

During his years at the Foreign Policy Association, McDonald developed the habit of recording daily activities in a diary, by dictating to a secretary or stenographer and then checking the typed text. Once he involved himself in the campaign to help victims of Nazi persecution, first independently and then as League High Commissioner, his diary entries became more and more detailed—and revealing. After he resigned as League High Commissioner, his diary entries trailed off. Following a respite in early 1936 McDonald took on a new and demanding job on the editorial staff of the *New York Times*, where he had neither a driving purpose nor the secretarial support for the diary-keeping he had done earlier. (He dictated readily but wrote slowly.)

Later, as a member of the Anglo-American Committee of Inquiry on Palestine, as American special envoy to Israel, and as the first American ambassador there, he resumed the habit of keeping a very detailed, day-to-day account that again offers a personal tour through momentous post–World War II events in which he participated. These diary entries will form the third volume in this series published by Indiana University Press in association with the United States Holocaust Memorial Museum.

This current volume covers a critical period in McDonald's humanitarian activities. To that end, McDonald tried to extract whatever remaining utility he could from his own position as High Commissioner for Refugees from Germany under the League of Nations. In an effort to demonstrate what the Nazi regime was like and in the hope of awakening consciences outside Germany, at the end of December 1935 he resigned in protest as High Commissioner, eliciting headlines in the United States and in parts of Europe. He also tried to get the League itself to take more direct responsibility for the condition of Jews in Germany. His diary entries show intricate diplomatic maneuvers at Geneva, important in what they reveal about European attitudes toward Jewish problems and toward the growing diplomatic crisis regarding Nazi Germany.

In March 1938 President Roosevelt decided, in response to the Nazi takeover of Austria, to launch an international refugee initiative. McDonald was an obvious source of information and expertise. Even though he had taken a new position as president of the Brooklyn Academy of Arts and Sciences, McDonald could not resist the opportunity to resume efforts on behalf of refugees from a new American vantage point. In the spring of 1938 he became chairman of President Roosevelt's Advisory Committee on Political Refugees, a position that gave him some influence on American refugee policy and some involvement in international negotiations too. Despite other professional obligations, he attended frequent meetings and took a stand on important controversies related to the pre-history and history of the Holocaust. He did not resume his diary, however, so we lack his day-to-day perspectives.

We have done our best to fill the gap by composing additional "substitute diary" chapters from other sources to fill the ten-year hole in the diaries. We do not mean "compose" in the sense of inventing, through our experience and imagination, how McDonald might have thought and written. Rather, we followed standard historical procedure by drawing upon McDonald's papers at Columbia University, government records, and a wide range of other private, mostly unpublished, collections to narrate his activities in their political context over the period until the end of World War II.

The first six chapters of this volume contain the last segment of McDonald's prewar diary. The last portion of chapter 6 and chapters 7 through 12 contain material written by McDonald, material written by others about McDonald, material written by other contemporaries about refugee policies, the political climate, the war, and the Holocaust, and, *in italics*, historical background, analysis, and comments inserted by the editors to stitch various sources together. All selections except the editors' comments in italics stem from the years 1936–1945: they are what the historian calls primary sources. They have the immediacy of firsthand observations written in the maelstrom of events.

We have continued our practice of providing in footnotes brief biographical information about the many individuals whom McDonald encountered, or who were engaged in related activities, in these years. For those persons whom we had identified at length in *Advocate for the Doomed,* we have kept our notes as brief as possible.

McDonald's earlier experiences conditioned his reactions to events in Europe and in the United States. They drove him to try to convince others of the urgency of the situation in Europe and of the need to extract as many as possible of those who were endangered. Some whom McDonald had contacted and inspired earlier carried on independently during this period; in chapter 11 we have devoted substantial attention to one such person, Mauricio Hochschild, whose activities are not widely known.

Advocate for the Doomed contained new information about the early history of Nazi Germany. This volume adds more such information for 1935 and 1936, but we have not tried to recapitulate basic events in Germany or German-controlled territories during the war and the Holocaust. The literature on the Holocaust is vast, and much of it is of high quality.[3] Many features of these terrible events are now well known to readers. We have drawn from documents or secondary sources—and added editorial analysis—where they illuminated events McDonald followed closely or with which he was directly involved.

America's response to escalating Nazi persecution and mass murder was McDonald's major focus during the years 1938–1945. Both in the realm of popular literature and scholarly works, interpretations of America's response to the Holocaust clash harshly. Scholars have described Franklin Roosevelt as everything from the savior of the Jews to one of the villains of the Holocaust. It should not come as a shock, given our previous works, that we believe the truth to be somewhere in between. By focusing on McDonald, we believe we have found some fundamentally new information about the president's views and policies before and during the Holocaust—and also about why American policies were so uneven and inconsistent.

Drawing on primary sources, we have here tried to show something of FDR's activities in refugee policy, adjudicating disputes between McDonald's advisory committee and the State Department. In this way readers can see a significant portion of the evidence in the political and bureaucratic context of the time and can use it to draw their own conclusions. They will not have to rely on our assertions.

The picture of Franklin Roosevelt that emerges is of a man who gave considerable attention to refugee problems, but who publicly shied away from seeming to champion a Jewish cause, even when he took positive steps in 1938–1939. And his willingness to take action varied sharply according to po-

---

3. The latest general treatment of the Holocaust, as of this writing, is Saul Friedländer's excellent work, *Nazi Germany and the Jews,* vol. II, *The Years of Extermination* (New York: Harper-Collins, 2007).

litical and military circumstances. Just before the Holocaust and during its first two years he was far more concerned about threats to American security than about humanitarian efforts.

We have tried, where possible, to give a little of the broader context of prewar diplomacy, American politics, and the war, as they appeared to government officials, McDonald, and his associates. Otherwise, readers cannot fathom the climate and constraints affecting refugee policy, and more generally, American reactions to the Holocaust. Government decisions about immigration and refugee problems were not made in isolation.

This volume starts, however, in Europe. In August and again in September 1935 McDonald traveled to Nazi Germany. (His September visit was his last.) All of his sources told him that the situation of German Jews was deteriorating. In retrospect, we know that, at that time, top officials of the regime were determined to segregate Jews from the rest of the German population and abetted local outbreaks of violence by SA members or other Nazi activists to help the process along.[4] McDonald did not stay long enough to witness very many individual incidents, but he certainly got the clear impression that emigration was the only option to save the lives of many German Jews. He wrote about it and, then and later, tried to do something about it. If the results were not nearly what he had hoped, they certainly made a difference for tens of thousands.

4. See Saul Friedländer, *Nazi Germany and the Jews: The Years of Persecution, 1933–1939* (New York: HarperCollins, 1997), 137–144, for a good description of the situation in Germany at the time.

1. From Germany to the Soviet Union: August 1935

August 1–17, 1935

In early August McDonald took a vacation in Austria and Italy. He then went to Lucerne, Switzerland, where the World Zionist Organization was about to have its biennial congress (August 20–September 14). Chaim Weizmann[1] was elected president at that meeting.

Lucerne, Sunday, August 18, 1935

On the way to lunch met Mrs. Stephen Wise,[2] who told me of her daughter being named as the first woman justice in New York City.[3]

Brodetsky[4] and I talked about the problems that were to come before the Zionist congress, the question of the Legislative Assembly, Trans-Jordan, and the executive. The latter evidently was the most important question.

Dinner with Laski[5] and his group.

Monday, August 19, 1935

Up to the Pilatus [mountain]. In the late afternoon conference with Miss Jaffe[6] of the JTA [Jewish Telegraphic Agency], and later, dinner with her. She was interesting about Jewish politics.

Tuesday, August 20, 1935

Long conference in the afternoon with Kreutzberger[7] and the young man who is to be his successor, Adler-Rudel.[8] They are particularly anxious that we

---

1. Russian-born British Zionist leader and a brilliant scientist. Later became the first president of Israel. Extensively treated in *Advocate for the Doomed*.

2. Louise Waterman Wise, wife of Rabbi Stephen S. Wise (president of the American Jewish Congress, extensively treated in *Advocate for the Doomed*), and a noted social worker.

3. Justine Wise Polier was appointed by Mayor LaGuardia to the Domestic Relations Court, where she served until 1973. She was instrumental in transforming the adoption and foster care systems in the United States.

4. Selig Brodetsky, president of the Zionist Federation of Great Britain.

5. Neville J. Laski, president of the Board of Deputies of British Jews.

6. Rebecca Jaffe became McDonald's secretary after he left the High Commission.

7. Max Kreutzberger, formerly a Jewish social worker and community leader in Berlin, head of the Reichsvertretung der deutschen Juden 1933–1935, the central body of German Jews.

8. Selig (Solomon) Adler-Rudel, originally a social worker and Jewish welfare official in Berlin. Became the administrator of the Central British Fund in 1935 and was prominent in rescue efforts during World War II.

should try to secure, or at any rate lay the basis for securing, permission from the Swedes and Norwegians for a certain amount of retraining there.[9]

Later we were joined by Otto Nathan,[10] when the discussion turned on the problem of transfers.[11] Nathan was completely pessimistic. He doubted the practicability of any suggestions made by the Germans. The basis for his doubt was primarily the unwillingness of the rest of the world to increase its purchases of German goods.

. . . .

Then with Rabbi Schulmann over to the Zionist congress. Chatted for a little while before with President Sokolow,[12] and was surprised at his extraordinary memory because he recalled our luncheon together several years previous. Chatted also with a number of other members of the executive. Apparently, Lipsky[13] and Rothenberg[14] are not nearly as important as certain other of the Zionist leaders outside of the United States.

The hall was crowded, and with the Klieg lights, which were almost blinding, the heat was excessive. Sokolow began by a brief speech in three languages, then called upon the British diplomatic representative from Bern, who made a wholly non-committal statement, then upon the representative of the Swiss authorities, who made a stirring speech of welcome in German, then they called upon me. I stuck closely to my text, though afterward I was somewhat sorry that I had not improvised a stirring peroration. However, perhaps it was just as well. But I did improvise a brief statement about Bentwich.[15] The talk was apparently well received.

Having spoken to Sokolow about the necessity of my leaving the next morning at 5:30, I slipped out at 10:30 and went back to the hotel.

Bad Kissingen, Wednesday, August 21, 1935

Called at 4:30, in order to take the 5:30 train for Zurich and from there on a fast train to Bad Kissingen. I was amused at the frontier to have my Swiss papers taken from me, and at the elaborate account which I gave of my supply

---

9. That is, retraining of young Jews into occupations (such as agriculture) in demand in potential countries of settlement.

10. Formerly a German economics professor. Close friend of Albert Einstein, and an old acquaintance of McDonald. Extensively treated in *Advocate for the Doomed.*

11. Transfer of blocked Jewish assets in Germany into some kind of asset that could be used by those able to emigrate. Germany's transfer agreement with the Jewish Agency for Palestine allowed German Jews emigrating to Palestine to extract some assets through increased German exports to Palestine. Proceeds from the sale of these goods were made available to the newcomers.

12. Nahum Sokolow, Polish-born president of the World Zionist Organization, 1931–1935.

13. Louis Lipsky, honorary president of the Zionist Organization of America, in 1935 president of the American Jewish Congress.

14. Judge Morris Rothenberg, on the board of the Zionist Organization of America and the United Palestine Appeal.

15. Norman Bentwich, McDonald's deputy at the League High Commission. Extensively treated in *Advocate for the Doomed.*

of money. Deliberately I refrained from using my *laisser passer*, because I wished to see what the frontier regulations are.

I soon knew that I was in Germany by the *Heil Hitler* salutations of the persons entering or leaving the carriage. At Stuttgart I bought a copy of the *Stürmer*.[16] More than ever before I was shocked by the use being made in that paper of children. Letters allegedly from youngsters of nine or ten were attacking and urging the extirpation of the Jews.

Reached Bad Kissingen in time for tea. My friends [Mr. and Mrs. Max Warburg[17]] seemed genuinely glad to see me. There was no sign on their part of the concern which I was told in Geneva they might feel at my visiting them there. After tea, while Madame played golf, Max and I walked in the woods. His estimate of ICA[18] and of Louis Oungre[19] and Sir Osmond[20] is identical with mine. But he hopes that perhaps through the association of K[21] with Oungre a gradual change might be worked out. I said I thought it worthwhile, but I was skeptical.

He outlined to me the program of emigration of fifteen to twenty thousand younger Jews from Germany. He said that he estimates that there are 450,000 real Jews, 300,000 baptized Jews, and 750,000 or more who have a Jewish grandfather.[22] In addition to his work with the Jews, he has been active in a non-Jewish committee.

He was interested to hear of our plans for reorganization under the League[23] and offered, if necessary, to discuss the matter with von Bülow,[24] with whom he is very close. For years he has been the executor of the von Bülow estate. He also knows von Neurath[25] well. He offered, if I would write him a letter explaining the proposal, to take the matter up with the German authorities.

He told me of his close relations with Dr. Schacht.[26] He sees him frequently and talks with him frankly. Indeed, he has been called to another conference within a day or so. He sees Dr. Schacht's position as constantly endangered by

16. Vicious, semi-pornographic anti-Semitic newspaper run by Julius Streicher, Nazi Gauleiter (chief party official) of Franconia.

17. Senior partner in M. M. Warburg, Hamburg, highly visible member of the German-Jewish elite, extensively treated in *Advocate for the Doomed*. McDonald avoided writing their names because of uncertainty about whether this meeting might be dangerous for them.

18. Jewish Colonization Association, extensively treated in *Advocate for the Doomed*.

19. Head of the Jewish Colonization Association, extensively treated in *Advocate for the Doomed*.

20. Sir Osmond Elim d'Avigdor-Goldsmid, chairman of the Jewish Agency for Palestine in London and president of the Jewish Colonization Association.

21. Probably Bernhard Kahn, European chairman of the Joint Distribution Committee, one of the best-informed specialists on the continent.

22. The number of baptized Jews is undoubtedly inflated.

23. McDonald's impending resignation as High Commissioner for Refugees provoked much debate about the High Commissioner's future existence, functions, and relationship to the League of Nations.

24. Bernhard Wilhelm von Bülow, state secretary in the German Foreign Office.

25. Konstantin von Neurath, German foreign minister, although not a Nazi.

26. Hjalmar Schacht, economics minister and head of the Reichsbank. Extensively treated in *Advocate for the Doomed*.

the ceaseless antagonism of his bitter enemies, who are alert for an opportunity to destroy him.

On the transfer problem he remains pessimistic unless much larger sums than now appear to be available are to be provided outside.

He expressed disappointment and disgust with the American corporation and seemed even to feel strongly toward Felix Warburg[27] for the latter's offer of a mere $10,000 toward the Cyprus project,[28] when he had expected many times that. He said, "We no longer need American advice. They cannot know our problem from the outside. Only we know it. We need from them nothing but money. My brother is too aloof. He tries to do too many things. And he is tempted to be dogmatic with inadequate knowledge."

Conditions internally are steadily worse. The cold pogrom is intensified. For example, in Bad Kissingen the Jewish families do not go out at night. In many districts it is unsafe for grocers or druggists to sell to Jews. The forces making for isolation are stronger and stronger.

He drew from all of this, however, the philosophic consolation that this persecution has probably saved Judaism for another hundred years; prior to this Jews were weakening—in Russia tending toward anti-religion, in Poland toward extinction through poverty, in Germany being absorbed through assimilation, in America forgetting their heritage in their concern for wealth. He said he would be willing to talk with Hitler, and that Schacht might arrange this, but that he would never talk to Goebbels because the latter was, from any point of view, an unspeakable person.

We talked about the Peace Conference, Paris, 1919 and the role which he played there in influencing Keynes. He told me of his remark to the French finance minister that France's bankruptcy would follow that of Germany. In his view, beginning with that fatal treaty,[29] nothing had ever been done since in time.

Economic conditions in Germany are bad, and may become worse, but they will not overthrow the regime. Indeed, at the moment there is a certain degree of war prosperity there as elsewhere.

He expressed the keenest pleasure and deep interest in my proposed last will and testament. And as we walked to the train, he talked to me as if I had been a member of his own family.

The train was a little late leaving Bad Kissingen, and I thought for a moment that I was going to miss my connection, but I did not and reached Bamberg in time to get the sleeper for Berlin.

27. Max Warburg's brother. One of the most important American Jewish leaders in the twentieth century and one of McDonald's main supporters. Extensively treated in *Advocate for the Doomed*.
28. An attempt by ICA, backed by Felix Warburg, to revive a 1906–1928 effort to settle Jewish refugees in Cyprus.
29. The Treaty of Versailles.

Reached Berlin exactly on time, at 8:02. . . .

To the Embassy, where I talked to Mr. White,[30] the ambassador not yet having returned from his holidays. White had arranged for me to meet Dr. Mackeben in the office of Barandon,[31] who is still away on his holidays.

Long conference with Geist[32] at the hotel. He spoke of the regime as one of gangster brutality, becoming worse, with increasing predominance of Goebbels and Streicher. The Jews are being fed to the lions to distract attention from the economic situation.

Schacht is still in a strong position, but is always in danger. Supported by the Reichswehr on special issues, he can only count on that support in a vital crisis if he can show that the policy of the extremists would endanger the sources of supply of the army. Otherwise, the army prefers to remain non-political. Schacht's Königsberg speech[33] was a sop to foreign opinion, but looked both ways. In this Geist agreed with Max Warburg that there was no real solace for the Jews in Schacht's statement.

New legislation is imminent, but it is difficult to tell exactly what the provisions will be. Certainly, they will tend further to differentiate the Jews from the mass of Germans and to disadvantage them in new ways.

There is the gravest danger if Italy stubs its toe in Abyssinia, that there will be a move [by Germany] to seize Austria. The only safety lies in keeping Germany poor and isolated. The Reich's foreign policy is controlled by Hitler and Goebbels, not the Foreign Office, except in routine matters.

I was much amused to hear the story of the fall of Hanfstaengl[34] from favor with the Führer. It appears that the former has not seen the latter since the end of last year.

Together Geist and I went over to meet the consul general, Jenkins.[35] He did not impress me as a man from whom I could expect much.

---

30. John Campbell White, counselor of the American Embassy, 1933–1935.

31. Both Wilhelm Mackeben and Paul Barandon were mid-level officials in the German Foreign Office.

32. Raymond H. Geist, American consul in Berlin and one of McDonald's best sources there.

33. On August 18, 1935, Schacht gave a speech to try to rein in Nazi extremists such as the rabid anti-Semite Julius Streicher, whom he explicitly criticized. On the other hand, he declared that the Jews in Germany had to recognize that their influence had disappeared permanently.

34. Ernst "Putzi" Hanfstaengl, of mixed German and American descent, Hitler's foreign press secretary and one of the most colorful figures in Hitler's inner circle. Extensively treated in *Advocate for the Doomed.*

35. Douglas Jenkins, in the Berlin Consulate since 1934, previously in the Far East for eleven years. Ambassador William Dodd had just recommended him for promotion to counselor, with Geist serving as acting consul general. Dodd opposed the sending of a new man to the Embassy in the following terms: "I have no objection to real American jews [*sic*], but I think six or eight here now, and another coming who would be counted as of the race, might raise a question." Dodd to R. Walton Moore, August 5, 1935, Moore Papers, Franklin D. Roosevelt Library, Hyde Park, N.Y. Dodd's statistics were a fantasy.

Lunch with Louis Lochner.[36] He was full of illustrative stories. On the religious problem he told the tale of the archbishop of Münster insisting that if he were to be arrested, he must be taken in the full robes of his ecclesiastical office. Told also of the Protestant, Niemöller, who, famous as a submarine commander, had refused to accept orders in religion as he had refused to obey the order of his superior when commanded to turn over his submarine to the British.[37]

Illustrative of the development of hatred among the children, he told of the stoning of some poor Jewish children, who had been brought to the country from the city, by other children.

He said that Hanfstaengl had lost his position because, when charged by Goebbels in Hitler's presence with having earlier been one of the supporters of Lüdecke,[38] who was then threatening to publish an exposé of the regime unless he were paid $35,000, Hanfstaengl is said to have lost his temper and to have used words in the presence of the Führer which had never been forgiven.

Foreign affairs are only nominally handled by the Foreign Office. Goebbels and the Führer are really in control, but Ribbentrop[39] and Rosenberg[40] also play important parts.

The Reichswehr wishes to remain non-political and, therefore, interferes only when its own interests are directly concerned.

There is increasing criticism of the luxurious life of Joseph Goebbels. Recently at a meeting of the old members of the Party, he was making a speech to the effect that in this revolution the leaders did not seek to enrich themselves or to beautify their homes. One of his old companions had called out, "Well, Joe, you must not have been home lately." Indeed, Louis's wife, who had been at Goebbels's house, said that it was the most beautiful house in all Berlin and furnished with the most exquisite taste, with beautiful and expensive things. Apparently too, Goebbels's wife has been criticized recently openly in public for her display of jewels.

Louis L. said that he has had amusing experiences with the wife of Göring, when, in conversation with her, she would, in moments of forgetfulness, tell about her travels with him before their marriage.

36. Louis P. Lochner, representative of Associated Press in Berlin, the senior U.S. journalist there.

37. Martin Niemöller, conservative Lutheran pastor who helped to found the Confessing Church, opposed to the Nazification of the German Protestant churches and to Nazi racial doctrines. In August 1935 Niemöller gave a sermon in which he stressed Jewish responsibility for the killing of Jesus.

38. Kurt Lüdecke, an anti-Semite who had joined Hitler in 1922 and helped him develop foreign contacts. Broke with Hitler later, was arrested, fled to the United States. Wrote a book entitled *I Knew Hitler*.

39. Joachim von Ribbentrop, Nazi official, appointed German foreign minister in early 1938. At this time advised Hitler on foreign affairs. In 1936 appointed German ambassador to Britain.

40. Alfred Rosenberg, head of the foreign policy office of the Nazi Party. At the start of the Nazi regime it seemed as if he might become a major figure in foreign policy matters, but his star faded. During the war became Reich minister for the Occupied Eastern Territories.

Conference in the late afternoon with Mackeben. I outlined to him the proposed reorganization under the League. He said that they had heard of it from the ambassador in London, that they were studying the question, and in response to my suggestion, said that they would send an answer through the German consul in Geneva by the opening of the Assembly.

Then Mackeben, on his own initiative, went on to tell me that having just returned from Central America, where he had had experience with the difficulties created by the restrictions on the renewal of passports of refugees, he had urged a more liberal policy on his colleagues. They, in turn, had instructed him to prepare a memorandum to make easier the granting of these papers. He had done this and expected his memorandum to be accepted and to be circulated soon to German consular authorities throughout the world. He made clear, however, that his simplified and more generous procedure could not apply to refugees guilty of political activities.

I was interested to note on the desk of Mackeben, along with other papers dealing with the refugees, the Diefenbach article from the *Christian Science Monitor* based on my talk on the *Ile de France,* which was not at all meant for publication.

Dinner with Enderis.[41] He said that things were getting worse and worse. The Reichswehr attends to its own affairs, is so absorbed in its gigantic task of rearming that it does not bother much about other things, unless, as happened during the Ribbentrop negotiations in London, the army's interest is directly at stake.

New legislation is certain,[42] but still not clear just what form it will take. Perhaps it will be announced at Nuremberg.

Copenhagen, Friday, August 23, 1935

Early plane for Copenhagen. There was an amusing search at the customs at the Tempelhof [airport] for money. Again, I did not use my *laisser passer.*

It was a beautiful trip, and only about an hour and a half.

Arriving in Copenhagen, I went directly to the Legation and chatted with Mrs. Owen.[43] Realizing that I was then running short of money, I arranged through her to cash my personal check at the bank.

. . . Then over to the Foreign Office for a very satisfactory talk with [the foreign minister] Dr. Munch.[44] He said unqualifiedly that the Danes would support the Norwegian initiative. He wanted, however, to know whom we had in mind for the High Commissioner. . . . He thought the personality very important.

. . . .

41. Guido Enderis, *New York Times* bureau chief in Berlin.
42. Legislation on the status of Jews in Germany.
43. Ruth Bryan Owen, American minister to Denmark. First woman to be named chief American diplomat in a country.
44. Peter Rochegune Munch.

Dinner with Miss Berg in the famous Tivoli Garden. Took the 8:40 night train for Oslo. On the way to the station I was interested to note the sale of Nazi—or rather Danish National Socialist—papers in the street.

Oslo, Saturday, August 24, 1935

Surprising amount of red tape at the frontier. Reached Oslo late in the morning. Went directly to the Legation. The new minister, a Mr. Drexel[45] from Philadelphia, had not yet arrived, but many vans of furniture from the States were cluttering up the courtyard. This was another illustration of why diplomatic posts are not for persons of limited means.

Then over to the Foreign Office, where I had a conference of nearly an hour with the foreign minister, Dr. Koht,[46] and the expert, Skylstad.[47] We covered practically all of the phases of the problem of the proposed central League organization. During the course of the talk the foreign minister tended to doze off a little, but Skylstad was keenly alert throughout. They too, as had Munch, expressed great interest in the personality of the possible new High Commissioner. I left feeling that the matter would be competently prepared on the technical side.

In the later afternoon I took a trolley ride up to Frognerseter. The view from there was lovely. I remained for dinner, and after the sun had set, it felt as if one were in the real mountains, and yet I was only thirty minutes from the heart of the city.

Sunday, August 25, 1935

Up early. Long letter to the office, and then the morning train to Sweden. It was a long trip and not very interesting, arriving at Stockholm about nine o'clock. . . .

Stockholm, Monday, August 26, 1935

The morning spent in getting pictures and visas, and money. Had a longish talk with Steinhardt,[48] the American minister. He still insists, I think rather optimistically, on the relative imminent breakdown of the Reich because of the economic situation. He insists that Swedish opinion, which is undoubtedly very well informed on German matters, is more and more bearish. He thinks the break may be postponed two or three years, but that it is inevitable.

Then to see [Rickard] Sandler, the foreign minister. He was very cordial, promised support for the Norwegian initiative; he questioned whether

45. Actually, A. J. Drexel Biddle, Jr.
46. Halvdan Koht.
47. Rasmus Ingvald Berentson Skylstad.
48. Laurence A. Steinhardt, American minister to Sweden, 1933–1937. Subsequently ambassador to Peru, the Soviet Union, Turkey, and after World War II, Czechoslovakia, and Canada. One of the few Jews among American career diplomats. Played an important role in 1940 attacking the President's Advisory Committee on Political Refugees. See chapter 9.

Germany might not object. He thought that he had gotten that impression from the Dutch. . . .

Beautiful flight across the Baltic Sea to Abo, and then on to Helsingfors. The last hour was bumpy, and I was uncomfortable. I was impressed by the progressiveness of Helsingfors.

The late train for Leningrad.

Leningrad, Wednesday, August 28, 1935

We reached the Russian frontier about eleven o'clock. There was a long wait at the station, much ado about money, and elaborate examination of all papers by members of the secret police who could read only Russian.

Met and chatted with Lady Houstoun-Boswall,[49] who had a particular amount of difficulty because of the insistence of the customs people on opening every toilet article.

We arrived in Leningrad about two o'clock and were hustled off in magnificent Lincoln cars by the Intourist representatives.

In the afternoon, the Houstouns and I, with an intelligent girl guide and our open Lincoln, made a general tour of the city. It has obviously been improved considerably since 1929. More than ever, I was impressed by the magnificence of the scale on which it is planned.

At night to the opera with the Houstouns. It was 100 percent Russian production, but performed with great skill and devotion.

Thursday, August 29, 1935

Most of the day spent in the Hermitage. It remains one of the world's greatest collections.

Spent the late afternoon and the sunset time on the quay of the Neva, and at the foot of the statue of Peter the Great, looking out toward the west. From that viewpoint it seemed almost like a dead city, because there is so little shipping. But in other parts of the town there was busy animation.

Somewhat earlier in the day I had visited the St. Isaac's Cathedral, one of the most costly in all Russia, now turned into a rather poor anti-religious museum.

Night train for Moscow.

Moscow, Friday, August 30, 1935

Arrived in Moscow on time, and again expeditiously conducted by the Intourist to the Hotel National. It proved to be an even better place than the Astoria in Leningrad.

---

49. Wife of British diplomat Sir Thomas Houstoun-Boswall.

The day of my arrival being the rest day, it was difficult to get in touch with anyone. Indeed, I was soon to learn that the Russians themselves have already forgotten the names of the days of the week. If you tell anyone that you will see them on Tuesday, for example, they do not know what you mean. They only use the dates. Sunday, therefore, has disappeared from the nomenclature and from the consciousness of all the young. This change had taken place since I was last there.

The city has been enormously changed, but the Red Square, the Kremlin, and St. Basil's [Cathedral] fortunately remain unchanged, except for the sacrilegious whitewash which some stupid person put on the red wall, presumably to make the Lenin tomb stand out more strikingly. Fortunately, white is gradually being washed off by the weather, and it is hoped will not be replaced.

At night I went alone to a workers' theater in the Hermitage gardens and stayed for the first act of *Carmen*. Then, without waiting for the car which the Intourist had said they would send me, I undertook to walk back to my hotel alone. I succeeded in getting more completely lost than I have ever been in a foreign capital. Moreover, I had nothing on me in Russian which would help anyone to tell me my direction. Fortunately, I occasionally met a person who knew a little German, and after an hour and a quarter or thereabouts, found my way near the Red Square, and then, with the aid of a taxi, got home. I had never before felt so helpless. Nonetheless, I was glad I had the walk, because I covered miles of streets which I would ordinarily never have visited. Men and women seemed on the whole better dressed than when I was there before, and one passed many new apartment buildings, but one could see that the bulk of the people probably were still living in as cramped quarters as formerly. But there was one striking difference with any other great city; there was not a single sign of prostitution. As I was later to learn from Wertheimer of the League Secretariat, the Russians have done perhaps the best job in this field of any country in the world, partly because of their excellent system of rehabilitation, and perhaps even more because of the fundamental levelling process which has gone on and of the new ideas as to marriage, etc.

Saturday, August 31, 1935

Visit to the Embassy. Bullitt[50] was busy, but a Mr. Henderson put me in touch with Stolyar in the office of Krestinsky.[51] I went to see Stolyar, told him what I wanted to take up with his chief, and was promised that he would let me know whether the latter would be able to see me. While going into see Stolyar, I fortunately ran into Maisky.[52]

---

50. William Bullitt, the first American ambassador to the Soviet Union.
51. Nikolai Krestinsky, acting commissar for foreign affairs.
52. Ivan Maisky, Russian ambassador to Great Britain.

Lunch with Grower.[53] He urged me to see the chairman of the Komzet,[54] which has to do with Biro-Bidjan.[55] He also told me of what has been done for the intellectuals in Russia, some thirty having been placed, and of the possibilities for perhaps one hundred more. He kindly offered me the use of his car the next day, which I gladly accepted.

To Bullitt's house for tea and a movie party. It is the house which the Soviet authorities had picked out years ago for the American Embassy. It had formerly been owned by a rich merchant who had made his money by exchanging vodka for furs. It was one of the most beautiful houses I have ever seen, classic in design with perfect proportions. The furniture, most of it at least, dates from the old regime.

The movies were *The March of Time*, showing most strikingly the maneuvers of the American fleet in the Pacific, and realistically depicting its plans for destroying the Japanese fleet. Next to me sat the Japanese ambassador. The tension was relieved at the end by the words of the Japanese ambassador in Washington to Secretary Stimson, "But you know, Mr. Secretary, navies will be navies."

The second movie was a thriller, and afterward we had a second tea. I had an amusing talk with the German ambassador,[56] who knew only that I knew a good many people in the German Foreign Office. He said, "We do not have two Foreign Offices, we have five. The Wilhelmstrasse, Rosenberg, Ribbentrop, the head of the cultural organization,[57] and the head of the religious organization." . . . Bullitt said that he was most anxious to have a real talk and would get in touch with me later. He certainly is a delightful person.

That evening at supper I spoke to three young Americans whom I had been meeting constantly for the last days in Moscow and Leningrad, and asked them if they would like to go to the country with me the next day. They were Harriet Todd, Frances Montangani, and Miss Todd's brother. The girls were going on alone through southern Russia.

53. Ezekiel Grower, Dr. Joseph Rosen's right-hand man at the American Jewish Joint Agricultural Corporation (Agro-Joint), which carried out settlement projects in Crimea and Ukraine.

54. Russian acronym for "Committee for the Settlement of Toiling Jews on the Land."

55. A "Jewish autonomous region" of the Soviet Union, in the Far East, near the Chinese border. Had about 14,000 Jews in 1935.

56. Friedrich-Werner Graf von der Schulenburg, ambassador to the USSR, 1934–1941. A conservative aristocrat, he later joined the anti-Nazi opposition. Executed after the failure of the plot to assassinate Hitler on July 20, 1944.

57. The Volksbund für das Deutschtum im Ausland, a long-standing organization to maintain cultural ties with ethnic Germans in other countries, was taken over by the Nazis and used to advance Nazi foreign policy interests.

2. Nuremberg Laws: September 1935

Moscow, Sunday, September 1, 1935

The day in the country at one of the Soviet recreation centers. It was a beautiful day. On the way back we ran into larger and larger crowds as we approached the city, [crowds] which were gathering for that night's international youth demonstration.

Unable to get tickets for the Red Square, we watched the three hours' parade from the other bank of the river. It was an impressive and, at times, extraordinarily beautiful show, with the minarets and the spires of the Kremlin silhouetted against the bright sky.

Unable to get home until the processions had passed, we went into the third-class hotel for tourists, and there I met and chatted for a moment with Michael Straight.[1] Shortly after ten the bridge across the river was opened for traffic, and we walked home through the Red Square. An hour or so later I walked out again, and then there were no signs of the great demonstration which had taken place so shortly before. Nor were there on the streets any crowds such as would inevitably have been present following a demonstration at home. It had all been very business-like, and when the workers and children had finished, they had gone to their houses.

Monday, September 2, 1935

Conference with Grower in the morning. Then to the theater to see an excellent performance of *Til Eulenspiegel*. However, in order to go to the French Museum I left early. Again, I was overwhelmed by the beauty and variety of the two collections now housed in one museum.

---

1. Michael Straight, son of Dorothy Whitney Straight Elmhirst. Mrs. Elmhirst had been a member of the executive committee of the Foreign Policy Association (FPA) and one of its largest financial supporters in the early years. In the mid-1930s Professor Anthony Blunt at Cambridge secretly recruited Straight into the Communist Party; he became part of the spy ring that included Blunt, Anthony Burgess, Donald McLean, and Kim Philby. Straight maintained a covert relationship with Soviet intelligence while serving as a speechwriter for Roosevelt and as a State Department official. After the war he became publisher of the family-owned *New Republic*, hiring Henry Wallace as editor. In 1963 he told Arthur Schlesinger, Jr., about his past Communist connection and thus led to the exposure of Anthony Blunt. Obituary by Richard Norton-Taylor in the *Guardian*, January 9, 2004.

Dinner with [Walter] Duranty.[2] He talked very indiscreetly about the *New York Times* and particularly of the "deadly feud between Arthur Sulzberger and Colonel Adler." I said that I knew nothing of such a situation.[3]

As to Russian conditions, Duranty was less optimistic than usual. He admitted the tendency toward luxury in high places, the slow progress in mechanization of the farm, the disastrous effects of these first efforts, but insisted that the regime was no longer in danger. Indeed, he said, that now the main lines of policy had been so clearly marked out that Russia was not nearly so interesting as formerly. He declared that the Russians were securing between two hundred and three hundred million dollars of gold from washings in the rivers, by employing about half a million men. He outlined also some of the large projects now under way, such as the Don Canal, the canal connecting the Volga and the Moscow rivers, which is to raise the latter as much as ten feet, and thus permit sizable barges to reach the capital.

Toward the end of our conference Duranty launched into a philosophical and scientific disquisition about the nature of man and his relation to woman. He spoke with great authority, but I was not convinced that he had learned the whole truth.

Tuesday, September 3, 1935

Grower called. Together we went shopping, and then he waited for me while I went to the Foreign Office. Stalyar acted as interpreter during my conference with Krestinsky. The latter was most emphatic in his opposition to the proposed reorganization of the refugee work under the League. He put it on two grounds: the practical one that the Germans would be disadvantaged by their association with the White Russians; and the theoretical basis that the Soviets could have nothing to do with an organization which had in it representatives of the White Russians. However, after he had spoken at considerable length, he said that these were only his personal views, and that he would not propagandize Mr. Litvinov.[4]

I asked him if there was any objection to my seeing the Komzet. He said not.

Lunch at Bullitt's. He has a charming daughter of about thirteen, but we had little chance to talk at lunch because the other guests included two society ladies who were not much interested in refugees. Bullitt emphasized the growing luxury in high places, and insisted that there was increasing anti-Semitism, which might become dangerous because of what he characterized as the "creep-

---

2. Foreign correspondent of the *New York Times*, 1913–1939. Subsequently became known for having played down the many negative features of Stalin's regime and accentuating positive developments.

3. After the death of Adolph Ochs in April 1935, a struggle for succession at the *Times* broke out. Sulzberger was pitted against Brigadier General Julius Ochs Adler. Those outside the Ochs-Sulzberger family were not supposed to know about it. Susan Tifft and Alex Jones, *The Trust* (Boston: Little Brown, 1999), 157–160.

4. Maxim Litvinov, Soviet commissar for foreign affairs, 1930–1939. Of Jewish origin.

ing in" of the Jews among the "interstices." Bullitt insisted on a long discussion about the reasons for anti-Semitism.[5]

Went directly from the Embassy to the office of the Komzet, where Mr. Grower and I interviewed Tshootzkaiev [the chairman].[6] The latter told of the plans for the development of Biro-Bidjan, the bringing in of 1,000 Jewish families from abroad in 1936. He said that most of these would have to be Polish peasants, but that there might be room for some German technicians. The immigrants are met at the frontier and personally conducted to Biro-Bidjan, where they are turned over to local Jewish organizations. The choice of immigrants, I judged, was partly the work of the Agro-Joint.

Chat with Smith, an American associated with the Railroad Administration. He told me interesting tales about favoritism in the railroad organization. He seemed to feel that the Russians were much less effective in administering the railway than they were in doing a stunt enterprise, such as building the Moscow subway.

Young Thayer[7] at the Embassy told an amusing tale of the difficulty of getting an extra spring for his Ford sedan, which had been broken the day before on the trip back from Nizhni Novgorod. He had found the greatest difficulty and had finally appealed to the commissar who would correspond to our secretary of commerce.

The night train for Warsaw.

I left Russia with a feeling of disillusionment very different from that which I had experienced on my two previous trips. I could not, of course, pretend to have made a study of the situation; nonetheless, I could not escape the impression that there has been a great deal of low-lancing in liberal and radical circles in the west about the epoch-making achievement under the Soviets.

Wednesday, September 4, 1935

Reached the Polish frontier about noon. It was startling—the marked change in the countryside almost immediately after one had left Russia. The farms were immeasurably better kept, there were more cattle, and in every way the standard of living seemed higher.

Changed trains in Warsaw, or rather, our wagon-lit was switched to another train, but I did not stop overnight.

---

5. Bullitt was known to blame Jews for a wide range of situations. In 1942 he spread the completely unfounded story that the United States was emphasizing the war in Europe (as opposed to the Pacific) because of the influence of Jews inside the Roosevelt administration. See Richard Breitman and Alan M. Kraut, *American Refugee Policy and European Jewry, 1933–1945* (Bloomington: Indiana University Press, 1987), 241.

6. Sergei Egorovich Tshootzkaiev.

7. Charles Wheeler Thayer, U.S. diplomat who served in Berlin and Moscow in the 1930s and worked for the Office of Strategic Services in Yugoslavia during World War II. Later headed the Voice of America.

Arrived shortly after eight o'clock in Berlin. Went directly to the Esplanade, then to the Embassy. Chatted with Mrs. Levine. . . . [8] She told me some amusing, but I am not sure that they were accurate, tales of conflicts between Goebbels and Göring. She had recently talked with Professor Fay,[9] whom she found much too "pro-German."

Ambassador Dodd[10] talked fully and frankly, but again, as in earlier talks with him, I did not get the impression that he was always realistic in his estimate of the situation. For example, he said that he thought the Catholics and the Protestants were about to make peace with the government on rather advantageous terms. Then he added what would undoubtedly be true—that if this were to take place, it could only disadvantage the Jews by diverting the full force of the Party dislike on the single group.

He thinks the economic situation is more and more serious, largely on account of the huge floating debt of many billions; but he does not feel that conditions are critical.

He emphasized that the radicals are strongly in power, that they had even gone so far as to propose through Goebbels in a recent meeting of the cabinet the confiscation of Jewish property. Schacht, however, had staunchly resisted this and had been supported by Hitler. Schacht had thus a sort of a victory, but since the radical pressure never relaxes, the net result is always to leave the Jews worse off than before.

He talked about the proposed new legislation and said that he had heard that it might include segregation of the Jews.

. . . .

In the afternoon Ebbutt[11] of the *Times* came to see me. He wished to learn what I knew about the proposed legislation. Then he went on to talk most interestingly for nearly an hour. As to the Church situation, he disagreed completely with Dodd. He sees no prospect of peace, for he is convinced that the ultimate objective of the regime is inconsistent with the established religions.

---

8. U.S. Embassy secretary, sister of Herbert and Gerald Swope. Herbert was a prominent journalist, and Gerald had been president of General Electric.

9. Professor Sidney Bradshaw Fay, American, German-educated diplomatic historian who taught at Dartmouth, Smith, and Harvard. His *Origins of the World War* (1928) held Germany among the countries least responsible for the outbreak of World War I. After World War II he moved to the fringes of the group of extremists who denied that there had been a Holocaust.

10. American Ambassador William E. Dodd, formerly a history professor, who got the position McDonald had originally wanted. Extensively treated in *Advocate for the Doomed*.

11. Norman Ebbutt, chief *London Times* correspondent in Berlin, 1925–1937. A strong anti-Nazi who was ultimately expelled from the country. William L. Shirer wrote, "Ebbutt has complained to me several times in private that the *Times* does not print all he sends, that it does not want to hear too much of the bad side of Nazi Germany and has been captured by pro-Nazis in London." Shirer considered him the best foreign correspondent in Berlin. William L. Shirer, *Berlin Diary* (New York: Knopf, 1942), 78.

As to the Jews, it may be that the legislation announced at Nuremberg will be the culmination of the present wave of anti-Semitism. But almost certainly, whatever lull follows will be only temporary. Moreover, each new attack begins from where the last left off. In this way, despite the efforts of Schacht, the radicals are able to register steady advances.

On the question of relations of the army to the Jewish question, Ebbutt was particularly convincing. He knows the army authorities very well and is convinced that, though they control the final authority, they are reluctant to intervene in matters outside their own immediate fields unless they can be shown that their interests are directly concerned. It is important to remember that the army is carrying through an enormous task of enlargement and reorganization which normally occupies all its energy. On the other hand, it cannot ignore any development which might seriously jeopardize the economic resources of the country or, more particularly, curtail further the supply of foreign exchange essential for the purchase of needed raw material. Hence, Schacht can probably count upon the army on particular issues. Indeed, Blomberg[12] and Schacht work together closely. After Schacht's recent speech at Königsberg he and Blomberg went together to Hitler to protest against Goebbels's interference by censoring Schacht's speech before it was printed.

Ebbutt admitted, however, that despite the encouragement which might be drawn from this attitude of the army, that the radicals would probably continue to register advances, because they had a positive interest in the attack, whereas the army bothers only occasionally to resist.

Ebbutt agreed with the German ambassador in Moscow that there are in fact not two, but five Foreign Offices in Berlin—the Wilhelmstrasse, Ribbentrop, Rosenberg, and the heads of the cultural and religious associations.

Ebbutt's estimate of the diversity of counsel and authority in foreign affairs confirmed the views expressed to me earlier by Geist.

. . . .

Lucerne, Friday, September 6, 1935

Reached Lucerne about noon. After telephoning a couple of times to my colleagues in Geneva, I had a long conference at tea time with Lola Hahn.[13] She told me of Max Warburg's visit to Schacht the day after I had seen the former in Bad Kissingen. Schacht had begun the conversation by reminding Warburg of an earlier statement about the possibility of organized mass emigration of the young [Jews], and wanted to know whether such a program was still possible. He thought that if it were and could be planned definitely, it might be used as a lever to secure better terms for those who must remain,[14] and perhaps even to modify somewhat the legislation soon to be enacted. Warburg had replied that

---

12. Werner von Blömberg, head of the Reichswehr and minister of defense.
13. Oldest daughter of Max Warburg.
14. In February 1934 McDonald had presented this notion directly to German Foreign Minister von Neurath. See *Advocate for the Doomed*, 292–293.

there was, of course, still this possibility, but that conditions in the meantime had materially changed, and it was more difficult now than two years earlier. Moreover, there was the almost insuperable obstacle of transfer. To this, Schacht had definitely replied that Max need not worry about that, because he, Schacht, would give the necessary permission. Schacht then asked Max if he would write him a letter outlining the conditions under which such an emigration might be carried through. Max had agreed to do so and had already sent the communication.

Lola told me that there had been considerable differences of opinion as to whether the communication should be sent. Erich had opposed it, not on the ground that it might endanger Max, but on the broader ground of policy that it might be interpreted as an admission that the emigration was inevitable and had been accepted as such. Lola said that she thought that this was an unrealistic view, because there is no good in blinking [at] the fact that such a transfer of the young is essential.

We talked about many other aspects of the general situation and also about personalities. She doubted that Kreutzberger would join the ICA; thought, instead, that he had already definitely decided on going almost at once to Palestine.[15] We talked on until after sunset, which, from the balcony of the beautiful sitting room which the hotel had given me and which looked out over the lake and the mountains, was extraordinarily beautiful. It seemed almost grotesque that in the midst of so much natural beauty one had to face the facts of such ugliness in human relations.

Laski and Joseph Hyman[16] came in. . . . Laski told me of his recent talk with Johnson[17] and of his own decision not to come to Geneva for the Assembly, because he thought it better for him not to be involved in the problem of reorganization. He wanted me, however, to know that he would come at any time if I felt he were needed, and that, moreover, he was at my disposal in London for anything that he might do in connection with the statement I am preparing. He suggested the name of a lawyer in London who, he said, would also be glad to help and whom he considers to be the most distinguished authority available—his name is Lauterpacht.[18]

Dinner with Max Warburg and his family. Was delighted to see Anita [Lola Hahn's younger sister], whom I had not met for several years. Others besides the family, Lady Erleigh,[19] and Laski.

---

15. Max Kreutzberger in fact emigrated to Palestine in late 1935.

16. Joseph C. Hyman, high official of the American Jewish Joint Distribution Committee.

17. Major T. F. Johnson, head of the Nansen Committee.

18. Hersch Lauterpacht, a Jew born in Bialystok, who became a professor at Cambridge University and one of the world's leading experts on international law. Served as a judge on the International Court of Justice.

19. Eva Violet Mond, daughter of the first Lord Melchett. Wife of Gerald Rufus Isaacs, Vicount Erleigh, who in 1935 became the second Marquess of Reading. Raised as a Catholic, she converted to Judaism and became an important figure in Jewish and Zionist circles. President of the British National Council of Women.

There was no opportunity at dinner for serious talk with Max Warburg. Instead, he seemed terribly tired. So I left without any chance to ask him about what Lola Hahn had told me.

I should perhaps add that Lola in the afternoon had deplored the tendency of Felix Warburg to act as though he knew more about the situation in Germany than he possibly could know from his beautiful but aloof study on Fifth Avenue. She emphasized the point of view which Max had put to me at our previous talk—a view based on the feeling that there is too much tendency to dictate from afar by well-intentioned Americans.

McDonald then returned to Geneva for the opening of the regular session of the League of Nations.

Geneva, Saturday, September 7, 1935

Early train to Geneva. Arrived about half past twelve. Went directly to the Bellevue, then to lunch with Bentwich, May,[20] Kotschnig,[21] and Miss Sawyer.[22] We had a general discussion of the situation, but concentrated on the immediate work ahead. It was decided that we should go at once to see Lange.

Kotschnig and I talked for nearly an hour to the Norwegian representative. We saw at once that the members of the Secretariat and the representatives of the Geneva organizations who have their own special formula had been actively at work educating him. He seemed more inclined to accept a weaker organization than seemed to us desirable. Nonetheless, he listened sympathetically to our exposition and was not unsympathetic to our contentions that it was essential that there be a reorganization under the League with effective leadership, and that the Assembly must give the direction to the Experts' Committee so that the Council could take prompt action.

Up to the Saléve for dinner. It was a marvelous evening.

Sunday, September 8, 1935

Worked in the morning with Miss Sawyer. Lunch with Janowsky and Fagen[23] and Miss Sawyer. General talk about our plans.

. . . .

Monday, September 9, 1935

This marked the beginning of a rather hectic two-weeks' period of lobbying for prompt and effective action by the Assembly. During this period all of

20. Herbert L. May, American lawyer and businessman involved in humanitarian causes. Close associate of McDonald.
21. Walter Kotschnig, born in Austria, secretary general of the International Student Service in Geneva, member of the League High Commission staff.
22. Ollve Sawyer, McDonald's regular secretary.
23. Oscar I. Janowsky and Melvyn M. Fagen, authors of *International Aspects of German Racial Policies* (New York: Oxford, 1937). They did the detailed research for McDonald's letter of resignation as High Commissioner.

us were to see many individuals, but the points of view expressed by them were often of only transient interest, so I will not attempt to set down any of them, except a few in detail.

To the Secretariat and then over to the Assembly. . . .

On this day McDonald wrote a long letter to Felix Warburg summing up his experiences and conclusions of the preceding few weeks. Excerpts include:

Here in Geneva the shadow of impending conflict in Abyssinia discourages most efforts even in those humanitarian fields that have not the slightest relation to the controversy in East Africa. . . . In Berlin at the Foreign Office they listened sympathetically to my explanation . . . of the reorganization of refugee work under the League. . . . In Moscow, unlike in the Scandinavian countries, I received a rather definite rebuff . . . for the proposal that I was urging. Krestinsky . . . was firmly opposed to cooperation by his government with any organization which included representation of the White Russians. . . . While in Moscow I visited . . . the office of the Comzed [Komzet]. The Chairman, Tshootzkaiev, . . . confirmed the impression which I had gotten from Rosen that Biro-Bidjan, so far as it is available to foreign Jews at all, is primarily for Polish Jews, and that only a very limited number of specially trained Jewish technicians from Germany could be expected to find homes in the Far East. . . .

A little about my impressions of Germany: there can be no doubt that the situation for the Jews has worsened [illegible word] during recent months. The extremists, Goebbels, Streicher, et al. have had their own way. It is true that Schacht's Königsberg address was a protest against irresponsible and unofficial actions; but one must be an incorrigible optimist to have gathered much satisfaction from the Reichsbank president's statement taken as a whole. At the best he can only hope to stem the tide of anti-Semitic outrages temporarily, and then only if he is able to make a strong case that such attacks seriously jeopardize the economic position of the country. Similarly, it is my impression that no effective or continuous help for the Jews can be hoped for from the Reichswehr. The army prides itself on being non-political. It has, of course, on occasions shown its dissatisfaction at some of the actions of the anti-Semitic extremists, and it might even in certain contingencies take a strong line against such outrages. But this would not be done as a matter of principle, or to defend the Jews, but only if Schacht and the military leaders were convinced that Germany's program of rearmament was being jeopardized by the world's unfavorable reaction to the Goebbels-Streicher program. . . .

From no one was I able to get a clear picture of what may be expected in the threatened new legislation. . . . One can only be certain that the result will be to penalize the Jews in various ways and on the basis of pseudo-legality, which causes grim forebodings. Surely there is no hope in the Reich for the younger generation of Jews. This time, more than during any of my several previous trips to Germany, have I been unable to find anyone who differed with this grim conclusion.[24]

Bentwich and I at twelve went to see Lord Cranborne[25] and Malkin.[26] They were as sympathetic as we had any reason to expect. They did not commit themselves definitely on specific programs, but indicated that they would support the Norwegian initiative and would not be petty on the question of somewhat larger appropriations. We stressed the importance of immediate action and of setting up an organization with a powerful personality at the head.

. . . .

With Kotschnig to see Dr. Krauel,[27] the German consul. He said that he had had a reply from Berlin, that though his government could not answer officially, he could let me know that they were not opposed to a reorganization under the League which would bring the German refugees within the competence of that new organization. He felt that this was a considerable concession on the part of his government, since it would mean that they would not object to having German refugees considered as eligible for the same facilities as are accorded the Nansen refugees. They were only concerned that the new organization would be non-political in its activities, as had been the Nansen Office and the High Commission.

He then went on to say that it would be looked upon with favor if the decision were to turn the German refugees over to the Nansen Office. He elaborated this point at some length, and though I listened very closely to what he said, I could not make out whether he was on this matter expressing a personal view or that of his government.

We parted with expressions of mutual regard, and I with a feeling that, for the time being at any rate, the situation was such that one could cooperate with Krauel on a friendly basis.

Wednesday, September 11, 1935

Morning conference as usual. Then to the Assembly to hear Hoare's[28] speech. It made a more profound impression on the audience as a whole than it did upon me. It was an excellent analysis of the responsibilities under the League and contained a more far-reaching commitment on Britain's part than

24. McDonald to Warburg, September 9, 1935, McDonald Papers, Columbia University, D361, Folder 158 (Warburg Special File).
25. Robert Arthur James Gascoyne-Cecil, Viscount Cranborne. Conservative politician and cabinet minister. From 1941, the Fifth Marquess of Salisbury.
26. Sir William Malkin, legal adviser to the British Foreign Office.
27. Wolfgang Krauel, German consul general in Geneva until 1943. Not a member of the Nazi Party.
28. Sir Samuel Hoare, British foreign secretary.

anything heretofore said by a responsible foreign minister. However, I was discouraged by the rather self-righteous tone.

. . . .

Friday, September 13, 1935

The Sixth Committee took up the Norwegian proposal.[29] Dr. Halvdan Koht presented the matter, not very effectively.[30] Then followed a public debate in which some sixteen countries participated. Among those who gave their support were the Swedes, the Danes, the Dutch, the British, the French through Herriot, the Czechs, and perhaps one or two others. But from the Latvians, the Yugoslavs, the Rumanians, the Greeks, and the Italians and Russians and some others came ominous signs of opposition. However, they finally all agreed to the naming of a subcommittee [to discuss the proposal], which, when its makeup was announced, was seen to include practically all of those who had spoken against the measure, leaving a bare majority of one or two for it. However, as the event will show, this was a good arrangement, for it permitted all of the opponents to vent their opposition in the private meeting.

. . . .

Saturday, September 14, 1935

I should have indicated earlier that on one of the previous days I had lunch with Sholem Asch[31] and Nahum Goldmann.[32] Asch talked extremely interestingly about Jewish problems in general and the Jewish situation in Poland in particular. He said that the German authorities had offered to allow his books to be published in Germany and even advertised there, since they dealt with Jewish life, as they feel Jewish writers ought to concern themselves with their own people; but that he must separate himself from the boycott movement. This he refused to do.

. . . .

Dinner at the Mays. It gave me a very welcome opportunity to have a long talk with Abraham about the procedure before the subcommittee the next week. I was again impressed with him as an honest, but extremely cautious and rather bureaucratic, official.

29. The Norwegian proposal was that the League set up a new umbrella refugee organization to take over the work of the Nansen Office (mostly Russian refugees), the High Commission (McDonald's organization), Assyrian refugees, and the flow of political opponents of the Nazis and Jews from the Saar region since January 1935.

30. The Norwegian foreign minister asked the League to "make a vigorous effort to enable these refugees from war and dictatorships to obtain a means of subsistence." *New York Times*, September 13, 1935, p. 12.

31. Sholem Asch, famous Yiddish novelist from Poland, author of *Three Cities*, *The Nazarine*, and *The Apostle*, among other works.

32. President and co-founder of the World Jewish Congress.

Amusing talks with Mrs. Abraham about her early work with the League to enforce peace. We also chatted about the Baruchs,[33] whom she knows intimately. She insists that Bernard is misunderstood, that really he is rather a shy, retiring individual. I could only reply that he manages most successfully to hide these characteristics.

. . . .

Monday, September 16, 1935

Worked all morning on my statement before the subcommittee.

In the afternoon conference with Antoniade, the Rumanian representative and a member of the Nansen Governing Body. He indicated approval of the reorganization.

A long and interesting session with Raphael, the Greek representative and the acting chairman of the Nansen Office. He was utterly defeatist. He said that in their office during the last three years they had not been able to settle more than 3,000 people; that their work was practically negligible; that they, of course, sought to avoid discouraging people by a too frank statement, but that in his view the refugee situation is absolutely hopeless; nothing real can be done unless there is a fundamental change in the economic conditions of the world. He argued that it was fallacious to assume that because you changed your mechanism and brought your organization closer to the League, you would thereby improve the lot of the refugees. It is not, he said, a question of mechanism at all. If, he argued, after eighteen years, during much of which time there had been world-wide prosperity and large sums available, so little progress had been made in the Russian refugee solution, what could be hoped for under the present circumstances? Anyhow, he said, the consular work on behalf of the refugees was not the function of the Nansen Office; it was really carried out by the Secretariat through the Nansen Office delegates abroad. Raphael did not express any directly personal views about Johnson, but it was clear that he was not enthusiastic about him.

Tuesday, September 17, 1935

Wurfbain[34] and I went in the morning to see the Italian delegate, Baron Basile. He was most unsatisfactory. Despite the proof I offered that Germany had no objection to the proposed reorganization, Basile launched into a long oration about fundamental principles involved in this question, which involved questions of sovereignty and could, therefore, only be decided upon by the governments themselves. All of this seemed to both Wurfbain and me to be a mere façade to hide Italy's desire not to have the categories opened so that Italians [Italian anti-Fascist refugees] might be included under the League

---

33. Bernard Baruch, of Sephardic origins, American Jewish financier and adviser to several presidents. Conservative non-Zionist.

34. André Wurfbain, Dutch, member of the League High Commission staff.

supervision. Anyhow, it was quite clear that we must count upon Italian opposition in the subcommittee.

In the afternoon I had an appointment with Bérenger[35] at 4:30 in the room where the subcommittee was to meet. He, however, did not appear until after the committee had met—indeed, not until after I had read my statement. He apologized to the committee, saying that he had been delayed by the meeting in honor of Chateaubriand where he had had to speak.

As soon as the subcommittee was called to order, M. Motta,[36] the chairman, asked me to make my statement, explaining that I had had it translated into French and suggested that members follow it in that language. After I had finished reading, there were a number of questions—two from Raphael—one to bring out that there was no advantage in tying up with the Nansen Office, which was a dying organization; the answer to that was that we hoped that our problem would be very largely solved before 1939. The Dutch asked if our organization had encouraged the refugees to take part in propaganda, or rather, if the work on behalf of the refugees lent such encouragement. My answer was no—that what drove refugees to agitation and intrigue was the failure to find work. A delegate asked about the plans for the High Commission and my own plans at the end of the year. I said that I hoped to go home, but that presumably an organization could be kept in being until the League reorganization had taken place. Later, I was to learn that it had been my reply on this point about my own plans that gave Bérenger an excuse for his savage attack in a later private meeting of the subcommittee.

Other questions brought out other aspects of the proposal, but none of the questions addressed to me were unfriendly except that of Bérenger when he asked caustically, "What has the United States government done?" When I replied that financially it had done nothing, he indicated his pleasure, but when I went on to explain concessions made in the granting of visas and the non-requirement of work permits, he was less pleased.

When I had finished, my colleagues and I were excused and left the room. On the way out I met Johnson and said I hoped we had not kept him waiting too long. As I shook hands with him, I noticed that he was trembling with excitement.

Dinner with Paul Schwarz.[37] We talked about all sorts of things and touched only indirectly on internal conditions. My faith in his essential honesty was confirmed. It was pitiful to hear him say that, though he had hoped to be able to play a role in avoiding the destructive results of disorganization at home, he was now doubtful, since the events of two or three days previous,[38]

---

35. Henri Bérenger, president of the Committee for Foreign Affairs in the French Senate and French delegate to the Governing Body of the League High Commission. Treated extensively in *Advocate for the Doomed*.

36. Giuseppi Motta, member of the Federal Council of Switzerland, four times president of Switzerland, and in December 1935 chosen vice president.

37. Paul Schwarz, former German consul in Chicago. Left his post after Hitler took power.

38. The Nuremberg Laws. See italicized insert immediately below this entry.

whether he could carry on. Delicately, he suggested that he would be grateful if I could find something [for him] overseas. The answer [which] was obvious but which I could not give, was that this would have been much easier two years ago than now. He is a broken and extremely sad man.

In September 1935 Hitler took the occasion of the Nazi Party's annual Nurem-berg Party rally to have the government bureaucracy issue laws with two different objectives: establishing racial criteria for citizenship and banning intermarriage and even sexual relations between German Jews and "Aryan" Germans. The Law for the Protection of German Blood and German Honor and the Reich Citizenship Law, both issued on September 15, 1935, and known as the Nuremberg Laws, also forbade Jews from employing female Germans under age forty-five, and relegated Jews (and Gypsies) to the status of subjects, rather than citizens. These laws were not, as was once supposed, the result of a spur-of-the-moment decision by Hitler, but rather the outcome of long-standing discussions within government and party circles. Hitler adjudicated the disputes, determined the timing, and authorized the laws. Advocate for the Doomed gives some occasional glimpses of the behind-the-scenes debate in Nazi Germany about how to regulate the status of Ger-man Jews.

Although some contemporary observers and German Jews hoped that issuance of these laws might at least stabilize conditions, it did not. (Germany's need to play down evidence of persecution of German Jews lasted only through the 1936 Berlin Olympics, which had been threatened by a boycott and which were an important showcase for the regime.) In a letter to James Rosenberg, McDonald correctly assessed the significance and likely impact of these laws: "The blow last Sunday, though it was more or less what was anticipated, took on an even more vicious form than the opti-mists had hoped." He went on to say that these laws were only the "basis for the devel-opment of a wide range of anti-Jewish attacks."[39]

We now know that a week later, Hitler privately warned against having party activists push to expand the new laws or undertake direct economic actions against Jews. At the same time, he promised that "in case of a war on all fronts, he would be ready for all the consequences."[40]

Wednesday, September 18, 1935

Long conference with Dr. Demuth,[41] at the end of which he strongly urged me not to return home until the new League organization had begun to function. He said that I was the only flag around which the work could center.

---

39. McDonald to Rosenberg, September 18, 1935. Copy in McDonald Papers, USHMM.

40. Quoted in Philippe Burrin, *Hitler and the Jews: The Genesis of the Holocaust* (New York: Hodder Arnold, 1994), 48–49.

41. Fritz Demuth, of the Association for Emergency Aid for German Scholars Abroad.

Dinner at the Sweetsers. . . .[42]

After dinner talked with Bonnet[43] about the French attitude toward our proposal and the attack of Bérenger on me that afternoon. It appears from what I was told by a personal friend present during the private session of the subcommittee of the Sixth that Bérenger, infuriated by some remark of the British delegate to the effect that it was desirable to hasten reorganization because the High Commission was winding up, launched into a vindictive personal attack on me and on the work of the office. He is reported to have said that I had insisted on the title of "High Commissioner" on the ground that it would enable me to secure large funds from America, and that I had failed completely; that so far as the High Commission was concerned, it wouldn't matter if it did go out of business, that it had accomplished nothing anyhow, etc., etc. My friend told me that he had never heard as bitter an attack during all of his years of the League. Apparently, Motta was so shocked by it that he asked the permission of the English members of the committee not to have the statement translated into English.

This account did not surprise me after my encounter with Bérenger that morning. When I went up to speak to him as he left the Sixth Committee, I said to him, "What do you think now about the reorganization?" His reply was, "I think that this is not a matter for dictation by Americans. There are no American refugees, they are European refugees, and we are big enough to look after ourselves. Goodbye." This may not be a literal translation, since it is dictated nearly a week later, but certainly it expresses the tone and the temper of the senator.[44]

His attitude indicates that the report we had a day or two earlier was probably true, that Laval[45] had said something to the effect that the French resented the Anglo-Saxon and North European attempt to monopolize the refugee problem.

Thursday, September 19, 1935

Echoes in the *couloirs* [corridors] of Bérenger's attack of the day before.

Conference with Motta by Bentwich and myself. We urged the importance of the principle of reorganization under the League so that the Experts' Committee would have a definite mandate. Motta referred deprecatingly to the Bérenger attack, and then outlined to us his compromise proposal, which was later in all its essentials adopted.[46]

42. Arthur Sweetser, an American in the League of Nations information section. Well-connected in Washington. Further discussed in chapter 7, pp. 125–127.

43. George Bonnet, French foreign minister.

44. Lord Cecil commented, "The French of the type of Bérenger are intolerable. They are obsessed with petty jealousies or dignities which make work with them a perpetual harassment." Cecil to McDonald, September 24, 1935. Copy in McDonald Papers, USHMM.

45. Pierre Laval, French prime minister, June 1935–January 1936. During World War II was the key figure in France's authoritarian Vichy regime.

46. The Sixth Committee refused to coordinate all refugee work under the League. Instead, it proposed that a small committee of experts (referred to here as the Experts' Committee) investigate the matter and authorized the Council to act on their advice without waiting for the

Ran into Hérriot[47] just before lunch, and urged him to be sure to attend the afternoon meeting of the subcommittee. Several other persons had done the same in the hope that his presence would restrain Bérenger.

. . . .

Friday, September 20, 1935

Early morning conference with Beneš,[48] accompanied by Bentwich. I explained that in view of the action by the subcommittee the previous day, one of the purposes of my visit had been anticipated. However, I added that we were anxious to have the whole matter expedited, and we would be grateful for his support.

Then we talked about the situation in Czechoslovakia and the possibility of some direct governmental subvention for travelling expenses of refugees to be evacuated. Beneš expressed complete understanding of the problem and said that he would talk to Kosé[49] about it just as soon as he had returned to Czechoslovakia.

As to the question of settlement in Czechoslovakia, Beneš was positive that it would be a mistake to attempt anything in the Carpathian region. He confirmed what we had heard from other sources, that already the territory there is so poor and the people so impoverished that they are migrating to other parts of the country.

The technical questions finished, I asked Beneš if he would talk to us briefly about the present European situation. He expressed himself as not worried by Hitler, that, on the contrary, the dictatorial regime in the Reich in a sense weakened Germany's possibility of attack because of internal divisions, and because a dictator invariably tends to become a prisoner of the forces which brought him into power. As to the Memel reference of Hitler,[50] this he interpreted as an obvious maneuver by Hitler to show the British that if they now committed themselves to an unequivocal policy of sanctions in the event of violations of the Covenant, they might soon be involved in the east. Beneš thought that this maneuver had been seen through by the British.

As to the Abyssinian situation, Beneš gave us little that was new. He did say that in some quarters it was suggested that Mussolini might be allowed a

approval of the next Assembly. It also refused to extend to the "stateless people" the status of refugees. It appropriated 5,500 Swiss francs for the expenses of this committee, but stipulated that there should be no other expenditure without explicit permission from the Assembly.

47. Édouard Hérriot, formerly French prime minister, now chair of the Foreign Affairs Committeee in the Chamber of Deputies.

48. Eduard Beneš, one of the co-founders of Czechoslovakia, became president on December 18, 1935.

49. Dr. Jaroslav Kosé, active in American-Czech trade relations.

50. On September 15, 1935, Hitler gave a speech in the Reichstag, referring to the theft of Memel from Germany. Lithuania had annexed Memel in 1923. Hitler may have wanted to influence the September 29, 1935, election in Memel, which pro-German forces won. The presence of a large number of ethnic Germans there led Nazi officials to agitate for its return to Germany. On March 22, 1939, just after Germany annexed Bohemia and Moravia, it also took over Memel.

victory of prestige in Adawa before effective sanctions were imposed, but he considered this a dangerous procedure.

. . . .

Sunday, September 22, 1935

Ten o'clock conference with the three foreign ministers of Denmark, Norway, and Sweden, Dr. Munch, Koht, and Mr. Sandler at the Richmond, with Bentwich and Kotschnig.

Full account of the conference is set out in an aide-mémoire sent to the foreign ministers later and need not be summarized here. On the whole, it was a very satisfying conference, and made one realize how much freer are foreign ministers whose governments are not vitally concerned in the political maneuvers which involve the Great Powers and many of the smaller ones.

A long distance telephone call from James Rosenberg[51] from London. He said that he was going to urge Sir Osmond to make the supplementary grant to our budget, but urged that I should take the line with Louis Oungre that if ICA were unwilling to do it, I would not worry because I could find it elsewhere. However, Rosenberg's real reason for calling up appeared to be his desire to emphasize again the importance of my final statement, and the desirability of having Cecil's[52] cooperation, but that, above all things, I should not permit any consideration to deter me from carrying that plan through. He also indicated that there had been some criticism of my trip to Russia. He did not indicate the grounds, but presumably on the theory that it had been too brief to be justified by any work done there, and he suggested that I should consider seriously whether I would not be more widely criticized if I made a trip to Palestine at the very end of my period in office. He felt too that it might put me too much in the hands of the Zionists; indeed, I am inclined to think this latter consideration weighed with him much more than the other, though he may not himself have realized it.

. . . .

Tuesday, September 24, 1935

Disturbed by the report that action was not being taken in the Fourth Committee to secure special action by the Council to make funds available this year for setting up the Experts' Committee, I called Burgin,[53] the British member on the Fourth Committee, and was rather shocked to have him say that he knew nothing about such an item. Then I called Malkin of the British delegation by mistake, intending to get Meakin, whom I finally did talk to. He

51. James Naumburg Rosenberg, American lawyer, on the boards of the Joint Distribution Committee and the American Jewish Committee. One of McDonald's patrons. Extensively treated in *Advocate for the Doomed*.
52. Lord Robert Cecil, Viscount Chelwood. One of the main supporters of the League of Nations from the beginning. Chair of the Governing Body of the League High Commission. A leading figure in *Advocate for the Doomed*.
53. Edward Leslie Burgin, member of the British Board of Trade.

assured me that Burgin did know about the matter and left me with the impression that it would be cleared up. Then I talked with Lange on the telephone. He said that Hambro was following the matter and would check with his British colleague. This seemed all that could be done.

Over to see Dr. Krauel, the German consul. We first talked about the reorganization program. Krauel said that he understood the chief opposition came from those who did not want their political refugees brought under a League organization. I agreed, but expressed the hope that the limited program would be pushed forward rapidly. I added that I hoped this might be possible so that our separate organization could disappear.

I then brought up the question of Gertrud Baer.[54] I explained that though she was a pacifist and active in that work, she was not a member of any political party and was not engaged in propaganda against Germany. In this connection I asked Dr. Krauel if he had had recent instructions from Berlin making the renewal of passports easier, explaining or rather referring to my previous talk with him in which I had reported on my interview in Berlin on the twenty-second of August at the Wilhelmstrasse. Briefly, I summarized the arguments advanced by Mackeben in the Foreign Office for a more lenient policy. Krauel answered that those were exactly his views; in short, that it would be better from Germany's own point of view to be more liberal.

Returning then to the case of Miss Baer, he suggested that it would be best if she came in to see him, for, he said, often in a case like this a relatively minor point makes all the difference. I promised to ask her to call him to inquire for an appointment.

. . . .

In the afternoon Miss Baer came to see me. She was inclined to feel that she ought to take someone with her when she went to see the consul. I argued that her only chance of success was to establish the right kind of personal relationship, and that this would be easier if she were alone. She agreed.

. . . .

Wednesday, September 25, 1935

Asked Miss Elisaberg to come to see me. She is a photographer from Germany, forced out. I had previously arranged for Mr. Hissman of the International News Service to try to secure for her a nominal position which would enable her to have press privileges and, therefore, to avoid the difficulties in connection with *carte de séjour* and *carte de travail*.

Dinner with Mrs. Wertheimer of Vienna. Then to the Bavaria. Pleasant visit with Derso,[55] who told me the very interesting story of his impressions of

---

54. Gertrud Baer, one of the founders of the Women's International League for Peace and Freedom and its co-chair, 1929–1946.
55. Alois Derso, a famous cartoonist.

Mussolini at the Stresa Conference.[56] He said that the latter could not coordinate his eyes with his other features, but they would flash in all sorts of directions as if the man were not well adjusted. Derso was confident that at that conference the English had gotten a more unfavorable impression of Mussolini, and at that time had begun the development which led to the English determination to finish with the Dictator.

As I was leaving the Bavaria, Dr. Krauel came up to me and said that the matter of papers for Gertrud Baer had been arranged, but that nothing should be said about it.

Thursday, September 26, 1935

. . . .

With Kotschnig to see the Austrian foreign minister [Egon Berger-Waldenegg]. We raised with him the question of expulsions, retraining, special treatment for Catholics, but received no very satisfactory response. He asked for an aide-mémoire, and it was sent him promptly.

I was dubious of his good faith because of his positive insistence that there is no Jewish problem in Austria. This statement was almost more than even Kotschnig could accept without protest.

. . . .

Friday, September 27, 1935

Dinner at the de la Paix as the guest of Mrs. Wertheimer. The guests included Madariaga[57] and the headmaster and mistress at Rolle, where Mrs. Wertheimer has her son. As was to have been expected, Madariaga did most of the talking. It is the first time in years that I have had a good chance to see him in such excellent form. He was gay and amusing. However, when he did speak seriously, he expressed complete pessimism about the possibility of Mussolini's yielding. He thought that conflict was inevitable.

Saturday, September 28, 1935

Miss Lucy Borchardt of Hamburg came in to tell me of the desire of the group which she represents to find a suitable agricultural country where they could work their own land and be freed of religious training in the schools or of obligation for military service. I told her of Inman's present investigation in

---

56. Britain, France, and Italy conferred at Stresa on April 11, 1935, prior to a League of Nations discussion about Germany's (illegal) introduction of the draft. The Stresa Conference condemned Germany, reaffirmed the Locarno Treaty, and restated the need to maintain Austria's independence and integrity. Britain's failure to bring up the subject of Ethiopia may have given Mussolini the impression that he had a "green light" there. Gerhard L. Weinberg, *The Foreign Policy of Hitler's Germany*, vol. I, *Diplomatic Revolution in Europe, 1933–1936* (Chicago: University of Chicago Press, 1971), 208–209.

57. Salvador de Madariaga, Spanish ambassador to France and Spanish representative to the League.

Colombia and promised to write him at once. I suggested also that probably Parana [Brazil], from the agricultural point of view, would be best, and agreed to put her in touch with the Parana Company in London.

Over to the Assembly just as it was adjourning, unexpectedly early.

Met Hammarskjoeld, registrar of the [World] Court. I told him briefly of the problem I was facing in connection with my final statement and asked his opinion. He talked freely and apparently frankly. According to his view, the recent German legislation [the Nuremberg Laws] offers no technical basis for legal action. It does, however, offer a basis for political action and could properly be considered by the Council. Denationalization, on the other hand, is a different matter and might properly come before the Court. It was not only Germany, but Belgium might be involved. So far as my action is concerned, there is no way of asking for an advisory opinion. However, in my communication to the Secretary General it would be possible to suggest that on the matter of denationalization by the Reich, an advisory opinion might be asked, and then by implication suggest that the German legislation should also be brought under review.

I asked Hammerskjoeld if he would be willing to discuss the matter with me further, when I had gotten farther along in the consideration and preparation of my brief. He said he would be delighted to do so and would be available to see me almost any time I might choose to come to The Hague.

Lunch at the Kotschnigs with Kosé from Prague. It had been suggested to the latter that he might be approached as a member of the Experts' Committee.

I fell in love with the Kotschnig children—a beautiful girl of about ten and two younger boys.

Dinner at the Plat d'Argent. My guests included the Mays, the Gerigs, Mr. Achilles[58] of the State Department, Sarah Wambaugh,[59] Helen Kirkpatrick,[60] and Carol Riegelman.[61] It was a gay party which threatened never to end.

. . . .

Monday, September 30, 1935

Dinner at Sweetsers. Others included the Mays, the Gilchrists,[62] and Eichelberger. I was shocked to have Arthur say that he had cabled urgently to the Rockefellers appealing to them to contribute toward the Assyrian refugee

58. Theodore Achilles, whom McDonald dealt with later in meetings of the President's Advisory Committee on Political Refugees, 1938–1939.

59. An American who had once worked in the League of Nations Secretariat. An expert on international plebiscites.

60. Correspondent of the Chicago Daily News and New York Post, later public affairs adviser in the European bureau of the State Department.

61. Carol Riegelman, in the Secretariat of the International Labor Organization.

62. Thomas Gilchrist, wealthy partner of the law firm Cadwalader, Wickersham and Taft, whom McDonald knew as a fellow Bronxvillian.

pool. I told him frankly that I thought this was nonsense, that it was absurd to hold up that arrangement as an example of desirable international cooperation; that, on the contrary, it had been a bludgeoning process by the English and the French, and that the result was entirely inconsistent with the action of the Assembly in reference to German or Russian refugees, or toward the women and children in eastern Asia. I did not add, but I thought, it was just another illustration of Arthur's permitting his enthusiasms to run away with his judgment.

3. Deterioration on All Fronts: October 1935

Very interesting talk in the morning with Frau Schreiber-Krieger.[1] Her point of view about the Nazi regime as being destructive of the free and creative individuals whom we had all been pleased to honor in the prewar days was especially striking. We agreed that we should talk again when I returned to Geneva.

Very pleasant lunch with the Mays. Besides the hosts were Prentiss Gilbert,[2] Helen Kirkpatrick, the Countess Murat and Mme. Ferriere. Gilbert was unusually amusing. His jibes at the English and mine along the same line went so far that Mrs. May, next to whom I was sitting, gave me a sharp push to indicate that she thought we had gone far enough. But I hope no one's feelings were really hurt.

Wednesday, October 2, 1935

With May over to 12 Place du Grand Mézel to hear the translation of Mussolini's broadcast[3] and to make my good-byes.

At the hotel I got Gerig[4] on the telephone and asked him excitedly what he thought developments of the day—the Italian general mobilization, the crossing of the Ethiopian frontier by Italian troops—would mean. He replied, "I think the Council will meet a day earlier."

Thursday, October 3, 1935

Lunch with Johnson. Our talk covered practically all aspects of the problem of reorganization. . . . As to the makeup of the committee, Johnson seemed to have no new information. As to his own budget, he said, of course, that had been voted in such a way as to make it available under any reorganization scheme. As to the most desirable form of a new governing body, he felt strongly that it should be wholly governmental. His own, which contains representatives of the private bodies, is weakened thereby. If, he added, it is insisted that there should be some representation of the private bodies, this should be in the form of assessors. One of the arguments against including the private bodies on

---

1. Adele Schreiber-Krieger, politician, journalist, and a leader of the German women's movement during the Weimar Republic. Served as a Social Democratic deputy in the Reichstag. Emigrated to Switzerland in 1933, died 1957.
2. Prentiss Gilbert, U.S. consul general in Geneva, also acted as liaison to the League of Nations, which the United States had not joined.
3. The reference is to Mussolini's broadcast announcing the Italian invasion of Ethiopia.
4. Ben Gerig, in the League of Nations Secretariat Information Section.

the Governing Board was that this would make the new organization more vulnerable from the point of view of attacks from the Russians, because of the presence of White Russian representatives, and later, from the Germans, because of the presence of Jewish representatives.

There should, of course, be an advisory council made up of the private bodies. As to executive representation, he recognized that there should be a Jewish executive on the staff, particularly entrusted with Jewish interests. As to funds, he recognized that the Jewish funds should be earmarked for Jewish purposes, and that such bodies could not be expected to pay more toward administrative costs than their proportionate share of the work done.

As we were concluding our talk, I raised the question: would Johnson care to come to London to discuss the question of reorganization with the Jewish leaders? He considered it favorably, and I said I would communicate with him about it later.

At the station Miss Ginsberg[5] introduced me to Dr. Alice Solomon,[6] with whom I talked briefly on the train. She was going back to Germany, despite the risk of imprisonment, but she said she could do nothing else because her funds were all inside the Reich, she needed medical attention, that she was too old—sixty-four—to begin life anew elsewhere. The talk of her experiences confirmed what I had heard so often of the complete disregard by the Nazis, in their discrimination against people of Jewish blood, of their previous records—no matter how distinguished these might have been. For example, Dr. Solomon had received very high distinction because of her work, had become Protestant, and yet was forced out of her position. She is anxious for an invitation from some of her friends—Miss Wald, et al.—to visit the States. But she, of course, recognizes that she would not be able to speak on the subjects which most people are interested in.

Arrived in Basel just before 7:00. . . .

Late night train for Paris.

Paris, Friday, October 4, 1935

Conference with Mr. & Mrs. Grzesinski.[7] She is English, speaking in rather cockney style. He speaks no English at all. We discussed possibilities of work for him in South America, and I promised to put him in touch with Alfredo Hirsch[8] or Hochschild[9] if they were in Paris. He is probably as able as

5. Marie Ginsberg, head of a committee to aid refugee scholars and an expert on refugee professionals.

6. Dr. Alice Solomon, well-known German feminist leader, educator, and pioneer social worker.

7. Albert Grzesinski, longtime German Social Democratic Party official. Former minister of the interior in Prussia and police chief in Berlin. Had favored a crackdown against Nazi Party violations of law in the years before Hitler came to power. Died in 1947.

8. Alfredo Hirsch, wealthy Argentinean Jewish businessman. Treated extensively in *Advocate for the Doomed*.

9. Moritz (Mauricio) Hochschild, born in Germany, influential Jewish metal-trader with extensive mining interests in Bolivia, Chile, and Peru. See chapter 11.

Wertheimer suggested, but rather old, it seemed to me, for beginning a new life in more or less a pioneer country.

. . . .

Conference with Robert de Rothschild[10] and Lambert[11] at the bank. Rothschild seemed almost dazed by the developments in Germany.

. . . .

Saturday, October 5, 1935

Conference in the morning with Professor Oualid.[12] At my suggestion he promised to write me his interpretation of the significance of the German laws in the field of culture.

Lunch with the Wertheimers at the Ritz. Mr. Wertheimer said that he was sure that if there could be developed a comprehensive scheme for the evacuation of the whole of the Jewish youth from Germany, much larger funds could be secured than had been forthcoming in response to the annual appeals. He, for one, would feel called upon to do much more than he had ever thought of doing.

Tea with Mlle. Rothbarth. Her tales of developments in Germany served only to strengthen my impressions of the ominous developments likely in the near future. Mlle. Rothbarth said that Schacht, in connection with his disregard of a financial arrangement worked out by Ulrich, the Jewish economic expert of the [German] Foreign Office, and Great Britain, said, "I am not bound by that Jewish agreement."[13] She also told me how Kaas,[14] the Catholic Center leader, justified their agreement with the Nazis in the spring of 1933 on the ground that there was a clause in the agreement to the effect that von Papen, on behalf of the Catholics, would have a veto power. She rightly emphasized that this showed how impractical were the Center leaders.

After a short visit to the Louvre, I took the 10:40 train for Savigny-sur-Orge to spend the day with the Pervys.[15] Their house is much too large for them and not very comfortable, but their grounds, which are extensive, are already beautiful and could be made much more so. We had a delightful visit.

I was almost surprised to see how changed he has become since 1929. There is in him now nothing at all of the intense French nationalism and of

10. Robert de Rothschild, French banker and Jewish community leader, president of the Consistoire Central des Israélites de France.

11. Raymond-Raoul Lambert, a leader in the French Jewish community. Headed the Union Générale des Israélites de France 1941–1943. Deported to Auschwitz, where he was murdered in December 1943.

12. Professor Israel William Oualid, Algerian-born French economist and legal expert.

13. This agreement must have preceded the Nazi regime.

14. Ludwig Kaas, Roman Catholic priest, German politician, and leader of the Center Party 1928–1933. Adviser to Cardinal Pacelli.

15. Adolph Pervy had travelled for four months in 1929 with McDonald and John D. Rockefeller III across Siberia to China and then to Kyoto as their French tutor. As it turned out, Pervy and John D. Rockefeller III did not get along well, but Pervy and McDonald remained friends for the rest of their lives.

that extreme sensitiveness which made him at moments a rather trying travelling companion. Instead, he rather bitterly expressed his disillusionment about statesmen in general and French politicians in particular. He spoke of the ruling class here as a group of men concerned only with keeping power or transferring it from one clique to another, while always profiteering from their special position. He criticized sharply the leaders of all of the middle or right parties, attributing to all of them a deliberate program of war scares and propaganda, with a view to making the success of the left parties more difficult and of giving continuous support to the war munitions industries.

As to French military training and service,[16] he said that it was unworthy of a human being, that it had almost no military value and tended to debase the individual.

Incidentally, from our talk about personal affairs I glimpsed something of traditional French economy. When I invited the Pervys to join me at the opera on Monday night, they begged to be excused on the ground that she had not had a new frock in many years, and that he had not worn his dinner jacket since he left America. Indeed, for months at a time they never went out in the evening, not even to a movie. On this basis of rigid economy, they managed to put aside enough to give themselves two or three weeks' holidays. His salary is 2,200 francs a month.

We spoke about John D. [Rockefeller] III and our experiences in Peking. Pervy told me what I had not known before, that my wife had written to him that John D., Jr., had told her that he was going to do something for Pervy. The failure of the latter to do this he attributed to John D. III's report to his father of the clash between them in Peking. Pervy said that he thought this had changed his whole career, and added rather bitterly that he had been a fool, that no one in his position then had the right to stand on his dignity or to be insulted by a Rockefeller.

I left shortly before eight o'clock, feeling that I had really known Pervy for the first time. His wife, too, bears up well under closer knowledge.

That evening McDonald sent a cable to his wife asking her to join him. It was not clear when he could return home, and he needed someone close with whom he could share his burden. She managed to arrive ten days later.

Monday, October 7, 1935

Jewish Day of Atonement, and, therefore, none of the offices were open. I lunched with Dr. Eisfelder of the Assistance Médicale, and Dr. Nettie Sutro, Ratzenstein Comité Suisse d'Aide aux Enfants d'Emigrés. . . .

Dr. Eisfelder told of a number of especially difficult cases involving children, for example, that of Mme. Schill née Hettinger, police dossier 86292.

16. Pervy had left the United States and had come back to France to do his national service.

This family, father and mother and four children, had come to France at the beginning of the exodus. Since then a new child had been born. Some time ago the father was expelled from France because of inadequate papers or for working without permission. He is now in Czechoslovakia out of work. A few days ago the mother received an expulsion order. In normal course if she does not leave, which obviously she cannot do, she will be arrested, and the five children will be left alone in the small hotel where they now live, the state not assuming any responsibility for them.

Dr. Eisfelder is anxious that the woman should be permitted to remain for some months, during which time efforts can be made to reunite the family. But since the family is not Jewish, Lambert would ordinarily not intervene on their behalf. I promised to ask him to do so.

. . . .

The opera at night, [Berlioz's] *The Damnation of Faust*. As my guests at the Rothschild box I had Miss Rothbarth, Miss Leet,[17] Mrs. Mead and her daughter, and Mrs. Malcolm Davis. . . . was a beautiful performance, marred only by the persistent chatter in the neighboring boxes.

Tuesday, October 8, 1935

Conference with [Bernhard] Kahn, at his office. We discussed various questions in connection with the reorganization. As always, he showed a complete willingness to cooperate.

Then over to see Louis Oungre. I explained to him what had happened in Geneva. He at once began to raise objections to the proposed reorganization. His main point was that it would be futile to have a new organization unless there could be assurances that it would be able to secure more from the governments than the High Commission had secured. He argued that our failure in this regard was not the result of lack of effort, or because of weak personalities, but because the circumstances were such as to preclude a greater measure of success. He doubted that a new machine with a new head would be any material improvement. Therefore, he did not see the advantage of setting it up.

He expressed the view that I had gone "perhaps a little far" in the statement in my report to the subcommittee of the Sixth Committee that the Jewish organizations could be counted on to cooperate with a central League organization.

He again expressed his skepticism about Johnson, but seemed a little reassured when I told him more about my talk with Johnson.

He emphasized that the one important task which the High Commission might perform during its remaining months would be to induce the governments to assent to the extension of the Nansen passports to the German refugees.

17. Dorothy Flagg Leet, director of Columbia University's Reed Hall Paris campus.

We might have continued our discussion much longer, but I had to leave to catch the 12:20 train to London.

The crossing was rough and its effect on me worse.

Miss Sawyer met me at the Russell [Hotel] and brought with her a cable from my wife telling me that she would arrive on the *Manhattan*. My cable to her of the previous Saturday had been more efficacious than I had dared hope.

London, Wednesday, October 9, 1935

Nearly an hour's conference with Lord Cecil at his house. We chatted first about the sanctions movement [against Italy], which I attributed in no small part to his initiative. He smilingly refused to accept credit for this and said that it was now wholly the government's responsibility. We then talked about the French attitude at Geneva. He again expressed his indignation at Bérenger's stand. He went further than that to generalize on what he declared to be the almost universal French tendency to allow personal jealousies to warp their judgment and to influence their actions. They are, he said, incorrigibly jealous of Great Britain. But it is not only in foreign affairs; their jealousies reach in the domestic field and embitter personal and party relationships. He added that he meant to tell Helbronner,[18] when he saw him, what he thought of the breach of faith involved in the stand at Geneva. He would not, he said, have urged his government to go as far as they did had he not had the assurance of French support.

Turning to the reorganization program, he said that he was fairly well pleased with what had been done at Geneva, that one must always remember that it is the first step which is the most difficult and the most important. If that is taken and is a success, the rest will follow.

In view of the French jealousy, I told him that I had to confess that he had been absolutely right in insisting that it would have been premature to have approached Lord Lytton in the matter of the new High Commissionership.

. . . .

Mr. Eric Mills of the Immigration Department of Palestine came in with Bentwich to tell me of his terrific impressions in Germany, and of his hope that a number of governments could be induced to make informal representations to the German authorities to the effect that Jewish emigration should be expedited. His plan also envisaged the cooperation of the government in such a scheme. He thought formal or open representations would be worse than useless.

I told him of my own concern about the situation and my anxiety to do anything that could be done, but I could not feel that the government could move.

18. Jacques Helbronner, counselor of state, vice president of the Consistoire, the central religious body of French Jews. Extensively treated in *Advocate for the Doomed*.

. . . .

Lunch at the Savoy with Siegmund and Erich Warburg.[19] The latter had a number of proposals to make:

(1) He was disturbed at the quality of the German refugees entering the United States. He suggested that a move should be made to modify the American regulations which made it easier for relatives of persons in the States to enter. I gave little sympathy to such a proposal on two grounds: (a) that it would be very difficult to achieve; and (b) that it would be a mistake even from the Jewish point of view to attempt.

The fact that Erich made this suggestion shows how deep-seated are the differences among the older, more aristocratic, and nationalistic German Jews and those from the East;

(2) Erich is much concerned that the funds heretofore available through the clearing arrangement to enable school children to remain abroad should be replenished. He pointed out that the flight of Jews in the smaller towns to the large cities had already so increased enrollment in the Jewish schools as to present an impossible problem. For example, in Berlin, in a school in which Lola Hahn is interested, there are now upwards of eight hundred pupils, instead of the normal three hundred;

(3) He emphasized the importance of making plans promptly in America for the shipment of food packets and other supplies to needy families if, as is to be anticipated, the situation becomes worse. He said that it would be most desirable to utilize the machinery already in existence in America, particularly since this agency is non-sectarian and has been doing work in Germany over a decade;

(4) The chief discussion centered around the problem of working out an arrangement to facilitate the transfer of Jewish capital. Both Erich and Siegmund had seen the cables from New York and had discussed the matter with New Court. Erich felt that arrangements should be made forthwith and for a minimum amount of £500,000. Siegmund thought that this would be difficult to raise, that it would be better to start with a smaller amount to get the experience in actual practice, and, if successful, to enlarge the operation. Both agreed that the scheme envisaged by Erich would in its final analysis be tantamount to financing German dumping. This, it seemed to me, raised two fundamental difficulties:

(a) The opposition of Jewish communities to any measure which would encourage German [export] sales;

(b) The probability of special anti-dumping regulations in countries of potential imports.

19. Siegmund Warburg, German-born British banker and investor, cousin of Erich Warburg.

Erich admitted these difficulties, but insisted that the effort must be made.

I further pointed out that the amount of money tied up in any such attempts to transfer capital would be very much larger, in proportion to the numbers of individuals enabled to leave Germany, than if applied directly toward the cost of emigration. This was admitted, but it was pointed out that often the individual for whom the transfer would be made might not himself go abroad, but instead use the funds made available for the emigration of relatives.

Erich explained the present proposed scheme so far as the machinery within Germany is concerned as follows: that there would not be created a German corporation to take over actual title to properties, but rather, there should be an agency in Germany, preferably a branch of a foreign [institution] or group of foreign institutions, which would act as trustee, holding mortgages on property as security against funds advanced outside. In this way it is hoped that the danger of concentrating Jewish wealth, and thus making easier its confiscation, might be avoided.

Erich reported that the present state of negotiations between Max [Warburg] and Dr. Schacht was that further progress waited on exchanges of views now taking place among the different governmental departments whose cooperation would be necessary to make the proposed transfer arrangements a success. If and when these departments agree, then Max is prepared to come to England or to go to the States for as long a period as may be necessary to carry the plan into operation;

(5) As to the general situation, Erich was more pessimistic than I had ever seen him previously. He confirmed stories I had heard from other directions about food and medical shortages, the probability of radical action in implementing the Nuremberg Laws, and the waiving of all favors on behalf of the front-line soldiers or their children. In short, he sees the situation as hopeless and as leading to the loss, not only of status but of practically the whole of Jewish capital, estimated at about three hundred million Marks.

After this meeting, McDonald wrote to Felix Warburg:

[I have just come from nearly two hours with Siegmund and Erich. Everything they had to say confirmed my own worst impressions and fears about the situation as it has been developing since the Nuremberg legislation. . . . The question on everybody's mind is what can be done. On only one point is there complete agreement—the need for immediate action is overwhelming. . . .

Certain of the governments, more particularly the British and our own, should be induced to make informal representations to the Reich authorities. . . . You will know whether anything effective can be accomplished in Washington. . . . Perhaps you will be good enough to talk over this situation with Governor Lehman and tell him that it is my opinion that he, more than anyone else, could convince the President of the emergency character of the present situation, and of the justification for informal representation through Dodd.

． ． ． ． ． ． ．

The Jewish communities, particularly in Great Britain and in the United States, must at last realize the truth, bitter and terrible though it is, which you and I and some of the rest of us have tried to drive home to them for more than two years—there can be no future for Jews in Germany.[20]]

New York Governor Herbert Lehman sent McDonald's letter on to President Roosevelt.[21]

Friday, October 11, 1935

Talked with James Parkes,[22] who said that the present German practices were following closely medieval precedents. He did not, however, know of any special decree of the year 1050 which might have been the basis textually for the Nuremberg Law. He anticipates that the present tendency in the Reich will continue, and perhaps be speeded up.

． ． ． ． ． ． ．

Lunch at New Court. Present, besides Anthony de Rothschild,[23] were Erich Warburg and two or three others.

Anthony showed that the latest happenings in the Reich had really touched him. Now there was no longer any easy assumption that Jewish needs here in England must occupy all of the community's charitable efforts. He remained skeptical as to the workableness of the proposed transfer arrangements, but added that it was, of course, not enough for British and American Jews to point [out] the difficulties. They must, instead, canvass every possibility to see if ways could not be found to rescue at least a portion of their fellow co-religionists and some substantial part of their property.

After lunch Anthony showed Erich and me the draft of the cable which had been prepared in answer to the inquiry from New York. The substance of the reply was that it was felt here that it would be desirable to wait until the pending negotiations within Germany as to transfer arrangements had issued in something tangible.

． ． ． ． ． ． ．

20. McDonald to Felix Warburg, October 10, 1935, McDonald Papers, Columbia University, D361 (Warburg Special File), Item 158.
21. McDonald's letter to Warburg, October 10, 1935, FDRL, Official File 133: Lehman to FDR, November 1, 1935, reprinted in *Franklin D. Roosevelt and Foreign Affairs*, vol. III, *September 1935–January 1937*, ed. Edgar B. Nixon (Cambridge: Belknap, 1969), 50–51.
22. Dr. James Parkes, worked with the International Student Services, did research on relations between Christians and Jews.
23. Anthony Gustav de Rothschild, British banker and Jewish community leader. Head of the emigration committee of the Council of German Jews.

Dinner at the Derenbergs[24] with the family, and then with them to the Curzon Theater to see a good movie, *Music in the Blood.*

Afterward we went directly to the BBC.

The announcer made no difficulties at all about admitting as many persons to the studio as could find seats. The others were shown to the listening room. The broadcast was without incident.[25]

. . . .

Sunday, October 13, 1935

Morning train to Tunbridge Wells, where I met Louis Oungre and drove out with him to Sir Osmond's. En route, Oungre told me that Lady Goldsmid had called him that morning to stress the importance of not tiring Sir Osmond. Oungre added that, of course, he had a very large dossier, but was expecting to return in the late afternoon. I replied that there were only two points that I wished to bring up with Sir Osmond, and that I expected to return immediately after lunch.

I was discouraged by Sir Osmond's appearance. He seems thinner; though his color is not too bad, his tendency to stumble is a bad sign. Oungre offered to allow me to have my talk alone, but I declined this, saying that I had no secrets. So the three of us went to the library together. The points covered in the hour and a quarter that we were there, were the following:

(1) Conditions in Germany. I summarized my impressions. Sir Osmond agreed. We did not, however, discuss action in detail;

(2) Developments at Geneva. I outlined these fully, including a frank statement about the attitude of Bérenger, and Cecil's and my reaction thereto. I indicated what were our hopes as to subsequent procedure. We did not discuss the details of the proposed reorganization, but I got the impression that Sir Osmond was essentially of our point of view;

(3) The ad interim period. I told Sir Osmond of my plan in reference to Bentwich. He agreed, but not enthusiastically. As to my personal plans, he still felt that it would be all right for me to leave at the end of the year;

(4) Final statement. I summarized my ideas on this point, and again Sir Osmond said that he thought that this was both my duty and my opportunity. Oungre questioned whether it might not make matters worse in Germany and also in the countries of potential immigration. Neither Sir Osmond nor I admitted that we were impressed by these arguments;

<hr />

24. Walter and Gabriele Derenberg were children of Louise Warburg, younger sister of Max and Felix.

25. In his broadcast beamed to the United States, McDonald said that he expected twenty thousand people, mostly Jews, to emigrate annually from Germany. He urged that the League take over the responsibility and warned that "a delayed or half-hearted solution of this problem by the League would be worse than nothing at all." *New York Times,* October 12, 1935, p. 12.

(5) The minor matter. I announced that after examining carefully the financial figures, it would not be necessary for us to have the supplementary grant from ICA for the last two months, and that therefore I was withdrawing my request. I added if the two unpaid pledges of $7,500 from the JDC and £1,000 from the High Commission were good (and I had reason to believe they were), we should have a slight balance at the end of the year.

Sir Osmond seemed a little embarrassed by this statement. He said that he had "with the loyal cooperation of Oungre," pressed his colleagues on the ICA board and had finally gotten their consent to vote the supplementary £600; but that he regretted to add that Helbronner and Gottschalk were insisting that the vote be coupled with the phrase that this be the last contribution from ICA to the High Commission. He was relieved therefore that he would be able to say that we would not need the money, for he intended now to ask his colleagues to make the grant to him personally, for use in his discretion. I replied that I thought this was excellent, because if an unexpected situation arose, I should not hesitate to try to convince him as to the desirability of making the money available to us, though I would not be willing to attempt to convince his colleagues.

During all this talk about the "minor matter" Sir Osmond and Oungre reiterated statements to the effect that, of course, the attitude of Helbronner and Gottschalk had nothing personal in it. My reply was, "I know perfectly well what the attitude of these gentlemen is. Indeed, I have had no illusions about their attitude for many months, any more than I have had about that of Bérenger. My knowledge of their position is one of the factors which makes me the more anxious to return home to work with and for people whom I understand and who understand me."

In the course of the discussion Sir Osmond expressed regret that the High Commission would disappear, saying that it was the one instance where the League of Nations had made what is primarily a Jewish cause the occasion for setting up a special institution.

After lunch I took the mid-afternoon train back to London.

To see Grace Moore in *On Wings of Song*. Supper alone at the Savoy, and home to bed.

Monday, October 14, 1935

Telephone call from Wilfrid Israel[26] to the effect that he was in town just for the morning on private business. I said that I would come to see him at once. This Bentwich and I did. He was at the house of Mrs. Frank L. with his mother and a woman doctor, Goldhaber. Mrs. Israel asked if I would be willing

---

26. Wilfrid Israel, born in England, close friend and co-worker of Lola Hahn in Jewish causes in Germany, and often Max Warburg's envoy to British Jews. Extensively treated in *Advocate for the Doomed*.

to be of help to Dr. Goldhaber if, as now seemed likely, she might have to go to the States, or at any rate, leave Germany. I said I would. She is reported to be one of the most brilliant women physicians specializing in functioning of glands in the whole of the Reich.

Wilfrid Israel's account of conditions was very similar to that of Erich Warburg, but rather more detailed and circumstantial. In particular, his own experience with a representative of the Party who had come recently to say that if he were not prepared to sell [the Israel Department Store] at once, then within a few weeks he might not be able to sell at all. This was put on the ground that within a few days, perhaps that very week, the cabinet would implement the Nuremberg Laws and so penalize the Jews as to confiscate in effect their property.

Meantime, Dr. Schacht is on his holidays in Italy. He is said to be very tired, if not worse off nervously. In any case, Israel does not think that Dr. Schacht will make any real fight against the prevailing tendencies; and, indeed, he might purposely absent himself from the decisive meeting of the cabinet. Moreover, Israel does not think that there are any real negotiations about transfer going on. He does not think there will be tangible results from the exchanges between Schacht and Max Warburg.

Israel told of the arrest of Dr. Baeck and of the continued detention of Dr. Hirsch.[27] He hoped that the latter might be released by the middle of the week. It appeared that if it were not achieved, then there would be long delay.

As we were leaving, Israel asked me to come into one of the adjoining rooms alone. He said he wished to thank me for what I had done during the past two years and to say that he was expressing the views of his colleagues and of the Jewish community in Germany. He spoke with real feeling, and I was touched by it. My only reply was that I regretted that I had been able to do so little.

He left immediately to fly back to his business.

. . . .

Tuesday, October 15, 1935

Advisory Council meeting in the morning. Everything considered, it went off with a minimum of friction. The only serious objection to any one of the proposals was that of Louis Oungre to the ad interim arrangement. But he made no violent opposition and at the vote merely abstained. He did make a rather gratuitous suggestion that perhaps our proposed resolution about reorganization under the League, in the paragraph referring to the need for repre-

27. Rabbi Leo Baeck had asked Germany's rabbis to read a defiant special prayer on the Day of Atonement as a protest against the Nuremberg Laws, including the statement "we pronounce our abhorrence and see trampled deeply beneath our feet the lies which are turned against us, the slander turned against our religion and its character." He was arrested and held for twenty-four hours. Otto Hirsch was held for eight days. Leonard Baker, *Days of Sorrow and Pain: Leo Baeck and the Berlin Jews* (New York: Oxford University Press, 1978), 204–205.

sentation on the administrative staff of persons acquainted with the German refugee problem, was designed to ensure places for members of our own staff. I at once caught him up on this.

At the afternoon's meeting it was stormy. Cecil had consented to come and, at my request, made an interesting statement of his reasons for feeling that a League organization would be material improvement over ours.

Then Helbronner began in a very unpleasant voice to criticize the inclusion of the recommendation for an Advisory Council in the action taken that morning. Cecil agreed that it would be better not to have two bodies. Then, though most of the persons present wished an Advisory Body, no one defended the proposal, and it was therefore withdrawn.

This was only a beginning, however, for Helbronner. He followed up his easy victory by attacking another resolution passed during the morning—that providing for a continuation of the High Commission with a reduced staff, pending action by the Council. Brutally, he announced that he had orders from his government to work for the complete dissolution of the Commission at the end of the year. He argued that since the High Commissioner was resigning, his colleagues must go with him, since they were dependent upon him and could have no independent existence.

I replied that technically there was substance in Helbronner's contention, but that practically it seemed to me more desirable to assume that I, following the precedent set by Nansen, could name an acting High Commissioner, and that, in this way, the interim period could best be handled.

After more discussion from Helbronner, Cecil intervened to suggest that it would not be necessary to name an acting High Commissioner, that since my resignation would be made to the Council, I would continue theoretically to be High Commissioner until my resignation had been accepted. He added that he thought it preferable that the office should continue during the interim until the new organization was set up.

It was at about this juncture that Louis Oungre intervened to declare, in a nasty tone, that the private organizations which had financed the High Commission had committed themselves only to the end of the year, and that so far as his organization—ICA—was concerned, he could make no commitment whatsoever for the so-called ad interim period. He implied, both by what he said and by the way he said it, not only that ICA would not make any further contribution, but that its attitude in the matter should be decisive. He could not have been more unpleasant.

In view of this and Helbronner's statement, I felt that I had to make at any rate two points: so I emphasized, first, that while of course the attitude of the French government was very important, France was only one of the governments on the Governing Body, and I was not responsible to it but to the Council of the League. Second, so far as ICA was concerned, though I was deeply grateful for its financial help in the past, I could not accept the assumption that I was limited in my work or that the High Commission was dependent upon a further contribution from ICA; that, on the contrary, I was sure funds would be available for the interim period.

It was at this moment that Cecil chose to slip out. There followed some rather tense moments, and later in the session I said that if I had offended Helbronner or Oungre, I was sorry. Finally a form of resolution continuing the, or rather recommending the continuation of the "services" on a reduced basis, was passed. Nonetheless, much harm had been done, and as Bentwich was to tell me later, he had definitely made up his mind during the discussion that he could not carry on, and I had to tell him that I felt he was right.

Toward the end of the meeting there was a longish discussion on what might be done to affect the German situation. We finally wound up in good temper at tea.

Walked out with Herbert May, who agreed that I could not have said less to Helbronner and Oungre. He, however, seemed a little sorry, as did some of the others, that I had softened my reply later. But I was not sorry I had done so, because there would have been no profit in leaving the situation such that Helbronner or Oungre would have felt called upon to break off relations altogether.[28]

Down to the Paddington Station. The boat train was fortunately on time, at 8:53. Ruth reported a crossing as good as she could expect at that time of the year. But her account of her exchanges with Ambassador and Mrs. Straus[29] did not surprise me.

Wednesday, October 16, 1935

The meeting of the Permanent Committee went off like clockwork. Thanks in considerable part to May's careful preparatory work, not even the complicated financial questions resulted in any debate. It was true that the meeting was something of an exchange between Cecil and Helbronner, but the latter was on his good behavior and made no trouble.

After the meeting Helbronner came up to me and said that he hoped there would be nothing in the minutes of the Advisory Council about the slight difference of opinion yesterday afternoon. I assured him on this point.

It was a great relief to have had Cecil agree to continue as chairman of the Governing Body until the meeting of the League Council. This action on his part removed the last doubt in my mind as to my being able to get away at the end of the year, since under his general responsibility all the essential moves in the transfer and in the winding up can be carried through.

28. Bernhard Kahn wrote, "I must say that I have attended many meetings in the thirty-five years of my service but never such a depressing one as that one in London. Our French friends treated Mr. McDonald like a small office boy whose services are no longer needed and who should be dismissed on the spot. I tried my best, even by using Mr. Nahum Goldmann as an ally, to correct the situation, but against French verbosity we could not do much. Even Mr. McDonald lost his temper and made some bitter remarks which he later withdrew." Bernhard Kahn to Joseph C. Hyman, October 30, 1935. JDC Archives, HC3/High Commission File, 1935.

29. Jesse Isidore Straus, American ambassador to France, 1933–1936.

Conference at the Foreign Office with Mr. Baxter. He apologized for not being informed in detail about the questions I wished to discuss, but said that all the other men were away on leave or in Geneva.

I told him that the first matter which I wished to urge had in a sense been taken care of by the decision of the Council to name the members of the Experts' Committee, and as I understood it, to call the first meeting of the Experts' Committee for the twenty-eighth of November. Nonetheless, since we felt that prompt action is so extremely important, I ventured to hope that the Foreign Office would miss no opportunity to press for speed at Geneva. Baxter seemed to agree that this would be desirable.

I then explained my desire to see Vansittart[30] to talk with him about the desirability of the British government making informal representations at Berlin about the policy of the German government toward the Jews. I said that I realized how busy the undersecretary must be at this particular time, but that the situation in Germany is so desperate that I felt that delay would be disastrous. Baxter promised to take the matter up with Vansittart and give me a reply.[31]

. . . .

In connection with my diary for Wednesday I should have included an account of a talk with Mrs. van Tyn,[32] . . . [who] expressed with evident sincerity her deep regret at the attacks from the French on Tuesday afternoon. I told her that I had not minded these so much for myself, as I had because of their seeming reflection on Bentwich, since I had at the morning session proposed him as my successor for the ad interim period.

I should also have included in the Tuesday's report of the afternoon session of the Advisory Council a statement of the remarks at the close by Dr. Cohen. He was kind enough to speak very sympathetically and appreciatively of my work. Though no formal action was taken, he seemed to express the sense of the meeting, with the exception of the French group.

Perhaps I should also add that earlier in the afternoon meeting Bernhard Kahn had also spoken warmly though briefly about the work of the Commission. Others had done the same, including Miss Pye, Goldmann, and Schevenels.[33]

---

30. Sir Robert Vansittart, British permanent undersecretary of state for foreign affairs.

31. In his minutes of the meeting Baxter wrote that he thought it would be awkward to start discussions, because Britain could be asked to take the Jews. It would be better to use their limited influence for British citizens. "We cannot refuse McDonald's request out of hand. We may be certain that if we did so, our action would be much criticized here." Baxter minutes, October 18, 1935 FO 371/18862. C7298/323/18, cited by A. J. Sherman, *Island Refuge* (London: Frank Casse, 1994), 62.

32. Gertrud van Tyn (also spelled van Tijn), born in Germany, social worker of independent means.

33. Walter Schevenels, Belgian, secretary of the [Socialist] Second International.

....

Lunch with Idelson[34] at the First Avenue Hotel. During the meal we talked about a number of phases of my work and did not come to the main subject until at the end. Then Idelson, as always, proved to be extraordinarily suggestive. He agreed that my report would come at a most opportune moment. Never before in the history of the modern world had a great state made hundreds of thousands of its citizens helpless prisoners, refusing them the means of livelihood within or the means of seeking a livelihood without. Nor had there been a period in recent history when the nations of the world generally practiced such extreme and heartless policies of exclusion as now. Is it any wonder that men turn to revolution and become anti-social? Many of the most fundamental values of nineteenth-century liberal civilization are today threatened or have already been scrapped. It is high time that the significance of these developments are [*sic*] pointed out.

Idelson said that he was just finishing a book on the history of mysticism, and added that there was a certain amount of mysticism in him. Therefore, it seemed to him that there must be some deep significance in the fact of my nomination for my present work. If I, of all the men in the world, had been chosen to direct this ungrateful task, and in so doing, to break with my own past, it must be that I was meant to perform a distinctive service—perhaps my final report would be the embodiment of this. In any case, he was completely at my disposition for any service that he could offer to me. I thanked him cordially and said that I would get in touch with him as soon as my own outline of my report had been further advanced.

....

On this day McDonald wrote Leland Robinson a very long letter about international relations, which is excerpted here:

[. . . I claim at present no adequate qualifications as an observer. Indeed, there are two considerations which tend to disqualify me: (a) my deep sense of pessimism, partly an outgrowth of my experiences with governments during the past two years, and; (b) my absorption in the refugee work which has kept me from devoting attention directly to international affairs as such.

The extent to which the Abyssinian crisis has overshadowed other issues is a striking illustration of the futility of prophecy—at least in specific matters. For example, if twelve months ago you had asked a dozen of the most experienced students of international affairs to name the foremost serious

34. Vladimir Robert Idelson, practicing in London (barrister since 1928), expert on Russian and international law.

danger spots in the world, I doubt if Abyssinia would have been included in the list of any one of these students. Yet today one hears in the press of little else.

In a sense this absorption in the Italian-Abyssinian controversy is justified. Undoubtedly it does offer the most flagrant recent example—after that of the Japanese in Manchuria and Northern China—of unashamed traditional imperialism. Unlike, however, the Japanese adventure, it has become international in the broadest sense of the word, because this time Great Britain has chosen to make of it a test case of the workableness of the League principles and machinery. Except for the British, nothing more would have happened at Geneva than happened there to retard the Japanese.

. . . .

Nonetheless, I cannot rid myself of the depressing conviction that the dominant motivation of His Majesty's Government is not different from that which has controlled the policy of that Government in the past—that is, essentially national self-interest, the control of the Mediterranean, the Suez Canal, and the upper waters of the Nile. . . .

I realize that it can be argued that just because the nations are actuated by enlightened self-interest, they are more likely to carry through to the end a policy of sanctions against Italy. But I remain skeptical as to the extent of the enlightenment in the countries' conception of their self-interest. Already there are many signs that can be read between the lines to indicate that narrow interpretations of national self-interest may more and more weaken the program of sanctions as it comes to be applied in practice.

Moreover, a system of sanctions applied against Italy to an extent sufficient to defeat the Italian ambitions in Abyssinia, unless it thereby laid a secure basis for a European peace system which would work with equal efficacy in another graver crisis, might prove in the end to have hastened the day, so feared by serious students of international affairs here—a European war involving most of the continent. I have no love for dictators, even less for totalitarian states, and no special affection for the Italian Fascist regime or for its leader. Nonetheless, I do not see how one can be sure that the weakening of Italy would not leave Germany so dangerously supreme on the continent as to hasten the time when the Reich will challenge the whole of the territorial arrangements in the East fixed by the treaties of 1919. And such a challenge can only mean war on a continental scale.[35]]

. . . .

35. McDonald to Leland Robinson, October 18, 1935. Copy in McDonald Papers, USHMM.

Over to Marks & Spencer's head office to see Simon Marks.[36] As I began to give him my impressions of the German situation, he called in Sacher,[37] and the three of us continued the discussion. Sacher, who is always most definite in his views, was most emphatic in declaring that there is neither the funds nor any practical scheme for effecting the transfer of Jewish capital on a large scale from Germany. Moreover, the principle is wrong, for, as he puts it, it would mean substituting good Jewish money outside for bad Jewish money within Germany. Moreover, it would mean applying money from outside not in proportions sufficient to bring individuals out of Germany, but in proportion to what the individuals have in Germany. I had to confess that I too had my very serious doubts about the practicability of all of the large transfer schemes.

We then discussed the problems of transferring the younger people to the number of 15,000 to 20,000 a year. This program both of them were prepared to support.

Meantime, Simon Marks outlined three or four instances where his firm had financed the setting up of new industries in England or in Czechoslovakia by German industrialists who, forced to sacrifice nearly all of their capital, had been able to bring out their plans and their knowledge of the business. Then assured of a market to the Marks & Spencer organization and financed during the first year or two by the same organization, they had succeeded.

In this way a good deal could be done, but this was a far cry from any of the comprehensive schemes suggested.

. . . .

Simon Marks suggested that we continue our discussion at lunch, at Claridge's, where the three of us were joined by Joseph L. Cohen, Bentwich, and Norman Laski, a cousin of Neville and another of the Marks brothers-in-law. Something of the same ground was covered at lunch, but the most interesting point was brought up inadvertently when I, in answer to a comment by Simon Marks about my apparent wide knowledge of Jewish affairs, had said, "But there is one thing I can't understand, and that is the irreligious Zionists." Little did I realize that I was sitting between two such—Sacher made some very pertinent and pointed remark to the effect that religion had nothing to do with it at all. Then Marks pooh-poohed Bentwich's talk about the mission of the Jews, saying that he was sick and tired of all this talk about a mission or the re-valuation of old values, that he was interested merely in seeing the Jews organized and living as a normal people, that the sooner they had rifles and machine guns and military support at their back, the sooner would they be respected.

36. Lord Simon Marks, chairman, Marks & Spencer department store chain, a Zionist.
37. Harry Sacher, *Manchester Guardian* journalist, married into the Marks family. An important British Zionist.

I ventured to suggest that this sounded very much like Jabotinsky.[38] Marks did not deny it, but nonetheless stood his ground.

Ruth and I went early to the Mayfair for the Anglo-Palestinian Dinner. Already a large crowd was there. Before dinner I met and chatted with Sir Robert Waley-Cohen[39] and members of his family, the Chief Rabbi and his daughter, Dr. Weizmann and Mrs. Weizmann, and some others. I sat between Mrs. Weizmann and Professor Haldane,[40] and Ruth next to Sir Robert Waley-Cohen.

There were many too many speakers, but considering that, the program was excellent. It began with a good statement by the chairman, James A. de Rothschild. Then Weizmann briefly proposed the toast to Malcolm MacDonald,[41] who replied in a brilliant and diplomatic speech of twenty minutes.

The archbishop of Liverpool, in a rather didactic talk, proposed the toast "Racial and Religious Tolerance." This supported by Professor J. B. S. Haldane and by the Chief Rabbi. The chief response was by Sir Arthur Wauchope,[42] who pleaded for the planting of the tree of mutual understanding between Arab and Jew in Palestine.

Sir Robert Waley-Cohen proposed the toast "The Jewish National Home." I supported it, and Mr. Simon Marks responded.

Perhaps the most striking speech of the evening was that of Lady Erleigh, who proposed the toast for the club. She took occasion to reply to Malcolm's suggestion that care should be taken lest they jerry-build in Palestine by pointing out that, during a war, you do not stop to rebuild the hospitals, but you bring your wounded into the corridors. Similarly, she deftly touched on the Trans-Jordan possibility and emphasized the importance to Britain of a Palestine hinterland developed by loyal Jews. Horowitz, chairman of the club, replied briefly. And finally, Barnett Janner proposed the toast to the chairman, who replied and the meeting was over, at 11:55.

Afterward Dr. Sokolow and his daughter were almost pitiably grateful to me, because I had been the one person in the whole evening who had mentioned the name of Sokolow, while speaker after speaker had paid brief or repeated tributes to Weizmann.

. . . .

38. Vladimir Zeev Jabotinsky, Russian-born Revisionist Zionist leader.

39. Sir Robert Waley-Cohen, Anglo-Jewish leader and chairman of British Shell Oil Company.

40. Professor J. B. S. Haldane, British biologist and professor of genetics at the University of London. He had been working to find jobs for refugee scientists.

41. Malcom MacDonald, son of former Prime Minister Ramsey MacDonald, had just become secretary of state for Dominion Affairs. In May 1939, as colonial secretary, he introduced the White Paper that severely restricted Jewish immigration to Palestine. In a letter to Felix Warburg, McDonald missed the mark in judging Malcom MacDonald, based on his speech at this dinner, sympathetic to Zionist aspirations. McDonald to Felix Warburg, October 23, 1935, McDonald Papers, Columbia University, D361 (Warburg Special File), Item 158.

42. British high commissioner of Palestine, 1931–1938.

Lunch with Bishop Bell.[43] We first talked about Germany. He told me of his conferences with [Rudolf] Hess and with Kerrl.[44] From both of these he had gotten the impression that they meant to do the right thing in the church controversy, but he could not be sure of their ability. I seized this opportunity to tell him of what was happening to the Jews, and of Ebbutt's conviction as to the fate of the church.

Then we talked about the appeal. He agreed that the most important thing was to find the right organizer, and that while it would be desirable to carry on the campaign nominally through one of the church organizations, there is no chance that the church secretaries or the existing organizations could themselves do the job effectively. I then asked him for suggestions for an organizer. He had none, but he thought that Miss Elenora Iredale, of the Student Movement House, and of Ammondale, Golders Green, who was a brilliant money-raiser, might know of someone. He volunteered to speak to her about it.

The bishop suggested that it might be possible to get the bishops of the Anglican Church to agree to take certain quotas in this campaign. He, for example, thought that a certain amount could be raised in his diocese, perhaps £2,000. However, he pointed out that it would be necessary to educate the other bishops. He added that to be a success the appeal would have to provide for the money being paid over a period of three years. This seemed to me rather difficult, but since he saw it as an essential element, I did not argue the matter.

In general, he said that he would be glad to help wherever he could, and would encourage the archbishop to take the lead.

While we were talking, Lord Lothian[45] came along. He was rather apologetic about not having replied to my letter, asked me how long I would be here, and said he would get in touch with me later. I took advantage of the occasion, however, to tell him that I thought he had a responsibility to bring influence to bear on Germany. His reply was that he doubted if anything could be done until Germany raised some such question as the return of the colonies, at which time the British government could very properly and should say, "We cannot sit down with you until you have changed your policy of intolerance."

. . . .

43. George Bell, Bishop of Chichester and pioneer of the Ecumenical Movement.

44. Rudolf Hess, Hitler's onetime secretary who had become his deputy and administrator of the Nazi Party organization. Dr. Hans Kerrl, Nazi lawyer, appointed minister for church affairs in July 1935. Kerrl oversaw the expansion of the pro-Nazi German Christian faction within the Protestant churches. See Doris L. Bergen, *Twisted Cross: The German Christian Movement in the Third Reich* (Chapel Hill: University of North Carolina Press, 1996).

45. Lord Lothian, Philip Henry Kerr, Marquis of Lothian. Long in the diplomatic service, he had been private secretary to Prime Minister Lloyd George, 1916–1921, in the cabinet of Ramsay MacDonald in 1931. His last posting was as ambassador to Washington (July 1939–December 1940), where he died.

Over to Woburn House to see Mrs. Schwab of the Children's Committee. I told her of my special interest in the Schoens and my anxiety that the children might continue to be cared for. She made no definite commitment, but I think it likely that her group will continue to support the children, and perhaps from time to time do something to help the parents.

. . . .

About three-quarters of an hour with Dr. Weizmann. Our views about the possibility of the transfer of capital from Germany on a large scale are nearly identical. I asked him about the rumor from Palestine that there would be a smaller proportion of certificates for German refugees than heretofore. He said that he did not think this would be the case; that only one member of the [Jewish Agency] Executive, a Pole, favored it. He continued to discuss the matter, however, at some length, emphasizing that one must have sympathy with the Polish point of view because of the terrible need in Poland and because of the unsympathetic way in which German Jews had always until the present crisis dealt with their eastern co-religionists. He himself remembered very well conditions in Hamburg thirty years ago when Jews of the type of Max Warburg treated Polish and Russian Jews like dirt.

We talked a little about the appeals for next year. Weizmann said that he, while favoring a separate appeal because he thought it would be more effective and because it was not good for Zionists to be inactive, would not give orders to his colleagues, but would allow them to decide for themselves, since they would have to be the ones who would carry through whatever program was agreed upon.

At length he outlined to me his conception of broad strategy in Palestine. He had regretted that Lady Erleigh went as far as she did in her talk the other night about Trans-Jordan and the reliance which the Empire could place upon a Jewish hinterland in Trans-Jordan. The development of Trans-Jordan will require a large-scale settlement of some thousands of persons, which, in turn, necessitates millions of dollars. Until those conditions are met, the British may continue to hesitate because of the defense problem.

Meantime, more immediately practicable would be the development in the neighborhood of Aqaba. This [Red Sea port] city, if it were properly connected with Haifa, would give the British an absolutely assured route to India, irrespective of what might happen to the Suez Canal. He had tentatively made this point with Malcolm [MacDonald], but the latter had refused to commit himself on the major question of making Aqaba, in effect, a part of Palestine, saying that he would have to refer this matter to the Foreign Office. Weizmann said that there is no doubt that Britain could, if it would, decree that Aqaba is a part of Palestine.

Weizmann used his very careful negotiations with the British in connection with Aqaba as an illustration of his extremely cautious methods with them. As he put it, each year in the tunnel which he is building, he advances in millimeters; to do more might do more harm than good.

Weizmann said that, after all, the fundamental difficulty, both with Trans-Jordan and with Aqaba, is one which must be faced. It is that the British might properly ask, "What guarantees have we that if we encourage the Jews to flow over into Trans-Jordan and southward and permitted them to make homes for millions, that in every crisis and at all times they would be loyal to Britain?" And, he added, one cannot give a categorical affirmative reply.

. . . .

As I was leaving him, he gave me his blessing, which seemed a little incongruous because of his emphasis on the non-religious side of Zionism. Nonetheless, his sincerity could not be doubted.

Friday, October 25, 1935

Half an hour's conference with Lord Cecil at his house. I congratulated him on having converted Churchill[46] to the League, as evidenced in the latter's speech in the House the day previous. He said that Churchill had always insisted that they were not far apart, but that he had remained rather skeptical.

I called his attention to the dispatch from Berlin in the morning paper to the effect that Goebbels had ordered that no Jewish names be included among those to be inscribed on the memorials to the war dead. Cecil said that this was the worst thing which would shock the average Britisher, and that he might write a letter to the *Times* about it. I told him that I hoped he would.

We then discussed the problem of attempting to influence the attitude of the Reich authorities through possible representations by the British government. Cecil felt that the authorities probably would not be willing to go further than they probably had been going—that is, not beyond expressing informally to the officials in Berlin the view that so long as Germany continued its intensive policy of discrimination, it would be difficult for Britain to adopt any program which might seem to be pro-German. Cecil said that if Eden or Hoare asked to see him, that he would emphasize the desirability of making this view clear in Berlin.

As to my attempting to see Hoare or Baldwin,[47] Cecil felt it would be a mistake to press such a request prior to the election. He also felt that there would be no value in attempting to get a group of powers to make representations. There would be much delay in the preliminary discussions, and even if one succeeded in having action taken, the net result in Germany probably would be bad.

46. Winston Churchill, Conservative politician, prime minister of Great Britain, 1940–1945.
47. Stanley Baldwin, prime minister of Great Britain, 1923–1924, 1935–1937.

I asked him if he did not think it desirable for me to see Rumbold.[48] He said by all means. He characterized him as a shrewd, though perhaps not driving, personality, a man who looks like a perfect idiot, but is far from that. He added that Rumbold hates the Germans and Hitler. Parenthetically, Cecil said, "I must confess that I do hate the Germans; they seem to me an unspeakable people."

In the course of our discussion something was said about Britain's foreign policy and the League and sanctions, etc. Cecil's comment was that his country ought never hesitate to carry out a policy irrespective of cost so long as it served the common interests of the nations and "our own national interest."

. . . .

Dinner at Mrs. Ernst Schiff's. Others there, besides the hostess and Ruth and I, were Otto Schiff,[49] Rosie Derenberg, Mr. Turk, a Jewish broker colleague of Schiff's, Mrs. Marion Warburg, Mrs. Schiff's mother, and Mr. and Mrs. Bulkeley-Johnson of the firm of Rothschilds. During the meal at our end of the table the atmosphere was almost riotous. But out of it all I got a promise from Mrs. Bulkeley-Johnson of an English fruitcake before Christmas.

After dinner the men remained in the dining room until nearly eleven. Our talk was about the German-Jewish problem. No one dissented from the view that the transfer of any considerable part of the Jewish capital was impossible. The suggestion in Schiff's cable to New Court about the shifting of Jewish merchants and traders into manufacturing was, according to Otto, wholly Felix's. The latter, he added, was extremely anxious to induce Max and the rest of the [Warburg] family to leave Germany.

The most interesting part of the discussion in the later part of the evening was Mr. Bulkeley-Johnson's long statement to me as to his attitude on the condition of Jews in England. I think his statement is important, because he seems to me to be peculiarly typical of that powerful section of British life made up of ex-soldiers of the officer class, ex–civil servants, the middle-class property owners, and those with fixed incomes and the aristocracy. As to the Anglo-Jews, like the Rothschilds, the Weizmanns, and the Simon Marks, he had his "fascist eye on them." At first, I did not sense the full significance of this reference about fascist eye. As he talked, however, it became clear that he meant this literally: that though, as he put it, nearly all of his British instincts abhor the idea of fascism, yet he realizes that he and people who feel as he does have in them something which will make them turn toward fascism in the event that all that they hold dear were threatened by the complete demoralization or the threat of something like communism in this country. In that contingency he would want to be prepared to be able to say whether the prominent Jews could probably be counted upon to give an absolutely undivided

48. Sir Horace George Montagu Rumbold, diplomat since 1891, British ambassador to Germany 1928–1933, by 1935 retired.
49. Otto Schiff, prominent merchant banker in London, cousin of Frieda Warburg, head of the Jewish Refugee Committee.

loyalty to Britain. If not, their position would be gravely jeopardized. Of course, as soon as the crisis would be over, the British sense of fair play would lead many influential people to rise to the defense of the Jews, and therefore one need never fear the abuses which stained Germany's honor so shockingly.

I asked him if he meant that the fascist regime might be built on Mosley's[50] organization. His quick response was no, but as he went on, he admitted that it might be very useful to have the Mosley organization in being. At any rate, in Mosley's group you had men whose views were certain, and upon whom you could count to defend to the utmost King, God, and country. In a crisis thousands of persons like himself would rally to that banner.

I was the more impressed by Bulkeley-Johnson's monologue because of the following considerations:

(a) His long association with the Rothschilds;
(b) His statement, which I must take as the truth, that he is one of the Englishmen most sympathetic with the Jews, and;
(c) The almost fanatical light which shone in his eyes as he warmed to his subject (in an Englishman fanaticism is a very dangerous sign!).

London, Saturday, October 26, 1935

Two years since I took on this job. What it has meant for me I already know in part, but not until long from now will I understand fully.

. . . .

In the afternoon Ruth and I went to the Weizmanns for tea. Others there, besides the Weizmanns and ourselves, were Mr. Ben-Gurion[51] and two other members of the Zionist executive. Again, the talk underlined the fundamental differences between the nationalist Jews and those who feel themselves primarily to be members of the communities where they live in the Diaspora. Weizmann again expressed his contempt for the Neville Laskis and the Rothschilds, saying that what he objected to in them was not their lack of Jewishness, but the fact that not being real Jews, they nonetheless continued to set themselves up as leaders of Jewry. In fact, they are relatively insignificant in England, and it is only because of their insignificance that they may be able to avoid the same kind of attacks here as the Jews in Germany have suffered.

We discussed the question of irreligious or anti-religious Zionists. The groups denied that they were really anti-religious, or that men like Simon Marks and Sacher were. They were opposed to medievalism and the obscu-

50. Sir Oswald Mosley, founder and head of the British Union of Fascists.

51. In his diary David Ben-Gurion wrote that he was amazed at McDonald's expertise in Zionist office gossip and annoyed at Weizmann for adding to McDonald's "already impressive and unnecessary involvement in internal Jewish conflicts." Shabatai Teveth, *Ben Gurion: The Burning Ground, 1886–1948* (Boston: Houghton Mifflin, 1987), 509.

rantism of reactionary orthodoxy, but they insisted that the Jewish nation is so closely associated with the Jewish religion that the two cannot really be separated. In other words, an intense nationalist is in a sense intensely religious.

With Ruth to see Fred Astaire in *Top Hat*.

Monday, October 28, 1935

Ernest Kahn[52] came in to report on the work and plans of the Refugee Economic Corporation. He told first, however, that he had recently conferred with Mauricio Hochschild in Paris, and of the latter's conviction that a very large number of young Jews could be placed in the Argentine, and of Hochschild's willingness to take an active part in that plan. This account confirmed what Hochschild had said to me in Buenos Aires in the spring. I was glad to know of Hochschild's whereabouts.

Kahn told of his forthcoming visit to Palestine as a housing expert in connection with the project of the corporation to finance the building of houses there for children.

The project of Zemurray[53] in Guatemala is going forward. It will involve the purchase at almost bankrupt prices of certain estates which should be in such a condition as to be put quickly on a paying basis. It is expected that most of the immigrants there would be not 100 percent Jews, but partial Jews and left-wing refugees. I asked specifically if the corporation would finance it on this basis, and Kahn said yes. He estimates that the per capita cost will be very low, perhaps lower than in any other country.

Kahn reported briefly on the project for the settlement of a certain number of refugees in south France. This is being handled very discreetly by Dr. Bernhard Kahn, and is not to be spoken of generally.

Kahn raised the question of the possibility of my intervention with certain American consuls general looking toward their making somewhat easier the granting of visas. I told him of what I had done, and that I would be glad to intervene in any particular case where it seemed clear that my action would be helpful.

As Kahn talked, I became more and more startled by his appearance and his manner of speech. He seemed to me almost like a man who was either on the verge of serious illness or who was suffering from a form of shell-shock.

. . . .

More interesting and encouraging to me than Kahn's visit was that of Dr. [Mark] Wischnitzer[54] of the Hilfsverein der deutschen Juden[55] in Berlin. Each

---

52. Ernest Kahn, a German Jew who became assistant to Otto Schiff.

53. Samuel Zemurray, a Bessarabian Jewish immigrant to the United States, who, in 1930, became president of United Fruit Company.

54. Dr. Mark Wischnitzer, author of (among others) *To Dwell in Safety* (1948), a history of Jewish migrations since 1800.

55. The Hilfsverein was a German-Jewish aid organization concerned with emigration.

contact with him strengthens my impression of his unusual ability. His account of conditions made clear that a state of panic may occur at almost any time. The Jews in the smaller places are selling their businesses and property for what they can get, and are fleeing to the larger cities, there anxiously searching for opportunities for emigration.

As indicative of the interest in finding ways and means to leave the country, Dr. Wischnitzer said that the new edition of their *Korrespondenzblatt über Auswanderungs- und Siedlungswesen* [circular on emigration and settlement] of 5,000 copies had been sold within three days, and that recent meetings called to discuss emigration possibilities had been over-crowded, even though only a few hours' notice had been given. These meetings had become increasingly necessary because of the springing up of irresponsible bodies with fantastic schemes of emigration and settlement. He listed among these the Ecuadorian project.[56] His own organization is in a difficult position since, though it is, of course, free to denounce and warn against such projects, it itself is subject to constant and sharp criticism, because it is unable to show at once opportunities for everyone to emigrate. As Dr. Wischnitzer put it, "These frantically anxious people cannot understand why we cannot by some formula change the attitudes of the governments throughout the world."

A significant illustration of the increase in German trade with Italy is the fact that the German government now encourages Jewish emigrants to go to Italy by offering them Devisen [foreign exchange] in the form of Italian lira for amounts as large as 15,000 to 30,000 Marks. Such recipients must pay 30 percent to the Reich Gold Discount Bank, and also take a certain other loss due to the differential in the value of the lira in Germany and in Italy. Those who ask for amounts smaller than 10,000 Marks escape the 30 percent tax. The emigrants to Italy must pledge themselves not to leave that country. It is said that as much as half a million Marks have been set aside for this purpose—more perhaps would be available. The necessary technical arrangements are put through quickly. I should add that from another source I learned a little later that for some time there have been special facilities for those who wished Italian Devisen.

Dr. Wischnitzer raised the question whether, since only a relatively few Jews could go to Italy even with these added facilities, might it not be worthwhile to inquire whether they could go on to Albania and still utilize their Italian lira? He seemed to assume that Albania was a sort of Italian colony. I said that I doubted if the Albanians would agree with this interpretation, but I suggested that he talk that matter out with Bentwich at lunch.

Returning then to the subject of Jewish emigration, Dr. Wischnitzer said that even at present with quite inadequate funds, it was going on at the rate of several hundred a month. Frequently, he is surprised at the extent to which

56. In 1935 a French Jewish organization negotiated an agreement with the president of Ecuador for the lease of 500,000 acres to be farmed by Jewish immigrants. The agreement fell apart when Jewish organizations deemed the land unsuitable for cultivation.

family connections throughout the world result in the calling of relatives. This is the normal Jewish method of emigration. He feels that if a large guarantee fund were available to meet the financial guarantee requirements in countries such as South Africa, the Argentine, Brazil, Chile, it would be possible through this very normal procedure to evacuate tens of thousands of people a year. He is, therefore, taking the matter up with the ICA authorities and those of the British Central Fund. I asked him if he had seen Sir Osmond. He had not.

Out to lunch with Lola Hahn. She confirmed all that I had been told during the morning about the growing tendency toward panic. She said it is no longer any use to discuss with the Allocations Committee the question as to whether they will assign, for example, £20,000 or £30,000 to Germany. It is a question of meeting the necessities of tens of thousands of persons.

The recent decree about obliterating the names of Jewish dead on the war memorials had been, she said, the last blow for persons like Erich, or even more for her husband. The latter is now much concerned about the future of his own business. It is a steel tube plant employing about 1,200 workers, three-fourths of whom are non-Jewish. It is a question whether he will be allowed to continue to direct his business, and if he is not, the security of the Jewish employees will be jeopardized.

It is expected that the new laws implementing the Nuremberg decrees will be issued within a few days. Meantime the negotiations about transfers have been turned over by Dr. Schacht to Dr. Dreyse of the Reichsbank. The prospects for success are not encouraging. She told me of the impressions gained from Drs. Baeck and Hirsch after their return from their recent experiences.[57] Though both were, of course, forced to sign definite commitments, they could not avoid giving some sense of the frightfulness of their days away. Dr. Baeck apparently was more shaken by his briefer period than was Dr. Hirsch by a much longer time.

She emphasized again the feeling almost of dismay of herself and her father at the inability of New York to understand and of the tendency of Felix Warburg to try to direct from afar. She cited the sending of Ernest Kahn to Palestine, about which he knows nothing, instead of accepting the judgment of persons on the spot about housing. Similarly, Felix's acceptance of the judgment of Hexter about Cyprus was illustrative of this same tendency. It is resented also in Palestine circles generally.

Father Ducey came in and brought the report he had been working on. . . . Unfortunately, he was not very informing on the question of kinds and numbers of Catholic refugees. On the contrary, he suggested that most of the Catholics who had been forced to leave Germany had been charged with one form or another of political activity or were to some small extent at least of Jewish blood. . . .

57. See entry of October 14, 1935.

At four o'clock went to see Mr. Sargent of the Foreign Office. Though I discussed with him last year the question of the British and the American ambassadors making certain informal representations in Berlin, he gave no indication of being really au courant with the German situation at present. I therefore outlined to him in some detail and with as much eloquence as I could muster the elements in that situation which threatened disaster. He seemed to become more interested as we talked. In the course of the discussion I told him of Lothian's suggestion that it would be necessary to wait until the Germans raised the question of colonies, and that then the British government could say that the question could not be discussed until wrongs within Germany had been righted. Sargent's comment on this was unequivocal. First, to wait until the colonial question were raised would be to wait for months, perhaps years—the longer period being more likely than the shorter one. Second, this is just the sort of bargaining which the government would not take part in.

In this connection Sargent said that one of the reasons the government might hesitate to approach the German government at all was that it would fear that the German reply would suggest that Britain take a definite quota. This he did not think they could consider doing, nor would they want to put themselves in the position of giving the Germans an opportunity to bargain.

Finally, Sargent suggested that perhaps it might be well if the British and American ambassadors in Berlin talked the whole matter over, and then expressed to their respective governments their views as to what from their point of view might be done. Since this seemed the most that one could hope to get from the Foreign Office, I agreed that this would be a desirable step. Then Sargent asked me if I would prepare a memorandum setting forth my views of the situation and of the dangers which threaten. He added that on the basis of this he would try to get Vansittart's attention as soon as possible. I said that I would supply the memorandum promptly.

In the course of our talk I told Sargent of the special Devisen facilities being offered to German Jews going to Italy. He made particular note of this, presumably for the information of those handling the sanctions proposals.

Since Sargent did not seem to know any of the details about the Geneva procedure, got Stephenson on the telephone, and I talked to him. In answer to my questions Stephenson said that the committee had not yet been completed, presumably because of delay in deciding on the French member, and that the first meeting would be held sometime between the twenty-eighth of November and the second of December.

Conference in the later afternoon with Miss Iredale of the Christian appeal. She talked at length about her own activities in the international student work, that of the Russian relief, and other forms of philanthropic endeavors. Apparently, she has been as successful as the bishop of Chichester indicated in raising very large sums of money. She was sharply critical of the failure of the non-Jewish bodies to make a really national appeal at the beginning of the crisis, and now saw nothing but difficulties in the way of success. In particular, she questioned the wisdom of trying to raise money for the Christians alone, saying that such an appeal never went well, that it was always easier if it were put on a non-denominational, non-racial, non-class basis. She felt that the church secretaries could not help, that organizations such as the World Alliance were of little value in this emergency, and that only a really national committee of responsible people could lay the necessary basis; but the organization of such a committee itself would take weeks, and the essential preparatory work for a national campaign months, even after you found the essential key person and organizer. Such a person she could not think of at the moment. She herself was completely swamped and could not add another responsibility. She promised to think the matter over and to make suggestions if any occurred to her. She agreed that the organizer must be English and the organization also.

She was skeptical of the bishop of Chichester's plan to have bishops assume responsibility for £30,000 or £40,000. She agreed that himself and certain other bishops probably could raise their quotas easily, but before you could get an agreement for this scheme, each of the bishops would have to be convinced individually. That, again, would take weeks of intensive personal activity.

In short, the net impression she gave was most discouraging. And what is also bad, her response tended merely to deepen my own pessimism in this matter.

I should perhaps add that the one hopeful note that she struck was the possibility that substantial amounts could be gotten from certain individuals. But here again she emphasized the necessity of careful preparation of the plan and the exactly right kind of personal solicitation.

. . . .

Tuesday, October 29, 1935

Conference with Max Warburg. I found him just finishing a talk with Ernest Kahn. As the latter left, Warburg said, "I have never been so disheartened by America as now. It seems as though the more desperate the situation becomes with us, the less response there is even from those closest to me. It is not so much that there is misunderstanding as that there is no understanding at all. For example, I urge strongly the project for Cyprus, which would care at first for twenty families, in the second year for forty, and so on. I asked for a meager $50,000 from the corporation. Instead of giving it to me, they send Kahn to investigate. He makes criticisms of the plan, and nothing is done. Always in response to my suggestions I get requests for additional statistics, data, etc. I have now gotten to the point where when any American asks me for more data, I say good-bye to him."

Then he outlined the development of his discussions with Dr. Schacht. It appears that the latter asked whether it would be possible to establish a sort of concordat. This was the last week in August. The reply was that it was too late for that, because there was no point from which to begin. First there must be a breathing space so that plans might be seriously envisaged. Then there must be a plan which would include the following:

(a) The abolition of the capital export tax. This, Schacht said, would be agreed to;
(b) The help in transfer. This, Schacht thought, could be worked out.

These suggestions were amplified in a formal letter, which Schacht expected to use prior to the meeting soon to be held. According to his account, despite his apparent failure, he had succeeded in checking some of the very worst proposals, which would have gone much further than those actually adopted. Indeed, the All Highest [Hitler] had for the first time said, "We must work out some sort of 'tolerable arrangement' with these people."[58] This had seemed to Schacht to be a great victory.

Warburg had pointed out how, on the basis of a five-year plan, evacuating 20,000 a year, and taking account of the abnormal death rate because of the over age of the bulk of the community, not more than 250,000 would be left at the end of the period. At that time if it was desired to continue the process, the country could be freed of Jews at the end of another five years. Then presumably the era of happiness for Germany would begin!

The details of transfer arrangements are now being worked out with Dr. Dreyse. There are, however, a number of technical hurdles still to be overcome. But more serious than these are the hurdles of a political nature. It is still uncertain whether those who wish to come to an arrangement can control the street. That is the gravest danger.

He had come to the City to test whether the scheme to finance the transfers was practicable. He had been much encouraged by the response from certain members of the community, and particularly by the response from one of the leading non-members of the community, Sir H. D.[59] The idea is that a certain number of individuals will make available subscriptions to the total of perhaps a million pounds, on the understanding that they would take the first losses incident to the loans advanced to immigrants against their property left in Germany and held there by a trustee. If this amount were available from individuals on this basis, then much larger amounts would be available from certain of the large insurance companies, notably the Prudential.

In connection with all of this he wanted to ask me my opinion on one suggestion which had been made to him. It was as to the desirability of tying up this scheme to the League. My reply was definitely negative on the ground:

58. There is no independent record of such a conversation, and it is unlikely that it occurred.
59. Probably Sir Henry Drummond-Wolff, Jr., a Conservative MP of Jewish descent.

puters and Family History

- Mike Dixon of dixonhistory-com//lab

sion of new data sources for
history. Hobbyist or pro, join
on in Bear's Computer
the latest library and
can use to expand your
research tool box
day, July 13, 2019 @ 11 a.m.

Info Desk or call 302-838-3300.

World reacts to the
Holocaust
940. 5318 W

The holocaust: a new hx
940. 5318 R   5318 H
. 5315

(a) of an inevitable delay of three or six months and probably more;

(b) the probability of final rejection; or

(c) the likelihood of its being merged and lost in schemes for the whole body of League refugees.

He welcomed this advice because it fitted into his own conception; but he had felt that he had to ask me because someone whose cooperation he was asking had put forward the League idea.

He plans to return to England as soon as and if the program on the other side is agreed to. Here he expects to raise from personal old associates the first substantial amounts, and only then to put it up to the States. Both his sense of the best probable procedure and his feeling that a sense of self-respect would not permit him to go to the States to ask for aid in initiating the project cause him to take this line. He added, with sadness which was tinged with bitterness, that he was utterly disheartened by publicity about a $10,000,000 corporation, when, in fact, it did not even have one mission, and when, as a result, he was swamped by letters from persons asking why some of the ten million was not available. He himself could not understand why the lack of response; it was utterly beyond his comprehension.

We talked a little about my plans, about Hochschild, on whose cooperation he is counting, and of Anthony de Rothschild, whose first response was more encouraging than he had anticipated.

Ruth and I went to dinner at the Sachers' house. Others there besides the hosts were Mr. and Mrs. Sieff,[60] Mr. and Mrs. Sidebotham ("Scrutator"),[61] Mr. Norman Laski, Miss Marks, Mrs. Simon, and two or three others.

Before dinner Mr. Sieff expressed his regret that we had not met before, and told me briefly of his work in Czechoslovakia for the settlement of certain German manufacturers in Slovakia. It was not possible to settle them in Bohemia itself, because of the overcrowding in that section already.

During dinner . . . Mrs. Sieff and I chatted for a little while, first about the lunch at the Savoy where Lady Astor, Smuts, and Mrs. Sieff had spoken; the latter was critical of the *Times* for its inclusion of herself in the news account as one of those who "had also spoken." She talked about her plans for a visit to South Africa on behalf of the Keren Hayesod. I told her that she should also go to South America. We discussed developments in Germany and Jewish problems in general, and I recommended to her Kastein's *History and Destiny of the Jews*.[62]

After dinner, as the men were grouped around their claret, there was no serious talk, but amusing tales by Norman Laski of Lancashire folk stories. He recited in a charming way one of these in an amusing illustration of Lancashire dialect.

60. Lord Israel Sieff, vice chairman of Marks & Spencer department store chain.

61. Herbert Sidebotham, military journalist, writing as "Scrutator" in the *Sunday Times*, also a Zionist.

62. Joseph Kastein's 1933 work was pro-Zionist.

When we joined the ladies, Norman Laski, as a result of the unanimous demand, recited what is perhaps the most famous of the Lancashire dialect stories, "Albert and the Lion." It deserves its reputation.

Then Mrs. Simon and I talked about the situation in Germany and the discouraging lack of response to the various appeals made outside for help.

Miss Marks told of her participation in charity drives here through her efforts to sell blocks of tickets which, in the end, she usually bought herself. She admitted rather gloomily that this was not the best way. But from what Mrs. Simon said of her husband's activities that night in one of the small Jewish sections of the town, it is evident that the Zionist organizers do not neglect the task of keeping alive the local units.

. . . .

On the whole, it was a very informal and friendly evening, despite the evidences of luxury everywhere in the house and at the table.

I should add that during the few minutes of general discussion the subject was the leadership of Jewry in England. I had suggested that inevitably the leadership would change. Mrs. Sieff remarked rather grimly that if she had her way, the present grand dukes of Jewry in this country would be deposed at once as unworthy of their responsibility. The way she said this throws light on the famous remark of her brother, Simon Marks, at a meeting of New Court when the first drive was being discussed to raise money for the relief of the German victims. Simon Marks was arguing that he and the Rothschilds should each give £20,000, instead of the £10,000 suggested by Lionel Rothschild. The latter had pointed out that New Court had many obligations. To this Simon Marks had replied, "Well if you haven't got the money, I'll lend it to you." This, coming from the son of a Polish Russian immigrant and addressed in the full meeting to the head of the house of Rothschild, left Lionel gasping and most of the group restraining with effort their pleasure.

. . . .

Thursday, October 31, 1935

Wurfbain and I met at the office of Dr. Sidney Berry, moderator of the Free Churches. With the latter was Reverend Maldwin Johnes.

I outlined briefly the needs of the non-Jewish refugees and my conviction as to the essentially non-Christian attitude of the Reich authorities. I also indicated what had been the preliminary steps looking toward a Christian appeal, noting especially the offers of cooperation of the archbishop of Canterbury and the bishop of Chichester. I stressed the likelihood in the near future of a definite plan of settlement based on Mr. Sams's work, and the archbishop's desire for a definite plan for the financial appeal. I added that, therefore, we were now primarily concerned to find the individual to organize the latter.

Dr. Berry expressed complete agreement with my interpretation of the German situation and deep sympathy with the object of the appeal. He could not, however, suggest to us the names of any individuals who might be able to organize the campaign. He thought it should be an Anglican, on the ground that the Free Churches would be more apt to follow such leadership than would the Anglicans to follow a leader from the Free Churches. He doubted that the World Alliance leadership would be effective. He also felt that little could be expected from the Catholics.

In this latter connection he told a story which is worth recording. At a recent meeting at Lambeth Palace of Anglican and Free Church officers, a letter was read from Pacelli[63] about the attitude of the Catholic Church in the German situation. According to Dr. Berry, the letter was so weak that, as it was read, there were bursts of laughter from all parts of the room. Nor is this surprising in view of the weakness of the statement made by the bishop of Winchester a few weeks ago about the reasons for the pope's non-intervention in the Italo-Abyssinian dispute.

Lunch with Leonard Montefiore.[64] On the way over to the Piccadilly Hotel he told me that he thought it probable that there would not be a united appeal in England, and, on the whole, he thought it was better so.

. . . .

With Ruth to see the production of *Julius Caesar* at the Old Vic. Had Brutus been more convincingly portrayed, the whole production would have been much more impressive. But Cassius and Mark Anthony and the excellent staging made the play worthwhile.

63. Cardinal Eugenio Pacelli, papal secretary of state. The future Pope Pius XII.
64. Leonard Montefiore, president of the Anglo-Jewish Association. An English aristocratic assimilationist.

4. How to Resign? November 1935

Friday, November 1, 1935

Bentwich reported on his recent conference with Mills of the Palestine Immigration Service. The latter was on the whole encouraged by the great interest shown in his reports about the German situation and his suggestions of the way out. Incidentally, what he told Bentwich gave the clue to the meaning of the rather cryptic statement in Cecil's letter to me of two days earlier. The luncheon therein referred to was one called by Mrs. Dugdale and attended by Lord Salisbury,[1] Cecil, Mills, and a number of others. It was there agreed that a private letter signed by thirty or more distinguished Britishers known to have been friendly to Germany should be addressed to Hitler, urging the advantage of a moderation of the intolerance of the Hitler regime. My guess is that this will be a futile gesture, for surely the time has gone by when Hitler will be influenced by private, unofficial views.

. . . .

Lunch with Rennie Smith.[2] We first chatted about the British political situation, concerning which he takes, for a politician, a very dispassionate view. He is not standing for election this time, but instead is going off to the States for a speaking tour and in connection with his own work.

He emphasized that in the States he will not be concerned primarily with finance, nor with the political aspects of the developments in Germany. He and his colleagues are now studying the deeper spiritual and intellectual aspects of the [German] regime, their work being done on the more obvious phases such as rearmament. In the States, therefore, he is anxious to get in touch with a few people who share genuinely his concern about those manifestations of the regime which make it such a menace to civilization.

It is in this connection that Smith spoke of Lord Tyrell[3] and the latter's intense interest in the work of the "Friends of Europe." Lord Tyrell looks upon modern Germany as the antithesis of civilization itself, and is therefore

---

1. James E. H. Gascoyne-Cecil, Fourth Marquess of Salisbury, Conservative, active in politics, leader of the House of Lords, resigning in 1931. He thought the British military preparations against Hitler were grossly inadequate.
2. Rennie Smith, involved with "Friends of Europe" publications—a series of pamphlets critical of Nazi Germany.
3. William George Tyrell, First Baron Tyrell of Avon, British ambassador to Paris, 1928–1934, and member of the Privy Council. In 1937 became Britain's chief censor.

prepared to devote his utmost energy to making clear to the world the menace.

. . . .

In answer to R. S.'s request, I suggested the names of a few persons at home, whose interest he might reasonably expect to elicit. Among these were Felix Warburg and Constantine McGuire.[4]

. . . .

Ruth and I picked up Lola Hahn at the Dorchester House on the way out to the Neville Laskis to dinner. Others there besides Neville, Cissie, and the younger daughter, were: young Baerwald (Paul's nephew); an older Russian Jew, Jacob Teitel,[5] who since the [Bolshevik] Revolution has, as president of the Comité de Secours aux Juifs Russes en Allemagne, spent his whole personal fortune in this cause; and six other personal friends of the Laskis.

. . . .

After dinner I took occasion to read a long letter from Louis Oungre to Sir Osmond which was handed to me by Lola Hahn. It was a rather amazing account that ran through two pages and a half of the activities of Representative Dickstein[6] in cooperation with HICEM,[7] looking toward the reform of American and Canadian immigration regulations. Read in the light of Dickstein's real position at home, the letter is a travesty on the facts, but taking it at its face value, as presumably any reader would take it who does not know Dickstein, it makes an impressive shnorring[8] for HICEM.

. . . .

On this day New York Governor Herbert H. Lehman wrote to President Franklin D. Roosevelt, enclosing a letter McDonald had sent to Felix Warburg on October 10 describing conditions in Germany.[9]

["I know that you are well acquainted with Professor McDonald and know how reliable he is.

4. Constantine McGuire, Boston-born lawyer. An influential Catholic layman with close ties to the Vatican. McDonald had known him since their days at Harvard.
5. One of the first Jews to become a judge in tsarist Russia, Teitel left the country in 1921 for Germany. President of the organization of Russian Jews in Germany, he became involved in refugee affairs. In 1933 transferred his base to Paris.
6. Samuel Dickstein (1885–1954), congressman from New York City, 1923–1945. Headed both the House Committee on Immigration and the House Special Committee on Un-American Activities. In his time this special committee investigated anarchist, communist, Nazi, and fascist groups operating in the United States. Known as a seeker of publicity and a sensationalist, Dickstein unwittingly stirred up xenophobic sentiments.
7. Acronym for European Jewish Emigrant Association, a joint venture of three separate organizations, one of them being the Hebrew Immigrant Aid Society (HIAS).
8. Scrounging, Yiddish slang for fund-raising.
9. McDonald's letter of October 10 is excerpted in chapter 3, pp. 44–45 above.

The situation which Mr. Warburg has asked me to take up with you is as follows: The present immigration quota from Germany is, I believe, 25,000. This quota has never been availed of and immigration has in the recent past been limited to about 2,500. Because of conditions in Germany with which you are familiar and which appear to be getting worse continually, it is imperative that the opportunity for immigration be given to as many of the persecuted Jewish citizens of that country as is possible.

. . . Mr. Warburg and those associated with him in caring for the unfortunate refugees are very desirous of having the very stringent regulations with regard to the immigration quota from Germany liberalized to some extent by the State Department. They would greatly appreciate it if you would ask the Secretary of State to make certain that our diplomatic and consular representatives show sympathetic interest in permitting immigration of German Jews into this country, providing, of course, they fulfill the immigration requirements in every particular. They ask that the immigration quota of German Jews to this country be increased from 2,500 to 5,000. This, of course, is almost a negligible number.

. . . I therefore can very strongly endorse the request of Commissioner McDonald and Mr. Warburg. The matter is of such importance that I feel justified in taking it up directly with you. I hope that it will receive your personal consideration and favorable action."]

The imprecision in Lehman's letter and the modest level of his request made it relatively easy for the State Department to parry this initiative.[10] But the State Department response did indicate that those obliged to leave or seeking to escape should receive "the most considerate attention and the most generous and favorable treatment possible under U.S. laws." This vague formulation at least offered an opening for later efforts.[11]

Monday, November 4, 1935

Stopped at the Dorchester House to talk with Lola Hahn before we were to go together to see Simon Marks. She told me of her conferences the previous day with Marks and with Anthony de Rothschild. She was pleased that the former had worked out a large-scale scheme for liquidation [i.e., exodus] of some 10,000 a year of the younger people from Germany to go to Palestine, and was prepared to urge at New Court[12] a financial program over a period of

---

10. On November 13 FDR responded with a letter drafted in the State Department, denying that there was any arbitrary limit within the German quota of 25,957, and arguing that all those who fulfilled the immigration regulations were already being given immigration visas. The number given to German applicants in the fiscal year 1935 was in fact 5,117. Lehman to President Roosevelt, November 1, 1935, and Roosevelt to Lehman, November 13, 1935, Official File 133, Franklin D. Roosevelt Library, Hyde Park, N.Y.—both letters reprinted in *Franklin D. Roosevelt and Foreign Affairs*, ed. Edgar B. Nixon, vol. III, *September 1935–January 1937* (Cambridge: Belknap, 1969), 50–52, 64–66.
11. See chapter 7, pp. 122, 127–129.
12. Headquarters of N. M. Rothschild and Sons Bank in London.

years that would cost several million pounds. The response of Anthony was more encouraging than she had hoped for.

We then talked about the need at home for some new elements which would galvanize the wealthy Jews into a much more generous response. I said that I thought Simon Marks might be useful; that I had two years previously urged him to go; and that I would be prepared now to urge Felix Warburg to invite him, particularly if, as a result of the meeting on Thursday, the British were going to be in a position to give a real lead. She agreed.

At Simon Marks's office I shook hands with Israel Sieff as he was coming out of a business conference, and spoke to Norman Laski. Only Sacher was with Marks as Lola Hahn and I talked with him. Most of the time was taken up by Marks's lengthy statement of his own position. He repeated what he had said two years earlier in response to the initiative which had been taken at New Court by Felix Warburg and myself, that he was interested only in making provisions for refugees in Palestine, for there only did he feel that the future was relatively assured. He still felt that way, but he was prepared that any large program should make provision for emigration elsewhere, and for the essential measures of training and relief in Germany. As he developed his program, Sacher interrupted to say that if there was to be [*sic*] these ambitious plans for Palestine, it would mean that no more money could go into Germany at all. I took issue with this sharply, as did Lola Hahn. We both pointed out that funds were absolutely necessary for training, and also for help to the population that must remain; that this did not mean the building up or enlarging of permanent institutions in Germany. Sacher seemed to assent, but not wholeheartedly.

Simon Marks asked what were the figures of emigration at present; did they indicate a panicky condition? Our answer was that the actual emigration, while larger than recently, was not yet of alarming proportions, but that many other signs in Germany showed unmistakably the danger of panic. I underlined the probability, indeed the virtual certainty, of the continuation and intensification of the anti-Jewish program.

As Marks was developing his general scheme, Sacher interrupted to say, "But where is all of this leading to?" I replied that I thought that we ought to concentrate on a plan for Thursday's meeting at New Court. The others agreed. I added that it seemed to me that it was of primary importance to get from the New Court crowd an acceptance, at least in principle, of the idea that a greatly enlarged program for next year is essential; that if this could be done, then much more might reasonably be expected from America.

The others assented to this view, but Sacher questioned the desirability of urging now a three or five years' program. He felt that it would frighten the conservatives. In this connection Marks paid his respects to Leonard Montefiore, by saying, "He is dead from the neck up." This statement recalled to my mind what Leonard Montefiore had said about Simon Marks a few days earlier: "Simon Marks knows nothing except how to buy and sell cheap furniture."

. . . .

Janowsky and Fagen came in about 6:30. They and I met Ruth at the Piccadilly Grill for dinner. We continued our talk until about quarter of eleven.

During the course of the evening we agreed tentatively on the following: They are to begin the dictation of their first draft on Thursday, to complete it by Monday. . . . They are to be submitted to the following: May, Idelson, Lionel Cohen, Lauterpacht, Neville Laski. These, of course, in addition to the staff. We did not discuss it, but I assume that late next week a draft will be mailed to Rosenberg, though my own statement will not be ready then.

. . . .

We discussed the general nature of the statement and some specific points in connection with it; but except for the emphasis which I made on the possibility of centering it on Article 11,[13] there was not much new in this aspect of the talk. However, they did say that they felt that they were able to build up a case which would prove the effect, if not the purpose, of the anti-Semitic legislation is to destroy the Jewish people in Germany. They felt that they had also found some significant new material on non-Jewish aspects of the problem. Everything they had to say made me the more anxious to see their draft.

Both men are prepared to stay on the job until it is finished.

. . . .

Wednesday, November 6, 1935

Conference with Bernhard Kahn in the office. We first discussed plans for the Experts' Committee meeting [scheduled for November 28–December 8]. . . . He said that there had been a meeting of the Jewish bodies where he had urged that they should unite in the formulation of a single proposal to the Experts. . . . He listed the main points that he thought should be covered in such a program. These were, in essence, those adopted by the Advisory Council, plus an additional emphasis on the necessity of having the department for German affairs manned by someone who would command the confidence of the Jewish bodies.

Dr. Kahn told me that in his recent talks in Paris he had underlined the mistake from the French point of view of the recent attacks by Bérenger and Helbronner on the High Commission, and, of the former, on me personally. Dr. Kahn had pointed out that if, as he had been told, the French government is anxious to win the sympathy of world Jewry, and particularly of American Jewry, it is a mistake to attack me, for the American Jews have had and still have complete confidence in me. Moreover, he said that he had added that I would not be going back to America to do nothing, but would probably be in a position to have a certain influence in foreign affairs, and that, therefore, it was

13. Article 11 of the Treaty of Versailles allowed each member to bring to the attention of the League any circumstance affecting international relations that threatened to disturb the peace.

all the less logical that the French should have attacked me personally. He seemed to feel that he had made some impression, and on the major issue that the French might be expected to be influenced by American Jewry. I remained skeptical.

It was on this basis that he had hopes that the French might consent to a limited settlement plan in southern France. He had told them that now most of the worthwhile material had gone overseas, and had suggested the possibility of permitting certain people to come in from Germany. This proposal had not been rejected. But I still remained skeptical.

Mr. Hochschild and his colleague, Heinrich Ellinger, came in. We talked about conditions in South America. Hochschild expressed the confidence that if funds were available, 3,000 people a year could be admitted to the Argentine. He himself had taken on a number of persons, and he was continuing to work on the larger scheme.[14] I asked him about Grzesinski. His reply was that Grzesinski was too old to easily be absorbed, but that he was going to study the possibility further when he returned to the Argentine.

Then followed a lengthy talk about the possibility of finding a place for Ellinger's brother, Friedrich, a specialist in ray biology, in the United States. I put him in touch with Adams and suggested that he send me a list of his brother's connections in the States.

Hochschild urged me to let him know when I was coming to Paris, that he wanted us to come to his house.

Thursday, November 7, 1935

Conference at New Court. For details of this, see letter of that day to Felix Warburg.[15] In addition to what is indicated in that letter, I should like to add merely that while the meeting as a whole was encouraging, nonetheless the attitude of Lionel de Rothschild gave one reason for a measure of pessimism.

. . . .

Monday, November 11, 1935

Armistice Day. Long conference with Sir Horace Rumbold at his house. We discussed almost every aspect of the refugee problem. I was enabled to present forcibly our point of view—in particular, the necessity of prompt action.

14. See chapter 11.
15. "I spoke for only a few minutes, saying in effect that it was now clear that the German Jewish population must be liquidated, and it was merely a question whether Jewry of the rest of the world would help to make possible an orderly liquidation [emigration]." In the end, a committee was set up to study major programs, including Max Warburg's and Simon Marks's, for Palestine. McDonald thought the most notable points of the meeting were the willingness of the group to talk in really large figures, three or four million pounds over a period of years, the conciliatory attitude on all sides, the recognition of the gravity of the problem, and the hope that if the English could give the lead, the Americans and others would follow. McDonald to Felix Warburg, November 7, 1935, McDonald Papers, Columbia University, D361 (Warburg Special File), Item 158.

Sir Horace, though he said he had no knowledge of the subject, will, I think, make an excellent member of the [Experts'] Committee.

. . . .

Tuesday, November 12, 1935

Long conference in the morning at the Parana Company office with General Asquith, Mr. Thomas, their field representative, and two other directors. The results of this I have set out in memorandum for the staff. On the whole, I was again impressed by the encouraging possibilities of that area and the fairness and reliability of the English organization. It was amusing to compare notes with Thomas about our impressions of Magalhães Agamemnon,[16] Vaz de Mello,[17] and other Brazilian personalities.

Mr. Hansen[18] came to the office. During more than an hour he talked about the work of the Experts' Committee as if he were going to be the new chairman of the Nansen Governing Body and my successor also in the work for the German refugees. He admitted that he expected to be named to carry on these activities. We therefore exchanged views quite frankly about what seemed to me to be the essential conditions for success. My net impression of him was that he is an honest and reasonably intelligent judge, who is prepared to give the rest of his working career to this new job. He insisted that if he took it he would be satisfied only if he were the active head.

Rabbi Raffalovich[19] of Rio de Janeiro came in. As we talked, it soon became evident to me that here was a man of great devotion and intelligence. We seemed to feel much the same way about most of the aspects of the Jewish situation in Brazil. I was especially struck by his attitude toward ICA. When he sensed that he could speak to me frankly, he disclosed his resentment at the bureaucratic centralization from Paris. In particular, he felt, as I do, that what is needed from the Jewish point of view in Brazil is a great leader who will not be tied to Louis Oungre's apron strings. I suggested that Dr. Raffalovich should see Sir Osmond. He said he would be glad to do so, and now that he is no longer an agent of ICA, he would be free to talk openly.

. . . .

Thursday, November 14, 1935

Election day.

Long conference with Kotschnig in the morning and then lunch with him. In our private talk it became evident that Kotschnig is flirting—indeed he said so definitely—with the possibility of remaining in Geneva either as the Ger-

16. Brazilian minister of labor, in charge of immigration.
17. Ildeu Vaz de Mello, chief of passport division, Brazilian Ministry of Foreign Affairs.
18. Hans Jakob Hansen, Danish diplomat, jurist, League of Nations official.
19. Rabbi Isaiah Raffalovich, longtime head of Jewish Colonization Association (ICA) operations in Brazil.

man refugee person in the Nansen enlarged office, or as the head of the proposed Christian committee. He said that he was being urged strongly for both positions, and that there was no chance for Wurfbain in the refugee work. He thought, however, that the latter might find a place in the legal section of the League, to succeed the Dutch member recently deceased.

I urged as strongly as I could that from Kotschnig's own point of view he ought not give up the idea of settling in the States; that it would be better for him to do that in the long run, even if at the beginning he had to accept something quite modest. But I am not sure I convinced him; on the contrary, I had the impression that his wife's desire to remain in Geneva was a primary factor.[20]

Saturday, November 16, 1935

Conference at the office in the morning with Congressman William M. Citron, Congressional member-at-large from Connecticut. If anything could make me anti-Semitic, it would be this conceited, ignorant, boresome politician, and worst of all, he is going back on the *Manhattan* on December 15. His questions, which were of the most elementary and naive sort about Jewish conditions in Germany, Romania, Poland, and elsewhere show that he knows nothing and is unwilling to take the trouble to read. Seemingly, he is just one more of the breed of cheap politicians who would capitalize for his own purpose [on] the plight of his fellows.

. . . .

James Rosenberg wrote to McDonald:

["Your letters give me pain and sorrow, but they are not new emotions, I am sorry to say. The failure of the whole world, Christian and Jewish, to sense the implications and the threats upon civilization of the German outrages is what shocks me and continues to do so as it does you. But I suppose it has always been that way in the world; people are concerned with their own immediate affairs and when it comes to the sufferings of other people, especially when the people are far away, most people . . . have not the imagination to be concerned."[21]]

Monday, November 18, 1935

Erich Warburg called me on the phone just after I had breakfast and asked me if I would stop at his hotel. I was delighted to know that he was in town and went over directly.

He told me that my interpretation of his father's attitude toward his plan and that of Simon Marks was correct; that his father had no idea at all that the capital plan should be a substitute for the other; that, on the contrary, his father

---

20. Kotschnig did go to the United States and became a professor at Mt. Holyoke College.
21. Rosenberg to McDonald, November 16, 1935, Felix Warburg Papers, Box 324, JDC (a), American Jewish Archives.

was most anxious that the other should be pressed forward in a modified form as urgently as possible.

Negotiations are still proceeding between Max Warburg and Dr. Schacht. The former hopes that there may be something definite within a week or two. At their last conference Dr. Schacht asked for a more detailed program.

Meantime, conditions worsen steadily. I could not, however, but be amused at the consideration which had led Erich to give up travelling on certain boats and to decide to take the *Manhattan*. It was because the name of the *Albert Ballin*[22] had been changed. He was also very much disturbed by the fact that the name of an institution in Hamburg called after one of the most distinguished scientists had recently been changed.

He still feels that something ought to be done to modify the present visa arrangements which give some an advantage to a person who happens to have a relative in the States. I again told him that I could do nothing about this, but that if, when he was in New York or Washington, he cared to raise the question, it might be helpful.

Tuesday, November 19, 1935

Full dress conference at the chambers of Lionel Cohen to go over the Janowsky and Fagen draft [of McDonald's final report]. Present were Cohen, Idelson, Lauterpacht, Laski, the two authors, Wurfbain, Bentwich, a Warburg (a distant cousin of Erich), and myself.

. . . .

We began by a consideration of general principles. After I had explained briefly the nature of my letter, then Lauterpacht made the far-reaching and, I thought, unacceptable suggestion that we should consider the memorandum as raw material, decide on what principles we wished finally to be incorporated, and then assign the various sections of the memorandum to individuals to revise or rewrite—the whole then to be brought back to a drafting committee. This proposal found no real support. . . .

Idelson seemed to me to be rather inconsistent, because, on the one hand, he urged a very strong form of attack, while, on the other, he felt that to leave the legal sections as they are, without also suggesting something like the Iraq scheme for League action, would be to leave us liable to the charge of indicting the Reich. This view was not accepted.

We then went through the material chapter by chapter, not with a view to verbal changes, but rather with the idea of determining whether in principle all were agreed on the substance of those sections. These criticisms were extremely helpful. But at the end it was felt that it would be desirable to have further con-

22. Albert Ballin, Jewish owner of the Hamburg-America Line, who had committed suicide when Germany was defeated in 1918.

ferences on details, and also an additional conference on final form. I was particularly grateful for the large amount of work which Laski had put on the job, and for his willingness to do more.

. . . .

Wednesday, November 20, 1935

. . . .

Lunch with Ferdinand Kuhn.[23] Talked at length about the publicity methods in connection with my final statement. He favored release simultaneously in London, Geneva, and New York. . . .

. . . .

Talk with Erich Warburg, who was very anxious that there should be an English High Commissioner. He suggested the possibility of Lord Halifax.

Dinner at Lord Bearsted's.[24] Present besides Lord and Lady Bearsted and their son were Simon Marks, Sir Osmond, Sir Stanley Cohen, Lionel Cohen, and myself.

For a full account of this session, see my letter of November 21 to Felix Warburg.

Bearsted told McDonald that he knew Bernard Baruch, Edward Harkness, and John D. Rockefeller, Jr., very well—he was willing to approach them for large sums. Bearsted believed that "the worst will happen in Germany," and that large-scale emigration was necessary. England should take the lead and then ask for U.S. cooperation. Bearsted wanted first to discover the level of openings in Palestine and elsewhere. McDonald disagreed. He specifically warned that attempts to get acceptance in principle from the governments in South America, South Africa, and the United States for the admission of a definite number of persons would only result in failure.

McDonald sounded out Simon Marks on a visit to the United States by Bearsted. They agreed that he might be able to raise money from non-Zionist sources, which had not yet been tapped. Marks hoped for two million pounds over a period of three or four years.[25]

During the next few days, culminating in an all-day session, Sunday, November 24, the texts of McDonald's letter of resignation and attached annex were extensively discussed. McDonald sought advice not only from his colleagues but also from international lawyers of note and others involved in the refugee crisis. J. F. Cohen ended

23. Ferdinand Kuhn, journalist and author on foreign affairs. Correspondent for the *New York Times*, 1925–1940, official in the Office of War Information, 1942–1945, diplomatic correspondent of the *Washington Post*, 1946–1953.

24. Walter Horace Samuel, Second Viscount Bearsted, chairman of British Shell Oil.

25. McDonald to Felix Warburg, November 21, 1935, McDonald Papers, Columbia University, D361 (Warburg Special File), Item 158.

up contributing to the first part of the draft by Janowsky and Fagen; a second part dealing with legalities was scrapped. The modified draft eventually became the basis of a detailed annex to McDonald's letter of resignation.

Monday, November 25, 1935

Lunch with Cecil at his house. During lunch, at which Lady Cecil was present, we talked about all sorts of things, including the situation in Germany. Not until afterward did we get down to the major purpose of my visit. I then explained to him what I had in mind in connection with my letter of resignation to the Secretary General, that I intended in that to speak with complete frankness about affairs in Germany which are making for the destruction of the whole of the Jewish people and, in addition, a certain number of non-Aryans. I realized this might be criticized as an improper use of my office and interference in the domestic affairs of Germany.

His first reaction was that if I emphasized very strongly the gravity of the problem, it might tend to frighten the governments off and cause them to do less, rather than more, at the League. In reply, I said in effect that that point could be worked in just the opposite way, that is, that the governments would agree to do something real only if they realized that if they did not do so, they would be burdened with tens of thousands of those forced out of Germany. Moreover, I added that it seemed to me the time had gone by for reticence, that here in the heart of Europe was being perpetrated an unspeakable crime.

Cecil replied, "I think you are right: you must tell the truth as you see it. The members of the Council of the League have a right to know it, and you must disregard the consequences." This statement on his part was a great relief to me, because I was particularly anxious not to go contrary to his considered judgment.

. . . .

The trip to Paris was uneventful, the Channel refreshingly quiet. Reached the Continental about 11:30.

Paris, Tuesday, November 26, 1935

. . . .

In the middle of the afternoon I went to Dr. Kahn's house, where Mrs. Kahn, he, and I had tea. We talked over the plan for Geneva and the possibility of the Jewish organizations presenting a united front. He said that the Oungres were resentful of the invitation issued by the [Jewish] Agency. While they did not say so, they were unwilling to accept that leadership and might not appear at Geneva in time for the conference of the other Jewish bodies. To both of us this seemed merely to be a reason to have a conference at Louis Oungre's office the next morning.

Conference of over two hours with Herbert May from 6:00 until dinner time. We went over in detail the draft of the letter [of resignation].

. . . .

After dinner the Mays and I went off to see the new Sacha Guitry play with Miss Leet. The play was amusing in the light French fashion: perhaps it would have been a little shocking had my French been better.

Wednesday, November 27, 1935

An hour and a quarter's conference in Louis Oungre's office. Those present besides Louis Oungre and myself were Dr. Kahn, Edouard Oungre, Mr. Schweitzer,[26] and James Bernstein. I outlined the points which I thought should be emphasized before the subcommittee. These seemed to represent the consensus of opinion. We then discussed the possible hope of the German department in an enlarged organization. Kotschnig's name was suggested, perhaps by me, though I added in that connection that I personally was advising him to go to the States. Louis Oungre at once raised objections—Kotschnig was too young, not a technician in emigration matters, etc. He suggested that Malméde and certain other persons associated with the HICEM would be the type. Dr. Kahn argued that technical qualifications were not the most important. The discussion seemed to indicate that Louis Oungre had something in mind—it was not disclosed. He and his brother did not indicate at what time they would go to Geneva.

11:30 over to see Osusky.[27] I found him, as always, friendly, intensely alive, and an excellent listener. I emphasized the main points in our thesis, but he did not commit himself. The only new light which his remarks threw on the situation was his statement that the Secretary General [Avenol] had told him that he had been chosen as a member of the committee [the Experts' Committee] because of his membership on the Supervisory Committee: that, in effect, he was the representative of the Supervisory Committee. I told him that I was delighted that he was on the committee, but that we hoped he would not think of himself as a representative of the Supervisory Body, but rather as the representative of Czechoslovakia and as a broad-gauged human being.

We chatted a little about the situation in Czechoslovakia. He said that there were two reports about the president and his resignation, that this would take place when his successor had been decided upon and the other, which he thought more likely, that the president had said he would resign when the parties had agreed on his successor. Until there was a decision on that major question, the matter of a successor to Beneš did not arise.

. . . .

---

26. David J. Schweitzer, experienced European official of the JDC.
27. Stephen Osusky, Czech minister to France and delegate to the League of Nations.

Into the Louvre for half an hour during the middle of the afternoon. Found it in nearly deep gloom, except for the new section, which was indescribably beautiful, particularly the Winged Victory lit up with the flood lights against dark blue background.

4:30 went to see P. Roland-Marcel, was delightfully surprised at his cordiality, his human approach to the problem. We did not discuss details, but said that we would see one another in Geneva.

Dinner with Mademoiselle Wurfbain, and then train for Geneva.

Geneva, Thursday, November 28, 1935

Arrived at the hotel at 10:00, and went directly to the Secretariat to learn that I would be called that afternoon [to the Experts' Committee[28]]. De Montenach[29] is acting as chief secretary and Coliat as assistant.

The Nansen people were heard most of the afternoon. I was called at 6:45. The chairman encouraged me to speak with frankness, which I did.

I first expressed the thanks of the High Commission, Cecil, and myself—our indebtedness to the Secretariat's preliminary work, and to the members of the committee for their willingness to meet us so promptly to expedite the matter. I then stressed the imperative necessity for speed, both on the ground of the urgency of the problem, and of the need which the Jewish organizations all feel for prompt decision in order to expedite their own plans.

Then after a brief reference to our work, I outlined the need of re-organization which seemed desirable:

(1) A League organization;
(2) A strong new head of an enlarged organization;
(3) A German department headed by someone commanding the confidence of the Jewish organizations;
(4) A Governing Body of the sort recommended by the High Commission;
(5) Finally, that in all respects the committee ought to do such work so that the Jewish organizations who had done and would continue to do the real work on behalf of the refugees should feel encouraged to carry on.

Toward the end I spoke with perhaps rather startling frankness about conditions in Germany.

---

28. The Experts' Committee consisted of Dr. Stephen Osusky, chairman; Sir Horace Rumbold; P. Roland-Marcel of France, formerly prefect of Strasbourg, where he worked on behalf of refugees; Senator Giuseppe de Michellis, formerly chairman of the Governing Body of the International Labor Office; and Michael Hansen of Norway, ex-judge in the Mixed Tribunals in Egypt.

29. Baron Georges de Montenach, Swiss League of Nations official.

There followed at that stage questions from all the members of the committee. The more important of these were:

(1) Sir Horace questioned whether a League organization would encourage Germany to throw the people out.

I replied that the forces at work for the destruction of the Jews were so powerful that even the government itself could not check them, that they would continue in all respects irrespective of what the League did, and that, therefore, the League must disregard the possibility he suggested. After the meeting was over, Sir Horace told me that his view about the situation in Germany was exactly the same as mine;

(2) The chairman, I think, asked a question which suggested the possibility of continuing the High Commission with a new head, at least until September. I strongly deprecated any such move, saying that I was sure the Jewish organizations would not want it;

(3) (?) asked about the plans for liquidating the High Commission. I explained these in detail, making it clear that everything could be turned over to a new organization by the middle or the end of January. I had, of course, to admit that it would be possible to continue the High Commission, since the Governing Body was continuing under Cecil until the time of the Council meeting, but I insisted that the others would not wish to continue;

(4) Someone asked about the willingness of the Jewish organizations to finance the supplementary work in the new organization. I said I could not, of course, speak for them, but that I felt confident that, if the work of the committee commanded the confidence of the organizations, the money would be forthcoming, at least up to the meeting of the Assembly when the matter could be reconsidered;

Later on, I spoke to Dr. Kahn about this, and he told me that he, too, felt this would be possible even if the ICA would be unwilling to go along;

(5) Someone asked about the non-Jewish refugees and their position in the proposed new organization. I admitted that less had been done for those than for the others, that I felt that they should all be included in the same committee.

There were a number of other questions, all of which indicated the alert interest of the members of the committee. I was much impressed by their attitude.

I did not speak of the church situation, partly because it had somewhat slipped my mind, and perhaps also because it might not have been best at that point. Later, de Montenach told me that he was sorry I had not mentioned it and hoped I would do so when I reappeared before the committee. I said I would gladly do that.

I did not finish appearing before the committee until about quarter or ten minutes of eight. Then hopped off to dress for dinner at Captain Walters. The other guests included Sir Horace Rumbold, Mr. Krauel, Mr. Johnson of the Nansen Office, and two or three others. The only serious talk I had was with Krauel. We chatted about Kiep, whom Krauel thinks will "come back" [and] about Luther,[30] whom Krauel thinks has developed and is now out of his place. But the important subject we discussed was church and state. Krauel said that this was, he thought, in the long run more important than the Jewish issue, that it would involve a greater readjustment. He said that [Alfred] Rosenberg in this field was simply systematizing the tendencies of many men before him who felt the need for church based on race and soil, that there would have to be a fundamental readjustment of the Evangelical and Catholic churches to meet the conditions of the new state.

I asked to be excused about 10:30 in order to attend the Thanksgiving party of the Americans. That was a delightful occasion where I met dozens of old friends. We danced until nearly two.

Friday, November 29, 1935

Long conference during the morning at the hotel with Dr. Kahn and Mrs. van Tyn. The Jewish bodies had not yet had a general meeting. The Oungres were not to arrive until Sunday morning. Meantime, however, there had been a sort of agreement of the Jewish bodies that the whole were to appear before the committee together. It was also agreed that there would be four spokesmen: Louis Oungre, Otto Schiff, Nahum Goldmann, and Bernhard Kahn, the latter to speak on behalf of the national organizations. These plans remained somewhat indefinite, because there had been no possibility of getting the views of the Oungres.

. . . .

Conference at teatime with Dr. Demuth. He reported the good news that Colombia [the country] had finally accepted ten of the professors and that more might follow. On the other hand, he added that Dr. Plaut (?), who had agreed to go to Peru and whose transportation had been set, at the last minute decided that he would not go. It is this sort of thing which makes Demuth's work more difficult.

Demuth is looking forward to moving to London, but does not expect to remain in his present work beyond six months more. He looks very badly and seemed to me unwell. But for that matter, so also does Dr. Bernhard Kahn, who never seems to be able to get away from his work.

30. Martin Luther, Nazi Party economic specialist and protégé of Joachim von Ribbentrop. After Ribbentrop became foreign minister in 1938, Luther became state secretary in the Foreign Ministry in charge, among other things, of Jewish issues. Attended the Wannsee Conference on January 20, 1942, as representative of the Foreign Ministry. See Christopher R. Browning, *The Final Solution and the German Foreign Office: A Study of Referat DIII of Abteilung Deutschland 1940–1943* (New York: Holmes and Meier, 1978).

Demuth gave me the impression of being genuinely distressed when I told him that my decision to resign at the end of the year was to be adhered to. I explained to him what would probably come out of the Experts' [Committee's] work, but he said that he did not think this would be adequate and that I ought to remain. Though I could not say that I would accept his advice, I was nonetheless touched by his attitude.

Later in the afternoon, Goldmann came to see me. . . . He told me of the preliminary work which had been done. Not unnaturally, he, in these preparatory efforts, did not neglect the Zionist interest. Indeed, I think that he may have somewhat over-stressed the Zionist aspects of the problem.

During the afternoon, Ruppin,[31] who had made a special trip to Geneva from Naples for the purpose, appeared before the committee to tell them of the work in Palestine. I was to learn later that this account, though doubtless impressive, tended to frighten the members of the committee because of their misunderstanding as to the possible part which the League organization might be expected to play in that area.

Goldmann told me of the difficulties he had in securing co-operation in the preparatory work of the Oungres. In passing, he told me that after a year or two he was going to concentrate on (blank, blank) treatment of those individuals.

After Goldmann left, Ruppin and Rosenblut came. . . . Dr. Ruppin was rather discouraged by the reception he had had before the committee. They did not ask as many questions as he had anticipated. This was explained to me later when de Montenach told me of the committee's fear that they might be expected to play a role in Palestine.

I was glad to have a chance of a talk with Ruppin and to explain to him what probably would come out of the committee's deliberations. Through him, one can have an access to the [Jewish] Agency, supplementing that of Goldmann.

. . . .

Saturday, November 30, 1935

Conference with the Secretariat during the morning, but they did not take me much further in knowledge of the committee's work. I did hear, however, of the impression made by the German commission. Heinrich Mann,[32] who presented an intensely polemic statement, was rather checked by the committee on the ground that they could not deal with German domestic affairs. They indicated nothing of this attitude when I spoke frankly about conditions in the Reich. It was, perhaps, a mistake for Mann to have appeared. On the other

31. Dr. Arthur Ruppin, German-born sociologist and Zionist leader in charge of settlement in Palestine.

32. Heinrich Mann, prolific German writer and social critic, elder brother of Thomas Mann. Attacked authoritarianism, militarism, capitalism, and social corruption in a number of works, the most famous of which, *Professor Unrat* (1904), served as the basis for the film *The Blue Angel.* Exiled by the Nazis in 1933, Heinrich Mann lived in Prague and Nice, then went to the United States in 1940. He died in Los Angeles in 1950.

hand, Bernhard[33] and the other German spokesmen made excellent impressions.

. . . .

Conference at 4:00 with Georg Bernhard. I told him the probable results of the committee's endeavors and urged him to support these. He had been favorably impressed by the committee and will, I think, use his influence to make their work effective.

He was generous in his remarks about my work and expressed most cordially his personal feelings. This was a considerable satisfaction to me because there have been times during the past two and a half years when he had been decidedly critical. Like Demuth, he is good enough to give considerable weight to my good will, which, they say, is everywhere recognized in the Jewish world.

. . . .

To the Rialto at six o'clock to see the private showing of the Palestine film. I was stirred by it. It is well done and gives a moving impression of the rebuilding of the national home. The most effective parts of the picture are those depicting the activities of the young people.

As I was walking out with one of my younger non-Jewish friends, I was somewhat shocked by her remark that she did not think much of the picture. Her reaction illustrates, I think, the fact that those who do not know Jewish history or who are not particularly sympathetic with Jewish problems may fail to get the meaning of the picture.

The audience was almost wholly a Jewish one. Their reactions were clearly those of men and women stirred by a new sense of their past and their possible future.

. . . .

About 9:30 Ruth dropped me at the Beau Rivage, where I joined Marion Warburg and Otto Schiff, the latter having arrived less than an hour previously from London. He outlined briefly to me what he expected to say before the committee. In substance, he was going to trace the need of the private organizations for League support in the juridical and consular field. His one point which was somewhat new was his desire that the German government should be induced to see to it that all new refugees had adequate papers. He felt that the League could properly urge this minimum condition. I think he will make a good impression.

With Otto Schiff over to Miss Ginsberg's a little after 10:00. There she had gathered most of the representatives of the committees interested in the

33. Georg Bernhard, former German Democratic Party politician and editor of the *Vossische Zeitung*. Lived in exile in Paris and edited the *Pariser Tageblatt*.

Jewish refugees. Also present were Miss Pye and other Quakers, Mr. Hansen of the committee, de Montenach, Johnson, and many others. I chatted with many persons, but my most important talk was with de Montenach. He at first gave me the impression of a man who was nearly overwhelmed with a sense of the technical and legalistic difficulties in the way of the committee's success. Moreover, he indicated that his ideas at the moment centered on the continuation of the High Commission in one form or another. He felt that it was not possible for the Council, under the terms of the Nansen Statute, to elect a president of the Governing Body of that organization, and that, therefore, it would not be practicable to work out a definitive incorporation of our work with the Nansen Office before the Assembly. Meantime, an ad interim scheme would have to be worked out.

I then suggested the possibility of someone like Hansen being elected, if not as president of the Nansen Governing Body, then as High Commissioner directly under the Council and charged, in addition to directing the work for the German refugees, with the carrying further of the League committee's investigations with a view to a definitive settlement at the Assembly. De Montenach thought this a possible way out.

He then asked me what about the possibilities of financing the continuation of the High Commission for the period prior to the Assembly. I said that I was confident that this would be done by the private Jewish bodies, provided they were satisfied with the setup; but, of course, they would want it understood that this was only a temporary arrangement, and that in September the question of League support for the whole administrative expenses, or at any rate the larger part of them, would be taken up anew.

De Montenach then indicated that the elaborate statement made by Ruppin, when the latter had appeared before the committee, had rather frightened them by the prospect of a large amount of work of training, re-training, emigration settlements involved. I pointed out that it was not the thought of the Jewish bodies, particularly in Palestine, that the League body should concern itself with these problems. This seemed to relieve de Montenach of one of his major worries.

Earlier, we had talked about the religious situation in Germany. His interpretation about that is the same as mine. Moreover, he said he was sorry that I had not stressed this in my first appearance before the committee. I said that I would welcome an opportunity to bring it up if I appeared before the committee again. This led him to say that he would arrange for me to be heard again on Tuesday. He expressed the hope that at that time I would not only speak of the religious matter, but also qualify the other points which we had discussed together. He seemed to feel that our talk had been extremely helpful.

After eleven o'clock Mr. Hansen, Senator François, and I started to walk away together. We were joined by a beautiful Polish lady who, as I discovered later, is Ada Halpern, a brilliant mathematician, assistant to one of the professors in the university. The four of us went to the Bavaria, where, in the midst of a crowd of people and a fog of smoke equal to the worst Assembly periods, our Polish friend entertained us with brilliant discussions of life in some of its more significant aspects. As one after another of the other men deserted me, I was left to be entertained alone by Mademoiselle!

5. Dramatic Protest: December 1935

. . . .

Dinner at the Vieux Bois for Otto Schiff. Besides Otto Schiff and Mrs. Marion Warburg and I, who were acting as hosts, there were present the Streits, the Tyrones, the Oungres, the Johnsons, Miss Hyatt, Arthur Sweetser, Mrs. Polachek, the Potters, and the Kotschnigs.

It seemed a really successful party. I am not sure, however, that the business end of it was a complete success, for there were no clear indications that Johnson and the Oungres had been brought closer together, though they seemed to be friendly enough.

Monday, December 2, 1935

About 12:15 I spoke to Miss Ginsberg, who had just come from the office of Mr. Rosenberg, the undersecretary general of the League.[1] She told me that she thought it essential that I should see Rosenberg before I appeared at the committee that afternoon at four o'clock. I said, all right, I will drop in and see him just before I go to the meeting. She answered that she did not think this would be sufficient; that I would not have time enough; that I had better call him and arrange for an earlier appointment. This I did, and he asked me to come and see him as soon as he had finished a telephone call which was then coming through from Moscow. It was arranged that I should to go Arthur Sweetser's office, who was to lunch with me, and wait there till Rosenberg called. I arrived at Arthur's office about a quarter of one.

Arthur told me amusingly of his experiences with Mr. Rockefeller, Jr., in reference to the [League] Library, when the two of them talked together in Paris. Arthur tried vainly to stir Mr. Rockefeller's interest in the building. The latter seemed to feel that it was all a dream—and one in which he was no longer interested at all.

Shortly before one o'clock Rosenberg asked me to go to his office. After short preliminary remarks about my visit to Soviet Russia, we got down to the matter in hand, which was the work of the Experts' Committee. It soon

1. Marcel Rosenberg, the Soviet Union's first representative to the League. In August 1936 became Soviet ambassador to the Spanish republic during the civil war. Tried to run the government there with advisers. Purged by Stalin in 1937.

became clear what Rosenberg wanted to say to me was in effect what the acting commissar for Foreign Affairs had said to me in Moscow a couple of months previous and what the Russian ambassador in Paris and Litvinov at the Assembly had been saying in September. In other words, Russia was still opposed [to], and I got the impression, would veto in the Council any proposal to link up the High Commission with the Nansen Office.

Rosenberg, during the first part of his talk, argued that such a continuation would be undesirable from the point of view of the refugees themselves; that the value of the League symbol is more theoretical than real; that London is preferable to Geneva for this work; that the League restrictions would cramp administration; that the seal of death is on the Nansen Office and would not be removed; that the problems of the two groups of refugees were basically different; and, in short, that the German refugees would be disadvantaged by fusion.

Later, Rosenberg emphasized the Russian determination to end the Nansen Office. A decision to fix the liquidation date had been taken before Russia came into the League; to extend the period now against Russia's opposition was unthinkable. Subventions go from the Nansen Office to individuals who, though nominally doing relief work, are actually members of White Russian military organizations. It would be absurd to have Soviet money turned over to irreconcilable enemies of the [Soviet] regime. Anyhow, everything has been done for the refugees that can be done. In this case it is now purely a problem of unemployment. No more persons are leaving Soviet Russia; nor would they expect any isolated cases to leave, even if there were no restrictions. Hence, the Russian problem is solved, or at any rate, as near a solution as can be hoped for.

On the other hand, the German refugee problem is still in the course of development. He emphasized the point I had made about the probability of large numbers of Jewish and non-Aryan, and even some religious refugees. Russia was anxious that everything should be done to care for these. He further argued for the continuation of the High Commission: the bringing of it closer to the League, if that were desired, but keeping its office in London and maintaining it separate from the Nansen Office.

I pointed out the difficulties of such a suggestion, but he was not convinced that these were insuperable. At any rate, he argued that it was much better to accept his suggestion as an ad interim solution, on a theory that by September, the German situation would be clearer and one could then plan a definitive scheme. I told him of the opposition to bringing the High Commission as a separate organ under the League, and of the possibility of German opposition. He belittled the former and said that the latter should be disregarded.

He pressed me to give my views on his suggestions. I hesitated to commit myself. Nonetheless, I suggested that if the Council should name a new High Commissioner and at the same time made that individual a representative of the Council in directing whatever further stage might be necessary to bring matters to a definite settlement at the Assembly, it might be acceptable to the

Jewish bodies. I was not, however, enthusiastic about it and hoped instead that some more satisfactory results could be achieved at this time.

It was a quarter of two when we had reached this point in our discussion. At that moment Arthur came into the room saying laughingly that he was tired of waiting for me, that he was hungry and was going to eat, if necessary, alone. Then all three of us went out together to the Bergues. We first went to the grill, but, in view of the rather crowded tables, Sweetser and I suggested that we go up to the restaurant. There for an hour and a half we had a very amusing conversation, little of it bearing directly on the refugee problem. Arthur was in excellent form, and, uncertain what to say about the refugee question, kept the talk on general subjects. I liked Rosenberg's brilliant, skeptical, almost cynical attitude about the League and the noble efforts of my American colleague. As we were breaking up, Rosenberg said that he was very anxious to see me again before I left.

Disturbed by Rosenberg's indication of Russian intransigence, I, even before we sat down to lunch, called Otto Schiff and arranged to see him and Kahn after my appearance before the committee.

While waiting for the committee after four, I heard more of the gossip about the morning's unfortunate developments which had been precipitated by Louis Oungre's vanity, which showed itself so overwhelming as to be tantamount to stupidity. He had called me up the previous morning on his arrival in Geneva and asked about the arrangements made for the Jewish organizations. I told him that I had nothing to do with these, but I understood that the Jewish bodies as a group were to appear on Monday before the committee and that he, Kahn, Goldmann, and Schiff were to speak. He replied that he had never given his assent to such a plan, and asked if it would be possible for him to appear separately. I told him that in reference to that, he had better get in touch with the secretary of the committee. From that time I heard nothing more about him.

On Sunday, however, at a long meeting of the Jewish bodies, at which two Oungres were present, the plans for Monday were gone over, the list of speakers was discussed, and Oungre said nothing then about wishing to appear separately from the general Jewish group. It was only on Monday morning, when the Jewish organizations were meeting before they were to be called, that following a series of conversations between the two Oungres and much going out and coming in of the room, that Edouard Oungre announced that his brother had been asked to appear alone to give certain special information.

At once the other bodies were furious. They had not been told of Louis Oungre's plan, and they resented the implication that he should not appear with them. Schiff and Kahn felt that at least Louis Oungre might have told them of his plans.

The resentment of the Jewish bodies was heightened when later in the morning they were asked by members of the committee, following their statement to the committee, if they disagreed with Mr. Oungre who, apparently, had given the impression that he did not think a central League organization to be important; that, on the contrary, the general work being emigration and colonization, this could be well left to HICEM and ICA. This, in view of the fact that the Jewish bodies had not only at our Council meeting, but also within the last twenty-four hours, reaffirmed their unanimous insistence on a League organization, seemed to them utterly inexcusable, as indeed it was.

I made no effort to discuss the matter with the Oungres, because there was nothing which could helpfully be said, but the more I heard of the echoes from their action, the more I felt that I had been exaggerating Louis Oungre's intelligence. Indeed, Kahn may be right when he puts it that the two brothers are merely glib. Certainly, their vanity is colossal.

On the defensive, Louis Oungre is said to have claimed that he had been misunderstood by the committee; that Hansen, who had asked the question implying that Louis Oungre had deprecated the need for a League organization, had not understood French. This is absurd, because Hansen speaks French perfectly. Moreover, Oungre is said to have argued that since Ruppin had appeared before the committee a couple of days earlier alone, and on behalf of the [Jewish] Agency, the ICA representative must appear alone. When someone replied that Ruppin was in Geneva for only a few hours and had to leave at once in order to catch his boat, which he had left at Naples to come to Geneva, Louis Oungre replied that he too had to leave promptly!

I was called before the committee about 4:30 and apparently was their last witness. De Montenach had given the impression that I had asked to be called, but he and I soon cleared up this slight misunderstanding. I took the occasion of this hearing to speak about the possibility of religious refugees, to say that the Jewish bodies would not expect the League organization to do the work of settlement and emigration and relief. I also said emphatically that the Jewish organizations—all of them—favored a central League organization; that even if one or two of the executives had indicated doubt on this score, I was sure that Sir Osmond, the head of ICA, was as enthusiastic about the League work as was Lord Cecil or I.

In answer to questions, I indicated that I was sure that, irrespective of the opposite attitude of one or two Jewish organizations, a fund would be available to provide for the administrative expenses of a League body at least up to the Assembly; that the Jewish givers would not insist that their fund be used merely for an office devoted solely to Jews. In reply to the question about the non-Jewish refugees, I spoke of the archbishop's appeal and said that what was needed was not a separate office for these refugees, but money to help them; that if the money were available, the new office could then carry on such relief, emigration, and settlement as might be required for this small group. In answer to Sir Horace's question, I said I was sure that the archbishop would not require a confession of faith from each of the non-Jewish refugees before the fund would be available for their care.

Then at the end, the ad interim chairman, P. Roland-Marcel, made a brief statement of thanks to me for my work. After saying good-bye to members of the committee, I hurried off to meet Kahn and Schiff.

Kotschnig, who had been present with me at the hearing and who handed me at the psychological moment a note about the archbishop, remained at the Secretariat to pick up what information he could.

Schiff, who had just been conferring with Sir Horace, reported that he had told the latter exactly the same thing about Sir Osmond that I had told. Both Schiff and Kahn were furious with the Oungres. We discussed the attitude of the Russians, but there seemed to be nothing to be done about it at the moment.

Dr. Kahn, with a show of feeling, again urged me to reconsider my decision about going home, but I told him that I could not—that both from the point of view of the work and from the personal point of view, I must go. . . .

I saw Miss Ginsberg for a moment. She said that she had never been so furious as she is with the Oungres; that she had tried to stop Louis Oungre's separate appearance and had even used what, under other circumstances, she would have considered dishonest means.

Goldmann and Rosenblut came to see me. In addition to being indignant with the Oungres, they were full of the story that Lambert, who had come to Geneva, was to be Roland-Marcel's assistant in drafting the report of the committee. After we discussed the matter, it appeared to me that it was not probable that Lambert was to do that work, but that, more likely, he had been asked by Marcel to make suggestions as to the work in France. Nonetheless, Goldmann was going to spend some time in calling the secretary's and members of the committee's attention to the danger as well as absurdity of having an employee of the Oungres in such a confidential position. Moreover, as Kahn put it, there is, from the point of view of the refugees, no man in the whole world whom they would resent more helping to write the report than Lambert.

Because of the developments during the day, I was forced to cancel a couple of late afternoon engagements, but had to keep the one with Johnson at his house at 7:30. He gave me copies of the material submitted by his bodies to the committee. We went over them briefly. I told him something of the attitude of the Russians. He told me that, of course, if they stuck to that, there was nothing more to be done, but he doubted if they would. He denied the suggestion that persons receiving subventions from his funds were in any way propagandists, pointing out that if they were, that was a matter which could be remedied and that it was not a proper ground for attacking the office with a view to destroying it.

Tuesday, December 3, 1935

Worked during the morning until nearly time for the luncheon at Major Johnson's.

Present at the luncheon, besides Major and Mrs. Johnson and myself were Senator François, Hansen, and de Montenach.

Most of the meal was given over to a frank discussion of different aspects of the work of the Committee of Five.[2] De Montenach had spent more than an hour with Rosenberg during the morning. The impression he received as to the Russian attitude was the same I had had. It is clear that the Russians will not admit of any solution which enlarges the Nansen Office. Major Johnson tried to argue the point and asked repeatedly what were the reasons for the Russian objections. But I remained convinced that the fusion idea must be given up.

There was a long discussion as to whether the Council has the authority under Assembly resolutions to elect a president of the Nansen Office. De Montenach and François say no; Johnson and Abraham say yes; Hansen does not express a view. But, irrespective of these opinions, the Council will probably not take any action which could be criticized in the Assembly as unwarranted. Everybody agreed that something had to be done to keep the work on behalf of the German refugees going. There is a general impression that the committee would recommend that the Council does not designate a special representative who might be called High Commissioner, or something else, to carry on for the German refugees until the Assembly would have the opportunity to make a definite scheme. Whether such an officer would have a mandate to study the whole problem of refugees, and, by implication, the possibility of some co-ordination with the Nansen Office, was not clear. Hansen evidently felt that this broader scope was desirable.

A report of the committee is being prepared in four sections—the first, historical, by the Frenchman. In this connection I became completely convinced that there is no real ground for the rumor that Lambert, as agent of Louis Oungre, is to have any important part in that work. The second is to be known as the legal section. The third, a more important general section, [will be] by the Italian nominally, but actually by de Montenach. The fourth, the vital section, the recommendations, [will be] by Sir Horace [Rumbold]. Osusky, being absent for several days, is returning in time to check the report. In effect, he will be acting, at least in part, as the representative of the Secretary General.

Three members of the committee, judging from the talk at luncheon, are anxious to take a broad line, but they are inhibited by the caution and timidity of the permanent officials.

I made a special point of checking with de Montenach and Hansen as to the attitude of Louis Oungre when he appeared privately before the committee. Both assured me that he had not given an impression of opposition to

2. On September 4, 1935, the League established a committee with representatives of Britain, France, Poland, Spain, and Turkey to try to prevent war between Italy and Ethiopia. This Committee of Five recommended making Ethiopia an international protectorate of the League, with Italy receiving significant territories in Afer and Ogaden provinces. Both Italy and Ethiopia rejected this proposal.

a League scheme—on the contrary. This information I was glad to have and, later on, told Goldmann of it, so that he might know that the stories about Louis Oungre's position were not justified. Nonetheless, these rumors are a part of the price Oungre pays for having allowed his vanity to lead him to insist on a separate appearance.

. . . .

Shortly after five I went to say good-bye to the Secretary General [Joseph Avenol]. He was ready to leave the office, so we had little time. I thanked him for the thoroughness and speed of the Secretariat work and for the admirable choice of the committee. I told him that I understood Osusky was a member of the Supervisory Committee, but that I hoped Osusky would take a broad view.

He then talked about the Russian attitude. It was clear that he shares the opposition to fusion. Whether he arrives at this view because of a desire to end the Nansen Organization, or because of hesitation to oppose the Russians, or for other reasons is not important. He did not indicate that he favored a separate body under the League of Nations for the Germans, nor did he indicate the contrary. This, I think, seems to indicate that he would not oppose. I said nothing whatsoever to him about my final plans in connection with December 30.

Then, with Walter Kotschnig, to see [Marcel] Rosenberg. He reiterated and made even stronger his former attitude. This time he said in so many words that the Russians would definitely block any proposition to add to the responsibility of the Nansen Organization. He went further and said that he thought the Jewish bodies had made a mistake in saying that they would be willing to accept fusion; that they should have insisted on a separate body under the League of Nations. When we explained that they had wished for a separate body and had agreed to consider the other plan only because they had been told by members of the Secretariat that this was the only practicable scheme, he asked: "What members of the Secretariat?" Naturally, neither Kotschnig nor I was able to reply. Then Rosenberg added, "That is not the view of the Secretary General and cannot be the view of the Secretariat." He then repeated his argument of the day before against the scheme from the point of view of its usefulness.

Kotschnig and I had our final long conference at the hotel, while I began my packing.

. . . .

Basel, Wednesday, December 4, 1935

To the Secretariat to say good-bye to friends, then with Kotschnig to the 11:10 train. Arrived in Basel at 3:32.

. . . .

. . . Then supper with another group, including Dr. Barth[3] and Dr. Ludwig representing the Basel government. I was glad to meet Barth; he is very pessimistic about church development in Germany.

We went directly from dinner to the meeting, which was in the same hall; there must have been 1,200 persons present. The chairman gave a brilliant translation and thus improved materially on my English talk. Mellon and Eisfelder were excellent; the latter's simple account of the tragedy of one family brought tears to the eyes of nearly everyone. Barth, whose talk closed the meeting, devoted himself to the intellectual side.

Afterward, there was a reception and supper, during which I had an interesting interview with the French Jewish rabbi of Basel. Excused myself and was back at the hotel and in bed by midnight.

Zurich, Thursday, December 5, 1935

After dictating my diary and letters to the office, took the midday train to Zurich. I was met at the station by Siegmund Schultze[4] and taken to his home. There I telephoned Kotschnig to get the latest news of the Experts' Committee. Schultze spoke to me about the Christian committee, indicated that he was considering the chance of going to Geneva for this work. I felt called upon to tell him frankly what I thought about the prospects for the various drives which are now either under way or in prospect. He asked me if I did not think that a specifically Christian colonization project would have a better chance of success than any other from the point of view of appealing to the Christian world for funds. I had to admit that this would be true.

I liked Schultze very much, but I could not feel that he would be justified in leaving his Zurich position at the university to undertake the work as secretary of the Christian committee.

Very short supper with Frau Schreiber. Then to the meeting at the university—or rather, at the Technische Hochschule. One of the large auditoriums seating perhaps four hundred was crowded, and several were turned away. Professor Brunner of the Theology Department presided. I enjoyed speaking to this audience more than to the one in Basel. Dr. Eisfelder was again movingly effective. The meeting was closed by a very well-organized and delivered appeal by Professor Brunner.

. . . .

---

3. Karl Barth, Swiss Reformed theologian, responsible for the Barmen declaration (January 1934) rejecting the influence of Nazism on the German Evangelical Church. This declaration became a founding document of the anti-Nazi Confessing Church. Barth resigned as professor of theology at the University of Bonn after refusing to swear an oath to Hitler.

4. Friedrich Sigmund Schultze, German theologian who opposed rearmament, advocated conscientious objection, and helped to found the International Fellowship for Reconciliation. Emigrated to Switzerland in 1933.

Bern, Friday, December 6, 1935

Met with some refugees in the morning. Then took the train at noon arriving in Bern just before two o'clock.

Went almost directly to Rothmund's[5] office. He, as usual, was extremely cordial, but in his long explanations of the situation in Switzerland he gave no indication whatsoever that additional facilities [for refugees] would be granted in Switzerland. I spoke to him in particular about Frau Schreiber, who was coming to see him the next day, and Kirkpatrick, whose work permit is in question. Later, I talked with Berchtold for a few minutes. He was also friendly but non-committal.

I did not see any of the members of the committee until shortly before the meeting. It was the least well arranged of the three. The program was as on the previous night. Afterward, I had to hurry off to take the night train to Paris.

Paris, Saturday, December 7, 1935

Arrived in Paris at ten minutes of nine, and after checking my trains, had breakfast with Bernhard Kahn at his house. There was nothing particularly new in our talk, but I was again impressed by his sadness, which is not surprising considering what he has been through.

A wonderful crossing, arriving in London just in time to miss the train out to Chesham—the Franklins. Took instead the next train.

After dinner Bentwich and I went over the letter [of resignation] again and made what I hoped would be nearly the final revision.

. . . .

After a four-day deadlock, on December 7 the Experts' Committee issued two reports, the majority signed by the British, French, Norwegian, and Czech members and the minority by the Italian. The majority report recommended the integration of all refugee work in a single office under some eminent personality. The work would be placed under the Council's direction, with one section specially devoted to German refugees. This office would liquidate the Nansen Office's work by 1938. The minority report would have left things unchanged, but limited even further the High Commission and made it more dependent on the private organizations.

Though Germany was no longer a member of the League, Italy and Russia had the power to block any real reform. Nothing substantial could be done before the Assembly met in September 1936. The committee agreed on a provisional arrangement up till that time.

---

5. Heinrich Rothmund, chief of police in the Swiss Department of Justice and Police. One of the most powerful men in Switzerland and one of those most responsible for closing Switzerland to most Jewish refugees before and during the Holocaust.

Lunch with Jordan.[6] He said that all of the information he had from Germany indicated that the church situation was becoming worse, not better. But there is no indication that Rome is any more inclined than before to take up the challenge at this time.

. . . .

Wednesday, December 11, 1935

Busy with this and that until, with Ruth, I took the 5:31 train for Tonbridge. Sir Osmond was not down until dinner, so we had an hour and a half or so of talk with Lady Goldsmid and her soldier son.

After dinner Sir Osmond read the letter [of resignation], seemed delighted with it, and said that he could not understand why Sir Herbert could have objected to the ninth section.

. . . .

Thursday, December 12, 1935

. . . .

Lunch at New Court. Present besides Lionel and Anthony were Lionel Montagu, Otto Schiff, Neville Laski, Leonard Montefiore, and perhaps one other.

Most of the talk which followed my brief report on the work of the Experts' Committee, was in reference to possible Englishmen for the position of High Commissioner. Everyone agreed that it should not be a Jew. . . .[7]

When this discussion was finished, to my complete surprise, Lionel rose to his feet to make a speech of presentation. One surprise followed another. Lionel could not have been more gracious. He began by saying that when I had first appeared in that room and had talked of the needs of the refugees in terms of millions of pounds, he and his colleagues had not believed either that so much was needed or that it could be raised. He was frank to confess that he had been wrong, and that I had understood the problem better than he. Then after some words of appreciation and of friendly regard on his own behalf and that of his associates, he gave me the silver salver on behalf of the Board of Directors and honorary officials of the British Central Fund.

I replied as well as I could on the spur of the moment, speaking more of the problem that remained than of my part during the past two years and a

6. Max Jordan, pioneer news broadcaster and, from 1934, NBC European correspondent, based in Basel. Always interested in religious matters, he eventually became a Benedictine monk.
7. The new High Commissioner, named later, was General Sir Neill Malcolm, a Scot, whose last post had been General Commanding Officer in Malaysia. He had had experience in Germany.

quarter. I urged them particularly to carry through the present projected plans in order that they might give a much-needed lead to America..

Bentwich and I met on the subway and went off to see Cecil. After he had read the concluding part of the Experts' report, we discussed it. He does not think much of it. He was disappointed at the failure to make a central organization and to bring it directly under the League.

. . . .

We then talked about steps toward liquidation. He agreed that the Governing Body could be dissolved by correspondence, if there were no objection, in reply to a letter which he would address to the other members. I reminded him of the arrangement by which he and Guani were authorized to complete the financial liquidation. He had forgotten this, but assented to it.

On the whole, he was not cheerful, either about the refugee prospect nor things in general.

. . . .

Back to the office, and worked until time to go home to dress for dinner. Otto Schiff was giving a small farewell party at the Savoy. Other guests, besides Ruth and myself, were Mr. and Mrs. Leonard Montefiore, and Lionel Montagu. It was a pleasant party, and broke up at a reasonable hour. As we were saying good-bye, Mr. Schiff said in substance what had been said to me by other individuals at the noonday meeting, that he felt a personal loss in my retirement, and hoped that I would be back soon; that in any case, he expected to be in the States in September.

Friday, December 13, 1935

Lunched with Simon Marks, Mr. Sacher, Mr. Cohen, and I think also Mr. Sieff, at Claridge's. It was a sort of a farewell party, but we also talked shop. During the course of it I said to Marks that I had now made up my mind what would be a fair sum for him and his group to give in the campaign just being envisaged. He asked me how much. I replied, "£100,000." He answered, "All right, but I would not do it alone. There must be others who will do the same Beaumont, the de Rothschilds." I questioned whether the de Rothschilds could afford it. He said, "certainly, if Jimmie[8] comes in, for he is the richest of the lot."

We parted feeling, at least on my part, that that group and I had become really good friends.

At four o'clock to the Foreign Office to see Sargent. He expressed keen personal interest in my letter when he was told about it and asked to receive a copy.

---

8. James Armand de Rothschild (1878–1957), heir to Baron Edmond de Rothschild (Paris), the wealthiest of the Rothschilds. Born in France, he acquired British citizenship and became a Liberal Member of Parliament and an ardent Zionist.

As to the subject which Bentwich went to talk to him about, that is, British cooperation with the United States in an appeal to Germany to bring about better conditions within the Reich, at least during the period of the carrying out of an organized emigration program, he was at first non-committal. Then, when he had thought it over, he said, "If there is worked out definitely the scheme which you refer to, it is possible that we might be able to go to the Germans and make informal representations along the lines you suggest." This reply seemed to both Bentwich and me encouraging.[9]

Then the two of us went over to see Lord Bearsted at the latter's magnificent house in Carlton Gardens. He said that for the moment nothing was being done on developing the emigration program, because Max Warburg had wired asking for delay until he had come to London for the holidays. This seemed to Bentwich and me a little disquieting, but obviously there was nothing to do about it. Bearsted seemed to have a wholesome skepticism about aid from the League. He repeated his hope that he would be able to secure funds in this country from the non-Jews. I again urged him strongly to come over to the States and, if possible, with Sir Herbert [Samuel] and with Simon Marks.

. . . .

Saturday, December 14, 1935

Ruth and I lunched with Mr. and Mrs. Geoffrey Dawson[10] at their home near Regent's Park. It is an old-fashioned English house, as cold as tradition would have us believe that English houses are. I was interested especially in Mrs. Dawson's suggestion that Britain ought to consider giving Germany a relatively free hand in the Near East or that, at any rate, Britain should remain neutral if conflict arose in that area. I jokingly asked whether this view was her personal view or that of her husband and of the *London Times*. He was quick to reply that it is his wife's personal view only. After a very pleasant lunch Dawson and I talked about my letter, which he had just read. He was enthusiastic about it. He asked to have another copy sent to him personally at the office so that he might assign the study and handling of it to one of his colleagues.

As we were leaving, he saw us to the door and picked up a letter lying on the stand. He said, "This looks like it were from a bishop." He opened it, and, sure enough, it was from the archbishop of Canterbury. He read it to us. It was a glowing tribute to the *Times'* attack the day previous on the Hoare-Laval

9. On December 10 Phipps had written to Anthony Eden at the Foreign Office that "the position of the Jews is becoming so desperate as to make it more apparent every day that . . . the present Nazi policy threatens the Jewish population in the Reich with extermination." He went on to say that they had no place to go, no way to take out enough money to live on. He thought there would be no success in approaching the German government in reference to softening their policies, and the government would only resent the interference. A. J. Sherman, *Island Refuge*, 63. The British government did not make informal representations to the German government about its treatment of Jews.

10. George Geoffrey Dawson, editor of the *Times*. A strong proponent of appeasing Nazi Germany.

agreement,[11] and begging Dawson to continue the effort to save Britain's honor.

Back to the hotel. Finished packing.

Sunday, December 15, 1935

At tea time we were joined by the Birchalls.[12] He looked through the letter and annex,[13] was enthusiastic about it, said that he would write [Edwin] James and suggest that it be given a column on the first page, with a full page inside.

. . . .

Nearly everybody from the office came down to the train to see us off. Such leave-takings are always rather sad, so in a sense it was a relief when the train finally pulled out.

To bed very shortly after reaching Southampton and after boarding the *Washington*.

At sea, Monday, December 16–Sunday, December 22, 1935

The voyage was uneventful. Most of our talk was with shipping people who were at the captain's table, as we were. The weather was not unusually bad, so the time passed enjoyably.

. . . .

New York, Christmas, Wednesday, December 25, 1935

Long session in the afternoon with [James] Rosenberg. He wanted me to hold a press conference at which I would stress again the Protestant and Catholic aspects of the problem and, "for my own sake," indicate that I was not withdrawing my interest. At the end of all our talk he was still rather gloomy.

Then over with Ruth to Lewis Strauss.

Thursday, December 26, 1935

It was either on this day or a day or so earlier that the first of the cables came from Bentwich urging delay and reconsideration on the letter. He was then up in Scandinavia and reported that the officials he saw there were of the view that the release of my letter at this time might be disastrous. I refused to yield and indicated so in my cables. Bentwich replied, repeating his recommendation and adding his own assent to the view of the Scandinavians. I still

11. The foreign ministers of Britain and France had agreed on a proposal to end the fighting in Ethiopia by offering a large region to Italy as an incentive. To many in Britain, this seemed like rewarding the aggressor, and the reaction was so violent that Hoare was forced to resign on December 19.

12. Frederick T. Birchall, *New York Times* Berlin correspondent and later bureau chief.

13. A thirty-four-page annex to McDonald's letter of resignation detailed Nazi Germany's discriminatory legislation, administrative measures and party activities, application of racial laws by the courts, and other forms of persecution.

refused to modify my plans. It would have been extremely difficult to do so because of the advance preparations, but I remained unconvinced that it was desirable to attempt to withdraw.

Lunched with John D. Rockefeller III and chatted about my work and about my new work, which interested him more than the old.

. . . .

Over to see Sulzberger. Our talk was all about the letter and the way in which it could be best handled. He said that he had not heard of any word from Birchall, but that he was prepared to start it on the front page and carry it over for a full page inside. He would have been willing to print the whole, were it not that this would probably be self-defeating. James was called in. I suggested that they assign a good man to it, and I would go over the matter with him.

Stopped in later to see Henry Ittleson[14] at their apartment in the Ritz Towers. Found him rather discouraged because of his impending new operation. [He was] intensely interested in what I had to tell him about my letter.

McDonald's letter of resignation described and condemned the discrimination, persecution, and humiliation of Jews and "non-Aryans" in Nazi Germany. He concluded on a personal note:

[Prior to my appointment as High Commissioner for Refugees Coming from Germany, and particularly during the fourteen years following the War, I gave in my former office frequent and tangible proof of my concern that justice be done to the German people. But convinced as I am that desperate suffering in the countries adjacent to Germany, and an even more terrible human calamity within the German frontiers, are inevitable unless present tendencies in the Reich are checked or reversed, I cannot remain silent. I am convinced that it is the duty of the High Commissioner for German Refugees, in tendering his resignation, to express an opinion on the essential elements of the task with which the Council of the League entrusted him. When domestic policies threaten the demoralization and exile of hundred of thousands of human beings, consideration of diplomatic correctness must yield to those of common humanity. I should be miscreant if I did not call attention to the actual situation, and plead that world opinion, acting through the League and its Member-States and other countries, move to avert the existing and impending tragedies.[15]]

14. Henry Ittleson, founder and chairman of the board of Commercial Investment Trust. A wealthy American Jewish philanthropist.
15. McDonald's *Letter of Resignation* (London, December 27, 1935), copy in USHMM.

Saturday, December 28, 1935

Brief conference with Hyman; then press conference in the library. I handed them a brief statement stressing the two points about the non-Jews and about my own continuing interest.

. . . .

Monday, December 30, 1935

On December 30 the New York Times *gave the letter of resignation full coverage: a story on the front page headlined "League Aid Asked by McDonald to End Nazi Persecution"; the actual letter printed in full; an additional page summarizing the annex; and finally, an editorial on German refugees, praising McDonald for the work he had done and for issuing the appeal.*

Was delighted with the space given in the *Times* and the *Tribune*. This was all the more welcome in view of the scare which we had had the Saturday previous when Popkin called me up to report that there had been a leak from the Havas Agency, which was releasing the letter for Saturday afternoon. Thanks to Popkin's energetic efforts and to the cooperation of the New York afternoon papers and the Havas Agency, this was stopped, and the release went off according to schedule.

Called Markel to ask him about the better picture in the Sunday paper. He said I had better take it up directly with Arthur Sulzberger, which I did.

Rosenberg called and indicated that he was more reconciled.

. . . .

In the late afternoon I went to Felix Warburg's house, where were gathered fifty to sixty members of the "high command" of the JDC and their wives and friends. I was then presented with a sterling tea service by Mr. Baerwald, and afterward made a relatively brief statement on the situation abroad. . . . Took the tea set home to surprise my family, and discovered that they had all known about it before I did.

Further reactions to McDonald's resignation:

Washington Post, *December 31: "One of the most powerful indictments of the Nazi regime of terrorism yet given to the outside world."*

San Francisco Chronicle, *December 31: "Perhaps it is nobody's legal business. It is certainly nobody's military business, but when a nation which once stood among the leaders of the world's civilization descends to this uncivilized course is it not the moral business of civilization?"*

New York Sun, *December 31: "Cold, deliberate, implacable persecution evidently designed not so much to wound the body as to crush every honorable aspiration of the soul is so inhuman as to be beyond the grasp of ordinary imagination."*

The Nation, *January 15, 1936: "McDonald . . . resigned with a bang. And the reverberations of the bang are still sounding in every corner of the world with results that have only begun to be felt. Mr. McDonald's departure from his post may well prove to be the most effective act of his two years' service, more effective perhaps than the whole period of heart-breaking labor. . . . His mission was an honorable failure."*

Likewise, newspapers around the world headlined the story. In Britain the letter was printed in full in several papers, and editorial comment supported action by the League.

The Manchester Guardian *editorialized that "For the Jew the Dark Ages have returned."*

In the German press, silence.

6. Aftermath: 1936–1937

Friday, January 3, 1936

. . . .

Lunched with the Zionists at the Aldine Club. Mr. Nathan Straus[1] called for me. Rabbi Wise presided. Afterward I was presented with the insignia indicating that my name had been inscribed at the opening of a new volume of the Golden Book in Jerusalem. I had a very cordial reception, but I was so tired that I was not, I am afraid, as alert as I should have been.

Saturday, January 4, 1936

Meeting at the Town Hall.[2] Then presided at the FPA luncheon, and afterward attended a tea given for me by Mr. Rounds, and was pretty much of a wreck at the end.

. . . .

At its annual meeting the American Jewish Committee passed a resolution asking the League "to call the German National Socialist Government before the bar of justice." The American Jewish Congress called upon the United States, as well as the League, to "make itself felt in unequivocal terms with respect to the monstrous wrong which the Nazi government is inflicting upon the Jewish people in Germany, upon Jews everywhere, and against the moral sense of mankind." Rabbi Stephen Wise called upon President Roosevelt to speak frankly to the German government.[3]

In a letter to Bentwich, McDonald wrote, "So extraordinary has been the response to my statement that I am inclined to feel that this results not so much from merit in the statement itself as from the intense desire in many quarters for a frank and authoritative indictment of the Nazi attitude toward the 'non-Aryans.'"[4]

1. Nathan Straus, Jr., grandson of the founder of Macy's, director of the Federal Housing Authority, 1937–1942. Teenage friend of Otto Frank (Anne Frank's father), he was unsuccessful in his 1941 efforts to arrange for the Frank family to immigrate into the United States. See chapter 10.
2. The headline of the article in the *New York Times,* January 5, 1936, p. 37, was "McDonald Gloomy on Hope for Peace" because of "mounting armaments, national fears and political demagoguery overshadowing the sincere desire of the masses for peace."
3. *New York Times,* January 6, 1936, p. 8.
4. McDonald to Bentwich, January 10, 1936, McDonald Papers, Columbia University, General Correspondence (Bentwich), Folder 38.

Sunday, January 12, 1936

Came into town to see Dr. [Albert] Einstein. He was most cordial and really enthusiastic about my letter. Then discussed various aspects of the general situation, and [we] seemed to be of much the same mind on all problems. He offered to write to some of the French authorities and to make an appeal for the doctors among the refugees in France. At my suggestion he said he would also write to the authorities in Brazil. . . .

We also talked about the transfer of Jewish capital from Germany. Einstein was firmly opposed as a matter of principle, and [Otto] Nathan remained convinced that as a practical matter it could not be worked out. I explained to them my understanding of the plans at the time I left London.

. . . .

Tuesday, January 14, 1936

Dr. Brooks examined me and said that I should go away for six weeks to two months. I was all right, except for the lowest blood pressure he had known me to have since he had been examining me.

. . . .

Wednesday, January 15, 1936

To see Felix Warburg. He shared my views about the terribleness of the *Times* article the previous Monday. Confirmed my opinion that it was not based on fact.

The January 6, 1936, front-page article in the New York Times *concerned an alleged German proposal for the mass exodus of 100,000–250,000 Jews from Germany, financed by world Jewry, combined with an increased volume of German exports. Germany allegedly threatened heightened persecution of the Jews if the plan were turned down. Sir Herbert Samuel, Lord Bearsted, and Simon Marks were supposedly bringing this proposal to American Jewish leaders when they sailed for the United States on January 15. The unsigned story, datelined London, cited sources "whose good faith is unquestioned and yet [offering information] in such an unofficial form that the advances may be disavowed at any time."*

In actuality, before leaving England, Bearsted and Samuel told the New Court Committee of the Central British Fund that Max Warburg's proposals to transfer Jewish capital out of Germany "or any scheme for the [increased] export of German goods would not be countenanced in America." While they felt that something like Warburg's scheme must be carried out, it had to be done by an independent organization, not by the Central British Fund.[5] Still, the Times *article was not as far off as McDonald believed. Max Warburg and Bearsted had hoped to convince Ameri-*

5. Archives of the Central British Fund, Roll 1, File A, Minutes of the Meeting of the New Court Committee, December 31, 1935.

can Jewish leaders that only an increase in exports of German goods—a modified version of the Transfer Agreement used earlier with Palestine—would persuade Nazi officials to allow German Jews to leave with some assets. But the premature publicity killed whatever slight chance there had been for favorable reception of this plan.[6]

Thursday, January 16, 1936

. . . .

Lunched at the *Times*. Was the guest of Arthur Sulzberger. Before we went in, I told him how bad I thought the Monday article had been. He said it had been checked in London, and that he had had it in his pocket from Friday until Monday. We then talked a little about my own future, but we were to continue this after lunch.

At lunch were present, besides Sulzberger and myself, Ogden, James, Merz, Adler, Finley,[7] and Mr. Riordan of Stern's [department store]. I told the whole group frankly my view of the article of Monday. After we discussed it at some length, James finally said: "Well, you know so much more about this than we do that there is nothing to do except to wait and see what the men themselves say when they arrive."

After lunch Sulzberger and I continued our talk. He was glad that I was going out of town, because he thought this would eliminate the continued discussion as to my view and also would take me out of the news. He liked the idea of my not speaking publicly on this question.[8] We agreed that I should begin not before March 25 and not later than April 1.[9]

. . . .

Sunday, January 19, 1936

Took the late afternoon train for Indiana.

Monday, January 20, 1936

Arrived in Muncie in time for Ruth's father's ninetieth birthday dinner at the church in Albany, where about 125 friends and relatives sat down.

---

6. Naomi Shepherd, *A Refuge from Darkness: Wilfrid Israel and the Rescue of the Jews* (New York: Pantheon, 1984), 110–111.

7. Senior editors at the *New York Times*.

8. In fact, Sulzberger insisted that the refugee situation be described as a general problem, not a Jewish one. He soon instructed McDonald to decline an award from the Jewish Forum for promoting the welfare of the Jewish people and humanity. Sulzberger to McDonald, February 1, 1936, AHS file, McDonald folder, New York Times Company Archive, cited by Laurel Leff, *Buried by the Times: The Holocaust and America's Most Important Newspaper* (Cambridge: Cambridge University Press, 2005), 33n47.

9. The original discussions with Arthur Sulzberger, as reported earlier in the diary, had McDonald's future role at the *Times* as a spokesman, making speeches around the country. As it turned out, he became a member of the editorial staff.

Train from Dunkirk to Chicago, arriving the middle of the afternoon [for a dinner and speech].

. . . .

Bloomington, Indiana, Thursday, January 23, 1936
Visited with my brother and his family, and dinner in the evening with the Kohlmeiers and Dr. and Mrs. Smith of the School of Education and Dr. and Mrs. Robinson of the School of Law. I was much interested and disturbed by the stories they told me of increasing anti-Semitism in the university because of the influx of Jewish boys from the east, where restrictions in professional schools had limited their admissions. This was only too sad a confirmation of the story I had heard from other sources as to the effect of this emigration from the east into the western institutions.

Friday, January 24, 1936
By bus in the morning to Indianapolis, and then took the train at two o'clock for New York, Ruth joining me in Muncie.

. . . .

Sunday, January 26, 1936
Informal dinner of about 150 at the Harmonie Club. Mr. Austrian presided. Arrangements had been made through Mr. Klein of Altman's [department store]. The knowledge gained during dinner that this [German-Jewish] club kept its doors closed against eastern and Russian Jews and the rather smug appearance of most of the audience drove me to be more frank and more "eastern" than I otherwise perhaps would have been in my attitude. Nonetheless, it seemed as though my evident sincerity avoided the danger of giving offense.

. . . .

Tuesday, January 28, 1936
Stopped at Mr. [Felix] Warburg's on the way down. Told him of my plans for leaving, and he agreed that there was nothing more that I need to do up here, and said that he would be glad if I were willing to cooperate in case he made some suggestions about seeing some people in the south.

. . . .

Mr. Baerwald called to ask if I would dine with him that evening before the meeting at the Temple Emanu-el. Said I would be glad to.

A few minutes later Rosenberg called to say he had definite ideas as to why I ought to speak. He wanted to discuss these with me at dinner that evening. I told him I had already engaged myself to Baerwald. He said he would call Baerwald and ask to have me excused, and so it was arranged.

. . . .

A delegation from the Committee on Fair Play in Sports came in, made up of Mr. Chamberlain, Mr. Harriman, and Dr. Spiro. They wanted suggestions from me as to the makeup of a delegation to go to Germany. I was of little help to them, for I had few suggestions and was not enthusiastic about the idea of sending a delegation at all.

At 3:30 to the Waldorf to see Bearsted, Sir Herbert, and Marks. They were still in conference, so I chatted a little with O'Connor, the representative of the *Times*. He said that he shared my view about the article in the *Times* the day before. He had criticized it to his colleagues when he had gotten back from St. Louis. They had told him it was from the same source as the equally bad one two weeks earlier.[10]

I should perhaps also note that Felix Warburg was as indignant as I when we discussed that article this morning. He added, half jokingly, that it was just as well that I should be over at West 43rd Street [the *New York Times*] to "protect us from mistakes of this sort."

The conference with the "three horsemen" [Samuel, Bearsted, and Marks] was rather unsatisfactory, because they were all evidently tired and pressed for time. They seemed reasonably satisfied with their visit, and felt that essential conflicts could be ironed out and that the financial response would be satisfactory.[11] They were divided as to whether I should speak at the Temple. They all spoke warmly of my letter and its success in England.

Over to [James] Rosenberg's for dinner, without an opportunity to dress. After some discussion I agreed to speak briefly at the meeting. After dinner I dictated my statement and followed it literally, except for a reference to Simon Marks and a request for a moment of silence in memory of the King.[12] Because I had to prepare my remarks after dinner, I was late arriving. It was nearly half past nine then. The meeting had been going on for more than half an hour. Sir Herbert was speaking when I came in. He spoke well. Then followed Lord Bearsted, who was less effective, then Jonah Wise, who made a fine speech. A little earlier Mr. Baerwald read a dull statistical account of the JDC. Simon Marks was witty and effective. While he was speaking, Rosenberg came over and showed me a note from Rabbi de Sola Pool to the effect that some reference ought to be made to the death of the King Jimmiu

---

10. This article described in detail an exchange plan between the Reich and wealthy Jews which, it claimed (inaccurately) had already begun. "The German Government profits by the system from whatever angle it is regarded. German industry is being pulled out of the slump into which it had fallen. The Jewish problem in Germany—as far as the prosperous Jews are concerned—is being solved. And the German Jew pays the entire cost." *New York Times*, January 27, 1936, p. 1.

11. Samuel later spoke about the thirty speeches and five broadcasts they had made in the United States; they had also met with President Roosevelt, McDonald, and Secretary of Labor Frances Perkins, assuring the Americans that "they were not acting as an Agent of the German Government to aid the export of German goods." Archives of the Central British Fund, Roll 1, File A, Minutes of the New Court Committee, February 13, 1936. Their backup plan was to raise enough funds for the exodus of 100,000 young German Jews over a four-year period. Half were to go to Palestine; half to other countries. Shepherd, *Refuge from Darkness*, 110.

12. King George V of Great Britain had died on January 20.

said he didn't know how to do it; would I? When he called on me, I asked for a moment of silence. The audience immediately rose and stood. It was, I think, a tribute which the Englishmen appreciated. Felix Warburg closed the meeting in good style. It was then already too late (eleven o'clock). Rosenberg was an enthusiastic but not a happy chairman. He has no sense of humor at all.

. . . .

On February 1 Sir Herbert Samuel met with President Roosevelt at the White House. There was again discussion of whether American consuls in Germany were using reasonable standards in deciding whether or not to grant immigration visas to applicants. Samuel later wrote, "I recall what was said in America with regard to the desire of the President that the rules should not be enforced too rigidly by the American Consuls in Germany."[13]

On February 4 there was a dinner in McDonald's honor in Philadelphia. Albert Einstein, who was unable to attend, wrote a tribute:

[. . . Through his capacity as High Commissioner for German Jewish refugees McDonald came to know intimately—more so than anyone not personally affected—the suffering and difficulties of the victims of the present political madness in central Europe.

Similarly, he experienced just as much the unwillingness to cooperate and the lack of feeling of responsibility and active will for justice that by and large prevailed in the rest of the world. With experiences and disillusionments, his striving for the innocent victims of persecution and in the interests of justice and tolerance unceasingly gained strength and purity. What he at first took on as a job became a matter of the heart. His letter of resignation to the League of Nations is one of those irrefutable masterpieces, which a human being can only achieve when he is consumed by his mission. This letter will go down in the annals of history as a lasting appeal to humanity's conscience.[14]]

. . . .

Wednesday, February 5, 1936

Back home [after speaking in Philadelphia], getting ready to go [back] to Philadelphia with the family [Ruth and Bobby].[15] Started the car in time to reach Philadelphia for supper and spend the night with my brother.[16]

---

13. Samuel to Felix Warburg, May 27, 1936, reprinted in *Franklin D. Roosevelt and Foreign Affairs*, vol. III, 324.

14. Einstein to Billikopf, February 3, 1936, McDonald Papers, Columbia University, D361 (Albert Einstein Special File). Original in German.

15. This was the first leg of a trip to Florida for a six-week vacation as guests of Henry Ittleson.

16. Edward McDonald, professor of English at Dropsie College.

Reached Washington at noon. Found an invitation waiting for dinner at the White House. I called to ask if I might bring Ruth. Mrs. Roosevelt's reply was she would be delighted. The dinner was for about twenty persons. During the meal I chatted most of the time with one of the younger Roosevelt boys, who is now at Harvard, John. He talked amusingly about Harvard affairs.

After dinner the President had an appointment, so Mrs. Roosevelt and the other guests went to one of the sitting rooms. There Mrs. Roosevelt, Judge Moore[17] of the State Department, and I did most of the talking. It all centered on the situation in Germany. I was delighted at Judge Moore's frankness. Then about 8:30 Mrs. Roosevelt said that I must see the President for a few minutes before the general reception. So I was taken to the President's study. The others present were two of the Roosevelt boys. They asked if they might be allowed to stay. I said so far as I was concerned I would be delighted if they would stay. Then the President and I talked for about twenty minutes on conditions in Germany. He doesn't seem to have become any more friendly to the regime. On the other hand, I had kind of an impression that he was not any more inclined to take an initiative in the matter than he had been previously. This was discouraging.[18] But he could not have been more cordial to me personally.

At nine o'clock all went downstairs to watch the beginning of the general annual department reception, at which the President received a couple of thousand members of the governmental departments. During that time I chatted with the secretary of the treasury [Henry Morgenthau, Jr.]—mostly about personal things, particularly the death of Jerome Straus.

Before going home Ruth and I danced for a little while.

Friday, February 7, 1936

Awoke in a terrific blizzard. It became apparent that it was quite impossible to think of leaving that day by car. I made various visits to the Department of State.

McDonald's most important meeting was with Undersecretary William Phillips, who recorded McDonald's purpose in his diary.

[Mr. James G. McDonald, who has just resigned from the International Jewish Relief Organization [!], dropped in. While in this office he dictated the following memorandum:

"The day before I sailed from London on December 15 last, I took up for the second time with the Foreign Office the possibility of informal representations at Berlin, preferably in cooperation with the Government of the United

---

17. Robert Walton Moore, former Virginia congressman, assistant secretary of state (1933–1937), then State Department counselor until his death in 1941.

18. McDonald was apparently hoping that the president would issue a statement denouncing Nazi persecution.

States, in reference to the situation of the Jewish population in Germany, as outlined in my letter of resignation addressed to the Secretary General of the League of Nations.

My appeal to the Foreign Office this time was on a different basis from my earlier suggestion. The new element is the large-scale plan which has been formulated and is being financed by Jewish groups chiefly in Great Britain and the United States to evacuate from 100,000 to 125,000 of the younger Jewish men and women from Germany within the next four or five years.

In view of this program of emigration and taking account also of the fact that the number of Jews in Germany is diminishing rapidly because of the abnormally high death rate and because there are fewer marriages and births than usual, I expressed the hope that the Foreign Office would consider the present to be an appropriate occasion to approach the German Government. I did not, of course, suggest that there should be any form of protest, but rather that the two Governments, speaking as friends of Germany, should, after calling attention to the program of emigration, make the point that it would be advantageous to Germany, because of the effect upon world public opinion, if the Reich were prepared to expedite the evacuation by certain concessions in the matter of transfer of property and also by making the lot of the Jews who must remain, either temporarily or permanently in Germany, somewhat easier.

The answer given me by the Foreign Office was that the proposed plan of evacuation did offer a possible basis for the representations which I had suggested and that the matter would be studied promptly and sympathetically.

It is my belief that, if now the American Government would indicate to the Foreign Office its willingness to cooperate, prompt action might be secured.

I am venturing to make the suggestion of this cooperation as a private American citizen. I have had no official responsibility since December 31. I can assure the Department that this is a matter which is not going to be broached in the press and will not even be discussed by me with any save two or three of the Jewish leaders, of whose confidence and discretion I am perfectly sure."[19]]

McDonald's diary entry of February 7 continued:

Late that night I decided to send the car by train and to go down south by train ourselves.

Saturday, February 8, 1936

Left on the afternoon train for Palm Beach.

19. Phillips Diary, February 7, 1936, call number bMS Am 2232, Houghton Library. By permission of the Houghton Library, Harvard University. McDonald did not know that the British government had already decided not to intercede with Germany. The United States decided independently not to do so. The reply came from Simons to Schoenfeld to Dunn to Phillips that the United States could not intercede for a non-American group and that the immigration laws admitted of no special privileges for any group. Schoenfeld to Dunn, February 17, 1936, NA RG 59, 150.626J/185.

Reached Palm Beach. Met at the station by Mrs. Ittleson, who took us to the lovely quarters at the Seaglade Hotel, where they had made reservations for us.

The next six weeks, from February 9 to Saturday, March 21, were a holiday. It is unnecessary to give details of what went on from day to day. Mostly it was golf, the beach, and friendly lunches and dinners. The new people whom I met and came to know best were Mr. Philip Block, president of the Inland Steel; Mr. Florsheim, president of the Florsheim Shoe Company, who thinks that he can make me the president of Northwestern University; Edna Ferber,[20] who wanted to talk to me about conditions in Germany; Mrs. Levy, with whom my family was to stay for a while; the McCormicks from Albany; Sam Lamport, enthusiastic golfer; Sam Harris, and a number of other theatrical people, but more interesting and [most] worthwhile of all, Eddie Cantor[21] and his family. His response at once to my suggestion that we cooperate in raising funds for the Assistance Medicale[22] did much to revive my faith in human nature. The net result of our efforts was $5,630.

On February 27 McDonald also gave a ten-minute speech by phone to a dinner meeting of the American Christian Committee for Refugees.

Among McDonald's golfing partners in Palm Beach was a man named Leo Butzel, who later relayed an account McDonald had given him. It concerned a luncheon meeting he had had in 1931 in Detroit with Henry Ford:

[Ford asked him if he knew who caused the last war. McDonald said he did not know and that he talked with leading historians and statesmen and they likewise did not know. Ford said, I can tell you in one word. McDonald thought that would be a valuable contribution to history and Ford answered, "the Jews."

Ford then asked McDonald if he knew who brought about the Russian revolution and killed the Czar, etc. McDonald said he did not know and anticipated Ford's one-word answer which again was "the Jews."

Ford then told McDonald that he had bought the original copy of the Protocols [of the Elders of Zion] from a Russian, that they were genuine and that he had them locked up in his safe in Dearborn. He said that he had paid $10,000 for them but that he could not reveal the name of the Russian who sold them to him[,] as the Russian pleaded with him not to divulge his name[,] for if he would, the Jews would murder him within 24 hours.[23]]

20. One of the best-read novelists in the United States during the 1920s and 1930s. Won the Pulitzer Prize in 1924 for her novel *So Big*. Her father was a Hungarian Jewish immigrant.

21. One of the best-known comedians in the United States during the twentieth century.

22. The Assistance Medicale was in Paris. The sum raised was enough to finance their dispensary for the rest of the year and thus help about a thousand children.

23. Abba Abrams to Morris D. Waldman, April 1, 1936, American Jewish Committee Archives, Morris D. Waldman Files, RG 1, EXO-29, League of Nations, James G. McDonald folder, Center for Jewish History, New York.

This was a shortened and slightly distorted version of McDonald's own account of his January 9, 1931, conversation with Henry Ford, which is found in the carbon copy of his diary for that date. This portion has been removed from the diary original. The carbon copy version follows here.

Reached the Dearborn research plant almost exactly at one, was shown in promptly to one of Mr. Ford's offices, where I found him with his secretary, Mr. Campsall. He was most cordial, introduced me as the man who had made a speech out at the Club the other night and who had put Tolstoi in his place.

Then, while we were waiting for lunch, Ford entertained me with some interpretations of world events. He said, "Do you know, Mr. McDonald, that the world war was caused simply by the desire of the Jews to get control of everything in Germany?" He said the situation was quite clear. The same way it is perfectly certain that the Bolshevik revolution was carried through by the Jews. "I have the documents to prove it. A Russian made a special investigation for me and gave me the documents, including photographs of people shot, bullets, etc. The evidence is overwhelming. I have it in my vault. The man who gave me the material, to whom I paid $10,000 for it, said, 'This has cost me much more than that, but I wanted to put it in your hands. My health is such that I will not be alive a year from now and I am better satisfied now that you have this data.'"

Ford continued, "You know practically all the leaders are Jews. I don't blame the Jews. They have a place in the world. That is what they are here for. Whenever a situation becomes inconceivably bad and has to be destroyed, it is for the Jews to destroy it, so that afterward others can come in and build it up again."

There was more along this general line when it was time for us to go into lunch.

. . . .

During the luncheon, which lasted until nearly half-past three, we discussed many, many subjects, but at no time did I hear any one of the executives disagree with him on any major point. Apparently, no matter how high you get in the Ford organization, you must not disagree with Henry. Among the subjects discussed were:

(1) <u>The Depression.</u> Mr. Ford said it was the best depression in history, much better than earlier ones, because they had been more or less local and this is world-wide. Out of it great good would come. He implied that in part it was more or less arranged by the financiers: that certain people would be cleaned out and the whole atmosphere more wholesome after it was all over.

. . . .

(2) As to <u>International Finance</u> in general, he seemed to feel that it is omniscient and omnipotent except as concerns himself. He seems sure that

international financial interests are going to be able to get into Russia and build on a substantial scale after the Jews had gotten through destroying the old regime.

. . . .

On the whole I had the impression of a man clearly a fanatic or, if you prefer, so much of a genius that he bordered on the insane. When he talked of the Jews, his eyes would light up and his face become tense, like, I can imagine, the head of the Inquisition in the Middle Ages.[24]

McDonald's diary entry continued:

During the whole of our stay the Ittlesons could not have been nicer. It was with great regret that I felt I had to leave on March 21 in order to keep an appointment at Montgomery, Alabama.

Montgomery, Alabama, Sunday, March 22, 1936

Was met at Montgomery by some of the members of the committee. Played golf for a short time before dinner.

There was an excellent audience, representing social workers of the whole of the south [Southern Regional Conference of Jewish Welfare organizations]. The chairman was Harold Hirsch.

Atlanta, Monday, March 23, 1936

The morning train to Atlanta with Mr. Hirsch and his son-in-law.

In the afternoon golf at Bobby Jones's course with three excellent players.

Six o'clock dinner with Mr. Hirsch as host, at which were present some thirty or forty of the dignitaries of the state, including the chief justice. I spoke briefly but frankly, stressing non-Jewish aspects of the situation in Germany. Then I went almost directly to the temple, where I spoke to a "full house."

Tuesday, March 24, 1936

Noon train for New York.

Wednesday, March 25, 1936

At FPA office early in the morning.

Here McDonald's prewar diary ends.

During the remainder of 1936 McDonald served on the editorial staff of the New York Times, *writing editorials frequently—but rarely about European matters, which were usually covered by Anne O'Hare McCormick. He also "put the paper*

---

24. McDonald Diary, Carbons, 3 January 1931–6 January 1932, McDonald Papers, USHMM.

to bed" on a regular basis. This was not at all the position he and Arthur Sulzberger had discussed initially, which would have had him serve as something of a spokesman and liaison for the Times. *Instead, he found a job that took most of his time and did not make use of his experience. It produced friction on both sides.*

In his spare time he kept up his contacts with those interested in helping German Jews and other victims of Nazi persecution leave Germany. His former deputy Norman Bentwich and his former secretary Olive Sawyer kept McDonald informed about League of Nations refugee activities. Newly appointed High Commissioner for Refugees Sir Neill Malcolm, a career Royal Army officer, interpreted his responsibility narrowly and distanced himself from the previous commission, deciding not to employ any of the staff. The League also restricted him: Malcolm was not to be involved with facilitating emigration from Germany or with the humanitarian side of the refugee problem.[25] The League Secretariat was to give him minimal funds for his office. McDonald, in turn, told Bentwich about controversy between Zionists and non-Zionists on his side of the Atlantic.[26]

In 1936 Bentwich became honorary director of emigration and training for a new international organization called the Council for German Jewry.[27] One of his early deft moves was to mobilize a Pittsburgh lawyer named David Glick. In early 1936 Max Warburg had suggested to his brother Felix that conditions for Jews had so deteriorated that an American citizen in Germany might do some good—particularly in view of the fact that German Jews were now barred from meeting with German officials unless summoned to do so.[28] JDC official David Schweitzer explained some of the reasons for Glick's mission to Germany to Bernhard Kahn in Paris:

Mr. Glick is sailing on the *Ile de France* tomorrow, April 4. He is going directly to London. He is well acquainted with Mr. Bentwich, whom he met years ago at Harvard University, and since then they have kept in touch with each other. Mr. Bentwich urged Mr. Glick last year to give some of his time to the German situation, and it was originally Mr. Glick's idea that he could be useful as a sort of liaison between Berlin and Geneva. Conditions have so changed since that time, however, not only in Germany (in view of the new regulations concerning foreigners),[29] but with respect to the whole setup of the High Commission, that Mr. Glick realizes that he will have to feel his way and see where and how he can be most helpful after he arrives on the other side. After seeing Mr. Bentwich in London, Mr. Glick plans to visit you in Paris.[30]

25. Olive Sawyer to McDonald, February 10, 1936, McDonald Papers, Columbia University, Correspondence 1936, H22.

26. McDonald to Bentwich, March 26, 1936. Copy in McDonald Papers, USHMM.

27. Norman Bentwich, *My 77 Years: An Account of My Life and Times, 1883–1960* (Philadelphia: Jewish Publication Society of America, 1961), 142.

28. David Glick, "Some Were Rescued: Memories of a Private Mission," *Harvard Law School Bulletin*, December 1960, 6.

29. German Jews were prohibited from meeting with foreign Jews without prior police permission. Bentwich, *My 77 Years*, 143.

30. Schweitzer to Kahn, April 3, 1936, USHMM, Glick Papers, RG 2004.320.1, Folder 6.

In 1960 Glick described his subsequent visit to Germany.

When I arrived in Berlin [in April 1936], I registered at the Esplanade Hotel, which was directly across the street from the United States Consulate. . . . I then called upon Mr. George S. Messersmith, the United States Consul General, an outspoken and fearless representative of our country, and his First Assistant, Raymond H. Geist, the United States Consul. I explained to both these officials the purpose of my visit to Germany [to bring to the attention of the Nazi officials any suggestion, recommendation, or assistance I thought should be given the Jews that would enable them to migrate to other lands]. . . . They reacted enthusiastically and immediately phoned Himmler without disclosing to him the purpose of the call, simply asking for an interview. The interview was granted and a few days later, I drove with Mr. Geist to the headquarters of the Gestapo, at No. 8 Prinz-Albrecht Strasse.

. . . .

Mr. Geist suggested that he do all the talking, that I was to give no indication to Himmler that I could speak German fluently. Geist was to tell Himmler my purpose in coming to Berlin in German, then relate to me Himmler's reply in English, and I would speak to Geist in English. This arrangement worked satisfactorily and gave a kind of semi-official appearance to my visit. Geist told Himmler that I was in Berlin at the request of two men [presumably the Warburg brothers]; that there had been no publicity given to my trip to Berlin; that no publicity was intended; that my work would be done quietly; that I would make no speeches or propaganda upon my return to America, nor write any articles. My purpose was specifically to give help to the Jews of Germany to assist them in leaving Germany for other parts of the world with as much of their property as possible under the laws of Germany. He also told them that arrangements for the Jews to migrate could be accomplished, but that they must take with them some property in order that they would not become a charge on the community to which they migrated.

After considering the matter, Mr. Himmler consented to the arrangement and called in Reinhard Heydrich, explained the situation to him, and Heydrich then took me into the office of the Deputy in charge of the "Juden Fragen" . . . , whose name was Dr. iur. Karl Haselbacher. I spent considerable time with Haselbacher, for he knew the important Jews in every large city in Germany. He had a filing card system that contained the names, addresses, activities, and occupations of thousands of the important Jews in Germany. Haselbacher was good enough to give me his calling card with his private phone number so that if I needed to call him for any reason, I would have no difficulty. He also furnished me with a list of leading Jews in the large cities of Germany. Geist and Messersmith were both amazed that permission was granted so quickly.

. . . .

Himmler, at first glance, appeared like an experienced title searcher in the office of the Recorder of Deeds of a country county seat. No pomp, no table thumping, no attempt to make an impression. He sat there with three SS men around him, but those eyes of his; those beady, button eyes, cruel as he was cunning and cunning as he was cruel. When Heydrich entered the room, my first thought was, "What a tackle he would make on a professional football team." He was a blond gorilla—big shoulders, long arms, powerful legs.[31]

During 1936 the chances for German Jews (and other victims of Nazi persecution) to emigrate to the United States were still limited. They faced a peculiar situation in which there was seemingly room for them under the relatively large immigration quota for Germany (25,957 annually), but U.S. immigration regulations, especially a clause barring those likely to become public charges, prevented most from qualifying for visas. Isolationists and refugee advocates in the United States each sought to modify this awkward and unstable arrangement.

The tendency in Congress and in some executive agencies was toward tighter restrictions. Key senators led by Senator Robert Reynolds of North Carolina engaged in serious discussions and hard bargaining to cut immigration quotas by 90 percent; Commissioner of Immigration Daniel MacCormack said the Labor Department could accept a 75 percent reduction on the grounds that no more than 25 percent had been filled in the last four years.[32] This statement was a technical disguise for Mac-Cormack's view that the country could not afford a higher level of immigration from Germany. Majority sentiment in Congress was most likely in favor of additional restriction, but influential liberals held some key positions. In the end, Congress was unable to agree on any remedy, so the formal quotas remained unchanged.

In mid-June 1936 Governor Herbert H. Lehman of New York reminded the president of his previous pledge to reduce the difficulties for Germans seeking to obtain immigration visas to the United States.[33] In the remaining months before the presidential election, President Roosevelt issued a statement favoring the rebuilding of a Jewish homeland in Palestine, and the United States urged Britain not to curtail immigration to Palestine, a step then under consideration.[34] But the president refrained from actions that might increase immigration to the United States. In light of his past experiences and his awareness of the public climate, McDonald declined to write to FDR again to ask him to issue a public statement on refugee matters.[35]

After Roosevelt and the Democrats won a resounding electoral victory in November, the political and bureaucratic balance in the State Department shifted. Foreign Service Inspector Jerome Klahr Huddle soon visited American consulates in

31. Glick, "Some Were Rescued," 7, 9.
32. Carr Memorandum, April 29, 1936, NA RG 59, Visa Division 150.01/2450.
33. Lehman to My Dear Mr. President, June 15, 1936, reprinted in *Franklin D. Roosevelt and Foreign Affairs*, vol. III, *September 1935–January 1937*, 323.
34. See Breitman and Kraut, *American Refugee Policy*, 48.
35. Frank Ritchie to Clarence Pickett, October 30, 1936, American Friends Service Committee Archives, Committees and Organizations, American Christian Committee for German Refugees, 1936.

Germany and reported that the character of prospective German-Jewish immigrants was unusual—many applicants were from the better classes, and even if they had only distant relatives in the United States, these relatives had sincere desires to assist them escape persecution. After some internal debate the State Department informed certain American consulates in Europe that they should reject only applicants who were probably going to become public charges: the possibility of becoming a public charge was not sufficient grounds for denial of visas.[36]

This new instruction led Consul General John Wiley in Antwerp to inquire of his colleague Homer Brett in Rotterdam, "Is there a radical change of policy with free and easy issuance of visas or is the [State] Department merely concerned over lack of proper efficiency in the field? . . . We have all, however, been of the opinion that the L.P.C. [likely to become a public charge] clause, in view of the widespread unemployment still existing in the United States, was not a thing to be taken lightly." On January 8, 1937, Brett responded: "Yes, we got it [the new visa instruction] too. . . . I understand it as a radical change of policy and I am sending in an enthusiastic acknowledgment. . . . I personally think that a strained definition of the L.P.C. clause has been enforced ever since September 1930 and that this instruction signifies that 'likely' is to mean what it meant when the law was written."[37]

Around the same time, McDonald wrote writer Dorothy Thompson about how many had managed to leave Nazi Germany since Hitler came to power. Combining information from governments and private organizations, McDonald estimated that through the end of 1936 about 110,000 Jews had left Germany, as had about 16,500 others—Christians considered non-Aryans, political refugees, Catholics, and Protestants. So the total number who had left to escape persecution was in the range of 125,000–130,000.[38]

The number of American immigration visas granted under the German quota to applicants inside and outside Germany increased substantially in 1937, largely the result of the new visa instruction. Joseph Hyman, executive director of the Joint Distribution Committee, wrote in June 1937, "Every month brings almost double the number of immigrants for the similar period last year."[39] By late 1937 even some of those advocates for refugees were satisfied with the level of immigration from Germany for the time being.[40]

Emigration options elsewhere also improved somewhat. Bentwich was able to go to Stuttgart, Breslau, Gleiwitz, and Frankfurt to look for promising Jewish candidates for admission to Australia.[41] The Reichsvertretung der Juden in Deutschland—

36. Breitman and Kraut, *American Refugee Policy*, 49. Barbara McDonald Stewart, *United States Government Policy on Refugees from Nazism, 1933–1940* (New York: Garland, 1982), 259–263.

37. Wiley to Brett, January 6, 1937, and Brett to Wiley, January 8, 1937, John C. Wiley Papers, Box 6, General Correspondence B, Franklin D. Roosevelt Library, Hyde Park, N.Y.

38. McDonald to Mrs. Sinclair Lewis, undated [January 1937], McDonald Papers, Columbia University (Dorothy Thompson), Folder G383.

39. Quoted by Stewart, *United States Government Policy*, 264.

40. See Breitman and Kraut, *American Refugee Policy*, 50, for details.

41. Bentwich, *My 77 Years*, 143.

the official leadership body of the Jewish community in Nazi Germany—estimated at the end of 1937 that since 1933, 127,000 German Jews had been able to emigrate throughout the world. Taken together with the death rate, emigration had reduced the German Jewish population to about 350,000 (from 501,000).[42] *Events during 1938, however, would make most of these Jews desperate to leave and added many others in Austria and part of Czechoslovakia to their number.*

42. Kurt Battsek to McDonald, June 22, 1938, McDonald Papers, Columbia University, D367 (PACPR—Evian Conference), Folder P15.

7. Refugee Politics and Diplomacy: 1938

In March 1938 Nazi Germany brought about the Anschluss (annexation) of Austria, which, by the standards of the Nuremberg Laws, had more than two hundred thousand Jews. Austrian anti-Semites, members of the Nazi Party, and police and SS officials immediately attacked, arrested, and humiliated Jews and political opponents in Austria. Confiscation of Jewish property and public scenes such as forcing Jews to scrub sidewalks were everyday occurrences. Hundreds of Austrian Jews committed suicide, and tens of thousands sought to leave as quickly as possible. A new stage of the European diplomatic crisis—and of the related refugee crisis—had begun.

Drawing upon his past experience with Nazi officials, McDonald recognized impending dangers in central Europe. Nazi measures against Austrian Jews—marked by greater violence, more immediate expropriation, and greater pressure to leave—only confirmed his previous view of where Nazi Germany was heading. In a speech to a small group of potential Jewish donors in New York City, McDonald explained (according to a later summary prepared by Joseph C. Hyman):

In Germany and spreading out from Germany all over the continent of Europe and across the waters to this country and other countries, is the oft-reiterated theory that Jews are parasites and that they are to be regarded, not figuratively but literally, as sub-humans. The attitude of many people, who are otherwise presumably intelligent, is that to crush a Jew is no more unworthy or reprehensible than to step on vermin and crush the life out of such creatures.[1]

The war that the Nazis are waging is not a war against the Jews of Germany, but against all Jews, whose influence must be obliterated and who themselves should either be exterminated or driven out of all civilized lands.

. . . If you think that because you live in the United States you are immune, you are very foolish. Nothing counts these days except money with which to carry on your work of relief, of emigration, and of service to your fellow Jews. Mass meetings, parades, demonstrations, resolutions, getting nice letters from friendly Christians, are all very well, but they don't actually save a single Jewish life, feed a starving Jewish boy or girl, train a single youth, pay for his emigration, or enable him to start life anew anywhere else.[2]

---

1. McDonald had told his American Jewish contacts as early as 1933 that the Nazis considered eliminating Jews like killing cockroaches. Although this analogy was not directly recorded in his diary, there is an oblique reference to it in his diary entry of November 2, 1933.

2. Hyman to Pell, March 30, 1939 (with the explanation that this meeting took place a year or so earlier), Joint Distribution Committee Archives, Box 31, Germany—Refugees 1939–1942, Center for Jewish History, New York.

In a March 29, 1938, address at the Jewish Theological Seminary (as summarized by an official of the Joint Distribution Committee) McDonald stated:

This problem will require thinking in terms not of a few million dollars, but in terms of tens of millions of dollars. Moreover, the problem is not a Jewish problem. The conscience of America has been stirred. Protestants, Catholics, men of all groups have expressed themselves as anxious to help in some way. It requires now the harnessing of all of these forces of Christian and American goodwill. This situation cannot be and must not be dealt with as a Jewish problem or as a Jewish organizational activity. It far transcends in its challenge and its implications anything specifically Jewish.[3]

Both Herbert Feis, an economic specialist in the State Department, and the writer Dorothy Thompson had urged the Roosevelt administration to respond directly to the Anschluss and its consequences.[4] According to an unofficial account of the cabinet meeting of March 18, 1938, President Roosevelt raised the idea of taking in more "Austrian political refugees," just as the United States had taken in so many fine Germans after the unsuccessful revolutions of 1848. This formulation expanded upon McDonald's notion that the Nazis had challenged all civilization, but wrapped it in precedent and language concealing the fact that most of the victims this time—and those in greatest need—were German and Austrian Jews.

The president was willing to consider some remedies. He suggested combining the German and Austrian quotas, which would give Austrians access to the unused portion of the much larger German quota. He also asked the cabinet whether an act to increase the German quota would get through Congress. The cabinet concluded that such a move would fail. The president then announced that he hoped to encourage other countries to take in at least ten to fifteen thousand families. In subsequent discussions with Morgenthau and Undersecretary of State Sumner Welles, FDR reaffirmed that congressional and public opposition ruled out new legislation, but that he hoped to liberalize U.S. immigration procedures and to persuade Latin American countries to take in additional refugees. He approved a formal list of American proposals on March 22 that implicitly involved full use of the combined German-Austrian quota.[5]

President Roosevelt then launched an initiative without consulting the State Department (though Secretary of State Cordell Hull had to follow up), inviting a range of other governments to attend a refugee conference to be held in Europe (later

3. Secretary to Mr. Hyman to Florence Stanford, March 30, 1938, Joint Distribution Committee Archive, AR 33/44 (Refugees), File 255, Center for Jewish History.

4. Breitman and Kraut, *American Refugee Policy*, 56. Stewart, *United States Government Policy*, 272.

5. Morgenthau Diaries, March 22, 1938, vol. 115, Franklin D. Roosevelt Library (FDRL). Harold L. Ickes, *Secret Diary: The Inside Struggle, 1936–1939* (New York: Simon and Schuster, 1954), II, 342–343. Welles's memo of March 22 bears a handwritten note that the president approved it that day. See U.S. National Archives and Records Administration (hereafter NA), Record Group (RG) 59, 840.48 Refugees/11 1/2.

set in the French resort town of Evian-les-Bains) and to set up an ad hoc international committee on refugee problems. This meeting and the committee would try to bring about and finance emigration of political refugees from Germany and Austria. But, mindful of political limitations at home, the administration explicitly stated that countries participating would not be expected to change existing immigration laws. The president selected as American representative Myron C. Taylor, a retired chairman of the board of U.S. Steel and a Quaker, a man of intelligence and goodwill, but with limited experience on emigration issues.

These moves brought some satisfaction to American Jewish leaders. On March 28 Judge Irving Lehman wrote to FDR:

In the autumn of 1933, I told you a story brought to me by a friend upon his return from a trip to Germany. In the synagogue at Nuremburg [sic] an aged Jew, seeking in meditation and prayer, comfort and courage, said to my friend: "Does your great leader in America know what is happening here? All those who are oppressed, all those who are deprived of freedom, are praying that, in God's name, he will speak to the world for them."

You have done that, more than once, during these troubled years. Conscious both of the responsibilities of your position and of your great official and personal influence, you have, when occasion offered, voiced for America the ideals and traditions which have made America great; and many Americans have felt proud and grateful that they had such a spokesman.

I feel that last week you have done much not only to rouse the conscience of humanity but to restore sanity to a world gone made [sic, mad]. I have in the past said to you that I am an "incurable optimist," that I cannot believe that force can for long dethrone right and liberty, but for a time my optimism was shaken. You have restored it. As an American and as a Jew I want to say "Thank you!"

President Roosevelt responded on March 30:

Dear Irving:-

I am grateful to you for that nice letter, and I think that our action in regard to political refugees will have far-reaching consequences even though, unfortunately, we cannot take care of more than a small proportion of them. It is my hope that the narrow isolationists will not use this move of ours for purely partisan objectives.[6]

On March 31 Assistant Secretary of State George S. Messersmith wrote Secretary of State Cordell Hull and Undersecretary Sumner Welles about the ripple effects of President Roosevelt's initiatives.

6. Irving Lehman to the president, March 28, 1938, and FDR to Irving Lehman, March 30, 1938, FDRL, Official File 3186, Box 1, Political Refugees, January–May 1938. Governor Herbert Lehman wrote a similar, shorter letter.

There is the great danger that if the matter is not handled carefully[,] false hopes may be raised[,] and that further demoralization instead of some constructive action may result.

. . . The other day Mr. Chamberlain[7] of Columbia, Paul Baerwald of the Jewish Distribution Committee, and Miss Razovsky,[8] who is one of the best-informed workers among refugees and emigrants, came to see me. All three have through continuous contact and close study of all aspects of the refugee problem a very intimate knowledge thereof. It is their settled conviction that the step which our Government has taken is encouraging and will prove useful if directed in the proper channels. They have pointed out, however, the danger which exists if various organizations in this country may become too active in propagating measures which would tend toward changes in our statutes liberalizing further our immigration practice. They are convinced that under our existing statutes and practice this country is able to receive as many immigrants every year as it can absorb.[9] They believe that certain changes can be made in immigration practice which are necessary. They envisage the problem as one in which other countries must cooperate by assuming at least a more liberal attitude toward receiving immigrants—an attitude somewhat approximating at least our own.

Rabbi Wise has been to see me and he agrees with all the others I have seen that the activities of Jewish organizations must be kept in the background. A number of members of Congress have been in touch with me and I have gathered uniformly from them that they realize that any proposed changes in our immigration laws might lead to more restrictive rather than to more liberal immigration practice on our part.[10]

Messersmith may have recorded accurately the climate in Congress. Yet his memorandum reflected his own views, probably more so than the views of American Jewish leaders. He recommended holding a White House conference with interested persons or groups. (He personally favored invitations to individuals as the best way to keep humanitarian aspects of the problem in the foreground "and religious, racial, and political considerations . . . in the background.") Messersmith nominated a list of individuals, including McDonald, some of whom were in fact invited, along with others.[11]

---

7. Joseph Perkins Chamberlain, professor of public law, Columbia University. Active in refugee work, 1933–1950. One of McDonald's longtime allies.

8. Cecilia Razovsky, from 1934 to 1939 headed the National Coordinating Committee for Aid to Refugees and Emigrants Coming from Germany.

9. This may have been Messersmith's impression. By late 1938 some American Jewish leaders wanted special measures beyond the quotas.

10. Messersmith to the Secretary and the Under-Secretary, March 31, 1938, NA RG 59, Lot File 52D408, Alphabetical Subject File, Box 9, Political Refugees.

11. Messersmith to the Secretary and the Under-Secretary, March 31, 1938, NA RG 59, Lot File 52D408, Alphabetical Subject File, Box 9, Political Refugees.

Before this meeting took place, President Roosevelt spelled out some of his thoughts about the refugee problem in an April 4 meeting with Arthur Sweetser,[12] the most prominent American connected with the League of Nations. Sweetser recapitulated the conversation in a memorandum apparently written some days later.[13] To the best of our knowledge, this is the first time this manuscript has been published or cited. As does no other document, it spells out President Roosevelt's private hopes for the refugee conference.

For the first time during the 20 years that I have been going to Washington since the creation of the League of Nations, I decided to write on [*sic*] in advance to the White House that I was en route. Accordingly, I wrote my friend Steve Early, Secretary to the President, who had covered the State, War, and Navy Departments with me for the AP during America's approach to the World War, when Franklin Roosevelt was Assistant Secretary of the Navy, that I was slowly and cautiously converging on Washington via Florida, Chicago, and New York. He evidently passed my letter to Marvin McIntyre, immediate Secretary, who telegraphed me to get in touch with him on my arrival as he had a message for me. That seemed to mean an appointment with the President. . . .

. . . .

The President greeted me very affably as I came in [around 3 p.m.] After the first few words, he quickly took the lead as he usually does by asking how I liked "my [FDR's] refugee proposal." I had not expected this, but as I had talked a good deal about it with the State Department people and others, felt quite prepared to answer. I said I thought it was grand, that I was very much for it, that I loved seeing our country take a like [line?] of that sort.

"That was my proposal," the President quickly interjected, tapping his chest with obvious pleasure. "I worked that out myself."

I said I had guessed as much; it was fine.

"We had the matter up at the Cabinet," the President continued, "to see if we could not do something for these unfortunate people. But some of them, particularly Ickes,[14] objected on account of the immigration laws, said it

12. Arthur Sweetser worked in the League of Nations information section. Also had close relations with the Rockefellers. Extensively treated in *Advocate for the Doomed*. Appears in chapter 2, n. 42.

13. Typos and punctuation have been corrected. Italics added. This document is consistent with expressions of opinion by FDR earlier in 1938. See Ted Morgan, *FDR: A Biography* (New York: Simon and Schuster, 1985), 499.

14. Secretary of the Interior Harold L. Ickes. In his diary Ickes had written a somewhat different version of the cabinet meeting of March 18: "It was clear that the President thought we ought to make it as easy as possible for political refugees to come into this country, leaving it for future determination whether we could keep them here under the quota laws. I interposed that I thought it might be a fine gesture if we should open our doors to political refugees even if this meant a temporary amendment of the immigration laws. I pointed out that we stood to have a fine class of citizen, similar to the type that we got after the abortive revolution of 1848. The Vice President was of the opinion that it would not be possible to get an amendment of this law. He said that if the matter were left to a secret vote of Congress, all immigration would be stopped." Entry of March 19, 1938, *Secret Diary of Harold L. Ickes*, II, 342–343.

couldn't be done. Then suddenly it struck me: why not get all the democracies to unite to share the burden? After all, they own most of the free land of the world, and there are only . . . what would you say, fourteen, sixteen million Jews in the whole world, of whom about half are already in the United States. If we could divide up the remainder in groups of 8 or 10, there wouldn't be any Jewish problem in three or four generations."

I was astonished at this and couldn't help remarking that the only difficulty I foresaw was exactly that, that you couldn't divide them up, as they always congregated in the great cities. I then quickly took the opportunity to say that there was just one thing I regretted in the refugee matter and that was that the government had completely overlooked the League in making its proposal, and, while saying that it did not want to embarrass other efforts, did not think to send the correspondence to Geneva as well as to many capitals. The League had, after all, I continued, repatriated some 400,000 prisoners of war under Dr. Nansen, who could well be called refugees; it had worked out with conspicuous success the greatest transfer of populations in history when it took a million and a quarter Greeks from Asia Minor to Greece and a comparable number of Turks from Greece to Turkey; it had established the Nansen office which was caring for certain categories of refugees; it had later established the office for Jewish and other refugees from Germany; and it was now in the midst of reorganizing and stabilizing its whole effort in this field. Here, it seemed to me, had been one of those opportunities where the United States could have made a very friendly gesture toward the League, recognizing the good work it had done and offering to cooperate further with it. Instead, it had taken no note of the League and even in some quarters created the impression that, at the last minute the United States was coming in with all its weight and power, to take over a problem others had been working on for years and thus[,] on the one hand[,] not getting the benefit of their experience and[,] on the other[,] leaving them out in the cold.

This was a much more positive picture of the League of Nations' refugee activity than McDonald had given President Roosevelt in the past. Moreover, FDR placed no great stock in the League generally, thinking it useless for any serious political issues or controversies. He told Sweetser this plainly later in their conversation (in a portion of Sweetser's summary not printed here).

Sweetser's memorandum continued:

The President made no direct comment on this very direct statement. He said, however, that he was much encouraged with the replies, that the governments were all apparently favorable, except, he added, Italy. At this point he smiled broadly, saying very pointedly: "I had an invitation sent her with malice aforethought. I knew she would refuse, but I wanted her on record. I'm not the least troubled by her not coming in.

"I've not yet heard from the British," he went on. "I'm having lots of difficulty with them. The trouble is that England is not really a democracy. We make a great mistake in thinking it is. Look at this," he added, handing me a page clipping from the *Washington Post* on the so-called "Cliveden set."[15] . . . "And look at this, too," he went on, handing me a *New York Times* story from London that "[Archbishop of] Canterbury Backs Seizure of Austria." "What can you do," he said, "with people like that?"

. . . .

Then the President himself held things [Sweetser's departure] up by asking about European possibilities. I said I had at last found something where I agreed with Mr. [Herbert] Hoover (the President smiled) and that was that there would be no war within a year in Europe. Nothing in Central Europe, I thought, could stop Hitler; nothing outside, I felt, would try to. He would thus have some time to organize Mittel-Europa [German domination of central Europe], and he would need it. The real question in my mind came not here but subsequently. When that was all done, would Hitler stay content, or would he lead his people, with its persecution, inferiority complex, either east or west into an inevitable clash with either the Russian or the Anglo-French Empires[?] German opinion at present was enormously exalted; Hitler could lead it where he liked; the collision point seemed to me to come later.

The President seemed to agree. He told of a letter from a friend who had dined in a company of 6 or 8 with Schuschnigg the day after Berchtesgarden [Berchtesgaden].[16] Schn [Schuschnigg] said he had never dreamt of anything like it; that Hitler was unbelievable, that in his long tirades two names kept repeating themselves, Julius Caesar and Jesus Christ. The President seemed to think you could do very little with a man like that.[17]

A week and a half later the group of people interested in refugee problems invited to the White House met with the president there. Samuel McCrea Cavert, general secretary of the Federal Council of Churches, wrote up a confidential account.

The President opened the conference by remarking that the United States has always been deeply sympathetic with political refugees and that the time had come when our country had another historic opportunity to show this sympathy. . . . He expressed the hope that the group whom he had invited to the White House would be willing to serve as a permanent committee of an

15. The "Cliveden set" is the term for an aristocratic circle around Viscountess Nancy Astor (whose country residence was called Cliveden, in Buckinghamshire). They not only supported Neville Chamberlain's appeasement policy but some wanted friendly relations with Nazi Germany.

16. On February 12, in a private meeting with Austrian Chancellor Schuschnigg at Hitler's Alpine retreat at Berchtesgaden, Hitler launched a tirade in which he said he was determined to end Austrian treason against Germany. He threatened to use force unless Austria gave in to his demands.

17. Interview with President Roosevelt, April 4, 1938, Arthur Sweetser Papers, Manuscript Division, Library of Congress, Container 34.

advisory sort, mediating between the international commission and the various administrative organizations carrying on relief programs for the refugees.

Professor [Joseph] Chamberlain raised the question whether the term "political refugee" as used by the President was accurate. The President replied that he felt the term was accurate if used in a broad sense to describe those who have become refugees because of political conditions in their own countries. While the President did not specifically say so, it was clear that he was anxious to avoid using the term Jewish refugees.

Mr. [Raymond] Fosdick[18] felt that the amount of money which would be needed would be so large that under present conditions it could hardly be raised by private organizations, and asked whether appropriations might not be made by the Government. The President replied, with a touch of humor, that that would require congressional action and that he did not seem to be very successful in getting congressional action. I [Cavert] followed up Mr. Fosdick's question . . . by asking whether it might be possible for loans to be made to refugees by some governmental agency if private philanthropic organizations dealing with refugees underwrote the loans. The President replied that he felt that at least for the present[,] it would be unwise to put forward any proposal which would occasion public dispute and controversy, such as a change in the immigration quotas or appropriations or loans from public funds.

Mr. [Bernard] Baruch expressed some doubt as to whether any such move should be made as the President has in mind. He wondered whether, under present conditions in this country, it would be wise for our Government to encourage the idea that more refugees should come here.

Dr. McDonald felt that while everything possible should be done for the refugees, the problem would involve terribly "rough sledding" so long as the people generally felt that European dictators were creating refugees faster than any human agency could care for them. The President agreed but remarked that even if we could not do anything about political conditions in Europe[,] we could take such steps as are possible for us, to show our sympathy with the victims of those conditions.

I asked what the relationships would be between the new international commission and the existing [League of Nations] Nansen Commission and the High Commission for German Refugees. The President did not seem to be very clear on this point and appealed to Dr. McDonald for his judgment, to which Dr. McDonald replied that the Nansen Commission and the High Commission for German Refugees would both go out of existence at the end of this year. . . .

Msgr. [Michael] Ready brought up the question whether something could be done to make it less difficult for prospective émigrés to secure admission to this country, and . . . I [inquired] . . . whether it is really necessary to have

18. Raymond Fosdick, director of the Rockefeller Foundation and president of the League of Nations Association of the United States.

two rather iron-clad affidavits from American citizens for each refugee. Miss [Frances] Perkins[19] explained that the present requirement was not a legislative one but was the result of instructions sent out by Mr. [President] Hoover in 1929 or 1930. She felt it might be possible to relax the requirement somewhat. Mr. Messersmith held, however, that if the impression got abroad that the present regulations governing immigration were to be modified[,] a storm of protest would arise from certain circles. Miss Perkins agreed that no public statement on this point should be made[,] but suggested that perhaps some informal advice could be given to American consuls indicating that they need not be quite as strict as some of them are now being.[20]

At the end of the hour the President asked the group if they would be willing to meet at the Department of State at three o'clock. . . . At three o'clock the entire group, with the exception of the President and Miss Perkins, met with Secretary Hull and Mr. [Undersecretary of State Sumner] Welles.

Mr. Welles stated that it is very likely that the international conference which the President has convened will be held in Evian, France, just across from the Swiss border and not far from Geneva. Dr. McDonald suggested that London might be better.

. . . There was a general feeling that Dr. McDonald should be the chairman. He felt that he could not accept such a position at this time but promised to take it under consideration. Professor Chamberlain was also proposed as chairman[,] but he insisted that Dr. McDonald was the right man.

. . . [With regard to discussion of additional representatives on this committee] Mr. McDonald nominated Mr. Paul Baerwald, successor to Felix Warburg as Chairman of the Jewish Joint Distribution Committee. I nominated Mr. James M. Speers, Chairman of the American Committee for Christian German Refugees. Msgr. Ready and Mr. [Louis] Kenedy suggested Basil Harris, a Roman Catholic layman identified with shipping interests. It was definitely understood that the nomination of these or other persons must come from the President himself and that the committee was doing no more than making these informal suggestions.[21]

In the spring of 1938 McDonald left the Times to become president of the Brooklyn Institute of Arts and Sciences. This organization, once envisioned as a vast museum and research institution, included the Brooklyn Museum of Art, the Brooklyn Academy of Music, the Brooklyn Children's Museum, and the Brooklyn Botanic Garden. McDonald's heart was not in administration, but this position left him freer to

19. Frances Perkins, secretary of labor, the first woman to hold a cabinet post. A consistent supporter of measures to assist German refugees.

20. According to Stephen Wise's account, Perkins said, "Mr. President, I have no doubt that we will have to relax the regulations with regard to affidavits[,] and that if we really want to be of help, we will have to permit the incoming of refugees without affidavits." Memo on the Conference with the President and State Department, April 13, 1938, Brandeis Papers, Louisville University Microfilm Series, VI, Roll 106.

21. JDC Archive, AR 33/44, File 405, Center for Jewish History.

pursue refugee issues in his spare time and speak freely about them. He no longer needed clearance from the Times.

At the first formal meeting of what was called the President's Advisory Committee on Political Refugees on May 16, McDonald was elected chairman, and Cavert was chosen secretary.[22] The committee soon set up an office at 122 East 22nd Street in New York. Expenses were covered by contributions from organizations represented on the committee.

On May 16 Messersmith laid out the State Department's approach to refugee policy—no American government participation in emigration or settlement projects, but full use of the combined German-Austrian immigration quota. Some of the discussion suggested that the committee members wanted more than the State Department was prepared to give.

Rabbi Wise wondered whether the American representative on the Intergovernmental Committee [the upcoming Evian Conference was expected to create a new international committee] might not discuss informally with the British representative the possibility of an upward revision of the schedule of March 6 for immigration to Palestine.

Mr. Messersmith questioned the advisability of the American representative taking up this question, even informally.

The Chairman [McDonald] interposed that he could see no reason why Mr. Taylor should not be brought up-to-date on the Palestine question. It might serve a useful purpose if Mr. Taylor could, informally, suggest to the British that the schedule might be revised upward.

Mr. Messersmith doubted whether Mr. Taylor could be given any such instruction. In any event, it seemed to him that any question such as that should be very carefully avoided.

Mr. Harris observed that when you sit down at a conference it is impossible to tell when a question of that nature will turn up. . . .

The Chairman said that we could be sure now that this matter would come up. It might be well to envisage the probability that the question would come up and to furnish the American representative with material in order that he may have some idea in advance as to the line which he should take.

Mr. Kenedy said . . . we must dispel the idea that the Committee will drown this country with refugees and emphasize that it will be called upon mainly to furnish financial assistance [for them to settle elsewhere].

Mr. Messersmith then read from a memorandum. . . . Although many of the countries represented on the Committee are deeply moved by humanitarian instincts, none of them is approaching the problem with enthusiasm and very few with the disposition to make sacrifices. The replies which we have

<hr>

22. Others present: Assistant Secretary of State Messersmith, Paul Alling, and Robert Pell from State; Hamilton Fish Armstrong, Baerwald, Chamberlain, Harris, Kenedy, James Speers, and Wise. Henry Morgenthau, Sr., Bernard Baruch, and Raymond Fosdick, who had attended the April 13 meeting, did not join the committee.

received from most countries indicate that they approach the problem and the Committee with much reserve. It is to be feared that some of the countries have agreed to be represented on the Committee only because they did not wish to appear before international opinion as completely standing aside. I think it must be recognized that, in view of the disturbed economic situation in practically every country, there is good ground for this reserve.

[Our announcement of the refugee conference] . . . created hopes which were out of proportion with the immediate results which can be realized. . . . I believe . . . that the work of this Committee will not be concluded during the next fiscal year but that it may be a continuing one for years to come.[23]

One country that approached the problem and the proposed international committee with much reserve was Great Britain, which insisted that invitations should go only to countries of potential immigration (and not to those wishing to rid themselves of minorities), that the conference limit itself to actual refugees and not those threatened by persecution, and that Palestine be excluded from the agenda.[24]

Rabbi Wise wrote Supreme Court Justice Louis Brandeis about some of the differences that had arisen at the committee meeting.[25]

[Messersmith warned against] trying to get Myron Taylor to . . . move Great Britain to open more widely the doors of Palestine. McDonald, who is fine, and I at once took exception. His [Messersmith's] reply was that Taylor had the rank of Ambassador for the time being, and it was not for him to urge policies upon other countries.

In other words, if we are going to pussyfoot about and say nothing to the countries that can give opportunities for outlet, then the whole thing becomes a farce. . . . I think that McDonald and I will be able to bring about a change in the arrangement.

Professor Chamberlain, who you know, stood with us. I find that the Catholic members are interested only in averting the spread of Communism, and they propose that lessons in "Americanism" should be given on all ships bringing refugees. The Protestants are all good—McDonald, Chamberlain, Spears.[26]

. . . .

At the May 19 meeting of the President's Advisory Committee, McDonald discounted the chances of getting the German government to cooperate with arrangements for orderly emigration. Chamberlain estimated that two hundred thousand

23. Strictly Confidential Minutes of PACPR, May 16, 1938, NA RG 59, Lot File 52D408, Alphabetical Subject File, Box 9, President's Advisory Committee—Minutes.
24. Mark Wischnitzer, *To Dwell in Safety* (Philadelphia: Jewish Publication Society, 1948), 201.
25. He misspelled McDonald as MacDonald: spelling has been corrected here for clarity.
26. Wise to Brandeis, May 17, 1938, Wise Papers, Box 106, Correspondence—Zionism, Center for Jewish History.

Jews would leave if they could, and he was not counting the substantial but difficult-to-determine number of non-Aryans (mostly non-Jews whom the Nazis considered Jews or part-Jews). Wise cautioned the group not to leak information about immigration plans: after some congressman had made public statements about immigrants being welcome in Cuba, the Cuban government cut off immigration. McDonald summed up the committee's immediate agenda: first, brief Myron Taylor and the American delegation to Evian on what had been done in the United States since April 1933; second, canvass the world for possibilities of settlement on a large scale.

Mr. McDonald suggested the possibility of the formation of a subcommittee to collect and furnish to the Department data regarding the entrance of refugees into the United States, their placement and their distribution. After some discussion it was agreed that Rabbi Wise, Mr. Baerwald[,] and Monsignor Ready would undertake this task. During the discussion Monsignor Ready pointed out that he had recently had information that there were about four thousand Roman Catholics who were seeking to leave Austria as refugees. Of these there were only six priests, a small number of members of various orders whose schools and charitable institutions had been closed, while the majority were simple laymen.

. . . .

Mr. McDonald then proposed the formation of another subcommittee to make a brief survey of the possibilities of finding a refuge in certain under-populated areas in Africa and elsewhere. After some discussion it was agreed that Mr. McDonald, Mr. Armstrong[,] and Professor Chamberlain would undertake this task.[27]

. . . .

Bentwich returned to Geneva in May 1938 to observe developments at the League of Nations. His report to the British Council for German Jewry cast light on the League, preparations for the Evian Conference, and McDonald's dealings with President Roosevelt.

The Council of the League accepted the proposal of the British Government that the activity of the High Commissioner for the refugees from Germany should be extended to the refugees from Austria. That implies that the Convention signed at Geneva in February of this year will be applicable also to refugees from Austria. I met a Deputation of Refugees from Austria, who were all political exiles and Aryans. They were specially concerned that the title of

27. Minutes, May 20, 1938. Copy in NA RG 59, Lot File 52D408, Alphabetical Subject File, Box 9, President's Advisory Committee—Minutes.

the High Commissioner's Office should be modified so as to refer expressly to Austria as well as Germany.

The Council accepted also the report of the Sub-Committee which was appointed some months ago to submit proposals for the future organization of the League for refugees. The Committee recommended that there should be a single League Organization after the Assembly of 1938, which would comprise the functions hitherto exercised by the Nansen Office for the Russian and Armenian refugees and the Office of the High Commissioner for the German (and Austrian) refugees.

. . . .

As regards the American President's proposal, the League and the Governments are mystified . . . although the principal American member of the Secretariat who saw the President after the announcement was made,[28] obtained an assurance that the League would be informed of the steps. Nor have the European Governments or the American Ministers in the Capitals any knowledge of the proposals to be made.

. . . .

An Advisory Committee has been appointed in the U.S.A. to assist the Department in the preparation for the Conference. J. G. McDonald, the former High Commissioner for the Refugees, is the Chairman of the Committee, and its Jewish members include Bernard Baruch, Mr. Morgenthau Senior, Dr. Stephen Wise, and Mr. Baerwald.[29]

. . . .

I was told by the American member of the Secretariat who saw Mr. Roosevelt that in his view the liberal countries should deal with the problem of the refugees on large lines, and be prepared to receive substantial numbers. The finance, however, should come from the private organizations. That, too, is the view of the European Governments; and Mr. Makins[30] thought that our Government would be unwilling to consider participation in any guarantee of a loan for the purpose of emigration and settlement. On the other hand, a large scheme would appear to require a loan guaranteed at least in part by some of the Powers, as was done for the Greek settlement, and before that for the reconstruction of Austria. Those, however, are matters which will have to be considered by technical experts.

It is generally felt that the American initiative has three great advantages:

28. On Sweetser's meeting with FDR, see pp. 125–127 above.
29. This listing was by this time inaccurate.
30. Sir Roger Mellor Makins, British diplomat, business executive, and atomic energy expert. A member of the British delegation to the Evian Conference in 1938, he was named secretary to the Intergovernmental Committee on Refugees. Served as British ambassador to the United States from 1953 to 1956.

(1) that the U.S.A. will be induced to give a lead in a more liberal admission of refugees, by granting facilities for the entrance of exiles from Germany and Austria, up to the combined quota for the two countries, which is about 28,000 a year;

(2) that the U.S.A. Government will be able to deal more directly and effectively with the Government of the Reich about the transfer of property, and facilities for emigration, than any European Government, or than the League; and

(3) that the U.S.A. Government has influence and authority with the Governments of the South American States, and can induce them to take a more liberal attitude.

At the same time, it is considered that the U.S.A. will expect the European Governments to contribute their part to a larger programme of emigration and settlement, through admission either to the European countries or to the Dominions and Colonies in certain cases. It will be important to marshal opinion in this country, and particularly to obtain some joint action of the Refugee Organizations, with a view to securing a liberal attitude by the British representatives of the Conference.

. . . .

Bentwich then sketched out a rough plan for the annual emigration from Germany and Austria of fifty thousand Jews and fifteen to twenty thousand "non-Aryans" for a period of four years. The financial assumption was that about half would be able to take assets with them, which meant that the United States would persuade Germany to allow the transfer abroad of some private Jewish capital.[31] This plan contradicted the basic British government position that the refugee problem could be limited to those who had already left Germany and Austria.

On May 20, 1938, Polish Ambassador Count Jerzy Potocki visited Assistant Secretary of State Messersmith to get some sense of how the upcoming Evian Conference might affect Poland's situation. Although Potocki did not say so explicitly, he hoped that it might be possible to resettle some of Poland's Jews. Messersmith gave him no encouragement.[32]

31. Note on Proposed International Conference called by President Roosevelt, May 15, 1938. Copy in NA RG 59, Lot File 52D408, Alphabetical Subject File, Box 9, President's Advisory Committee—Minutes.

32. Memo of Conversation, May 20, 1938, between Messersmith and Polish Ambassador Count Jerzy Potocki, Messersmith Papers, University of Delaware, Item 995. On September 20, 1938, Polish Ambassador Józef Lipski met with Hitler at Obersalzberg and reported to Foreign Minister Józef Beck that Hitler told him that he had in mind an idea for solving the Jewish problem by way of the colonies (Madagascar) through understandings with Poland, Hungary, and perhaps Romania. Lipski wrote, "at which point I told him that if he finds such a solution we will erect a fine statue of him in the heart of Warsaw." Wacław Jędrzejewicz, ed., *Diplomat in Berlin, 1933–1939: Papers and Memoirs of Josef Lipski, Ambassador of Poland* (New York: Columbia University Press, 1968), Document 99, 411.

At the third meeting of the President's Advisory Committee in early June, sharp differences emerged between State Department representative Robert Pell (who wrote the summary) and many of the committee members. The following excerpt gives a muted sense of the clash, which reflected different views about how much the committee and the Evian Conference could, or should try to, accomplish.

The Committee did not seem to have a very clear idea as to precisely [what] was expected of it, so that Mr. Pell, after emphasizing that it was an informal document prepared by several members of the Department's staff, which had not received the approval of anyone in high authority, [read] from a draft letter of guidance which is in course of preparation by the Departmental Committee.

This confidential memorandum included a section (reprinted below) that paralleled the British position with regard to Palestine:

> It is highly probable that various groups will endeavor to induce the representatives of the governments participating in the meeting to take up the question of immigration into Palestine. It is felt that the Committee should reject any attempts to inject into the considerations such political issues as are involved in the Palestine, the Zionist[,] and the anti-Zionist questions. These questions could stir up bitter passions and might even lead to a disruption of the Committee's labor.[33]

The Secretary of the Committee took note of various points embraced in this document. The members of the Committee then agreed to consider their recommendations in executive session, without the presence of Departmental representatives, and to convey their decisions to the representatives of the Department at a meeting to be held on June 10.

. . . A sharp difference of views arose with regard to the scope of the Intergovernmental Committee's work and the injection of political issues. Some members of the Committee insisted that the scope should be as broad as possible and should include refugees from all countries. Other members of the Committee insisted that the scope should be restricted to Germany alone.

Rabbi Wise was most outspoken in insisting that the question of Palestine should be considered at the intergovernmental meeting [at Evian] and seemed to have the support of a majority of the members of the Committee.[34]

Mr. Pell reported that after further consideration in Washington on this problem the decision had been reached to leave the door open in every possible way to include consideration by the Intergovernmental Conference of the

33. Quoted in Murray to Wadsworth, July 2, 1938, *Foreign Relations of the United States,* 1938, vol. I, p. 752, quoted by S. Adler-Rudel, "The Evian Conference on the Refugee Question," *Leo Baeck Institute Year-Book,* vol. XIII (1968), 238.

34. Memorandum, June 4, Third Meeting . . . , NA RG 59, Lot File 52D408, Alphabetical Subject File, Box 9, President's Advisory Committee 1938—Minutes.

problems of refugees from all countries.[35] Mr. Chamberlain suggested that it might prove practical at the Intergovernmental Conference, in order to secure concentration on consideration of German refugees, to suggest a recommendation that the refugee problems of other countries require further study and might be the subject of later conferences, particularly in view of the fact that the ensemble of refugee problems will require long-range planning.[36]

In June McDonald was appointed as an unpaid technical adviser to American envoy Myron Taylor.[37] On June 14 the United States sent out a proposed agenda for the Evian Conference reflecting a compromise between the Advisory Committee and the State Department. Against the British view, the United States included persons seeking to leave Germany and Austria under the rubric "political refugees." In keeping with the State Department view, the conference was to consider what steps might be taken within existing immigration laws and practices. The United States called for each government to spell out its present policies and state how many immigrants and what type of immigrants it was prepared to take in. The agenda also included the thorny question of substitute documentation for those would-be emigrants who were unable to secure passports or normally required paperwork (certification of no police record, etc.) from Nazi authorities. Finally, Palestine was not excluded from consideration.[38]

McDonald's 1935 experiences discussing immigration issues with officials of several South American countries undoubtedly convinced him that the way immigration laws and regulations were applied mattered at least as much as the letter of the laws themselves. So he probably felt that there was some scope for progress even within the restrictions laid down for the Evian Conference.

On June 28 Assistant Secretary of State Messersmith wrote to John Wiley, consul general in Vienna, about preparations for the Evian Conference. Wiley had raised the question of whether any American contacts with Nazi officials in Vienna might smooth the emigration of Jews. Messersmith responded:

Certainly the authorities have not shown any disposition to talk reasonably about this matter[,] and when James McDonald used to try to talk with them about the Berlin situation, he could make no progress whatever. As what they are doing in Austria far exceeds anything in ferocity than what they did in Germany, I think they could be even less inclined to talk to anyone now than they were to McDonald. It is true that they had a certain prejudice against McDonald in those days, but I think they would have prejudice against anyone who would come to talk about this matter in a reasonable way. . . .

35. The phrase "after further consideration in Washington" in this context very likely meant after consulting the president. See pp. 125–127 above.

36. Minutes, June 6, 1938, NA RG 59, Lot File 52D408, Alphabetical Subject File, Box 9, President's Advisory Committee—Minutes.

37. Welles to FDR, June 9, 1938, and FDR to Welles, June 11, 1938, FDRL, OF 3186, Box 2, Political Refugees, June–December 1938.

38. *Foreign Relations of the United States 1938*, vol. I (Washington, D.C.: U.S. Government Printing Office, 1955), 748.

. . . We are very much of the opinion that we should first see what the Evian meetings may do. It is our intention that the first meetings at Evian shall be rather of a confidential character because it is only in that atmosphere that the question can be explored usefully at this stage. We have done everything possible to keep down publicity for we are convinced that publicity at this stage is as dangerous as it is undesirable.

. . . .

We are really the only country which is following on the whole a humane policy. Unfortunately there are those who are beginning to question as to whether our own policy may not be too liberal. I think you know my own views on this subject and how definitely I have always felt that we must maintain our liberal immigration practice. I must confess that even a person like myself has had some rude shocks recently. There are an increasing number of these refugees who seem to feel that the United States owes them a debt of some kind[,] and that we of all countries are the one chosen to be their savior and that we owe it to them to give them an opportunity to start life where they left off in Europe, or perhaps even on a better scale. I have had some of the most extraordinary letters from professors and others who seem to be very resentful that we are not giving them on a golden platter a position which native-born Americans would be glad to get at the end of a long and hard-fought career. I get other letters from really intelligent people abroad who are seeking immigration visas who are already highly critical of everything that is happening in this country and who are telling me how we ought to run things here. I get other letters from persons who have been admitted into this country and who are not yet American citizens who tell us just how we ought to run the country, how we ought to change our laws[,] and what we owe to the rest of the world. Unfortunately that these people are doing these things and saying these things is beginning to become known in certain quarters in this country[,] and it is not doing any good. . . . We have among some of these refugees a group who consider themselves privileged and who are doing things the repercussions of which may be very dangerous in the end for less fortunate ones. In any event, this problem is not as simple as it seems. Because some people are foolish, unreasonable, prejudiced and bitter, this is not any reason for us to change our liberal views and practice. It is, however, a situation with which we have to reckon[,] for I am glad to say that this country still belongs to the native-born American and I am hopeful that the ideals of our native-born Americans may continue to control.

. . . It is really unspeakable what Germany is doing to these people and I am one of those who believe that this movement toward discrimination will not be eliminated until this regime in Germany is eliminated.[39]

39. Messersmith to Wiley, Personal, June 28, 1938, Messersmith Papers, University of Delaware, Item 1012.

On July 1, 1938, Felix Frankfurter wrote McDonald about the planning of refugee resettlement:

(1) . . . The situation in cities like Vienna is largely chaos. There are wholly unregulated heart-breaking individual applications and appeals for help both to Jews and non-Jews throughout this country as well as in Great Britain and I assume other countries. And the whole refugee problem is on an absurd and impossible basis of individual charity. I don't have to tell you the very large proportion of Catholics in Vienna who suddenly find themselves outcast. The conclusion seems to me inevitable that there must be established an international agency, non-sectarian of course, entrusted with the whole refugee problem from the place of departure of refugees to their settlement in the various countries. Branches, of course, will be necessary in the receiving countries, but it is indispensable to have some central direction for administering a situation that cuts across the boundaries of all nations. It is not for me to sketch the detailed administrative standards to be enforced by such an agency, but clearly the granting of visas should be subjected to some generalized standards and not left at present to the individual discretion, however conscientious, of a particular consul or vice-consul in a particular city.

(2) Needless to say, such an international agency should be invested at the very outset with as much prestige as eminent executive leadership and unstinted moral underwriting by the leading democratic nations, among whom I include the Scandinavian countries, can endow it.

(3) But moral underwriting is not enough. The problem has come too interpenetrating for the welfare and the responsibility of the world, too vast, to be left to the resources of private philanthropy. The problem may not unfairly be likened to our own unemployment problem. Government, both federal and local, had to step in to deal with the relief problem when it assumed dimensions that it did in 1933. It exceeded the capacities of a mere private effort.

(4) Finally, I am sure you have not left unconsidered the task of serious[ly] exploring opportunities for negotiating with some of the countries in Central and South America for available large tracts for mass settlement not unlike the settlement of the refugees in Asia Minor made under the auspices of the League of Nations.[40]

Frankfurter's ambitious sketch was not realized at the Evian Conference, although the conference did create a small new body—called the Intergovernmental Committee on Refugees—to try to negotiate with Germany. (The Intergovernmental Committee was temporarily represented by Washington lawyer George Rublee.) The State Department's hope to avoid publicity was also frustrated.

40. Frankfurter to McDonald, July 1, 1938, McDonald Papers, Columbia University, General Correspondence (Felix Frankfurter), Folder 146.

Some two hundred delegates, diplomatic observers, journalists, and representatives of Jewish organizations from various countries, including Germany, gathered in the small town on the French side of Lake Geneva, creating a circus atmosphere in which public speeches took on a larger-than-anticipated role. The high point was perhaps the offer by the representative of the Dominican Republic to take in one hundred thousand refugees, which turned out to be a huge exaggeration of what his government was willing and able to accomplish. There were a number of low points, among them a joint statement by Nicaragua, Costa Rica, Honduras, and Panama that they wanted no traders or intellectuals, and the open hostility of League of Nations High Commissioner Sir Neill Malcolm.[41]

Jewish representatives testified before one of the subcommittees on which McDonald served, which met in executive session. Representatives of the Reichsvertretung der Juden in Deutschland, whose families were in effect hostages in Germany, submitted a subdued memorandum that nonetheless pledged to do everything possible to assist any far-reaching plan for emigration from Germany. So many different organizations insisted on being heard that they each had little time, and some of the subcommittee members lacked the experience to appreciate the details.

Still, on the biggest controversies among governments—the question of whether "refugees" would include Jews still in Germany, and the question of whether a new international organization would be established—the liberal American view won out over the conservative British one.[42]

Near the conclusion of the Evian Conference, the executive secretary of the President's Advisory Committee, George L. Warren, wrote Professor Joseph Chamberlain about the outcome.

[The] Continuing Intergovernmental Committee will meet in London, August 3, appoint a Director, determine expense, and apportion it among the governments. . . . Otherwise the resolution provides for approaches to Germany and the countries of immigration, to work out methods to supplant chaotic exodus with orderly migration.

We have discarded the word "refugees" and have used the term "involuntary emigrants[,]" hoping that these will be more palatable to South American governments.

Mr. [Myron] Taylor has won the confidence and respect of the delegates and has demonstrated his ability as a negotiator. He has worked quietly and incessantly[,] and his sincerity and dignity and singleness of purpose will win the day.[43]

41. Stewart, *United States Government Policy,* 298–305.
42. Adler-Rudel, "The Evian Conference," 235–260, and Stewart, *United States Government Policy,* 298–315, give more detailed description and analysis.
43. Warren to Chamberlain, July 13, 1938, Joseph Chamberlain Papers, YIVO Institute for Jewish Research, RG 278, Folder 67.

In an August 1938 speech at Vassar College, McDonald noted the cruel disparity between hopes and results at Evian.

The very desperateness of conditions within the Reich caused those men and women so anxious about their future to build up false hopes that somehow at Evian ways would be found to place at once, or in the near future, two or three hundred thousand additional refugees in new homes. Those of us who worked on this problem were nearly heartbroken at these exaggerated expectations because we knew . . . that no such achievement was possible. Hence, we knew that inevitably Evian would create bitter disappointment.[44]

McDonald hoped that his long-standing efforts to enlist the support of Catholic Church officials for resettlement of refugees in the Western Hemisphere would finally bear fruit. Once again, he hoped to begin with a sign of approval from the Vatican. On July 1 Enrico Galeazzi had written to McDonald about McDonald's hope to meet again with Eugenio Cardinal Pacelli.

Although it is not possible to state any exact date when His Eminence the Cardinal Secretary of State will be able to fix an audience for you, I have been authorized to assure you that His Eminence will be happy to meet you again, should you pay another visit to Rome.

In case you let me know the exact date of your arrival, I shall see with pleasure that possibly the audience is arranged so as not to compel you to wait too long here for it.

Please remember me kindly to my very dear friend Basil Harris; I was delighted to see him on your committee.[45]

McDonald, then at Evian, responded with a telegram on July 12 asking for a meeting on July 18. The only information about the results of this meeting comes from a brief letter McDonald sent to Archbishop Rummel of New Orleans. It is clear from that letter that McDonald wanted to inform Pacelli about the results of the Evian Conference and the work of the President's Advisory Committee on Political Refugees. It is possible that McDonald also asked for Pacelli's assistance.

Immediately after the Evian Conference, I went to Rome where His Eminence, the Cardinal Secretary of State, again did me the honor of granting me an opportunity to talk over with him the refugee problem (three times previously when I was High Commissioner for German Refugees, Cardinal Pacelli received me on a similar mission).

---

44. Address before the World Youth Congress at Vassar College, August 19, 1938, quoted by Stewart, *United States Government Policy,* 317.
45. McDonald Papers, Columbia University, D367 (PACPR), P47.

His Eminence asked me to transmit to the members of our committee and to heads of other organizations working on behalf of refugees his thanks for this "truly Christian charity."[46]

In a subsequent letter to Monsignor Michael J. Ready, chairman of the National Catholic Welfare Conference, McDonald added that during his talks with Pacelli he gained a "deepened impression" of the danger Nazi "racial primitivism" posed to the Church.[47]

McDonald went from Italy to England, where he joined comedian Eddie Cantor on a fund-raising effort. In the course of a ten-day trip Cantor obtained pledges of £100,000. McDonald later wrote that the money was for the Youth Aliyah—for sending young German Jews to Palestine.[48]

On August 31 George Rublee, the new director of the Intergovernmental Committee on Refugees, conferred in London with McDonald's old friend Max Warburg about how to proceed. McDonald's executive secretary George Warren attended the meeting and wrote a summary of it.

Mr. Warburg first began to talk about his idea of a transit or emigration committee, to be set up in London under the Chairmanship of Mr. Anthony Rothschild. The function of this Committee would be [to] sift all schemes of international transfer of property from Germany and other matters in connection with involuntary emigration which are being suggested by individuals and private organizations. Mr. Warburg suggested that such a committee might be a great help to Mr. Rublee[,] who lacks the necessary technical staff, and further would be a means of putting at his disposal in fact the best of Jewish brains and experience in this matter.

Mr. Warburg said that he had spoken to Lord Winterton on this matter, and that after some discussion the latter appeared to agree as to the advisability of such a committee. . . .

Mr. Rublee said to Mr. Warburg that he welcomed this suggestion very much[,] as he, Mr. Rublee, was very much in need of expert advice especially in connection with the transfer problem.

Mr. Warburg then outlined the following points which he considered should be kept in mind as of major importance:

(1) The question of passports.

Mr. Warburg emphasized the importance of this, stating that practically all recent involuntary emigrants either have no passports at all or passports

46. McDonald to Rummel, August 22, 1938, McDonald Papers, Columbia University, D367 (PACPR), P20.

47. McDonald to Ready, November 22, 1938, McDonald Papers, Columbia University, D367 (PACPR), P40.

48. Bentwich, *My 77 Years* 148–149. McDonald's review of Marvin Lowenthal, *Henrietta Szold: Life and Letters* (New York: Viking, 1942), McDonald Papers, Columbia University, D355, MS19 (Manuscripts and Speeches).

which shortly expire and which the German Government will not renew. It was agreed that Mr. Rublee probably could not do much in this connection[,] as it is a question which has always come particularly within the purview of the League. From the standpoint of involuntary emigrants[,] it will be very important if something like the Nansen passport system is continued upon the reorganization of the Nansen and High Commissioner offices at the League this September.

(2) Mr. Warburg especially emphasized the need for time in solving the problem of involuntary emigration. Time is essential to permit an orderly emigration, and in order to permit training in Germany and in transit countries so that the involuntary emigrants may be acceptable to the countries of final settlement. Mr. Warburg stated that when pressure was first put upon the non-Aryans in Germany[,] he had told the Government his unequivocal opposition to their racial theories, and further that, assuming their position, the problem could only be solved in a reasonable way if the non-Aryans were given time. He said that all reasonable elements in the Government realized that time was essential, and that prior to the Anschluss it looked as if sufficient time was going to be afforded by the German Government to solve the problem of emigration from Germany proper. Since the Anschluss the whole aspect appears to have changed, and for the first time Mr. Warburg was pessimistic as to the outlook for his people in Germany. He said that unless the restrictions against the right to work and continue in business [were removed], and unless the burden of discriminatory taxation was relaxed, there would shortly be practically no Jewish resources or morale left in Germany.

(3) Mr. Warburg mentioned as another subject of negotiations the necessity of persuading the German Government to allow communication and co-operation between the Jewish organizations in Berlin and in Vienna, which at the present time is absolutely prohibited.

(4) Mr. Warburg mentioned the problem of finding out from the countries of settlement what contribution they are prepared to make as another job before the Committee. . . .

I [George Warren] got the impression from the above discussion and the nature of the points raised by Mr. Warburg that, although he realized the paramount importance of the transfer problem, he was not hopeful that the German Government could be persuaded to make any contribution in free foreign exchange. His view quite clearly was that any realistic approach to the transfer problem would be in connection with German exports. Mr. Rublee told him the position of our State Department in this matter. Mr. Warburg said that he quite realized that there could be no direct connection in any negotiations between a commercial treaty with the United States and attempts to secure better treatment for Jews in Germany. Mr. Warburg felt[,] however[,] that it could be indicated that the latter is necessary to create a better atmosphere so that the former might possible [*sic,* possibly] eventuate later.

. . . .

On the question of personalities [in the Nazi regime who might be approached], he thought either Goering or Hess, probably the former, and definitely not Himmler. He was quite clearly of the opinion that it was hopeless to try to change Mr. Hitler's views or even to talk to him.

Mr. Warburg is on his way to the United States and will be back in November.[49]

On September 10 State Department official Robert Pell, then detailed to the Intergovernmental Committee on Refugees (based in London), wrote to Jay Pierrepont Moffat, head of the Division of European Affairs, about the difficulties the Intergovernmental Committee on Refugees was experiencing.

Meanwhile, we have been having visitation from Ben Cohen[50] of the W[hite] H[ouse], who has gone through the files with a fine tooth comb. He claims to be satisfied with what we have done and with the course we are steering. He has given a strong hint, however, that this whole affair was planned by [Felix] Frankfurter et al. to be a demonstration by the Democracies against Germany—and was turned from its course by the Fascists in the State Department plus by Mr. Taylor who, very suspiciously, lives at Florence, Italy.

I told him that had there been any suggestion at Evian that we were to "demonstrate," the British would have walked out forthwith, with the small European [countries] and the Latin Americans close on their heels. And there would have been no "demonstrating" from the French without their British cousins. C. agreed that this would have been so, but said that others view the affair in somewhat different terms. Even B. C. believes that there should be a "demonstration if and when the negotiation with Germany fails—so do bear this in mind. He differs with his friends only in believing that we should go through the gesture of a negotiation with Germany before "demonstrating."[51]

The German annexation of the Sudeten region of Czechoslovakia, brought about through the Munich Agreement in October 1938, made the Nazis less concerned about foreign opinion and more eager to get rid of the increasing number of Jews within their reach.
On October 28 American Consul General Raymond Geist described the difficulties faced by German Jews seeking to emigrate to the United States.

During September we had to deal with thousands of desperate people, who stormed the Consulate General day after day. At times it seemed that we

49. Memorandum of a Conversation between Rublee and Warburg, August 31, 1938, NA RG 59, Lot File 52D408, Alphabetical Subject File, 1938–1941, Box 14, Warren Memoranda.
50. Benjamin V. Cohen, key figure in the Roosevelt and Truman administrations, member of FDR's "brain trust."
51. Robert Pell to Moffat, September 10, 1938, Moffat Papers, call number MS Am 1407, Houghton Library. By permission of Houghton Library, Harvard University.

could not control the situation any longer; but we kept our heads and finally brought the applicants under control and now everything is going smoothly again. The quota is now insufficient to accommodate the applicants who number about 125,000 against the available numbers of 27,300 for the fiscal year. Applicants who newly apply must now wait three or four years. This is a desperate situation for many, who are sure [that] unless they can effect their emigration to the United States, they cannot survive. We can only be sympathetic and kind; in most cases little practical help can be given. I am still hoping the Intergovernmental Committee will be able to open a few doors into other countries.

With regard to George Rublee's hope to come to Germany to gauge Nazi Germany's interest in negotiating an arrangement on emigration, Geist urged caution:

Hitler [should] not be approached, as he is now in the mood to defy any group of nations which desired to do something to help the refugees. I am of the opinion that it would be better to let the moderates around Hitler get some approval of a reasonable proposition than to approach him directly. This is a very grave business and the success of the enterprise is a matter of life and death for thousands of worthy and innocent people.[52]

On October 24 and 25 a group of State and Treasury Department officials met to consider German and outside proposals with regard to the transfer of German Jewish assets. State Department official Moffat described these meetings in his diary:

At four o'clock [October 24] we had a meeting in Sumner Welles' office wherein Shepard Morgan of the Chase National Bank presented a scheme to finance German emigrants by means of a new type of Mark with which they would be paid for their property and which would be used in payment of certain types of additional exports. The difficulties were obvious: goods bought by such means might run up against our Treasury regulations in the matter of appraisals; goods bought by that means in third countries would be competitive with our own products; it would be a dangerous precedent to start at the very moment when it was clear that the world would be faced by recurrent waves of refugees from Central Europe. . . . It is obvious that the omelet cannot be made without breaking some eggs. In other words, that we cannot help the refugees without surrendering some commercial advantages. The question is how much the country is willing to let profits interfere with its emotional desire to be of help.

For October 25 Moffat wrote:

52. Geist to Messersmith, October 28, 1938, Messersmith Papers, University of Delaware, Item 1051.

We also suggested that Mr. Rublee, instead of asking different countries how many refugees they would admit, should ask a series of contingent questions: "How many refugees would you admit without property?" "How many with $1,000 per family?" "How many with $5,000 per family" et cetera. . . . Meanwhile the British are not trying to help because they are endeavoring to give the Sudeten refugees a preferred status over other refugees from Germany.[53]

Moffat's diary entries for October 29 and 30 gave a somewhat jaundiced picture of domestic reactions to international events.

The pressure from Jewish groups all over the country is growing to a point where before long it will begin to react very seriously against their own best interests. The Poles and the Germans start expelling each other[']s Jews and immediately we are flooded with protests and requests for intervention. The German Consul General makes an offensive speech and we are bombarded with demands that we ask his recall, quite oblivious of the fact that Ambassador Dodd's was equally offensive on the other side of the picture. On Palestine the pressure has been so great that one can now buy a form telegram to the President or the Secretary of State for twenty-five cents in the Postal Telegraph Office. The Jews are demanding that we go more strongly to the bat with Italy, et cetera, et cetera. They are going through a horrible persecution and there is nothing within reason that one would not want to do to help the human misery, but no one likes to be subjected to pressure of the sort they are exerting[,] and the American public does not like pressure in favor of one particular population or group.[54]

On November 6, 1938, McDonald gave a speech at the First Presbyterian Church on Henry Street in Brooklyn. The text of this speech no longer survives, but the New York Times *quoted excerpts:*

Too many people have been making fun of Hitler. They pick on surface things that do appear ludicrous but in doing so tend to overlook his mysticism, fanaticism[,] and singular capacity for judging how far he can go—and when.

Hitler, to my mind, is one of the greatest living organizers. There is a conscious attempt in intellectual circles to belittle this man. Now, as you know I am second to none in denouncing what I believe to be a reversion to something close to barbarism in Germany[,] nor do I accept his degradation of his own people.

53. Moffat Journal, October 24–25, 1938, Moffat Papers, call number MS Am 1407, Houghton Library. By permission of Houghton Library, Harvard University.
54. Moffat Journal, October 29–30, 1938, Moffat Papers, call number MS Am 1407, Houghton Library. By permission of Houghton Library, Harvard University.

But no good can come from hiding the reality of the man's strength. Today he dominates Europe.[55]

On November 9, 1938, came a nation-wide eruption of violence against German Jews, set off by an incident. A distraught young Polish Jew named Herschel Grynzspan, whose parents had been among a large group of Jews suddenly deported from Germany back to Poland, assassinated a German diplomat in Paris. This shooting gave certain Nazi officials a convenient ground for punishing German Jews; the German press declared that this act was part of an international Jewish conspiracy against Germany.

After receiving a signal from Hitler, Propaganda Minister Joseph Goebbels seized this opportunity to suggest "spontaneous" outbreaks against the Jews, for which the SA [storm troopers] seemed the most appropriate force. In a process that began on the night of November 9–10 and extended over several days, more than one thousand synagogues and many Jewish shops or businesses across the country were destroyed. (The event has become known as Kristallnacht—night of broken glass.) Approximately one hundred Jews were killed, and thirty thousand were quickly sent to concentration camps. Foreign observers, newspaper reporters, and diplomats gathered extensive firsthand information about what was happening and spread it to the rest of the world.

On November 14 Undersecretary Welles wrote to President Roosevelt's appointments secretary Marvin McIntyre:

In accordance with our conversation on the telephone, I am writing to tell you that the President's National Advisory Committee on Refugees [*sic*], of which Mr. James G. McDonald is Chairman, had a meeting of the full committee today in New York in the office of Mr. Myron Taylor. At the end of the meeting Mr. McDonald called me on the telephone and said that the committee was unanimously of the opinion, as was Mr. Taylor, that it would be very desirable for a sub-committee of the National Committee to have an opportunity of conferring with the Department of State and, if it could be arranged, with the President as soon as might be possible.[56]

Following a State Department recommendation, on November 15 President Roosevelt held a press conference at which he read the following statement:

The news of the past few days from Germany has deeply shocked public opinion in the United States. Such news from any part of the world would inevitably produce a similar profound reaction among the American people in every part of the nation.

55. *New York Times*, November 7, 1938, p. 14.
56. Welles to McIntyre, November 14, 1938, FDRL, OF 3186, Box 2, Political Refugees, June–December 1938.

I myself could scarcely believe that such things could occur in a twentieth-century civilization.

With a view to gaining a firsthand picture of the current situation in Germany I asked the Secretary of State to order our Ambassador in Berlin to return at once for report and consultation.[57]

The reporters pressed for more details.

Q: Would you elaborate on that, sir?

The President: No, I think it speaks for itself.

Q: What about the talk or rumors or report that that is called a "recall?"

The President: Technically speaking, in diplomatic parlance, it is not a recall; it is a summons to come home.

. . . .

Q: Have you made any protest to Germany?

The President: Nothing has gone that I know of.

Q: There are reports from London that Mr. [Joseph] Kennedy[58] has made a suggestion to the British Government concerning a place wherein the Jewish refugees would be taken care of.

The President: I cannot comment on the report, because I know nothing of what has been happening in London. We do know that the International Refugee Commission is at work trying to extend its help to take care of an increasingly difficult situation.

Q: Mr. President, can you tell us whether you feel that there is any place in the world where you could take care of mass emigration of the Jews from Germany—have you given thought to that?

The President: I have given a great deal of thought to it.

Q: Can you tell us any place particularly desirable?

The President: No, the time is not ripe for that.

Q: Have there been any comments or protests made to you concerning the destruction or damage of American property in Germany?

The President: Nothing has come through on that; I imagine the Embassy is checking up on it.

57. The president toughened the original State Department draft, adding, among other things, the modifiers "deeply," "profound," and the one-line second paragraph.

58. Joseph P. Kennedy, prominent American businessman with strong political interests. Father of John Fitzgerald Kennedy. Named ambassador to Britain in 1938, he supported Neville Chamberlain's appeasement policy and the American isolationists. He resigned under pressure in November 1940. German Ambassador Herbert von Dirksen reported to Berlin on June 13, 1938, that Kennedy had told him that "it was not so much the fact that we want to get rid of the Jews that was so harmful to us, but rather the loud clamor with which we accompanied this purpose. (Kennedy) himself fully understood our Jewish policy." Edward Renehan, *The Kennedys at War, 1937–1945* (New York: Doubleday, 2002), 29.

Q: You said nothing as yet on a possible protest to Germany; is there anything on that?

The President: I cannot say anything on that.

Q: Would you recommend a relaxation of our immigration restrictions so that the Jewish refugees could be received in this country?

The President: That is not in contemplation; we have the quota system.[59]

The next morning Secretary of the Treasury Henry Morgenthau, Jr., telephoned the President to congratulate him on the statement he issued with the summoning of Ambassador Wilson home. In his diary Morgenthau continued to recapitulate their conversation. Punctuation here has been adjusted slightly.

I said, "I have the first concrete suggestion to make for the Jewish refugees." He [FDR] said, "Well for Heaven's sake, what is it?" I said, "Constantin Maguire[60] [Constantine McGuire] has sent me a letter suggesting that we make a settlement with Great Britain and France on their war debts for British [Guiana] and French [Guiana], and then somehow or other raise enough money to buy off Holland for Dutch [Guiana]."[61]

He said, "It's no good." He said, "It would take the Jews from 25 to 50 years to overcome the fever." . . . He said, "What's the matter with the idea I have been talking to you about for a long time and," he said, "that's the Cameroons." He said, "The Cameroons was a former German colony and now belongs to France and," he said, "the same suggestion that you have of giving these countries a credit on their debt to us would apply there and," he said, "I know from explorations that have been made in the Cameroons that they have some very wonderful high land, table land, wonderful grass and very thinly populated and" he said, "all that country has been explored and it's ready."

Then he said, "Adjacent to the Cameroons, the Portuguese have a territory and," he said, "that could be included."[62] But he said all the Cameroons have been explored and he said it's a good climate.

59. *Franklin D. Roosevelt and Foreign Affairs*, ed. Donald B. Schewe, Second Series, *January 1937–August 1939* (New York: Clearwater, 1979), vol. 12, 83–86.

60. On February 22, 1935, McDonald had recruited Constantine McGuire for the refugee cause. (See *Advocate for the Doomed*, 628.) See also p. 71 above.

61. Another who raised the same idea, suggesting even a U.S. protectorate and then an independent Jewish state in the Guianas, was Dr. Benjamin Akzin, a young professor at Harvard Law School. State Department official Theodore Achilles wrote up a sketch based on Akzin's notion and sent it to Undersecretary of State Sumner Welles. Welles quickly rejected the idea of a U.S. protectorate, which would cast doubt on U.S. motives, but substituted a temporary protectorate under all the American republics. He was moderately supportive: "The war debt question which comes into the picture in the case of France and Great Britain might still form our contribution as a government toward the realization of the project. . . . While the difficulties are tremendous and while I am by no means over-sanguine as to the possibility of working out some scheme of this kind, it should nevertheless, I think, be given careful study and the plans should be revised, as the first step, along the line I have indicated." Achilles to Welles, December 9, 1938, and Welles to Achilles, December 12, 1938, NA RG 59, Lot File 52D408, Country File, Box 1, British Guiana.

62. The Portuguese government firmly opposed the entry of Jews into Angola. A couple of years later, after an inquiry in Washington, the Portuguese minister to the United States said that

The thing to do is for us to get some geographer that Mr. Bowman[63] can recommend and look over all of the colonies belonging to France and England wherever they are and see which of these could take a population, and I want to say here that in discussing this with Mrs. Morgenthau, I think it is most important that whatever is done is opened up to all refugees irrespective of religion; that it should not be just for the Jews.[64]

Using British and French war debts as leverage to obtain a colony dedicated to resettlement of refugees was an idea that had surfaced earlier in 1938, shortly after the Anschluss and FDR's refugee initiative. One proponent was Thomas J. Watson, founder and chairman of International Business Machines (IBM). On March 31, 1938, Watson had sent a letter and memorandum to Secretary of State Hull:

It is the responsibility of the world to provide a permanent home for the Jewish refugees who find it necessary to leave Germany and Austria, and also for the ones who may possibly find it necessary to leave other countries, where the matter is being seriously discussed at the present time.

My plan is to make arrangements, through the cooperation of Germany, England, France and the United States, to turn over the former German colonies as a country for the Jews, not only for the refugees, but for all Jews who would like to participate in the building of a Jewish nation.

It seems to me that the right way to approach this subject would be for Germany to request England and France to turn over the colonies, which, of course, would mean building good will throughout the world for Germany, also for France and England. The United States could participate in this through making some concessions in regard to the International debts.

Right-thinking people in all countries are willing to contribute money for temporary relief, but that is not the answer to the Jewish problem as it exists today.[65]

Watson's notion involved Germany requesting the use of a former colony as an independent entity—a substitute Jewish homeland. It may have reflected his hope to improve the reputation of (and keep himself on good terms with) a regime which regulated an important IBM subsidiary.[66] It was based on the assumption that

Portugal had no Jewish problem because it had expelled the Jews in the Middle Ages [*sic*] and that it was making every effort to prevent the entry of Jews into any of its territories. Memorandum of Conversation re Attitude of the Portuguese Authorities to Jewish Immigration, September 20, 1940, NA RG 59, Lot File 52D408, Country File, Box 1, Angola.

63. Isaiah Bowman, president of Johns Hopkins University, a noted geographer. More on Bowman follows.

64. Morgenthau Diaries, November 16, 1938, Roll 40, FDRL. This entry also contains the transcript of Morgenthau's subsequent conversation with Bowman that same day.

65. Attached to Watson to Hull, March 31, 1938, NA RG 59, Lot File 52D408, Alphabetical Subject File, Box 6, Jewish Refugees.

66. Edwin Black, in *IBM and the Holocaust* (New York: Three Rivers Press, 2002), discusses the relationship, but does not mention the document included here.

Germany wanted to ship its Jews out somewhere and would cooperate with others in the process. But the Nazi regime never supported the concept of a Jewish state in Palestine, and some of its same objections applied to a Jewish homeland anywhere else.[67] *By December 1938 Hitler, strengthened by the Munich Agreement, had decided to put in a demand for the return of former German colonies without any compensation.*[68]

In late 1938 American efforts toward supplementing Palestine centered, perhaps slightly more realistically, on other locations in Africa. Herbert Hoover and Bernard Baruch wanted Jews to raise about $300 million to establish a republic open to those discontented in Europe: they foresaw a British protectorate out of parts of Rhodesia, Kenya, and Tanganyika. Undersecretary of State Sumner Welles focused increasingly on Angola, the area next to the Cameroons to which FDR had alluded on November 16.[69]

Looking for an immediate step, not a long-range solution, Secretary of Labor Frances Perkins wanted to extend the temporary visas of German Jews visiting the United States so that they would not have to return to Germany—a move the State Department opposed.[70] *On November 18 President Roosevelt held another press conference at which German matters came up.*

Q: On Tuesday, Mr. President, you intimated that you did not propose, or would not consider, lowering the immigration barriers for the benefit of German refugees. Since that time a good deal has been said in print that you might do so after all. Have you changed your mind?

The President: No. There is one other factor that was brought up that is a brand-new one which I did not hear about until yesterday. There are in this country at the present time quite a large number—I think you had better check these figures through the Secretary of Labor but I am inclined to think that they run as high as twelve to fifteen thousand—[of] refugees from, principally, Germany and Austria—what was Austria—who are in this country on what is called "Visitors' Permits," I think that is the word. In other words, they are here, not on a quota but as visitors with proper passports from their own

---

67. Hitler had written in *Mein Kampf:* "It doesn't even enter their heads to build up a Jewish state in Palestine for the purpose of living there; all they want is a central organization for their international world swindle, endowed with its sovereign right and removed from the intervention of other states; a haven for convicted scoundrels and a university for budding crooks." *Mein Kampf,* tr. Ralph Manheim (Boston: Houghton Mifflin, 1971), 324–325. See a discussion by Jeffrey Herf, "Convergence: The Classic Case: Nazi Germany, Anti-Semitism and Anti-Zionism during World War II," *Anti-Semitism and Anti-Zionism in Historical Perspective: Convergence and Divergence,* ed. Jeffrey Herf (London: Routledge, 2007), 55–60.

68. On the return of German colonies, Gerhard L. Weinberg, *The Foreign Policy of Hitler's Germany,* vol. II, *Starting World War II, 1937–1939* (Chicago: University of Chicago Press, 1980), 512. After the German conquest of France in June 1940, Nazi officials drew up a contingency plan for a forced transfer of the French colony of Madagascar and its use as a site for millions of Jews to be deported from Europe. The conditions envisioned in the plan would have made it a huge penal colony and would have brought about huge mortality.

69. Henry L. Feingold, *The Politics of Rescue: The Roosevelt Administration and the Holocaust, 1938–1945* (New Brunswick, N.J.: Rutgers University Press, 1970), 102–105.

70. Breitman and Kraut, *American Refugee Policy,* 62. Assistant Secretary of State Messersmith called Perkins's plan illegal.

governments. . . . A great many of these people, who are not all Jews by any means, since other religions are included in very large numbers among them, if they were to go back . . . , their treatment on reaching home might be a very serious problem. In other words, it is a question of concentration camps, et cetera and so on. . . . I don't know, from the point of view of humanity, that we have a right to put them on a ship and send them back to Germany under the present conditions. We can legally—the Secretary of Labor can, legally, give six months extensions so that they can stay in this country under the six months extension provision. As I understand it, the law does not say how many six months extensions there can be. . . . I have suggested to Miss Perkins that they be given six months extensions. Under those extensions they cannot, as I understand it, apply for American citizenship; they are only visitors and there-fore, there being no adequate law on the subject, we will simply present the facts to the Congress. If the Congress takes no action, these unfortunate peo-ple will be allowed to stay in this country.

Q: Will you repeat that, Mr. President?

The President: They will be allowed to stay in this country under the six month extension law because I cannot, in any decent humanity, throw them out.[71]

On November 16 McDonald, Hamilton Fish Armstrong, and George Warren from the President's Advisory Committee visited the White House to join the lobbying for American action to assist actual and potential refugees. It is logical to assume that McDonald had a general sense of the president's ambitious original hopes for the Evian Conference.[72] (McDonald had long-standing ties with both Arthur Sweetser and Norman Bentwich.[73]) The terrible events of Kristallnacht must have seemed like a favorable moment to press for further action.

This private meeting in the White House was described in the minutes of the next meeting of the committee.

Mr. McDonald opened the discussion by reporting on the visit of the sub-committee consisting of Mr. McDonald, Mr. Armstrong and Mr. Warren to Washington on Wednesday, November 16th.

The Committee called first on Under-Secretary of State Welles, who ac-companied the Committee to the White House. The Committee suggested to the President that in view of events of the past week in Germany a new impetus should be given to the efforts of the Intergovernmental Committee. Appar-ently the German Government had not responded satisfactorily to Mr. Rublee's

71. Press conference, November 18, 1938, *Franklin D. Roosevelt and Foreign Affairs*, vol. 12, 132–134.

72. See above, pp. 125–126.

73. There is strong evidence that Sweetser sent McDonald a copy of Sweetser's account of his meeting with the president on April 4. See McDonald to Sweetser, May 25, 1938, McDonald Papers, Columbia University, D367 (PACPR), P48.

request for a conference and the imposition of the fine had reduced the possibility of arranging that emigrants should leave Germany with sufficient of their capital to make settlement in other countries possible. The suggestion that Mr. Taylor return to London immediately grew out of the discussion and the President stated that he would request Mr. Taylor to go at the earliest possible moment.

Thereafter the discussion turned to the matter of the appropriation of funds by Congress. The President pointed out that as yet no practical suggestion for colonization had been developed. The President suggested that an appropriation by Congress might be conceivable when practical plans emerge if other Governments and private agencies participate.

Although not recorded in the minutes, this discussion became more specific, as McDonald later related: "The President told him that there was a possibility of governments supplying $400,000,000 for refugee settlement, $150,000,000 of which might be contributed by the United States Government over a four-year period." This information was not shared with State Department officials (other than Welles), but it was at some point given to Myron Taylor. There are traces of this conditional commitment in Taylor's later efforts.[74]

Mr. McDonald also reported on discussions with Mr. Welles, Secretary of State Hull, Mr. Messersmith, Mr. Moffat, and Mr. Achilles after the interview with the President. These discussions had to do with the study of projects of colonization, the Lima Conference, and the possibility of securing funds for the Committee's work in exploring projects. Both Mr. Welles and the President had urged speed to the Committee's efforts to explore possibilities of colonization in Latin and South American countries. With this in mind Mr. McDonald had communicated with the Rockefeller and Carnegie Foundations requesting an appropriation of funds for this purpose and had also secured the consent of Dr. Isaiah Bowman of Johns Hopkins University to head up the inquiry.

. . . .

The Committee thereafter devoted some time to the discussion of plans for raising money on a countrywide nonsectarian basis, Mr. Taylor expressing the opinion that such plans should be developed in preparation for the time when a general appeal would prove practical.[75]

74. George Warren, who had also been present, backed up McDonald when McDonald related FDR's November 16 statement on this point to a surprised State Department official seven months later. Morris to Hickerson and Dunn, Governmental Participation, June 29, 1939, NA RG 59, Lot File 52D408, Alphabetical Subject File, Box 3, Coordinating Foundation. On Taylor's subsequent use of this discussion, see chapter 8, p. 178.
75. Twelfth Meeting of the President's Advisory Committee on Political Refugees, November 21, 1938, NA RG 59, Lot File 52D408, Alphabetical Subject File, Box 9, President's Advisory Committee—Minutes.

On November 19 Supreme Court Justice Louis D. Brandeis, a Zionist, met with the president to discuss possibilities for resettlement of Jewish refugees. Brandeis subsequently summarized this meeting in a conversation with White House adviser Ben Cohen, who created a written version for Felix Frankfurter. Although this account of FDR's comments is secondhand, his reported views are roughly consistent with other sources included here.

Isaiah [nickname for Brandeis] saw the Chief [FDR] Saturday . . .

The Chief said he wanted to make a complete report before going South [to Warm Springs, Georgia] on the refugee situation. He had called in Lindsay[76] shortly after his previous talk with Isaiah. He had told him that he wanted to give him his ideas of the Palestine situation, and that he had no objection to his making a report of their talk to London.[77] He told Lindsay that he thought the British should call in some of the Arab leaders from Palestine and some of the leaders from the adjoining Arab countries. The British should explain to them that they, the Arabs, had within their control large territories ample to sustain their people. Palestine and Transjordan constituted only a small portion, probably not over 5% of their territories. Some Jews were in Palestine and others were clamoring to go there. Their coming to Palestine and Transjordan would not hinder the Arabs as there was plenty of land for all. Some of the Arabs on poor land in Palestine could be given much better land in adjoining Arab countries. The struggle between the Jews and the Arabs in Palestine was self-defeating for both Arabs and Jews. Lindsay spoke of the opposition of the Arab world and the Moslem world, and the Chief belittled this opposition and thought it due largely to British indecision and conflicting policy.

Lindsay spoke of possibly providing land for the Jews in [British] Guiana, but the Chief did not think this amounted to anything, and it would take 25 years to do anything there. The Chief suggested that if the British really wanted to do something there, they might turn over all the former German colonies for Jewish settlement. If the Germans wanted to get rid of the Jews they could not object to Britain and France opening these lands to them. Lindsay had very little to say and indicated that perhaps other places could be found.

76. Sir Ronald Lindsay, British ambassador to the United States, 1930–1939.

77. The White House Usher's Diary (FDRL) shows that President Roosevelt met with the British ambassador on November 19, from 4:45–5:05 P.M. We did not find Lindsay's written record of this conversation. But there is independent evidence of Roosevelt communicating his views on Palestine to the British at this time. "The United States Ambassador in London chose this moment [November 17, 1938] to press His Majesty's Government to assist German Jewish immigration into British territory in consideration of financial assistance from private sources in the United States. This approach was apparently made by Mr. Kennedy without instructions, but it reflected the ideas of President Roosevelt, to whom the refugee problem was known to occasion great concerns though mainly in the sense of expecting His Majesty's Government to increase Jewish immigration into Palestine." National Archives (Kew), FO 371/21538. We are grateful to researcher Stephen Tyas and Robert Clark of the FDRL for their help in getting this information.

The Chief said something might be done in Tanganyika and possibly also in Cameroons.

Then the Chief spoke to Isaiah about financial aid. He thought that if a plan was devised for a settlement of 100,000 families costing $3,000 a family or $300,000,000, the funds might be raised in the following manner:

$100,000,000 from the American Government

$100,000,000 from the British and French Governments

$100,000,000 from private subscriptions—largely Jewish.

The Chief said he had been deeply moved by events [Kristallnacht], that he had done all that he could think of for the moment, that he was going South for ten days, that if there was anything that Isaiah thought he could do in his absence Isaiah should communicate with him and, if need be, he would come back to Washington on short notice.[78]

After President Roosevelt's mid-November meetings and news conferences, he headed off to his retreat at Warm Springs, Georgia. He invited Messersmith, William Phillips, now ambassador to Italy, and Ambassador to Germany Hugh Wilson to join him. One topic of discussion was resettlement in Africa.[79]

In a memorandum asking Myron Taylor to return to London to facilitate negotiations with Germany or to undertake independent action, President Roosevelt then set forth his views of the refugee situation in late 1938.

The most urgent aspect of the problem is obviously the fining [*sic,* finding] of substantial opportunities for settlement. It is in this field that concrete results are most urgently necessary. There are many parts of the world which could accept substantial numbers of these people without injury to their economic or demographic organisms. It is rather to be anticipated that absorption of the special skills, intellect and energy of these people, especially if they bring with them a reasonable, if limited, amount of new capital, would be of definite benefit to the receiving countries through the development of new fields of activity. It is essential to create the proper spirit in the countries of potential settlement and to lead them to see this problem as one which is humanitarian in its urgency but from which they can draw ultimate practical benefit. Every effort should be made to develop this concept of the problem. Once it is created the development of concrete opportunities for settlement should be a comparatively minor problem.

(a) This Government is already accepting involuntary emigrants to the fullest extent permitted by law. I do not believe it either desirable or practicable

78. Cohen to Frankfurter, November 21, 1938, Felix Frankfurter Papers, LC, Box 45, Benjamin B.

79. Feingold, *Politics of Rescue,* 103–104.

to recommend any change in the quota provisions of our immigration laws. We are prepared, nevertheless, to make any other contribution which may be in our power to make. You are authorized to make a public statement that this Government can, under its existing law, accept annually 27,370 persons from Germany. This does not include certain members of the learned professions whose admission is not subject to numerical limitation. While this Government is thus apparently doing as much, if not more, toward a solution of the problem than any other Government, you may add that it is nevertheless continuing to study actively any other possible means by which it might be able to contribute further toward a solution.[80]

On November 25, 1938, Isaiah Bowman wrote to FDR through Secretary of the Treasury Henry Morgenthau to inject a note of caution about resettlement in the Western Hemisphere.

I have pleasure in handing you herewith a map consisting of two sheets of the Millionth Map of Hispanic America pasted together to show the whole of Costa Rica and parts of adjacent states. The map should be examined in the light of McBride's telegram and my earlier comment of which copies have been sent you.

. . . .

I have not spoken of the political difficulties which a large foreign immigrant group would create if planted in this small Latin American country, assuming that Costa Rica is willing to receive them. The effect of such a group upon the state, and the possibility that through the presence of the group we might become seriously involved in European quarrels, are matters upon which reflection is needed. My own feeling is that we keep our position uncompromised in the Western Hemisphere only so long as we do not interest ourselves directly in the importation of European population elements. The moment we do so we are likely to be charged with the importation of a European quarrel into America. Even if we are right about such importation from the humanitarian stand point, we thereby give the other fellow a chance to claim that we are wrong. Do we want to run that risk? Do we wish to confuse our position and dilute our argument respecting the Monroe Doctrine?

Why not keep the European elements within the framework of the Old World? Even if we do not favor migration to Latin America, but allow it, difficulties will arise. If we both favor and allow it, we commit ourselves to the consequences. These consequences will surely involve us in the rightness or wrongness of acts of the governments of the states of Central Europe.

80. FDR to Taylor, November 23, 1938, Myron Taylor Papers, Box 3, Folder 1: Correspondence, FDRL.

All this is gratuitous advice. I am forwarding my letter through Secretary Morgenthau, together with the map in question, so that he may make his own independent comment on the contents of this letter.

The African material is now in course of rapid compilation and will be sent the moment it is ready. It will be illustrated with clarifying maps.[81]

In a December 1 letter to George Rublee, George Warren explained how the President's Advisory Committee was following up leads for resettlement projects, giving more details about how Bowman had become involved in resettlement planning.

Study of Projects:

Mr. McDonald and I have an appointment this morning with Mr. Appleget of the Rockefeller Foundation to discuss our appeal for $25,000 to advance the study of projects.[82]

On Friday evening the attached list of men[83] are meeting at my invitation at the Harmonie Club to discuss colonization and resettlement projects. I expect to review such general findings and impressions of the many conferences which we have had to date and to secure from the discussion some leads on our future efforts.

Last Sunday, Secretary of the Treasury Morgenthau was in New York and called to his home Mr. Baerwald, Mr. Liebman, and Dr. Rosen. As a result of this conference Dr. Rosen went to Baltimore yesterday to confer with Dr. Isaiah Bowman, who, you will recall, agreed with Mr. McDonald over a week ago to participate in our efforts. Secretary Morgenthau has recently become more deeply interested, knows Dr. Bowman personally, and of course is frequently in touch with the President.[84]

On December 24 Secretary of the Interior Harold Ickes reflected on the repercussions of his speech to the Cleveland Zionist Society a week earlier.

My speech at Cleveland Sunday night on the subject "Esau, the Hairy Man"[85] had so outraged Germany as to create an acute diplomatic situation between that country and the United States. Under-Secretary Welles called

81. Bowman to My dear Mr. President, November 25, 1938, FDRL, PSF, Box 177, Refugees.

82. The Rockefeller Foundation never supplied any money.

83. The list included Paul Baerwald, John Bass (interested in the Dominican Republic), E. C. Bataille (interested in French Guiana), Chamberlain, David Heyman (New York Foundation, interested in settlement projects within the United States), Alfred Houston, Hyman, Jaretzski, Liebman, Edward Norman (interested in Iraq), Clarence Pickett, Ready, Rosen, Rosenberg, Eustace Seligman, Max Warburg, and George Warren.

84. Warren to Rublee, copy to Myron Taylor, Myron Taylor Papers, Box 8, President's Advisory Committee, May–December 1938, FDRL.

85. Ickes had said: "It seems to be all too easy to arouse prejudice and passion against the people who so long ago struggled out of the ford of the Jabbok to meet Esau, the hairy man. . . . Today the Jew in certain areas is a political eunuch, a social outcast, to be dragged down like a mad dog. . . .

me early Thursday morning to tell me that a protest had been filed with the State Department. . . . This Government was asked by the German Government to disavow my speech. Welles, having consulted with the President on Wednesday, sternly and categorically refused. I don't care very much for Welles, and the State Department has not been very friendly to me, but I must say that it did a good job on this occasion. Welles flung back at the Chargé d'Affaires that what I had said represented the overwhelming opinion of the people of the United States, and that in any event it did not lie in the mouth of the Germans, who were constantly criticizing our Government, to question our right to criticize theirs. He refused any retraction or repudiation.

For the last three or four days a great storm has raged over the incident. . . . Hitler himself is supposed to be handling the matter for Germany, and the papers have been carrying the suggestion, doubtless inspired by Hitler, that Germany might sever diplomatic relations. Steve Early told me yesterday that the President had said to Sumner Welles that "it would not hurt us if Germany should sever diplomatic relations. So what?"[86]

At the December 23 meeting of the President's Advisory Committee, State Department official Theodore Achilles noticed rising political pressure for American government action to aid Jewish refugees.

The interest of the Committee in legislation to permit the ex-quota admission of children has increased and consideration was given to a direct recommendation to the President that he sponsor legislation providing for the admission of up to 27,000 children.

The view was expressed that all manner of unsound bills for modification of the quotas would be introduced and that such action by the President might avert many more undesirable proposals. Mr. McDonald stated that former President Hoover was very anxious to "get into the picture" and suggested that he be asked to head a campaign to care for refugee children here and abroad. I [Achilles] suggested the desirability of assuring your and the President's approval before approaching Mr. Hoover. . . . The Committee agreed to take no action for the time being but requested an expression of your opinion both as to

"How can any American . . . accept a decoration at the hand of a brutal dictator who, with that same hand, is robbing and torturing thousands of fellow human beings? Perhaps Henry Ford and Colonel Charles A. Lindbergh [both decorated by Germany in 1938] will be willing to answer. . . . The bestower of [these tokens] counts that day lost when he can commit no new crime against humanity.

"We have seen free countries deteriorate into dictatorships ruled by the heavy hand of voodoo high priests. . . . To seek a true comparison it is necessary to go back into that period of history when man was unlettered, benighted and bestial" (*Time*, January 2, 1939).

86. *The Secret Diary of Harold L. Ickes*, vol. II, *The Inside Struggle, 1936–39* (New York: Simon and Schuster, 1954), 532–533.

legislation for the admission of children and as to the advisability of bringing Mr. Hoover "into the picture."[87]

McDonald had always understood the political significance and humanitarian need to deal with non-Jewish refugees. In late November he tried to assuage the president's most prominent Catholic opponent, telegraphing for an appointment with Father Charles Coughlin, whose writings and speeches contained a heavy dose of anti-Semitism. Since July, Coughlin's newspaper Social Justice *had printed excerpts from the infamous and spurious* Protocols of the Elders of Zion.[88]

As chairman President's Advisory Committee on Political Refugees, I am very anxious to talk with you about problem of Catholic refugees as I have done three times with his Eminence, the Cardinal Secretary of State Pacelli. Stop. Shall be in Detroit on other business all day Tuesday, November 29 at Hotel Book Cadillac. Grateful if you would fix appointment.[89]

It is not known whether McDonald succeeded in meeting with Coughlin, or if so, what the results of the meeting were. But the day after McDonald's telegram, Coughlin, in his regular radio broadcast on the CBS network, declared that there was no doubt that Jewish influence had been behind the Russian Revolution. In early December Coughlin's newspaper Social Justice *nearly copied a September 1935 speech Joseph Goebbels had given, denouncing Jews, atheists, and communists.[90]*

On December 17, 1938, McDonald wrote to Archbishop Rummel of New Orleans about a piece of anti-religious Nazi propaganda.

With this note I am enclosing a translation which I have had made of what seems to me to be a[n] extraordinary document—sacrilegious, even blasphemous, but extraordinarily interesting. It sets forth with brutal frankness the Nazi conception that it is Christianity which has defiled the race and that only through the destruction of the Church can the pristine purity of the German folk be restored.

87. Achilles to Welles, December 24, 1939, NA RG 59, Lot File 52D408, Alphabetical Subject File, Box 9, President's Advisory Committee—Minutes. Regarding the prospect of legislation, Assistant Secretary of State Messersmith had written two months earlier:

> [A]fter exploring the situation I and others who were interested found that the sentiment was such that if any question of revision of the immigration laws came up, it was likely that there would be revision in the sense of further limiting immigration rather than in liberalizing our present practice. I am inclined to think that when the Congress meets again in January this situation will be found unchanged.

Messersmith to Brandeis, October 24, 1938, Messersmith Papers, University of Delaware, Item 1054.

88. Michael Kazin, *The Populist Persuasion: An American History* (New York: Basic Books, 1995), 131.

89. McDonald telegram to Coughlin, November 26, 1938, McDonald Papers, Columbia University, D367 (PACPR), P8. Original in all-caps; punctuation added here.

90. Sheldon Marcus, *Father Coughlin: The Tumultuous Life of the Priest of Little Flower* (Boston: Little, Brown, 1973), 169–170.

My attention was called to this pamphlet when I was last in Washington for a series of conferences at the White House and the State Department. It was pointed out to me then that this unrestrained assault upon the Church is typical of what now goes on with the Reich with the connivance of the government and through the active propaganda of the extremist Nazis. This was, of course, not news. I thought it significant that Washington should be concerned.

As I read this document the second time, it occurred to me that members of the Hierarchy in this country might be interested to see it. If as chairman of the Bishops Committee on German Refugees [you] should care to distribute copies to your fellows, I should be glad to supply as many additional copies in this form as you might desire to use.

While waiting on your reply, I shall meantime do nothing about distributing the pamphlets except to send it to four or five personal friends.[91]

If Archbishop Rummel sent a written response, it was not found in McDonald's correspondence. But on December 21 Archbishop Mooney of Detroit responded to a similar letter from McDonald:

Many thanks for your kind letter of December 17th and the enclosed pamphlet. The pamphlet is only one more proof of what any discerning observer can readily see—that full-flown Nazi ideology is diametrically opposed to the fundamentals of historic Christianity and historic Judaism. The pity is that a third factor—Communism—enters in to complicate the picture and that it is either directly or indirectly fostered by those who have given up the fundamentals of historic Christianity and historic Judaism. I wonder[,] did the world ever present a more discouraging picture to men of good will?[92]

91. McDonald to Rummel, December 17, 1938, McDonald Papers, Columbia University, D367 (PACPR), P47.

92. Mooney to McDonald, December 21, 1938, McDonald Papers, Columbia University, D367 (PACPR), P22.

8. Toward War and Catastrophe: 1939

At the start of 1939 McDonald hoped to raise much larger sums to resettle refugees. On January 17, 1939, in a letter to comedian Eddie Cantor, he also gave some political background about both settlement efforts and resistance to fund-raisings:

Until the British government makes up its mind to resist firmly and consistently Arab terrorism and policies which are rooted in terrorism, it is only wishful thinking to plan for an additional 100,000 refugees in the Holy Land during the next few months. Similarly, settlement on a considerable scale elsewhere is dependent upon the attitude of governments which are little influenced by humanitarian factors. Hence, the imperative need is the formulation of plans which will appeal to the self interests of the potential immigration countries.

Throughout the whole period of Nazi persecution and the resultant need for new homes for hundreds of thousands of people[,] some of us have been convinced that very large funds ranging into the tens of millions of pounds must be in sight before large scale projects of settlement would be seriously considered by the immigration countries, or indeed before the plans themselves could be formulated. Others, including the Rothschilds and in general the heads of the Jewish financial communities throughout the world have insisted until very recently that the rest of us exaggerated the scope of the problem, that it was alarmist to speak about the need for hundreds of millions of dollars, that it was fantastic to think that these sums could be raised. . . . Today, these reluctant financial leaders are being forced to see that they have been taking counsel with their fears and that they must approach the problem with a much larger degree of boldness and generosity than heretofore.[1]

A few days earlier President Roosevelt had written to Prime Minister Neville Chamberlain:

I cannot emphasize too strongly the importance which I attach to the creation of a supplemental Jewish homeland as a step essential to the solution of the Jewish problem or my belief that Angola offers the most favorable facility for its creation.[2]

---

1. McDonald to Cantor, January 17, 1939, McDonald Papers, Columbia University, D361 (Eddie Cantor Special File).
2. FDR to Taylor for Chamberlain, January 17, 1939, *Foreign Relations of the United States*, II, 66–69, quoted by Feingold, *Politics of Rescue*, 105.

At its January 23 meeting the President's Advisory Committee considered the prospects for placing Jews in various parts of the world and for taking more into the United States. By this time the American immigration quota for Germany was being used in its entirety. There was interest in the possibility of bringing some children into the country outside the quota—children raising fewer objections than adults who needed jobs.

Children

Mr. McDonald then requested Mr. Achilles to report on the present status of the movement to secure the admission of a substantial number of children [from Germany to the United States] beyond the present quota limits. Mr. Achilles stated that the Wagner Bill[3] embodying this proposal had been presented to Mr. Messersmith, who had commented on its technical features. Mr. McDonald reported that a number of bills had already been introduced in Congress proposing reductions in present quotas. A general discussion followed but no formal action was taken.[4]

In a private conversation Messersmith had strongly discouraged McDonald and the Advisory Committee from pursuing or endorsing legislation to expand the quota, even for children. As in the past, Messersmith predicted that, given the chance, Congress would cut the quotas instead. State Department official Theodore Achilles thought that this warning deterred McDonald from bringing the question to a vote in the Advisory Committee. McDonald countered by asking whether Herbert Hoover should be "brought into the picture" to sway public opinion. Messersmith was opposed to any overture to Hoover, but McDonald wanted to know the president's views. Since Hoover and Roosevelt were not on good terms, and since the former president was likely to be a factor in the 1940 election, this inquiry was a way of increasing pressure on FDR to do more for refugees.

In February Senator Robert F. Wagner of New York (Democrat) and Representative Edith Nourse Rogers of Massachusetts (Republican) introduced identical bills in the Senate and House to admit 20,000 German refugee children to the United States over two years above and beyond the immigration quota for Germany.[5] McDonald was aware that pressing hard in Congress might create trouble, and Undersecretary Welles later added to his concern.[6]

---

3. See immediately below.

4. Sixteenth Meeting of the PACPR, January 23, 1939, NA RG 59, Lot File 52D408, Alphabetical Subject File, Box 9, President's Advisory Committee—Minutes.

5. Achilles to Welles, January 24, 1939, NA RG 59, Lot File 52D408, Alphabetical Subject File, Box 9, President's Advisory Committee—Minutes.

6. After a conversation with McDonald, on February 28 Eleanor Roosevelt wrote to Justice Justine Polier (the daughter of Rabbi Stephen Wise) about the Wagner-Rogers Bill (see n. 2 above):

> And he [McDonald] told me he is in favor of the bill personally, but he has been told that pressing the President at the present time may mean that the people in Congress who have bills to cut the quota will present them immediately and that might precipitate a difficult situation which would result in cutting the quota by 90%, and that, of course would be very serious. Therefore, the Committee hesitates to recommend

After several months of political maneuvering the Senate Immigration Commit-
tee amended the bill to give these children preference within the quota, not to admit
them outside it. The House Immigration Committee declined to report out any ver-
sion of the bill, which died in the rush to summer adjournment. An April 1939 poll
conducted by Fortune *magazine indicated that 83% of Americans were opposed to*
any increase in the quotas.[7]

On January 28 Jay Pierrepont Moffat, head of the European Division of the
State Department, wrote to Undersecretary Welles:

Mr. James G. MacDonald [*sic*] plans to telephone you Monday morning
on the following matter. Later on he will probably telephone the President, but
wants your views first. He says that he is under great pressure to urge the extension of the work of the Intergovernmental Committee to cover all refugees,
including Spanish refugees, just as soon as this can be done. Personally he is
entirely in sympathy with this idea, which he believes was the President's original idea which was blocked, first, by the State Department and, secondly, by
the British. He thinks that there is a distinct probability that the British, in
view of the debacle in Spain, will alter their position toward the extension of
the Intergovernmental Committee's terms of reference, and hopes very much
that we will urge them to do so.

To [adopt] the Committee's terms of reference to take care of Spanish
refugees would, it seems to me, (a) be the straw that might break the camel's
back; (b) create an addition of work which the Committee and the Directorship, as at present set up, is not competent to deal with; (c) would certainly
make it more difficult . . . to extend the work of the Committee to all other
countries in Central Europe; and (d) might give the Latin American countries
an excuse to refuse to receive German refugees on the ground that they preferred to concentrate on Spanish refugees.

McDonald's long experience with resettlement led him to completely different
conclusions—namely, that it would be easier to find places for a larger number of
people (and a larger number of Jews) if there were non-Jews among them.

On January 30, 1939, during a long address to the Reichstag, Hitler raised a
connection between impending war and killing of Jews, prophesizing that if interna-

support for the bill when they do not know whether this will be the result or not. . . .
Mr. Welles feels that strongly pressing the bill at the present time might do exactly
what Mr. McDonald says, because his desk is flooded with protests accusing the State
Department at conniving in allowing a great many more Jewish people than the quota
permits to enter the country under various pretenses.

Quoted by Joseph P. Lash, *Eleanor and Franklin* (New York: W. W. Norton, 1971),
576–577.

7. See Judith Tydor Baumel, *Unfulfilled Promise: Rescue and Resettlement of Jewish Refugee
Children in the United Sates, 1934–1945* (Juneau: Denali Press, 1990), 27–31; Breitman and Kraut,
American Refugee Policy, 73. There are differences of interpretation between these two sources.

tional Jewry brought about a world war, it would result in the destruction of the Jew-ish race in Europe. Hitler declared:

The German nation has no feeling of hatred toward England, America, or France; all it wants is peace and quiet. But these other nations are continually being stirred up to hatred of Germany and the German people by Jewish and non-Jewish agitators. And so, should the warmongers achieve what they are aiming at, our own people would be landed in a situation for which they would be psychologically quite unprepared and which they would thus fail to grasp. . . . The German nation must know who the men are who want to bring about a war by hook or by crook.

. . . .

In accordance with their [the rest of the world's] own declarations they cannot find a single reason to excuse themselves for refusing to receive this most valuable race in their own countries. Nor can I see a reason why the members of this race should be imposed upon the German nation, while in the States, which are so enthusiastic about these 'splendid people,' their settlement should suddenly be refused with every imaginable excuse. I think that the sooner this problem is solved the better; for Europe cannot settle down until the Jewish question is cleared up.

. . . .

One thing I should like to say on this day which may be memorable for others as well as for us Germans: In the course of my life I have very often been a prophet, and have usually been ridiculed for it. . . . Today I will once more be a prophet: If the international Jewish financiers in and outside Europe should succeed in plunging the nations once more into a world war, then the result will not be the bolshevization of the earth, and thus the victory of Jewry, but the annihilation of the Jewish race in Europe![8]

At the time, this speech was widely viewed as conciliatory, partly because of Hit-ler's declaration of peaceful intentions (quoted above), and in part because of a passage where Hitler claimed that nations must trade or die, supposedly an admission of Ger-man economic weakness.[9]

Was Hitler's comment about the Jewish question a device to pressure Western countries to admit German Jews as immigrants, or a forecast of what might happen if all of Germany's potential enemies joined against her? In a February 5, 1939, speech

8. Hitler's Reichstag speech of January 30, 1939, from *The Speeches of Adolf Hitler, April 1922–August 1939*, edited by Norman H. Baynes (New York: Howard Fertig, 1969), vol. 1, pp. 736–741.

9. Wesley K. Wark, *The Ultimate Enemy: British Intelligence and Nazi Germany, 1933–1939* (Ithaca, N.Y.: Cornell University Press, 1985), 218.

at Hadassah, the Women's Zionist organization, in New York, McDonald gave his interpretation; excerpts appeared in the New York Times.

Disagreeing with those "who thought that Chancellor Hitler's speech was pacifistic," James G. McDonald . . . said yesterday that the Fuehrer's declarations from the point of view of the Jewish situation and international relations was "the most threatening he had ever made."

. . . .

According to Mr. McDonald, the German Chancellor has accomplished the first phase of his program, the destruction of German Jews, and has begun his second phase, "extension of Nazism in the international sphere." Declaring Hitler used the Jews as "a shield for the Nazi program," he said Germany appeared to be at the height of her power, but "she might be near her downfall."[10]

Nazi Germany was rapidly moving toward launching a war and was not terribly interested in international negotiations about extracting German Jews. State Department official Robert Pell reviewed the problems that the Intergovernmental Committee on Refugees had had in making direct contact with the German government.

Attempt after attempt to establish contact with the German Government failed. There was, first of all, the Sudeten crisis; then, just as the situation was returning to normal, the Secretary of the German Embassy in Paris, vom Rath, was murdered, and a carefully organized attack on the Jews throughout Germany ensued. . . . Finally, however, word came that Dr. Schacht, who was at that time President of the Reichsbank, would be visiting London and would establish contact with Mr. Rublee.

On December 15, 1938, Lord Winterton and Mr. Rublee met Dr. Schacht . . . [who] suggested that a loan should be raised outside Germany to furnish the foreign exchange required for immediate emigration and settlement needs, and that this loan should be serviced by the proceeds of additional exports from Germany. . . . Mr. Rublee . . . [as well as Robert Pell and financial adviser Joseph Cotton] went to Berlin in order to explore the possibilities with the German authorities and to report to, but not to bind, the Intergovernmental Committee.

The conversations which were begun with Dr. Schacht were interrupted when he was dismissed from the Reichsbank and then resumed, under the aegis of Marshal Goering, with Mr. Wohlthat of his staff. These conversations covered the whole field of migration of minority elements in Germany and, on February 1, 1939, Mr. Rublee received the detailed program which the Ger-

10. *New York Times,* February 6, 1939, p. 6.

man Government, acting unilaterally and independently, was prepared to adopt. . . . The essence of the program was the desire of the German government to emigrate an aggregate of 150,000 persons, consisting of men and single women between the ages of 15 and 45, who were individually capable of earning a living and were otherwise fit for emigration, over a period of three to five years. In addition . . . the German authorities desired that their dependents, estimated to approximate 250,000 persons, should follow the wage earners when the latter were established and able to receive them.[11]

As part of the arrangement also, Germany was to set up a trust for a significant proportion (at least 25%) of the remaining assets of German Jews, with the assumption that it might serve as a source of some funds for emigrants under certain conditions or as collateral for loans or funds raised abroad for refugee resettlement. But such a trust would have been under Nazi control. No one outside Germany had much hope that this trust might really benefit emigrants, but the alternative seemed to be outright Nazi seizure of all Jewish assets.

On March 8 Robert Pell wrote from London about the degree to which the German government was committed to this agreement in principle:

My impression is that Goering wishes to go ahead with his program, but desires ammunition with which to justify his activities to Hitler. This ammunition in the first instance is to take the form of the memorandum on settlement projects which I am to take back to Berlin in a fortnight's time. Goering's other preoccupation is that the financing machinery on the inside of Germany and on the outside shall come into being simultaneously, that is, that the private corporation shall be set up at the same time. In studying the situation it seems to me that the clue to the timing lies with the appointment of the third or foreign trustee. When he has been approved by both sides, his appointment can be held off until both corporation and trust can be announced to the public. It is my impression that Wohlthat is in agreement with this way of proceeding.

As I indicate in my memorandum, I had a long secret conference with the Jewish leaders in Berlin. They are, of course, very nervous and jumpy, and inclined to discount much of what we are doing. At the same time, they are ready to acknowledge that there has been an easing of the situation, and that it is all to the good that Goering is centralizing the administration of the emigration. They were quite frank about the ship loads of their co-religionists which they are heading in various directions such as Shanghai, the Mediterranean and the Caribbean. They said that they had to get their people out, whether there was an easing of the tension or not. At any moment an incident might occur which would endanger the very lives of their people. They could not afford to take

11. Pell's analysis, Intergovernmental Committee, undated, NA RG 59, 840.48 Refugees/2122.

chances with the consequence that they were very ready to yield to the pressure of the secret police and the enticement of the shipping companies and to emigrate their people without papers and without a fixed destination. They said that no opportunities for infiltration existed any longer, with the exception of the American quota and the refuge opportunities offered in England. The rest of the world had dried up. They had, therefore, to fall back upon force majeur[e], and reveal to the world in this dramatic fashion what was their plight. I pleaded with them that they were doing more harm than good by this way of proceeding, that they were defeating our efforts to open up places in Latin America, but they laughed in my face. After six years of dealing with this problem they are very hard. They do not believe in promises. Too many promises have been broken. They want action and are in a state of mind where they will force action.[12]

McDonald and George Warren were eager for the quick establishment of a private organization to fund resettlement efforts on a large scale—in conjunction with the Intergovernmental Committee on Refugees. But some American Jewish leaders were wary. On March 6, State Department official Theodore Achilles wrote to his superiors:

He [Warren] stated that he and Mr. MacDonald [*sic*] had sensed a hesitancy on the part of the Jewish members to proceed with plans for the private international corporation or to take any other action pending the return of Rabbi Wise from London and a further opportunity to ascertain his reactions, as a Zionist leader, to the Rublee memorandum.

Mr. Warren and Mr. MacDonald sensed a general feeling in Jewish circles, particularly in those advocating the boycott, that action by governments or private organizations to facilitate the program of emigration outlined in the Rublee memorandum would (1) condone the policies of the German Government, and (2) perhaps eventually assist Germany through promoting exports.

They did not believe that either contention was well founded, but wished to let us know that such a feeling existed.

Mr. Warren pointed out that no authoritative public statement concerning the Rublee memorandum or the action of the Intergovernmental Committee concerning it had been made. He believed that a public statement by Mr. Rublee or someone else giving an authoritative picture of the situation might do much to dispel such criticism.[13]

12. Pell to Moffat, March 8, 1939, NA RG 59, Lot File 52D408, Alphabetical Subject File Box 14, Wohlthat-Berlin folder.

13. Achilles to Messersmith and Welles, March 6, 1939, NA RG 59, Lot File 52D408, Alphabetical Subject File, Box 9, President's Advisory Committee—Minutes.

On March 14, based on his telephone conversation with George Warren, Achilles gave an update of efforts by McDonald and Warren, starting with their conversation with Lewis Strauss:[14]

It developed that the feeling in New York in opposition to proceeding along the lines of the Rublee memorandum originated largely with the *Times* editorial staff and particularly with Arthur Sulzberger. Mr. Straus[s] had been influenced by Mr. Sulzberger and had talked to Mr. [Herbert] Hoover, who had the same feeling.

Mr. MacDonald [*sic*] and Mr. Warren had emphasized to Mr. Straus[s] that the memorandum represented the most that could at present be obtained from the moderate Göring group, that by putting the plan into operation and strengthening the hand of that group it might be possible to obtain more favorable conditions later, whereas failure to follow up the procedure contemplated would almost certainly bring down the lightning on the Jews remaining in Germany, and that failure to follow up would represent a totally defeatist attitude.

Straus[s] was apparently convinced. . . . The same arguments had been used by Mr. MacDonald on Mr. Sulzberger[,] who indicated that, while he would not support the plan, he would not actively oppose it.[15]

On March 15 the German army moved into Bohemia and Moravia,[16] *allowing Slovakia to set itself up as an independent state. Having surrendered its frontier defenses in October 1938 after the Munich Conference and lacking outside support, the Czechoslovakian government did not go to war. The state was dismembered.*

This was the effective end of British efforts to appease Germany. Aware that a larger army might be needed in the near future, Britain quickly introduced its first peacetime draft.

British and French representatives on the Intergovernmental Committee thought that Germany's new aggression ended any chance that the Rublee agreement might be carried out. But after some discussion Myron Taylor and Undersecretary Sumner Wells argued that the Intergovernmental Committee should carry on anyway.[17]

In a March 17, 1939, letter to Henry Ittelson, McDonald described his conversation with New York Governor Herbert Lehman about the prospects for the Rublee agreement.

14. Lewis L. Strauss, partner in the investment firm Kuhn Loeb. Wealthy Jewish philanthropist, influential figure in the Joint Distribution Committee. Later had a distinguished career in government, including chairing the Atomic Energy Commission.

15. Achilles to Messersmith and Welles, March 14, 1939, NA RG 59, Lot File 52D408, Alphabetical Subject File, Box 9, President's Advisory Committee 1939.

16. Bohemia and Moravia contained 118,000 Jews, as defined by Nazi standards, many of whom now sought to find havens elsewhere.

17. Welles to Pell, March 23, 1939, NA RG 59, 840.48 Refugees/1520: Stewart, *United States Government Policy*, 432.

What Mr. Lehman had to say merely confirmed my impression gained from many other conferences that the task of implementing the Rublee program is going to be one of great[,] though not necessarily unsuperable[,] difficulty. And in frankness, one must recognize that the latest Hitler conquest complicates the problem both by increasing the number of victims and by diminishing almost to the vanishing point any confidence that one might have in any promise made by the Reich.[18]

On March 22 the new director of the Intergovernmental Committee on Refugees, Sir Herbert Emerson (who had replaced Rublee), wrote McDonald:

I am writing to thank you for your kind letter and good wishes. I appreciate them the more since not long ago you occupied the seat I am now trying to fill. Even before I took over the Directorship of the Intergovernmental Committee I was working in close cooperation with Mr. Rublee, and I saw many of the letters addressed to him by Mr. Warren regarding the activities of your Committee. May I say how highly I value the practical work it is doing and its readiness to help on all occasions. I am particularly interested in the Commissions that are now investigating conditions in British Guiana and San[to] Domingo.

. . . .

At the moment it is most difficult to work out any orderly scheme of emigration in the absence of sufficient outlets. There would be definite relief even if only one considerable opening was found, and with two or more the problem would be brought within manageable dimensions. I am therefore very glad to hear that another Commission is being arranged to visit the Philippines, where the prospects appear to be favourable.

. . . .

Pell hopes to make contact with Berlin again in the near future, but recent events in Czecho-Slovakia made it desirable not to proceed without consulting certain Governments, including of course the Government of the United States, regarding the exact form which the memorandum should take describing the prospects of emigration. It is of course clear that if, as seems probably, persecution in Czecho-Slovakia increases the number of refugees by anything up to a quarter of a million, the period of emigration contemplated in the Rublee conversations will not be sufficient.[19]

In the early years of the Nazi regime McDonald had valued the insights and sources of Raymond H. Geist, American consul in Berlin. On April 4, 1939, Geist,

18. McDonald to Ittelson, March 17, 1939, McDonald Papers, Columbia University, D 367 (PACPR), P24.
19. Emerson to McDonald, March 22, 1939, NA RG 59, Lot File 52D408, Alphabetical Subject File, Box 14, Warren Memoranda.

now consul general and with even better sources high within the SS,[20] *wrote to Assistant Secretary of State Messersmith about the need to proceed, regardless of the problems with the Rublee agreement. Geist's prognosis of the worst case was astonishingly accurate.*

The agreement which Mr. Rublee took away with him was undoubtedly the best that anybody could obtain from the Germans and represented the limit of cooperation (if one might even call it cooperation) which the radicals would agree to. Göring made these concessions, but I have reason to know that the Secret Police were not in favor of going so far. . . .

I am afraid that in the end the Germans will consider that the efforts of the Intergovernmental Committee have produced so few results that they will consider the agreement off and will proceed to handle the Jewish problem entirely in their own way. There can, of course, be only an internal solution of the Jewish problem in Germany, and I believe they are preparing to solve the problem in this way. It will, of course, consist in placing all the able-bodied Jews in work camps, confiscating the wealth of the entire Jewish population, isolating them, and putting additional pressure on the whole community, and getting rid of as many as they can by force.[21]

Myron Taylor's efforts[22] *to carry out the Rublee agreement set off a flurry of meetings in late March and April 1939 involving prominent American Jews, Taylor himself, McDonald, and George Warren. Taylor repeatedly expressed his own conviction that there was a need to move very quickly to establish a new corporation to fund resettlement under the conditions arranged by Rublee in Berlin, that it was less a matter of the amount of money infused into this organization (perhaps a million dollars would suffice as a first step) than it was of convincing the German government to take this organization seriously. An April 15 meeting at the home of James N. Rosenberg, however, selected a committee, which then drafted an aide-mémoire, part of which is reproduced here. Expressing gratitude to President Roosevelt, Taylor, Rublee, and their associates, it, however, stipulated limits on cooperation:*

We believe that we should take no steps that directly or by implication would give recognition by the Jewish community as such to the validity of any expropriation of private property or of the requirement that German citizens who are Jews, shall be driven into exile. We should particularly refrain from

---

20. For the International Military Tribunal at Nuremberg, Geist submitted an affidavit stating that his prewar information about Nazi plans to kill Jews came from SD and Gestapo official Karl Haselbacher. See Richard Breitman, *The Architect of Genocide: Himmler and the Final Solution* (New York: Knopf, 1991), 64.

21. Geist to Messersmith, April 4, 1939, Messersmith Papers, Item 1139, University of Delaware.

22. Described in some detail in Taylor to Hull, March 30, 1939, Taylor Papers, Box 3, Intergovernmental Committee on Political Refugees, January–April 1939, FDRL.

undertaking, as a Jewish group, any step which might tend to induce any other government to follow the German program.[23]

We further note that these principles and the problem involved must necessarily concern all of the persecuted of every race and creed and that the problem of resettlement assumes such magnitude and complexity as to place it beyond the power of individuals alone to solve and to make it necessarily a subject for the concern and active aid of governments.

If in the judgment of Mr. Taylor, despite the conduct of Germany since the date of the Rublee memorandum, the effort should be made to effectuate it, and if in his judgment it would be helpful to form any organization to implement the plans, and keeping in mind the reservations mentioned in the foregoing paragraphs, we suggest that it should be formed, financed and operated under general, and not Jewish auspices. We are confident that this would evoke the cooperation of a number of individual Jews.[24]

On April 25 Judge Joseph Proskauer,[25] Harold Linder,[26] Henry Ittleson, and Lewis Strauss told Taylor about this aide-mémoire. Taylor quickly agreed with the stipulations and urged the American Jewish group to contact its English friends to get this corporation organized. In a memo summing up their conversation Proskauer praised McDonald and passed along his worries about undermining or failing to support Myron Taylor.[27]

On April 29 Sumner Welles sent a memorandum to FDR to prepare him for his meeting on May 4 with Myron Taylor and a small group of those involved in refugee matters.

You will recall that as a result of Mr. Rublee's [George inserted in pencil] negotiations in Berlin the German Government agreed to create a trust fund from Jewish property in Germany for the purpose of facilitating emigration. It was also contemplated that a private international corporation for the financing of refugee settlement should be set up concurrently outside of Germany. The carrying out of orderly emigration from Germany and the amelioration of the lot of Jews remaining in Germany are to a considerable extent dependent upon the early establishment and successful working of these two organizations.

23. The concern here was about Poland's government imitating Germany's forced emigration policy.

24. Highly Confidential, April 4 Memorandum re Conversations Concerning Proposals of Mr. Myron Taylor and later additions, Archives of the Joint Distribution Committee, AR 33/44, no. 255.

25. New York State Supreme Court judge, a major figure on the (non-Zionist) American Jewish Committee.

26. Harold Linder, president of General American Investors, official of the JDC.

27. Proskauer memorandum, April 25, 1939, Stephen S. Wise Papers, American Jewish Historical Society, Box 127, Roll 74, Center for Jewish History, New York.

This Government and the Intergovernmental Committee [on Political Refugees in pencil] have consistently made clear that this plan involved no "agreement" between the Intergovernmental Committee and the German Government. On the contrary it has been distinctly understood that the Germans would carry out unilaterally a program of emigration and that the Intergovernmental Committee and the private corporation would unilaterally carry out a parallel program of settlement.

In attempting to set up this corporation, Mr. Taylor has encountered great reluctance in Jewish circles to take definite action for the following reasons: (1) fear of accusation that there is such a thing as "international Jewry," (2) fear that creation of the corporation in accordance with the Rublee program would constitute an agreement with the German Government and consequently a condonation [condoning] of the racial policies of that Government, including confiscation of Jewish property, and (3) fear that the carrying out of the program might in some way assist the German Government.

Mr. Taylor has made great progress in convincing representative Jewish financiers that each of these fears is groundless. On April 15 a meeting of some seventy representative Jews agreed unanimously to proceed with creation of the corporation. This meeting appointed a sub-committee consisting of the following persons who will accompany Mr. Taylor on May 4: Edward Greenbaum,[28] Alfred Jaretzki,[29] Henry Ittleson, Harold Linder, Judge Joseph H. Proskauer, James N. Rosenberg, Judge Samuel I. Rosenman (chairman),[30] Lewis L. Strauss, Solomon M. Stroock,[31] Paul Baerwald, Rabbi Stephen Wise.

Mr. Taylor contemplates that the corporation, which he suggests be called the "Refugee Foundation,"[32] will have a capitalization which will at first be limited but which will be capable of indefinite expansion to meet actual needs. He envisages a high official of the Bank of England as chairman, to be assisted by well-known American, French, and perhaps other vice-chairmen, a small directorate of very prominent persons, and large national advisory committees which will also consist of prominent persons. All of these bodies will be widely representative of the Jewish, Catholic and Protestant faiths.

Mr. Taylor contemplates that the Foundation, or smaller organizations affiliated with it, will carry out the financing and execution of settlement projects, and that it will take over from the Intergovernmental Committee all dealing with the German Government.

The present status of mass settlement possibilities may be summarized as follows:

28. Partner in the law firm Greenbaum, Wolff & Ernst. Appointed chairman of the Alcohol Control Commission.
29. Partner in Sullivan and Cromwell law firm.
30. Speechwriter and adviser to President Roosevelt.
31. Wealthy New York attorney, influential member of the American Jewish Committee.
32. The name was soon changed to the Coordinating Foundation.

British Guiana. The survey commission's report recommends experimental settlement as soon as possible of from three to five thousand carefully selected and supervised young persons in camps similar to C.C.C.[33] camps. The estimate is that from three to five million dollars will be necessary to bring those numbers to British Guiana, establish them, and maintain them for two years. The experience of these groups should indicate within two years whether or not settlement on a much larger scale is practicable.

Dominican Republic. The survey commission has returned and its report should be completed shortly. It also will probably recommend experimental settlement by carefully selected and supervised pioneering groups along C.C.C. lines, with somewhat more assurance that large scale settlement will be practicable. Comparatively large sums will be necessary in carrying this out.

Mindanao. The survey commission is at work and should report within six weeks. In view of the favorable attitude of the Philippine Government and of the favorable climate of Mindanao, it is believed that at least ten thousand settlers may be colonized there and that the work may proceed fairly rapidly as soon as the preliminary planning has been completed. Large amounts of capital will be necessary.

Angola. The matter is in suspense pending the tentative mobilization of sufficient capital to enable someone to go to Lisbon to offer the Portuguese Government a very large sum either for the outright purchase of Angola or for the creation of a chartered company along the lines of the old British East India Company. There is no present indication, however, that an offer along either of these lines would be accepted.[34]

On May 1 Robert Pell wrote Myron Taylor:

Sir Herbert [Emerson] and I have lunched with Mr. Max Warburg and Mr. Wilfrid Israel, who has succeeded Mr. Warburg as head of the Hilfsverein at Berlin. Sir Herbert . . . said that he had reluctantly come to the conclusion that Jewish finance had no intention of setting up a private corporation and was just playing for time and finding excuses. Mr. Warburg, after some hesitation, admitted that that was the case. He said that he had conferred at great length with Lord Bearsted, Mr. Anthony de Rothschild, etc., etc., and this was the situation: (1) they did not wish to set up any corporation; (2) if they were forced by circumstances to set up a corporation it would have to have (a) a shadow capitalization and (b) Aryan direction, preferably by Mr. Taylor. Mr. Warburg said that he and the others concerned were opposed to the idea of a trust in Germany and wished to do nothing which would encour-

---

33. Civilian Conservation Corps, a work relief program for unemployed young men, established on March 19, 1933. Men were enrolled by the Labor Department, the camps run by the U.S. Army. At its peak, in August 1935, there were 502,000 men in 2,006 camps. It was disbanded in June 1942.

34. FDRL, Official File 3186, Political Refugees, January–June 1939.

age the creation of it. He said that if a project, such as the British Guiana project, were opened, financing should be only partly by private subscription and predominantly by governmental subscription. He said that there was no reason why the Jewish community should bear the burden of a situation which it had not created.

Mr. Israel, who is on the spot in Germany, took a very different point of view. He said that he was convinced of Wohlthat's sincerity and good faith. He said that he was having a difficult time battling against radical elements. He, Israel, had conferred with him last Wednesday, when Wohlthat had pleaded for some action in the way of a private corporation or else, he said, his position with the Führer would be rendered impossible, and Israel was of the opinion that a least a holding company should be set up urgently on the outside or else the battle inside Germany for the improvement of the condition of the Jews would be lost. He said that he found that the Jewish leaders here did not have, or did not wish to have, any realization of the situation inside Germany. He said that he sincerely felt that a great opportunity was being thrown away.[35]

Taylor, McDonald, Judge Samuel Rosenman, Judge Joseph Proskauer, Lewis Strauss, Henry Ittleson, Sol Stroock, Paul Baerwald, Nathan Straus, Jr., George Warren, and Rabbi Stephen Wise all attended a meeting at the White House on May 4. An unlisted participant was Jay Pierrepont Moffat, head of the Division of European Affairs in the State Department. A press release revealed the scope of the meeting,[36] but in his journal Moffat gave more pointed detail:

Mr. Taylor made the customary speech reporting of what had been done to date, and pointing out that he considered the setting up of the Refugee Foundation of utmost importance. In fact, he pointed out that Goering had as much as said that he had been given six months to come to an understanding with outside Jewry, and that if nothing happened by the end of that time the authorities would chart another course. Sumner Welles then read the latest telegram from [Raymond] Geist indicating that in his opinion unless places of settlement were opened up very shortly the radicals would again gain control in Germany and try to solve the Jewish problem in their own way.

35. Pell to Taylor, May 1, 1939, Myron Taylor Papers, Box 3, IGCPR May–June 1939, FDRL.

36. Mr. Taylor and Mr. MacDonald [*sic*] then said that they were happy to report that the results will soon be known of the splendid work done by the several commissions which have been sent out to explore the possibilities for large scale settlement of political refugees in British Guiana, the Dominican Republic, the Island of Mindanao in the Philippines, as well as in other areas. They indicated that it was their belief that should these reports prove favorable, progress toward a permanent solution of the refugee problem will have been made, though at the same time they warned against undue impatience, saying that in order to insure ultimate success short periods of experimentation may be necessary before any great mass settlements can be made. As the Intergovernmental Committee has continually emphasized, it has not asked nor does it expect any country to make any changes in its existing immigration legislation.

Copy in FDRL, Myron Taylor Papers, Box 3, IGCPR May–June 1939.

Judge Rosenman then recounted the efforts that had been made to set up the Foundation, pointing out the difficulties that had been encountered in reaching a meeting of minds. . . . He said that there was now universal agreement that the time had come to go ahead, but he made it clear that the Foundation should be interdenominational, with the Jews probably in a minority.

At this Mr. Taylor intervened, and said that while he agreed that the Foundation should be interdenominational, yet in all fairness he must point out that the greatest burden must be borne by the Jews, as it was largely their problem and their people who were in the greatest danger.

The President then pointed out that the conversation had convinced him of one essential fact,—namely, that haste was essential. Perhaps some existing organization could be used which would obviate the long delays necessary to setting up a new body. As this was a new idea to most of those present, there was considerable emotion and all the disadvantages were brought out toward using a foreign organization, or a relief organization, or an organization with existing commitments. The President, however, stuck to his point, and said that in his opinion we should tell the Germans in a fortnight,—not one day longer,—that an organization was in existence which could deal with the German Trust. It was not so much a question of the money as it was of actual lives, and the President was convinced that the warnings given by our Embassy in Berlin were sound and not exaggerated.[37]

There were also difficulties in Britain, with British Jewish leaders having their own objections. On May 12 British Prime Minister Chamberlain issued a statement approving the idea of an experimental refugee settlement in British Guiana and offering the lease of land on generous terms.[38] Private funds would be needed for any economic enterprises for this settlement. British Jewish leaders wanted to keep such an experiment relatively small.[39] On May 15 Robert Pell (in London) again wrote Myron Taylor.

My candid impression is that our business is becoming a tug of war between the Governments and our Jewish financial friends. The Governments are striving hard to shift the major part of the responsibility to Jewish finance and Jewish finance is working equally hard to leave it with the Governments. Some of our friends at New Court are, as usual, extremely frank and say that the whole object of the Evian movement was to bring about governmental in

---

37. Moffat Journal, May 4, 1939, Moffat Papers, vol. 42. Call number MS Am 1407, Houghton Library, Harvard University. By permission of Houghton Library, Harvard University. On the warnings from the Embassy, see Geist's letter to Messersmith, April 4, 1939, quoted above.

38. Kennedy to Secretary of State, from Pell, May 12, 1939. Copy in Wise Papers, Box 65, Roll 77, Center for Jewish History.

39. See Anthony de Rothschild to George Warren, May 26, 1939, Wise Papers, Box 65, Roll 77, Center for Jewish History.

place of private financing of the evacuation of the Jews and their resettlement and that they intend to maintain this objective.[40]

On May 20 Sumner Welles reported to FDR that Taylor now had a list of ten Jewish and non-Jewish nominees, McDonald among them, for a board of directors of a refugee foundation. Taylor also offered to go back to London to link this new organization with the Intergovernmental Committee on Refugees.[41] McDonald was heavily involved in these international efforts, all the more because Taylor soon had an operation and, on medical grounds, had to delay his trip until July.

McDonald was not prominently involved with the nearly simultaneous crisis and controversy involving the SS St. Louis, a German ship with 937 passengers, mostly Jewish refugees, which docked in Havana harbor on May 27. Cuban President Laredo Bru issued orders barring the passengers from disembarking, although they had tourist visas to Cuba and hoped to wait there for American visas. This ship with nowhere to land set off a media spectacle, which ended only when the ship returned to Europe and, at the last minute, Britain, Belgium, France, and the Netherlands agreed to divide and absorb the desperate passengers.[42]

On June 5 Myron Taylor's secretary had a long telephone conversation with McDonald and recorded McDonald's account of his recent activities.

Saturday, May 27th, although it was the beginning of a long weekend, I induced Mr. Ittleson to see me at his office . . . and he got in touch with a number of his colleagues. They agreed to hold a meeting the following Monday, May 29th.

At the Monday conference, at which Baerwald, Max Warburg, Ittleson, Linder, and I were present, there was a rather comprehensive review of the program Mr. Baerwald and Mr. Linder were to take with them to London. They were to sail on the *Normandie* the following Wednesday.

40. Pell to Taylor, May 15, 1939, Myron Taylor Papers, Box 3, IGCPR, May–June 1939, FDRL.

41. Welles to FDR, May 20, 1939, FDRL, OF 3186, Box 3, National Campaign, January–June 1939. But McDonald was eventually dropped as a director. The final list included the Earl of Bessborough, former Governor General of Canada; Paul Baerwald, chairman of the JDC; Viscount Bearsted, chairman, Shell Transport and Trading Company; Harold Butler, warden, Nuffield College, Oxford; Lionel L. Cohen, lawyer for the Rothschild interests; John W. Davis, former U.S. ambassador to Britain and Democratic presidential candidate in 1924; Simon Marks, Marks and Spencer Department Store; Nathan L. Miller, former governor of New York; Dave Hennon Morris, former U.S. ambassador to Belgium; Joseph Proskauer, former justice of the New York State Supreme Court; Lessing Rosenwald, chairman of Sears Roebuck; Lionel de Rothschild, of N. M. Rothschild and Sons; Sir Horace Rumbold, former British ambassador to Germany; John Hope Simpson, author and member of the Royal Institute of International Affairs; Lewis L. Strauss, Kuhn, Loeb and Co.; Rabbi Stephen S. Wise; and Owen D. Young, chairman of the board of General Electric Company. List in Morris to Berle, August 22, 1939, NA RG 59, Lot File 52D408, Alphabetical Subject File, Box 3, Coordinating Foundation.

42. Sarah A. Ogilvie and Scott Miller, *Refuge Denied* (Madison: University of Wisconsin Press, 2006). The passengers petitioned for entry into the United States on an emergency basis and were denied because the immigration quota for Germany was then full.

In the course of our discussion a cable reply was drafted to the cable message just received from Rothschild. The latter had again urged tying up the new Foundation with British Guiana and with the raising of a very large sum of money for settlement in Guiana and elsewhere. Our group decided to resist this British pressure. The cable which was sent and the instructions which were given Baerwald both insisted on the separation of the Foundation from other projects. This separation seemed to us essential, if anything tangible were to come out of Mr. Baerwald's visit.

. . . .

Last Thursday, June 1st, I made a special trip to Washington to see members of the State Department. While there I urged Mr. Welles to ask the President if the latter would be willing to pick up the telephone and urge Proskauer to go to London. I took this step because it had become clear to me by that time that nothing short of presidential pressure would move Proskauer.

While in Mr. Moffat's office he read to me a communication just received from Pell. It emphasized again the need for prompt action. It was particularly significant[,] however[,] because in it he disclosed the fact that the British officials, including Winterton, were now strongly of the opinion that it would be a mistake to make any commitment about a meeting of the Intergovernmental Committee. They were not willing to go beyond committing themselves to a meeting of the officers of that Committee, . . . Wohlthat would not be coming to London before the 10th or so of July.

This delay obviously gives a little more time, but I have not passed on this information to the Jewish groups here. It seems to me that there is no need to relax any of the pressure.

Last Friday, June 2, I went to see Rabbi Silver,[43] head of the Zionist portion of the United Jewish Appeal. I did this at the special request of Mr. Baerwald, who thought that my intervention might clear up the Zionist assent to the earmarking of a half million dollars by the United Jewish Appeal for the proposed Foundation.

Though I had known Rabbi Silver rather well and had been associated with him in various efforts at raising money, I was shocked by his attitude toward not only the earmarking of this fund, but also toward the Evian effort and everything which has followed it. In substance, Mr. Silver not only said that he was personally opposed to earmarking the fund, but that he had been opposed to the Evian effort; that he saw no particular good in it; that he thought the work of the President's Committee was useless, and that it was only with considerable difficulty that he had been able to induce his Zionist colleagues to vote a few thousand dollars to contribute toward the expenses of the President's Committee. As to the proposed earmarking of the funds for the Foundation,

43. Lithuanian-born Cleveland Reform rabbi and American Zionist leader. More militant than Wise, and just as fiery an orator, he played an important role in the creation of Israel.

he stated there was no one in this country who could give such an O.K. on behalf of the Zionists. This must wait on the action of the Zionist leaders in Palestine or in London. Finally he said that if Dr. Weizmann and Ben Goren [David Ben-Gurion], both now in London, were to assent to the earmarking, the Zionists in this country would agree. Dr. Silver suggested that I get busy to secure this assent. I told him that I did not think it my business to do this, nor the business of anyone on the President's Committee; that it was a Jewish matter and for the Jewish leaders themselves to settle. Nevertheless, I confess that even I, after seven years of experience, was a little shocked by Rabbi Silver's attitude. He asserted that Rabbi Wise, though admittedly the outstanding Zionist leader in this country, does not represent the Zionists on the President's Committee.[44] He implied that nothing Rabbi Wise said or promised binds anyone else.

Back of this attitude of Rabbi Silver is a long story of rivalry between him and Rabbi Wise for Zionist leadership. . . .

Immediately following my conference with Silver I got in touch with Mr. Ittleson, who was to see Silver that afternoon. I warned Ittleson as to what he should expect. . . .

Last Friday I also saw and had a long talk with James Rosenberg. You will recall that Rosenberg was not very enthusiastic about the venture, but, as I thought would be the case, he is better than his word. Rosenberg is prepared, should Baerwald urge him to do so, to do everything possible to persuade the Joint Distribution Committee to put up the whole half million dollars should the Zionists continue recalcitrant. In such an effort Rosenberg's leadership would be invaluable.[45]

Rabbi Wise was unable to persuade the Zionist Organization of America to supply one-half of the total American contribution to the proposed Coordinating Foundation. As a result, the Joint Distribution Committee decided to contribute $500,000, with British Jewish organizations and others contributing at least $300,000.[46]

McDonald was eager to bring the new foundation into existence in part because the Intergovernmental Committee was nearly paralyzed, with the British in frequent disagreement with the Americans, and with the French representatives Henri Bérenger, particularly vocal in his criticism of the Rublee-Wohlthat agreement: "the French Jews were not stupid little fish. . . . Mr. Taylor could have his trap. He could put his head into it."[47]

At the July 19–20 meeting of the Intergovernmental Committee on Refugees, Director Sir Herbert Emerson reviewed the offer of facilities for refugee resettlement

44. That is, that Wise, although a Zionist and on the President's Committee, did not represent all Zionists.

45. Fitch to Taylor, June 5, 1939, McDonald Papers, Columbia University, D367 (PACPR), P61.

46. Warren to Taylor, June 6, 1939, NA RG 59, Lot File 52D408, Alphabetical Subject File, Box 9, President's Advisory Committee, 1939.

47. Stewart, *United States Government Policy*, 462–463.

in British Guiana, a commission having recommended an experiment of three thousand to five thousand people supported privately for two years. Emerson also suggested that given the level of private support for maintaining and settling refugees since 1933, it was time to add new sources of funds. He then summarized the proposed organization of the Coordinating Foundation.

Representing Britain, Lord Winterton stated that his government was now considering an offer of financial support to the Coordinating Foundation, possibly proportionate to the amount raised privately. Emerson had raised this idea a month earlier and persuaded the British government to support at the July meeting. The proposal raised numerous difficulties—in fact, Robert Pell believed that this suggestion was an effort to sabotage the Coordinating Foundation, letting refugee matters revert to the League High Commission.[48] But it was roughly consistent with what President Roosevelt had discussed with McDonald and Warren shortly after Kristallnacht. (Pell was not aware of the president's willingness to go to Congress for funds under the right circumstances.)[49]

Winterton encouraged the representatives of other governments to solicit the views of their own officials. Myron Taylor followed immediately:

Under the American Constitution any contribution of funds by the American Government would necessarily be subject to the decision of our Congress. Moreover, I am certain that if such a proposal were to be considered favourably by public opinion in the United States and by Congress it would have to apply to a project of such a nature and extent that, instead of being a palliative, it would be considered as initiating a basic solution of the problem.[50]

At a dinner discussion on July 19 Emerson briefed Wohlthat and German Embassy officials in London on the day's proceedings. Emerson complained that Germany's forced emigration had grown faster than the capacity of private organizations to absorb refugees. As Myron Taylor summarized his remarks,

Emerson was most emphatic that, while the mere proposal by the British Government of governmental participation in financing was a substantial step, realization of such participation was dependent upon favorable action by various Parliaments and that there was perhaps one chance in ten that substantial governmental aid would materialize.

Wohlthat seemed definitely impressed and said that he would do his utmost to accelerate action with regard to the internal trust [composed of assets of German Jews]. Emerson emphasized that it would be the greatest possible

48. Stewart, *United States Government Policy*, 458.
49. See chapter 7, p. 152.
50. Inter-Governmental Committee to continue and develop the work of the Evian Meeting, London, 1938: Stenographic Notes of the Seventh and Eight Meetings of the Committee, held in the Locarno Room at the Foreign Office on the 19th and 20th July 1939. Copy in NA RG 59, Lot File 52D408, Alphabetical Subject File, Box 7, July Meeting London 1939.

mistake for the Germans to delay setting up the trust while waiting for governmental arrangements for financing. He stated that, while the chances of such aid were admittedly slight, the prompt establishment of the trust in Germany would tend to create an atmosphere more conducive to its materialization while failure to set it up would be fatal.

. . . .

Late this afternoon Abshagen telephoned an authorized message from Wohlthat that in view of the conversation which had taken place last night he was confident that the internal trust would be set up in the immediate future.[51]

Germany, however, failed to set up the trust for Jewish property: it was busy instead preparing to attack Poland. The Nazi-Soviet Pact, announced to the world on August 23, was additional diplomatic preparation for war. That same day McDonald met with Undersecretary Welles to discuss the president's call to the Intergovernmental Committee on Refugees to meet in Washington. McDonald summarized their conversation.

Mr. Welles was cordial as usual and his manner betrayed nothing of the anxieties which the European situation has brought upon him. Nonetheless his eyes told the story of deep concern lest the next few hours precipitate what he later referred to as the "dash off the precipice" which might engulf us all.

At the very beginning, I told him that in the midst of the crisis I wished to save his time as much as possible, and therefore suggested that he tell me in just a few minutes what the President had in mind when he issued the invitation for the October meeting. This he did in his usual succinct and perfectly organized manner.

The President, impressed by what he had come to believe was the increasing defeatism of all of the other countries on the Intergovernmental Committee, and convinced that a new initiative had to be undertaken, chose to invite the officers of the Committee to meet in Washington. He assumed that the following ends might be served by such a conference: (1) dramatization of the needs of the refugees and the urgency of a comprehensive settlement; (2) creation of an opportunity for a fuller study of (a) places of settlement; (b) methods of intergovernmental cooperation; (c) possibilities of governmental financing.

The Undersecretary gave me no indication that the President had any more definite program in mind than this.

I pointed out to Mr. Welles that unless the United States were prepared to throw something substantial into the common pot, the chances for the success

51. Kennedy to Secretary of State, from Myron Taylor, July 20, 1939, NA RG 59, 840.48 Refugees/1799.

of the Conference were slight, and that the final result might be worse than if the Conference had not been held. He agreed unequivocally.

I underlined the opportunity and the necessity which the British financial offer created of matching that proposal. Mr. Welles then spoke of what the President had said to some of us about six months ago, to the effect that he was prepared to consider a request to Congress for a substantial appropriation under certain circumstances.[52] The Undersecretary said that of course since then Congressional willingness to follow the President's lead in appropriation matters had noticeably diminished, and that Mr. Roosevelt would not be likely to ask for an appropriation unless he were convinced that he had at least an even chance of securing Congressional approval. Mr. Welles agreed that it would be desirable to canvas the possibilities of money or surplus commodities through the R. F. C.[53] or the Export-Import Bank. Pell is to do this.

In connection with our talk about projects and settlement areas, Mr. Welles indicated that he still hoped that something new might be developed, adding that he personally considered Angola more promising than anything that had been formerly suggested.[54]

I inquired whether it might not be desirable for the President to consider taking into his confidence a group of representative men of both parties from the Hill, well in advance of the Conference. Mr. Welles thought this might be a good idea.

The Undersecretary said that he knew the President would be anxious to talk to me about the program of the Conference just as soon as he had gotten out from under his immediate critical responsibilities. It was clear, however, from the Undersecretary's attitude that should worse come to worse in Europe, all consideration of intergovernmental activity on behalf of German refugees would be abandoned.[55]

George Warren wrote Myron Taylor two days later, sending a copy of McDonald's account of his meeting with Welles and adding details about efforts to move the State Department toward a more positive stance:

Mr. McDonald telephoned Mr. [Lewis] Strauss in Virginia while in Washington and they agreed that such a memorandum [from the President's Advisory Committee to the State Department] should not be presented now

---

52. See italicized insert into the minutes of the November 21, 1938, meeting of the President's Advisory Committee (chapter 7, p. 152).

53. Reconstruction Finance Corporation. Independent government agency established by Herbert Hoover in 1932. It gave aid in the form of loans to state and local governments, banks, railroads, and business. Adopted by the New Deal, it existed in some form until 1948.

54. Welles was following the president here. See FDR's conversation with Secretary Morgenthau on November 16, 1938, reproduced in chapter 7, pp. 148-149.

55. Warren to Taylor, August 25, 1939, and McDonald memo of conversation with Welles, August 23, 1939, FDRL, Myron Taylor Papers, Box 8, President's Advisory Committee, July–December 1939–1942.

Plate 1. At the Phoenix Club, Baltimore, March 30, 1936, *left to right*: Eli Strouse, clothing manufacturer; James G. McDonald; Sidney Landsburgh; and Maryland Governor Harry W. Nice. USHMM/McDonald Family.

Plate 19. Rabbi Aaron Kotler, eminent Talmudist, was rescued with the help of McDonald's President's Advisory Committee.
Orthodox Jewish Archives, Agudath Israel of America.

but soon after Labor Day, assuming that the international situation has calmed down. Mr. McDonald's original wording of paragraph IV of the memorandum to be submitted to the Department was as follows:

IV. For the United States to insist upon a comprehensive large-scale program as a sine qua non of government financial aid would be to postpone such assistance, perhaps indefinitely. Repeated canvasses of the possibilities of mass settlement have been made during recent years, and intensively during the last year, under the direction of the President's Advisory Committee on Political Refugees. In the light of those studies, there is slight likelihood of new areas being opened up besides those now envisaged—British Guiana, Santo Domingo, the Philippines and Northern Rhodesia—unless Alaska can be made available through being placed on an ex-quota basis.

The reference to Alaska was timely. In August 1939 two officials in the Interior Department, Felix Cohen and Nathan Margold, had written up a detailed proposal for a privately funded development enterprise that would employ substantial numbers of refugees, along with American citizens, in Alaska. Undersecretary of the Interior Harry Slattery signed off on it (Interior officials dealing with Alaska would not do so), and it became known as the Slattery report. A copy was sent to the President's Advisory Committee on August 28,[56] but it appears that McDonald had earlier access to it.

The basic idea resembled the Refugee Economic Corporation and the immigration financing concept McDonald had promoted since 1934, and he was undoubtedly familiar with this Alaskan initiative. It had the enthusiastic support of Secretary of the Interior Harold Ickes—and the hostility of Ickes's political enemy, newly appointed Alaskan governor Ernest Gruening.

At the time the Slattery report was released, the American immigration quota for Germany was fully used. Any refugees admitted to Alaska, therefore, would have been barred from entering the United States proper unless they went through the usual procedure for applying for a temporary visa. The notion of introducing restrictions on travel would have made refugee settlers into second-class residents and increased the political obstacles to acceptance of the plan. But the main roadblocks seemed to be the opposition of many Alaskans to an influx of Jews and Gruening's negative stance.[57]

On September 1, using a staged incident on the German-Polish border as a pretext, Germany invaded Poland. Two days later Britain and France declared war on Germany—although they did little to help Poland withstand the German onslaught. On September 17 the Soviet Union invaded Poland from the east. The fighting quickly created desperate conditions for millions of civilians.

---

56. Morris to George Warren, August 28, 1939, NA RG 59, Lot File 52D408, Alphabetical Subject File, Box 9, President's Advisory Committee 1939.

57. Feingold, *Politics of Rescue*, 94–95. Tom Kizzia, "Sanctuary: Alaska, the Nazis, and the Jews: The forgotten story of Alaska's own confrontation with the Holocaust," May 16–19, 1999 (four-part series), *Anchorage Daily News*.

World War II began with the United States remaining neutral—and with continuing diplomatic and media presence in Germany. A solid majority in Congress was opposed to American entrance into the war or to measures that might easily draw it in. But there were fears that the United States would have no choice—and that Germany was already thinking of how to stretch its reach across the Atlantic.

On September 9 Secretary of the Interior Harold Ickes wrote in his diary:

The President related to us that someone who knew Goebbels well had talked with him recently and had just brought back word to the President of what was running in Goebbels' mind. That gentleman believes that Germany will overcome Poland within a very few days and will then quickly smash both France and England, largely from the air. His interlocutor asked him: "What next?" Goebbels is said to have replied: "You know what is next, the United States." He was told that he could hardly expect to conquer the United States from a distance of thirty-five hundred miles of ocean. Goebbels' reply was: "It will come from the inside."[58]

On September 19 William Bullitt, American ambassador to France, sent a telegram marked secret and personal for the president, concerning detailed information about Hitler's intentions. Otto von Habsburg had received the information from a confidant in Vienna, who had heard it on March 12 from Hitler's economic adviser Wilhelm Keppler and German business executive Albert Vögler:

On Wednesday March 8th a conference was held at the Fuehrer's which was attended by personalities from the army, economic circles and the party. 'Austria' was represented by Gauleiter Buerkel in addition to those mentioned above. . . .

Then the Fuehrer spoke. First he declared that the four year plan was a last resort. The real problem for the German people was to assure for itself the sources from which could be obtained the raw materials necessary for its well-being. In addition[,] in order to enjoy this well-being enemies of the German people must be exterminated radically: Jews, democracies and the 'international powers.' As long as those enemies had the least vestige of power left anywhere in the world they would be a menace to the peace of the German people.

. . . .

Orders have been issued to the effect that in a few days [and] not later than the 15th of March Czechoslovakia is to be occupied militarily.

Poland will follow. We will not have to count on a strong resistance from that quarter. German domination over Poland is necessary in order to assure for Germany Polish supplies of agricultural products and coal.

58. *The Secret Diary of Harold L. Ickes,* II, 720.

As far as Hungary and Rumania are concerned[,] they belong without question to Germany's vital space. . . . The same may be said for Yugoslavia.

This is the plan which will be realized until 1940. Even then Germany will be unbeatable.

In 1940 and 1941 Germany will settle accounts once and for all with her hereditary enemy: France. That country will be obliterated from the map of Europe. England is an old and feeble country weakened by democracy. With France vanquished Germany will dominate England easily and will then have at its disposition England's riches and domains throughout the world.

Thus having for the first time unified the continent of Europe according to a new conception[,] Germany will undertake the greatest operation in all history: with British and French possessions in America as a base we will settle accounts with the 'Jews of the dollar' (dollar Juden) in the United States. We will exterminate this Jewish democracy and Jewish blood will mix itself with the dollars. Even today Americans can insult our people, but the day will come when, too late, they will bitterly regret every word they said against us.[59]

Millions of people besides Jews were now threatened by Nazi Germany, and many of them were desperate to find havens. In early 1940 McDonald wrote:

During the year 1939, parts of Europe were overrun by over a million refugees: about 500,000 from Spain poured into France; over 100,000 from Poland crossed into Rumania, Hungary, and the Baltic countries; of the 400,000 that had fled from Greater Germany by October, 1939, about 140,000 remained dispersed in Europe under the necessity of re-emigrating . . . and just as the year closed, about 400,000 Finns, mostly women and children, crossed into Norway and Sweden.[60]

There was no longer any talk of Germany's establishment of a trust for Jewish property or of German cooperation with the Intergovernmental Committee. McDonald, who had long seen war on the horizon, must have felt that the best chance to resettle large numbers of Jews and others victims of persecution had been lost. What was left was the chance to rescue smaller numbers.

59. Bullitt to Secretary of State, September 19, 1939, NA RG 59, 740.00/2138 Confidential File. After a meeting with Otto von Habsburg, Harold Ickes later wrote:

> Otto verified a story that Bullitt had told Jane and me when he was at our home on his last trip to the United States. Hitler had disclosed to a very confidential group, which included two Austrian-Germans, one of whom is in the confidence of Otto, that his ultimate objective is the United States, after he has conquered Europe.

The Secret Diary of Harold L. Ickes, vol. III, *The Lowering Clouds, 1939–1941* (New York: Simon and Schuster, 1954), 149.

60. "Refugees," manuscript submitted to the *New International Year Book,* January 19, 1940, McDonald Papers, Columbia University, D355, MS17 (1940).

Differences of opinion within the President's Advisory Committee emerged about a strategy for moving forward, as revealed at the committee's meeting on September 14. Pell wrote:

The "professionals" such as Mr. James G. McDonald and Mr. George Warren, the Secretary, wish to continue to develop the settlement projects such as British Guiana and the Dominican Republic and produced considerable evidence to justify the continuation.

The moderate Jewish leaders such as Mr. Baerwald and Mr. Lewis Straus[s] felt that in view of the outbreak of war settlement projects should be held in abeyance. Mr. Straus[s] contended for this group that one of three things would happen: (a) Germany would win the war; (b) there would be a draw; (c) the Allies would win the war. He said that in the event of the realization of (a) or (b) the refugee problem would assume such enormous proportions that a fresh approach would have to be made. In the event of (c) there would be no refugee problem and in fact the majority of Jews now located in other countries would wish to return to Germany. He said that this was no time in which to make or continue with settlement plans. He approved of the White House meeting as marking the continuity of the work and demonstrating to the Germans and also to the refugees that it had not been abandoned. He did not believe, however, that it should attempt to formulate programs and particularly should not go into the matter of settlement.

The Zionists constituted the third group and their spokesman was Rabbi Wise. The Rabbi made a long speech to the effect that many thousands of Jews interested in Palestine would be resentful if the President did not take this opportunity to raise the Palestine issue with the member of the British Government, Lord Winterton, who was most notoriously anti-Jewish, pro-Arab and anti-Zionist. He said that the President had indicated more than once that he was sympathetic with the work in Palestine[,] and if he passed up this opportunity to speak directly on the subject to a member of the British Government[,] there might be the most unhappy repercussions. Rabbi Wise differed radically with Mr. Straus[s] and said that the Jews would not wish to return to Germany even in the event of a defeat of that Power. The majority of them would wish to go to Palestine[,] and the others would for the time being remain where they have established themselves. Rabbi Wise remarked that it was futile to talk about settlement projects such as Guiana and the Dominican Republic when Palestine, under the arrangement with the British, could absorb 75,000 people in five years in a developed country at very little cost.

There was no agreement between the three groups, and they have decided to set up a subcommittee which will try to iron out the difference.

Everyone agreed, however, that if settlement projects were to continue[,] there would have to be some degree of governmental financing. In other words the challenge of the British proposals at the July meeting of the Intergovernmental Committee would have to be met. It was felt that a recommendation to this effect should be made to the President and the Department of State and that the Government should begin immediately to study ways and means of making contribution in this sense.[61]

In spite of a multitude of difficulties the White House wanted to carry on with the planned October meeting of the officers of the Intergovernmental Committee on Refugees in Washington. On September 19 Pell wrote about a telephone call he had just received from McDonald:

He said that a meeting had been held of the active group on the President's Committee, consisting of Messrs. Straus[s], Baerwald, Wise, Armstrong, Warren and himself, to consider the present situation of the refugee work in the light of the little that is known of the actual situation. Mr. McDonald said that it was the consensus of this group that the meeting called by the President for October 16 and 17 at the White House should be cancelled. The three main reasons . . . are: (1) If the meeting were to take place in the midst of the neutrality debate[62] and it was known that the President was closeted with representatives of the belligerents, including Lord Winterton, a member of the British Government, a ready handle would be given to the President's opponents to say that he was unneutral and this might affect the debate in Congress.

(2) It was the conclusion of those who participated in the meeting that the chances of doing anything at this time are to say the least slight. It is fairly obvious that the American Government is not preparing to meet the British challenge on governmental financing and the American private groups in this country, who were short of money already, have now so much war work to which they wish to subscribe that they do not see how they can raise funds requisite to develop settlement projects.

(3) Despite the efforts of all interested persons to describe this movement as a refugee movement[,] it is clear that it is primarily a movement on behalf of Jews and it is usually identified in the public mind with the relief and rescue of Jews. The Jewish leaders feel that it would be misunderstood if a matter which is primarily a Jewish matter should be picked out for special attention during a war crisis. It is felt that this might have a boomerang effect on the Jewish community and should be avoided.

Mr. McDonald asked me to convey these decisions to the Secretary of State and to ask him to repeat them to the President.[63]

61. Pell Memo to Moffat, undated, NA RG 59, Lot File 52D408, Alphabetical Subject File, Box 9, President's Advisory Committee 1939.

62. Neutrality Acts passed in 1935 and 1936 prohibited the United States from selling war materiel to belligerents. Exports to belligerents had to be paid for in cash and carried away by their ships. These laws were part of congressional efforts to minimize U.S. involvement in European conflicts and prevent the United States from being drawn in. Over time President Roosevelt became increasingly unhappy with these restrictions and sought to loosen them.

63. Pell Memorandum of Conversation, September 19, 1939, NA RG 59, Lot File 52D408, Alphabetical Subject File, Box 14, Warren Memoranda.

The next day Pell added:

Mr. Baerwald lunched with me today. He confirmed the impression which Mr. McDonald gave me over the telephone last night, namely, that the inner group at least of the [President's] Advisory Committee is now opposed to the holding of the refugee meeting at the White House in October. Mr. Baerwald, however, was not quite as sweeping as Mr. McDonald[,] who had said that the meeting should be "called off." Mr. Baerwald believed that the meeting should merely be postponed until the debate in Congress was safely out of the way. He believed that there was some advantage in holding the meeting. At least it would emphasize the fact that the work was continuing and that it still had the good will of the President and Government of the United States and other Governments.

I asked Mr. Baerwald if his objection was to the holding of the meeting or to the holding of the meeting at the White House. He said it was the latter. He said the Jewish leaders were very grateful to the President and did not wish to do anything which would cause him embarrassment.

. . . .

He did not like to discourage an initiative taken by the President, but at the same time he had a duty to warn the President if he felt that he was taking some measure which might prove to be imprudent. He said he would give further thought to the whole situation and [would] certainly not encourage McDonald, who was in a bad huff anyway because he had not been consulted about the White House meeting, to take any rash action. Mr. Baerwald said that in general it was most unfortunate that the President had not consulted more often in the past year with the Advisory Committee[,] which could have been extremely helpful to him. As it is, he has offended some of the members who have come to feel that their names were being used but not their services.[64]

The President's Advisory Committee decided to compromise on the issue of the October meeting: it recommended against holding the meeting, but said that if the president decided to go ahead with it, the committee would support him. Pell recommended to Secretary of State Hull to proceed with it.[65]

On September 5 McDonald had written to Norman Bentwich in London to ask his view about what might be accomplished in the near future. On September 21 Bentwich responded that the new director of the Intergovernmental Committee on Refugees, Sir Herbert Emerson, was planning to go to Washington for the October meeting at the White House. He added:

64. Pell memo regarding proposed cancellation of October meeting of the Intergovernmental Committee on Political Refugees, undated, NA RG 59, Lot File 52D408, Alphabetical Subject File, Box 5, Jewish Joint Distribution Committee.

65. Pell to Secretary of State, September 25, 1939, NA RG 59, Lot File 52D408, Alphabetical Subject File, Box 9, President's Advisory Committee 1939.

I should hope that the Conference will try and push forward to execution one or two of the colonization projects. That must depend on the willingness of the American Government and the American Jewish and Christian public to make a substantial contribution. I fear there is no hope that the British Government or the Jewish or general community in England will be able to help substantially during the war in that part of the problem.

So far as British Guiana is concerned, the plans which had been worked out so carefully may have to be suspended. There are two difficulties at this end: (1) whether, during the war, the Government will allow those who are technically enemy aliens to emigrate to British colonies and (2) whether any money can be obtained from the organizations in England for settlement, if it were allowed. But I cling to the hope that the New World will redress the bankruptcy of the Old.

. . . .

The main effort during the next period should be to increase the possibilities of emigration to the American continent, and particularly, of course, to the U.S.A., if there is any chance of getting some relaxation of the quota rules. If we cannot save more from Germany and Austria, it may be possible to press on with the settlement of the large numbers who are waiting in the European countries of refuge for their emigration. The American Jewish and Christian communities will have also to bear the greater part of the burden of those groups of refugees who have to be maintained in Europe. It is pretty clear that it will be impossible to raise in England and in the other countries sums for the help of refugees, approaching those which have been available during the last years.

As regards the new mass of Jewish misery which has been created in the war zones, particularly in Poland, it is just impossible to see, anyhow, so far as we are concerned in England, how anything can be done. America again is the only hope. For the moment . . . one should endeavour to facilitate movement from the existing reservoirs in the Western European countries and from places like Shanghai, where there are large pockets of destitute refugees. And for the larger problem there should be planning of the big systematic effort that must be made when the war is over.

I would only add that we have hopes that emigration to Palestine of those who had certificates before the outbreak of the war will be possible, and that the [British] Government during the next period may allow a modest emigration to go on of those who have escaped from the enemy countries.[66]

McDonald was able to secure a meeting at the White House with President Roosevelt on September 26. He gave FDR a memorandum apparently incorporating his

66. Bentwich to McDonald, September 21, 1939. Copy in NA RG 59, Lot File 52D408, Alphabetical Subject File, Box 6, Jewish Refugees.

ideas that it was better to move ahead with settlements in those areas already identi-
fied than to do nothing, and government financing was needed.[67] *To allay opponents*
in the President's Advisory Committee, the president invited McDonald to sit in on
the Intergovernmental Committee meeting.[68]

McDonald also conferred privately with Eleanor Roosevelt on a suggestion he
did not put on paper.[69] *Two days later George Warren summarized the situation for*
Columbia University professor Joseph Chamberlain.

There is much to tell you as a result of our visit in Washington Tuesday. Briefly for the moment, the British have indicated that they will not make a proposal of public funds for settlement at the Washington conference and, further, that emigrants of German citizenship will not be admitted to British colonies for political and financial reasons during the war. This cancels the British Guiana project. Otherwise they see the problem very much as we outlined it at the meeting at Mr. Taylor's office. Lord Winterton, Sir Herbert Emerson and Mr. Van Zeeland[70] will attend the Washington conference. The British point out also that the concern of the Intergovernmental Committee for refugees within Germany is now inconsistent with the major policies of five member governments at war. This attitude, however, does not necessarily condition the action of any individual member government, but it may operate to exclude from the concern of the Intergovernmental Committee during the war the refugees still within Germany. Until some response is received to the memorandum left at the White House we must proceed on the assumption that the conference will be held.[71]

On October 4 McDonald delivered a speech at the Midday Club in New York City.
In the course of it he reviewed his past impressions of Nazi Germany. The speech came
after Germany and the Soviet Union had overrun all Poland—the Polish government
reconstituting itself in London—and just before all fighting in Poland ended.

I am not going to tell you that I was a prophet; I wasn't. I was merely a pessimist. It seemed to me, from the very beginning of Hitler's rise to power, however, that sooner or later a clash was inevitable. I had not then read

67. A copy of this memorandum has not been found.
68. Stewart, *United States Government Policy*, 491.
69. McDonald to Ittleson, September 27, 1939, McDonald Papers, Columbia University, D367 (PACPR), P24. It may be that McDonald was lobbying for administration endorsement of the Slattery Report—introducing refugees into Alaska above and beyond the quota. Eleanor Roosevelt responded on October 12 that she had spoken with the president about the suggestion, but he said that until revision of the neutrality legislation was settled, he could not do anything else. McDonald Papers, Columbia University, D361 (Eleanor Roosevelt file).
70. Paul van Zeeland, former premier of Belgium. A Catholic, van Zeeland had been named president of the Coordinating Foundation.
71. Warren to Chamberlain, September 28, 1939, YIVO Institute for Jewish Research, RG 278, Joseph Chamberlain Papers, Folder 68.

Rauschning's book,[72] but I sensed something of the things which Rauschning develops so fully in this volume—the dynamic, revolutionary, driving force of this new regime.

I first came into contact with it in the fall of 1932, before Hitler was in power. Then I heard Hitler speak in September 1932, saw his regime at close range in April 1933, the fall of 1933, and repeatedly during 1934 and 1935. I never could understand, during those days, why everybody didn't feel this dynamic force at work within the Reich; hence it didn't seem to me that it required any particular intelligence to conclude that at some point this expanding power would come into conflict with the nations of Western Europe, that at some point Britain and France would have to fight.

A year ago last fall came Munich. Nearly all of my leftist friends could not find words adequate to denounce Chamberlain and Daladier, and yet I think that those men in that period were truly representative of British and French public opinion. The French and British people had not yet been convinced that Czechoslovakia was a vital frontier for France and Britain: so the main result of Munich, to my mind, was not the gain which Hitler made when he incorporated the Sudetenland and made ready to absorb Bohemia and Moravia and to enslave Slovakia. It was rather that Chamberlain and[,] with Chamberlain the British governing class[,] and Daladier[,] and with him the French governing class[,] at last became convinced that Hitler was a menace not merely to his Eastern neighbors but to Britain and to France.

. . . Chamberlain completed his education at Munich. Fortunately for France and Britain[,] I think[,] they did not accept the German challenge a year ago because it seems to me, on balance, they are better prepared to meet that challenge today. . . . Poland could not be turned over to Germany without inflicting a serious blow on France and Britain itself. Hence the alliance with Poland was not so much to defend Poland as it was to defend France and Britain.[73]

Except for the oblique comment about his leftist friends, McDonald did not express his own view of the best course for the United States to take toward the war, but it was likely the dominant view. Although an overwhelming majority of Americans blamed Germany for the war and wanted Britain and France to win, the same majority also wanted to stay out.

Beyond that feeling, there was vehement disagreement. The Roosevelt administration and the liberal-internationalist groups wanted to assist Britain and France, initially through revising U.S. neutrality legislation barring those involved in war

72. Hermann Rauschning, *The Revolution of Nihilism: Warning to the West* (New York: Alliance Book Corporation, 1939). A former Nazi who had headed the Danzig Senate, Rauschning became a conservative opponent of Nazism in 1935. He argued that the Nazi revolt did not represent nationalism, but rather a form of revolutionary extremism.

73. Copy in McDonald Papers, Columbia University, D355, MS16 (1939). This was a sophisticated, even astute analysis that stands up well in light of subsequent scholarly studies.

from buying American armaments. Led by the America First Committee, isolation-
ists saw such change as leading inevitably to entrance into the war, which, in their
view, was not in America's interest. After a tough battle, in early November Congress
passed a bill to allow "cash and carry" purchases of arms.[74]

The war had not yet deflated all hopes of resettlement, nor had Germany prohib-
ited Jews from leaving the country—though in practice, it became much more diffi-
cult. On October 9 George Warren, on the basis of information received from the JDC
in Europe, told Robert Pell that it was urgent to remove Jews from countries of refuge
in Europe. The following day Warren added:

Mr. Baerwald had had a long telephone conversation with Mr. [Morris]
Troper in Paris. Troper had said that the situation of the refugees in Europe
was chaotic. The British and French had backed out of the picture completely
so far as finances were concerned. Regulations were piling up against the refugees and their life was becoming harder day by day.

Troper reported that van Zeeland was coming to the meeting with gran-
diose ideas for great undertakings, naturally at the expense of American
contributors.

Mr. Baerwald and Mr. Straus[s] felt that it was essential to deflate van
Zeeland before he reached Washington. They would meet him at the dock and
attempt to impress upon him the realities of the financial situation here.

Mr. Warren said that a friendly battle had broken out between Mr. Taylor
and Mr. McDonald as to who should make the statement to the meeting with
regard to the Dominican project. Mr. Warren said that as an impartial observer[,] he felt that Mr. McDonald should make the statement since the
Commission of Inquiry was sent to the Dominican Republic under the aegis of
the President's Advisory Committee and at the expense of the members of the
committee. Mr. Taylor had had no connection with it whatsoever and when
called upon last week would not even write a categorical letter favoring it. Mr.
Warren thought that it was most unjust on Mr. Taylor's part to insist on making this announcement.[75]

The officers of the Intergovernmental Committee—Lord Winterton (chairman),
Sir Herbert Emerson (director), Myron Taylor (vice president and American repre-
sentative), and McDonald—joined diplomats from Argentina, Brazil, France, and
the Netherlands at the White House on October 17. The first day was largely given
over to speeches. President Roosevelt delivered an address in which he claimed that
things had been going well, if slowly, until war broke out. He then called to redirect
immediate attention to those in countries of refugee who were in need of permanent
homes. This short-range program, he said, involved perhaps two or three hundred

74. Gerhard L. Weinberg, *A World at Arms: A Global History of World War II* (New York:
Cambridge, 1994), 84–86.
75. Pell Memoranda of Conversations, October 9 and 10, 1939, NA RG 59, Lot File
52D408, Alphabetical Subject File, Box 14, Warren Memoranda.

thousand people. The long-range need was to plan for the future, at the end of the war, when perhaps ten or twenty million people would need resettlement. The president pointed to sparsely settled areas of the world, many of which would need substantial economic and engineering studies before settlements could be established.[76] *He wanted the planning to begin during the war.*

A second session that afternoon, which some State Department officials attended, considered how the war had changed the refugee problem. Even before then the British representatives had convinced Myron Taylor that an Allied victory would mean that refugees could return to Germany—to plan for large-scale resettlement after the war was contrary to Allied war aims.[77] *Taylor's defection turned out to be temporary, but it left McDonald isolated at this meeting. The third session the next day concentrated on possibilities of moving refugees from countries of refuge to those places of settlement which had opened up so far (the Dominican Republic and the Philippines). The fate of Jews still in Germany was essentially left out of consideration.*

A few days later Secretary of the Interior Harold Ickes wrote in his diary:

At my last conference with the President we discussed the possible further development of Alaska, in which he has always been very much interested. He had seen and read the report of the Department on the subject [the Slattery Report] which grew out of the idea of taking care of a certain number of refugees despite our quota laws.

The President's idea is that we ought to try to take care of ten thousand settlers a year in Alaska for the next five years, although he said that this number was only a guess and that we might not be able to do as well as that. Of this ten thousand he would have five thousand from the United States, and those from foreign lands would be admitted in the same ration in which they can come into this country, based upon the quota law. He estimated that, on this basis, not more than ten per cent would be Jews, and thus we would be able to avoid the undoubted criticism that we would be subjected to if there were an undue proportion of Jews. Another, and a particularly valid, reason for following the quota ration would be that a preponderating number of settlers would not come from one foreign country, thus avoiding the danger of setting up in Alaska nationalistic groups that, through adherence to their own language and customs, might resist the process of Americanization.

Once again I was astonished at the thought that the President had given to a comparatively minor problem, from his point of view, and his cleverness in working it out. Of course we are a long way from getting this whole matter started, but before I left Washington I was gratified to learn of one local promi-

76. Press release, October 17, 1939. Copy Harry Hopkins Papers, Box 118, Refugee Problems, FDRL.

77. Moffat Journal, October 23, 1939, Moffat Papers, vol. 43, Houghton Library, Harvard, and Berle Memorandum for the President, October 23, 1939, FDRL, PSF Diplomatic, Box 64, Palestine folder. Berle wrote to FDR, "We are somewhat embarrassed by the fact that Taylor committed himself to the British and French thesis before the meeting. If the British and French want to kill the idea, they ought to take the responsibility, without hooking you in on it."

nent Jew who wants to talk to me about financing or helping to finance one group in Alaska. I also had a letter from Bayard Swope[78] expressing great interest in this plan and volunteering to help.[79]

If McDonald was shifting his attention more and more toward short-term possibilities, others held onto hopes for larger solutions. Paul van Zeeland expressed the goal of raising twenty million dollars "immediately" from a limited group of interested persons, supplemented by another eighty million to be raised from the general public as a loan. Governments would have to guarantee repayment of this loan, which would eventually be repaid from the proceeds of enterprises established by refugees. Van Zeeland recommended a central holding company to finance individual settlement corporations, some of which would be agricultural and some industrial or commercial.[80] In a detailed memorandum to Undersecretary of State Welles, President Roosevelt commented:

Mr. van Zeeland's plan is on the whole good but I think misses the <u>psychology</u> which is necessary to success. . . .

In other words the outline does not stimulate my imagination or that of the average individual in the civilized world to picture the huge rounded out project which could affect many millions of our fellow beings. Most people would regard it as a large series of small individual projects and would mentally miss out on the conception of the whole. For example, nothing is said about the possibility of one or two very large areas which would take hundreds of thousands of people through a course of years and develop a wholly new rounded civilization.

. . . .

Somebody has to breathe heart and ideals on a large scale into this whole subject if it is to be put into effect on a world-wide basis.[81]

Roosevelt's long-term vision assumed that there would be millions of non-Jews as well as Jews eager to leave places where they had suffered for new opportunities. Their diversity might reduce some of the political barriers in places of settlement. Arthur Krock, columnist for the New York Times, *praised it for this reason.[82]*

Concentration on what could be done in the postwar period was too detached for McDonald. In a December 21, 1939, speech at New York's Town Hall that was

78. Herbert Bayard Swope, editor and journalist, winner of the first Pulitzer Prize for journalism in 1917.

79. *The Secret Diary of Harold L. Ickes:* vol. III, 56–57.

80. Pell Memorandum of Conversation with van Zeeland, November 8, 1939, NA RG 59, Lot File 52D408, Alphabetical Subject File, Box 3, Coordinating Foundation.

81. FDR to Undersecretary of State, December 4, 1939, NA RG 59, Lot File 52D408, Alphabetical Subject File, Box 6, Jewish Refugees.

82. "The New 'Golden Doors' of Liberty and Refuge," *New York Times,* October 19, 1939, p. 22: Stewart, *United States Government Policy,* 492.

broadcast on radio (part of a symposium on what Americans could do for humanity),
McDonald tackled the myth that the country was being inundated by refugees. The
following summary appeared in the New York Times.

James G. McDonald, chairman of the President's Advisory Committee on
Political Refugees, said that Americans can do most for humanity by remaining true to their heritage—"hospitality for the victims of foreign oppression,
equality of opportunity at home, and aid in proportion to our means for the
needy of other lands."

. . . .

McDonald said the United States is the product of refugees and their de-
scendants, he denied this country was being flooded with German refugees.
He said that in seven years since Hitler came to power the number of German
refugees arriving here has averaged about 12,500 a year, while 4,000 Germans
a year have been returning to the Reich for permanent residence.

He said that total immigration of all nationalities into this country in the
last ten years has been less than in any other decade in the last 100 years, and in
the six-year period from July 1932 to June 1938 more aliens left this country for
permanent residence abroad than arrived for permanent residence here.[83]

McDonald's speech reflected his view that the United States could and should
do more for refugees., American action was all the more needed, because wartime
conditions and constraints had dashed virtually all short-term hopes for large re-
settlement projects in the Western Hemisphere, and for British-American govern-
ment financing.

McDonald's unhappiness with President Roosevelt was based on differences of
strategy and priorities. FDR was far more interested in refugees than most of the
State Department, but wanted to focus on big plans outside the United States—
whenever they could set in motion. McDonald doubted the utility of continuing to
work on such plans in the midst of war, and wanted to do something to save some
people before it was too late. The issue of whom the United States could afford to take
in during a time of war and concern about national security would consume much of
McDonald's time during the next two years.

---

83. "Roosevelt Aide Says Refugee Flood Is Myth," *New York Times*, December 22, 1939,
p. 10.

9. Refugees as Spies: 1940

On January 24, 1940, President Roosevelt told Secretary of the Treasury Henry Morgenthau, "I do not want to run [for president again] unless between now and the convention things get very, very much worse in Europe."[1] But he was certainly aware of the possibility that conditions would deteriorate and that he would run for an unprecedented third term. In late January he also noted the need to strengthen security measures in ways that affected immigrants and aliens.

For some time it has been becoming more clear that in view of extraordinary world conditions and dangers[,] the easy identification of persons who travel from one country to another is unfortunately more and more necessary. While this is true from the point of view of national defense and protection of our own citizens, it is at least equally necessary for the protection of law-abiding citizens against all forms of disaster, accident, mistaken identity, detention and the guarding of their civil liberties.

At the present time American citizens going to any part of Europe must be finger-printed in addition to being photographed. This is being done to prevent the obtaining of false passports and to protect Americans who may be killed, meet with accidents, or be arrested or detained in foreign countries. It is a wholly reasonable provision in view of these unusual conditions.

By the same token, it seems necessary that we should finger-print aliens coming to this country on quota visas in addition to having their photographs. It is entirely possible that although the overwhelming majority of quota immigrants come here with every honorable intent, it is also possible that[,] because of conditions in other nations[,] some of them may be criminals, some of them may be spies, and some of them may be coming here with the definite objective of commiting [*sic*] acts of sabotage, etc. Furthermore, some of these quota immigrants may be political refugees marked for destruction in this country by agents of the governments from which they are fleeing. These people deserve all possible American protection, and the first element of such protection is ready identification.

The Attorney General has rendered an opinion that it is wholly legal for the Commissioner of Immigration to require finger-printing of quota immigrants by Executive Order. Please have such an order issued, after consultation

---

1. Quoted by Ted Morgan, *FDR: A Biography* (New York: Simon and Schuster, 1985), 520.

with the Attorney General and the Secretary of State, and let me have a copy of
it when issued.

F. D. R.[2]

*In early February the President's Advisory Committee met with Visa Division
Chief Avra M. Warren. Their assumption was that, with fewer German Jews able to
get clearance and transportation to leave Germany for the United States, a greater portion of the immigration quota for Germany could be made available to German refugees who had gone to temporary havens elsewhere. In turn, that step might have
created room for new refugees in European countries and in the Western Hemisphere.
But Avra Warren apparently declined to transfer German quota numbers to other
locations. George Warren, executive secretary of the President's Advisory Committee,
wrote:*

Our conference with Mr. [Avra] Warren in Mr. Rosenwald's office a few
days ago did not materially change the situation as you already know it. The
pressure is still great for emigration from Germany and the gains which we
anticipated under the quota for those outside of Germany have not developed.
Our friends, therefore, in Havana will have to remain patient.[3]

A few weeks later George Warren added:

You know that Cuba has been virtually closed as a place of temporary asylum for some months. Miss Razovsky told me yesterday that there is a new
Immigration Commissioner and there are signs that the old practices are beginning again under the new administration.[4]

*In early March the State Department's Division of European Affairs recom-
mended American disengagement from the Intergovernmental Committee on Refugees, President Roosevelt responded with a memo to the secretary of state:*

2. Memorandum for the Secretary of Labor, January 27, 1940, FDRL, Official File 2030.
In July Congress passed and the president signed the Smith Act, requiring the registration and
fingerprinting of all aliens. It also imposed fines or prison sentences for speech or writing that
could subvert the armed forces.
3. "Our friends in Cuba" meant German Jews who had gone to Cuba on temporary visas
and were on the waiting list for American immigration visas. George Warren to Joseph Chamberlain, February 10, 1940, YIVO, RG 278, Joseph Chamberlain Papers, Folder 69.
4. Warren to Chamberlain, March 1, 1940, YIVO, RG 278, Chamberlain Papers, Folder
69. On July 3, in a memorandum for Secretary of State Hull, President Roosevelt wrote:

> I think you might consider the possibility of saying something at Havana in regard to
> the ancient principal [sic] of political asylum. I think the Latin American governments
> have long adhered to the principal. There will, undoubtedly, be many political refu-
> gees from many parts of Europe and it occurs to me that a kind word in behalf of these
> unfortunate people might be an act of humanity as well as being strictly correct under
> international law.

FDRL, Official File 3186, Box 3, Political Refugees, July–September 1940.

I do not agree with the memorandum from the Division of European Affairs. The American position from the very beginning has been far broader than a mere negotiation relating to German pressure on the Jews or the problem of political refugees. Nor can I agree with the statement that "When the war broke [out] the principal justification for the continued existence of this consultative body ceased." . . . The Division, I fear, . . . fails to appreciate the long-range view. . . . I am not yet ready to "put the Intergovernmental Committee quietly to sleep."[5]

On April 9 Germany invaded Denmark by land, sea, and air, and German troops began to land in Norway, which took a little longer to subdue. Neutrality protected neither country. The expansion of German control added to nervousness in the United States. Greenland was under Danish sovereignty, and Iceland also had a tie with the Danish crown. The United States took steps to make sure that neither island could be used by Germany.[6]

On May 8 Assistant Secretary of State Breckinridge Long wrote:

At the request of the President, Welles called a few of us this morning to consider ways and means of preventing the further inflow of German and Russian propagandists and agents and of attempting to attend to those who had filtered through. About 16,000 aliens have forfeited their bonds at the end of their period of temporary domicile. Amongst these are known to be a number of German agents. The Department of Labor is very non-cooperative. Our Department's Visa Section and Passport Division and the F.B.I. have been quite cooperative and active, but no help is received from Labor except through the Commissioner of Immigration, who happens to be under that Department and who is himself in sympathy with the movement now under contemplation. Avra Warren in charge of the Visa Section is very well versed in it, and he is preparing the letter directed to the President after the conference outlining the situation and proposing to him possible remedies. . . . To my mind it is certain that if we have any trouble with Germany[,] every Russian agent will become a German agent, and it is now time to begin the steps to offset the effects of our laxity.[7]

On May 10 Germany invaded neutral Belgium and the Netherlands and launched a major assault against France that broke through French lines and created panic. The German aim was to dominate France and use it as a base for an invasion of Britain.

5. FDR to Secretary of State, March 7, 1940, FDRL, President's Secretary's File, Diplomatic, Box 64, Palestine folder.

6. Weinberg, *A World at Arms,* 121.

7. Breckinridge Long Diary, May 8, 1940, LC, Container 5. There is a similar, follow-up entry on May 10 that again praised Warren as efficient and competent and raised the prospect of new legislation to stem the influx of "undesirable persons whose purpose is contrary to the best interests of the United States."

The second-most powerful nation on the continent suffered a military and politi-
cal collapse within five weeks. Between May 26 and June 4 about 340,000 surrounded
British and French troops were evacuated from Dunkirk across the English Channel.
On June 14 triumphant German troops entered Paris. A new authoritarian French
government quickly replaced the collapsed Third Republic and set up headquarters in
the resort town of Vichy (in the portion of France not occupied by the Germans).

Many contemporary observers believed that disloyal elements within France
sowed dissension and prepared the way for the German conquests. How else could one
explain such an ignominious collapse? (In retrospect, these claims have proved highly
exaggerated: France's defenses and military strategy were fatally flawed.)[8] American
officials did not want this supposed "Fifth Column" to inflict similar damage in the
United States or in the Western Hemisphere.

American Ambassador to Cuba George S. Messersmith, formerly assistant secre-
tary of state, was one of many at that time associating refugees with the "Fifth Col-
umn" threat.[9] He wrote:

It is a fact that some of the Germans and Italians who left their countries
in recent years because of persecution by their governments have, nevertheless,
become in our country strong defendants of their native governments and the
practices of their present governments. Among the so-called refugees in our
country is a fair number who can be depended upon to act as agents of their
government and who will violate in any way the hospitality which they are enjoying among us.

. . . .

Most of the aliens in the United States, irrespective of their origin, have
near relatives in their native countries. The German government, in particular,
and the Italian government, in a lesser degree, have been exercising direct pressure on their nationals in the United States, this extending even to those who
may have become naturalized American citizens. . . . Some of these nationals
do not need the pressure from European governments, as they are fanatics,
critical of the institutions of the country which has given them a refuge; and
there is no doubt that, under given circumstances, they would become willing
and dangerous elements, being so widely scattered over our country and employed in all kinds of key industries in all kinds of capacities.[10]

Two days earlier, on May 20, Tyler Kent, a code clerk in the American Embassy
in London, had been arrested by British authorities. Kent was of elite background—a

8. See a brief, cogent discussion in Weinberg, *A World at Arms*, 127–129.
9. For a general discussion, see Wyman, *Paper Walls*, 188–191.
10. Strictly Confidential Memo attached to Messersmith to Welles, May 22, 1940, Messersmith Papers, Item 1360, Delaware. See also Messersmith to Secretary of State, June 21, 1940,
"Confidential" Letter, Subject: "With reference to the alleged pro-German attitude on the part
of Jewish refugees in Habana awaiting an opportunity to proceed to the United States on immigration visas." NA RG 59, 150.626J/798. Copy in McDonald Papers, USHMM.

graduate of St. Albans School in Washington, D.C., and Princeton. He had copied hundreds of confidential Embassy documents and given them to a female friend, who passed them on to the Italian military attaché. Some of the documents concerned President Roosevelt's consideration of ways to evade the restrictions of the Neutrality Acts in order to assist Britain further. The Italians (and Soviets, who had penetrated the Italian ring) and the Germans all gained knowledge of American codes, as well as of American foreign policy. Kent said he was motivated by a desire to keep the United States out of the war; he was also an intense anti-Communist and anti-Semite. A right-wing British MP was also implicated in the affair. President Roosevelt ordered tighter FBI surveillance of isolationists as a direct result of this episode.[11]

At the end of May McDonald wrote to Norman Bentwich in London:

In these tragic days it may seem almost frivolous to write about the documentation of the High Commission. None the less, I felt that I ought to ask you whether you do not think it would be wise either to remove the files from Woburn House to some place in the country or to destroy them. I don't remember that they contain anything which might interest the enemy, but one can never tell. In any case, I hope you will feel free to do whatever you may think best with this material. . . .

To you in Britain it may seem that American public opinion is responding very slowly to the terrible developments of the last weeks. In one sense that is true. But viewed against the background of staunch American isolationism, the progress of American thinking and feeling about the war has been more rapid than any save very few of us anticipated. And you may be sure of this, the United States is becoming more and more aware that the British Fleet is an essential factor in the defense of the Americas.[12]

On June 3 Secretary of the Interior Harold Ickes wrote in his diary:

There was a good deal of talk [at a cabinet meeting a couple days earlier] about aliens and the fifth column. There is a bill pending in Congress now which would forbid the employment of any alien beyond ten per cent in any plant if naturalized or native-born citizens were available for the jobs. Some of our superpatriots are simply going crazy.

. . . .

To regard every alien as a possible enemy spy or saboteur is the height of asininity. [Yet] I believe that there should be a careful scrutiny of aliens.[13]

11. Weinberg, *A World at Arms*, 156–57, 977n145. For broader treatment, Ray Bearse and Anthony Read, *Conspirator: The Untold Story of Tyler Kent* (New York: Doubleday, 1991).

12. McDonald to Bentwich, May 31, 1940, McDonald Papers, Columbia University, D367 (PACPR), P5.

13. *Secret Diary of Harold L. Ickes*, III, 197.

According to one biographer, President Roosevelt received daily reports on Nazi and Communist subversion from the FBI. Even though some of them were "far-fetched," they influenced him.[14] On June 5 President Roosevelt received a question about refugees at a press conference:

Q: Mr. President, one of the main groups that suffers from or is in danger of suffering from the fifth column talk is the group of refugees in this country. I know in working with church groups who are trying to place refugees, that recently the groups that would naturally take and try to fit in refugees have been very much disturbed as to whether or not these refugees, driven out by injustice, were not likely to be fifth columnists. . . .

P: Well, we are trying to be just as fair on that proposition as we can. Luckily, the refugees have got interested in them a good many private organizations. Now, it is up to those private organizations to see to it that no discrimination is shown to the refugees. Now, of course, the refugee has got to be checked because, unfortunately, among the refugees there are some spies, as has been found in other countries. And not all of them are voluntary spies—it is rather a horrible story but in some of the other countries that refugees out of Germany have gone to, especially Jewish refugees, they have found a number of definitely proven spies. It sounds like a horrible thing, but in most cases, the reason for that is this, that the refugee has left Germany and has been told by the German government "You have got to conduct this particular spy work and if you don't make your reports regularly back to some definite agent in the country, you are going to—we are frightfully sorry, but your old father and mother will be taken out and shot." It has been spying under compulsion, and it is an amazing story that we have rather fully. Of course, it applies to a very, very small percentage of refugees coming out of Germany, but it does apply, and therefore, it is something that we have to watch. Isn't it rather a horrible thing?[15]

An immigration crackdown related to national security came from different sources and for different reasons. For example, German applicants for visas to the United States had to provide police certificates to verify they were not criminals in their homelands. This was particularly difficult for German Jews, some of whom were arrested on false pretenses, and others were unable to count on police cooperation even when they had unblemished records. Yet some American consuls feared the opposite situation—that German police were giving whitewashed certificates to those who were criminals in order to get rid of them. This fear supplied another reason to crack down on issuing immigration visas. An American consul in Berlin wrote to the State Department:

14. Morgan, *FDR*, 524.
15. *Complete Presidential Press Conferences of Franklin D. Roosevelt*, vol. 13–14, 495–96, June 5, 1940.

For the reason that it is almost certain that the German authorities are issuing clear police certificates to aliens who have been convicted of crimes or
misdemeanors, there is a very good chance that alien criminals are finding
their way into the United States from this country. Practically since the incep-
tion of the present hostilities, this office has been requiring applicants for passport visas, in nearly every case, to submit police certificates as well. It would
appear that the only effective measure which could remedy the present situation would be the refusal on the part of the Embassy and other visa issuing es-
tablishments within the Reich and the territory occupied by the forces of the
Reich, to issue immigration or passport visas to residents of Germany or the
other countries involved in the absence of a definite assurance by the competent
German authorities that henceforth great care would be taken in the preparation of police certificates of conduct.

. . . The reaction of the German police authorities might be the refusal to
issue police certificates at all. However, it would appear that the prevention of
the entry of criminals into the United States would outweigh other considerations and that the desire of the German Government to hasten the emigration
of Jews from Germany might result in cooperation in the premises.[16]

*In June 1940 the State Department sent a series of circulars to its consulates in
Europe, ordering a tightening of visa controls. Applicants had to show a legitimate
purpose for entering the United States; it was no longer enough to show that he or she
had a good reason for leaving Europe. Consuls had to establish that applicants were
not likely to engage in radical activities that might endanger public safety. In order to
"safeguard the best interests of the United States" consuls were not to grant visas unless
they had "no doubt whatsoever concerning the alien."*[17]

*On June 14 Assistant Secretary of State Breckinridge Long wrote to Ambassador
Messersmith:*

We are communicating with the Consuls to be stricter in their interpretations of the law, and we have clamped down in various ways. . . . All the gaps
are being stopped up. I have had a good deal to do with it, and it has taken a
considerable bit of time.[18]

*In mid-June the Soviet Union occupied Estonia, Latvia, and Lithuania, quickly
bringing them formally into the USSR as republics. These Baltic states had fallen into*

16. Hodgdon to Secretary of State, June 20, 1940, NA RG 59, 811.11 Germany/14. Copy
in McDonald Papers, USHMM.

17. State Department Circular Telegram to Consuls, June 5, 1940, Quoted by Pell to Secretary of State, September 6, 1940. NA RG 59, 811.111 Refugees. Copy in McDonald Papers,
USHMM. State Department Circulars to Consuls, June 5, 1940, June 29, 1940, described in
Letter from Ambassador Steinhardt to Secretary of State, October 2, 1940, Telegram, NA RG
59, 811.111 Refugees/397.

18. Long to Messersmith, June 14, 1940, Long Papers, General Correspondence, 1903–
1947: M-Q Miscellaneous, Container 133.

the Soviet sphere of influence under the August 1939 German–Soviet pact and subsequent modifications. This Soviet takeover seemed to be another piece of evidence of coordinated German–Soviet aggression.

The Soviets began to deport Jewish professionals and rabbis to Siberia and other interior locations. Immediately, Orthodox rabbis and rabbinical students who had friends, colleagues, and relatives in the United States turned to them for assistance in getting visas to the United States. Eventually, their American sponsors turned to McDonald and the President's Advisory Committee.

On June 17 the President's Advisory Committee discussed how to best assist refugees given the worsening situation in Europe. The next day McDonald wrote to President Roosevelt:

The British and French Ambassadors have appealed to our Government for help in removing political and war refugees from their territories. The appeal has the same urgency as the appeal for military equipment and supplies which are already moving under your leadership. Our limits of material assistance may be supplemented effectively by prompt and practical action in helping the Allies to remove the refugees who[,] by their very presence[,] impede military operations, consume precious supplies of food, create problems of control embarrassing to the war effort and are themselves in great physical danger.

Your Advisory Committee on Political Refugees has sought ways and means of implementing your assurances of assistance to England and France. It respectfully recommends the following:

1. We urge that within the authority of our present immigration laws administrative measures be worked out to admit children either as temporary visitors or as permanent entrants.

    We recognize that the transfer of the Immigration and Naturalization Service to the Department of Justice presages a tightening of control on immigration and that this action has been taken to protect the country from "Fifth Column" activities.[19] Children do not constitute such a danger.

2. Beyond this we urge that in your good judgment a recommendation be made to the Congress that legislation be passed providing for the admission of a specific number of children each year for the next two years.

3. The British and French Governments should be informed on the maximum number of children admissible by administrative action under existing laws and the number recommended for admission under new legislation.

4. Because these steps will prove inadequate[,] we believe that the British and French governments should be urged to make available (in addition to outlets in Canada) their island colonial possessions in the Caribbean

19. In May responsibility for immigration issues was removed from the Department of Labor to the Justice Department, and plans were made to put the State Department in charge of the board that was to have oversight over alien issues. Long Diary, May 22, 1940, LC, Container 5.

(Bermuda, Jamaica, the Bahamas, Martinique, Guadeloupe) on the promise of assistance in maintenance of the refugees by our Government through an appropriation by the Congress of relief funds for the purchase and delivery or surplus food commodities and materials for housing and clothing to the American Red Cross.

5. We think it appropriate, too, to call to your attention the case of various individual political refugees now in an especial and immediate danger in France. Certain Italian, German, Spanish, Czech and Polish patriots are marked men because of their long leadership in the intellectual and political struggle against Fascism and Nazism. Undoubtedly outstanding French intellectuals are also already in immediate danger. We suggest that the diplomatic and consular officials of the United States might be able to be of assistance to outstanding individuals in this emergency. If their lives can be saved, many of them will prove useful in the future in preserving and promoting the democratic policies and principles in which this country has a direct and vital interest.

. . . .

We are convinced that substantial private funds will become available immediately in the United States to provide for the children admitted under the suggested administrative and legislative actions.

In offering the foregoing suggestions we are deeply conscious of the many responsibilities you are now facing. We hope that in fulfilling our function as your Advisory Committee[,] we may be practically helpful to you in this desperate hour.[20]

President Roosevelt asked McDonald and George Warren to confer with Undersecretary of State Welles, and Francis Biddle, solicitor general in the Justice Department. Afterward Warren reported to the President's Advisory Committee:

This conference proved satisfying. . . . We have been hopeful that administrative procedures under the immigration laws would be modified with particular reference to intellectual and political refugees caught in France and children in the British Isles.

Since then Mr. McDonald and Mr. Warren have had conferences with Mrs. Roosevelt[,] and Mr. Warren has participated in the organization of the United States Committee for the Care of European Children.[21]

McDonald also hoped that the Catholic Church would take part in assisting refugees. On June 25 State Department official Robert Pell wrote to Undersecretary of State Welles about a call he had just received from McDonald:

20. McDonald to President Roosevelt, June 18, 1940. Copy in Wise Papers, American Jewish Historical Society, Box 39, Roll 71, Center for Jewish History.

21. George Warren to members of the President's Advisory Committee, July 9, 1940. Copy in Wise Papers, American Jewish Historical Society, Box 39, Roll 71, Center for Jewish History.

Mr. McDonald . . . asked me . . . to request you to have this government intercede with the Vatican to appeal to Franco to give asylum to some of the political refugees, other than Spaniards, now in France. Mr. McDonald thought that the President might be willing to consider a personal appeal to the Pope.

Mr. McDonald wished me to thank you for receiving him on Saturday and to tell you how tremendously impressed he was with the progress that was being made. He was particularly pleased with the cooperative spirit shown by Mr. Avra Warren.[22]

McDonald was trying to be hopeful—or diplomatic—about Avra Warren's cooperative spirit. In April 1935, when McDonald was League of Nations High Commissioner for Refugees, he had visited Argentina, where Warren was an American diplomat. Warren had tried to sabotage McDonald's efforts to persuade Argentinean officials to accept German-Jewish refugees.[23] Now Warren was in a critical position to curtail the flow of immigrants to the United States.

A June 26 memo written by Assistant Secretary of State Breckinridge Long outlined two approaches he and Avra Warren had discussed, the first for restricting "nonimmigrants"—visitors or people en route to another country, and for full-fledged immigrants:

Nonimmigrants

Their entry into the United States can be made to depend upon prior authorization by the Department [State]. This would mean that the consuls would be divested of discretion and that all requests for nonimmigrant visas (temporary visitor and transit visas) be passed upon here. It is quite feasible and can be done instantly. It will permit the Department to effectively control the immigration of persons in this category and private instructions can be given the Visa Division as to nationalities which should not be admitted as well as to individuals who are to be excluded.

. . . .

Immigrants

We can delay and effectively stop for a temporary period of indefinite length the number of immigrants into the United States. We could do this by simply advising our consuls to put every obstacle in the way and to require additional evidence and to resort to various administrative advices which would postpone and postpone and postpone the granting of the visas. However, this could only be temporary. In order to make it more definite it would have to be

22. Pell to Welles, June 26, 1940, NA RG 59, 840.48 Refugees/2182.
23. See *Advocate for the Doomed*, 705–706.

done by suspension of the rules under the law by the issuance of a proclamation of emergency—which I take it we are not ready yet to proclaim.

Summing Up

We can effectively control nonimmigrants by prohibiting the issuance of visas unless the consent of the Department is obtained in advance, for universal application.

We can temporarily prevent the number of immigrants from certain localities such as Cuba, Mexico and other places of origin of German intending immigrants simply by raising administrative obstacles.[24]

Long soon wrote in his diary: "The cables practically stopping immigration went!"[25]

By this time McDonald's disillusionment with the Roosevelt administration had coalesced with his positive personal and political feelings for Republican presidential candidate Wendell Willkie. During his tenure at Indiana University, McDonald had taught Willkie, who later praised him as one of the best professors he had ever had.[26] McDonald sent a telegram to Willkie, congratulating him on his success at the Republican convention:

Your nomination is vindication of faith in Democratic processes and your election will prove that totalitarianism is not inevitable here.

At this time McDonald clearly preferred Willkie to FDR.[27] A Willkie victory seemed quite conceivable. On June 9 Ickes had written in his diary:

And if he [Wendell Willke] does come out as the Republican nominee, who knows that he will not defeat the President? Who even knows that the President would run against Willkie? With the running start that he will have and with his appeal to the imagination of the people as a strong, forceful leader—which is the kind that they want in a national emergency—no one can safely predict that on January 22, next, our Government, after eight years of New Deal, will not go into the hands of Willkie, the utilities, the First National Bank of New York, and the Morgans.[28]

---

24. Long to Berle and Dunn (then political adviser), June 26, 1940, Long Papers, LC, Container 211, Visa Division file.

25. Long Diary, June 29, 1940, LC, Container 5, quoted by Wyman, *Paper Walls*, 174.

26. "I have frequently said I never had a better instructor than you and few as good." Willkie to McDonald, December 3, 1937, McDonald Papers, Columbia University, D361 (Willkie Special File), Item 164.

27. McDonald to Willkie, June 28, 1940, McDonald Papers, Columbia University, D361 (Willkie Special File), Item 164. See also, McDonald to Knollenberg, June 29, 1940, D361, ibid.

28. *Secret Diary of Harold L. Ickes*, III, 208.

But by the fall FDR showed more indications of willingness to help Britain against Germany, and Willkie became critical of FDR's foreign policy. Family lore has it that McDonald ended up voting for FDR in spite of major disagreements on refugee issues.

On July 15 Avra Warren arrived in Lisbon and, according to American Minister Herbert Pell, "explained in detail the policy which had been adopted by the Department to meet the situation caused by the turn of military events in France. . . . Visas should be granted only when there was no doubt whatsoever concerning the alien."[29] *Although documentation is partial, it appears that Warren went on to the American consulates in Switzerland, Germany, Sweden, and perhaps elsewhere, where he gave out the same tough interpretation of previous State Department instructions and telegrams. Consul A. Dana Hodgdon in Berlin wrote in October 1940:*

Mr. Avra M. Warren, Chief of the Visa Division . . . recently inspected this office [and] stated that the instruction under reference had been correctly interpreted here as being highly restrictive. . . . The present period of emergency seem[s] to indicate the need of examining immigrants of Central European background with great care to determine whether, for instance, their disaffection toward certain countries is not directed merely toward the present governments rather than the country itself, to which some degree of allegiance may still remain.[30]

Margaret Jones, representative of the American Friends Service Committee in Vienna, encountered Avra Warren there, apparently in August:

I had a conference with Warren when he was in Vienna a few weeks ago—there is absolutely no chance for <u>anyone,</u> except in most unusual cases. FDR doesn't want any more aliens from Europe—refugees have been implicated in espionage—and so forth. All part of the spy hysteria. (What kind of a USA am I coming back to??? I am almost afraid to face it.) . . . The criterion is "what remarkable contribution will you make to the US?" So you see, I must get home and try to do something about easing this up somewhat. The strain of the past month has been something. Day after day men and women just sat at my desk and sobbed. They are caught and crushed, and they know it.[31]

29. Pell to Secretary of State, September 6, 1940, NA RG 59, 811.111 Refugees/2599. Copy in McDonald Papers, USHMM.

30. Hodgdon to Sholes, October 15, 1940, NA RG 84, American Consulate Basel, General Files 1941, 123-L. Records of the American consulates in Germany and of the Embassy for this time were destroyed. Rabbi Stephen Wise later wrote McDonald about the hopeless feeling among the Jews in Germany, "which the other Warren [that is, Avra Warren, not George Warren] seems to have created in Germany." Wise to McDonald, September 30, 1940, McDonald Papers, Columbia University, D361 (Stephen Wise Special File), Item 165.

31. Quoted in Clarence Picket to Evelyn Hersey, September 23, 1940, American Friends Service Committee Archive, Philadelphia, Refugee Service 1940, Committees and Organizations.

A little later another Friends worker in Vienna wrote:

The American Consulate goes on refusing giving out visas. People are examined, and a few days later they get letters informing them that either there is danger of their becoming a public burden, or that their husband in the United States should send an affidavit himself, or simply stating: "We do not see our way to give you a visa. . . . Yesterday I saw a form with a post scriptum saying that the people must bring a notarized statement signed by two friends in which they certify that the applicants for a visa have never committed any crime. Besides this the people have still to bring police certificates of good conduct. . . . He [the consul] said that this is done by order from Washington.[32]

The President's Advisory Committee decided it must somehow take charge of organizing refugee advocacy. On July 24 George Warren met with State Department official Robert Pell, who wrote after their meeting that:

The President's Advisory Committee had more or less come to the conclusion that it would have to assume direct responsibility in the matter of political refugees in Europe who were desirous of seeking asylum in the United States. Committees were springing up on every hand, each committee with a list of candidates for admission to the United States, and already they were beginning to fight among themselves and accuse the Government of favoring one side or the other.

. . . .

In short, there will soon be a highly chaotic condition which may give rise to political embarrassment if the situation is not taken in hand.[33]

On July 26 McDonald and Warren met with State and Justice Department officials to work out new visa procedures for political, intellectual, or other refugees in "special peril" in Spain, Portugal, southern France, or in French colonies in North Africa. Nazi Germany might have reached into any of these areas—either with or without the cooperation of the Spanish, Portuguese, or Vichy French governments.[34]

The meeting covered several different categories—visitors' visas, transit certificates, and immigration visas. For those deemed visitors, the Advisory Committee would carry out some of the preliminary investigation and the obtaining of affidavits of support and/or good character from American citizens; then State and Justice would consider whether such individuals could and would leave the United States at

---

32. Neumayer to Rogers, September 26, 1940, AFSC, Refugee Service 1940, Letters from Austria.

33. Pell Memo on Refugee Committee, July 24, 1940, NA RG 59, 840.48 Refugees/2220.

34. On Germany's intentions and efforts in this region during 1940, see Norman J. W. Goda, *Tomorrow the World: Hitler, Northwest Africa, and the Path Toward America* (College Station: Texas A & M, 1998).

the appropriate time. Immigrants also needed a place within the annual quota and evidence that they were likely not to become public charges. Once State and Justice approved individuals, their names would be sent to the consuls where they were applying for visas with the expectation of expedited approval. For those admitted to the United States temporarily or on transit visas, the Advisory Committee had additional work.[35]

On August 5 Attorney General Robert Jackson approved this proposed agreement.[36] *Assistant Secretary of State Breckinridge Long did not want the Advisory Committee to be the conduit for all names of threatened individuals, though he agreed with the rest of the procedures.*[37]

On August 7 McDonald telephoned Long regarding

the plight of a number of Jewish Orthodox Rabbis who are being taken into Russia from occupied parts of Estonia, Lithuania and other places. He said a committee of Jewish rabbis had called upon him yesterday to state that he or they make an engagement to see Mr. Welles or me in connection with it and to explore the possibilities of being of assistance to them. He suggested that Mr. Warren of his committee make the preliminary investigation of the names on the list. I told him I thought that was the proper thing to do. . . ."[38]

On August 13, Long advised Rabbi Meier Schenkolewski that he had to get approval of each name from McDonald's committee first, but that, in general, such rabbis could be considered political refugees.[39]

During August Rabbi Max Nussbaum and his wife arrived in the United States from Berlin. Nussbaum brought information about Nazi intentions—they were considering a plan to ship four million Jews to the island of Madagascar. He was able to get an appointment very quickly with New York Times *publisher Arthur Sulzberger and told him about the Nazi Madagascar Plan.*[40] *Years later Nussbaum recalled that Sulzberger set up a luncheon for the foreign policy experts at the* Times, *and Nussbaum spoke there about conditions in Germany. Then Sulzberger arranged for*

35. McDonald and George Warren to Undersecretary of State and the Attorney General, July 31, 1940, McDonald Papers, Columbia University, D367 (PACPR), P70.
36. Jackson to McDonald and George Warren, August 5, 1940, McDonald Papers, Columbia University, D367 (PACPR), P25.
37. Long to George Warren, August 13, 1940, Letter. NA RG 59, 811.111 Refugees/194. Copy in McDonald Papers, USHMM.
38. Long Memo, August 7, 1940, LC, Long Papers, Container 211.
39. Long to Schenkolewski, August 13, 1940, McDonald Papers, Columbia University, D367 (PACPR), P28. McDonald said that these rabbis were unlikely to be able to make it to the United States: their visas were a gesture of sympathy that might improve their treatment. See, for example, McDonald and Warren's memorandum to the president, October 8, 1940, FDRL, Official File 3186. Long later, however, used these visas as evidence that the President's Advisory Committee had gone too far.
40. Leff, *Buried by the Times*, 49, had access to the memo Nussbaum wrote in September 1940, which is in private hands.

Nussbaum to go to Washington in September to brief Treasury Secretary Henry Morgenthau, Jr., about the dire situation for Jews within Nazi reach.

Nussbaum came at the height of the "Blitz," intensive bombing of London and other British cities by the Luftwaffe. As Nussbaum later recalled, people in the United States believed then that any Jews the Gestapo let out of Germany were working as spies. The first question Morgenthau asked Nussbaum was how many Jews did he know who were working for the Gestapo. Nussbaum conceded that in Paris the Gestapo did put pressure on Jews who had relatives remaining in Germany—mostly to carry out small tasks, such as reporting on conversations of emigrants in cafés. In Germany their target was Polish Jews who needed official permission to stay, but some of those reported Gestapo pressure to the Jewish leadership, and they were helped to escape into Lithuania. The Gestapo had other (and better) ways of sending spies abroad—such as giving Gestapo agents the names of Jews who had died in concentration camps and equipping them with false passports stamped with the J.[41] Nussbaum's explanation of the real situation could not have entirely reassured Morgenthau.

Rabbi Stephen Wise soon sent McDonald a copy of Nussbaum's written statement:

Here is the statement, carefully written out, of Dr. Nussbaum, after he had seen A. H. S. [Arthur Hays Sulzberger] and A. K. [Arthur Krock] in Washington. After reading the statement, would you be good enough to send it on to F. F. [Felix Frankfurter] . . . ? He may wish to share it with L. D. B. [Louis D. Brandeis].[42]

On the day Nussbaum was received by Morgenthau, one small piece of the refugee problem had arrived, literally, on America's doorstep. The Portuguese steamship Quanza docked in Norfolk, Virginia, with a number of refugees aboard. Although all of them had been granted Mexican transit visas, they had been turned away when they arrived in Vera Cruz in Mexico: hence their arrival in Norfolk. Before the ship's arrival, a number of refugee agencies had contacted the President's Advisory Committee, asking it to intervene on behalf of these passengers, and during September 9–12 Justice had agreed that the passengers should be admitted to the United States. The President and Eleanor Roosevelt had indicated their interest in the matter. As McDonald wrote to Stephen Wise on September 10, he anticipated State's favorable decision:[43]

Just a few minutes ago I talked with Breckinridge Long on the telephone after twice being in touch with [George] Warren, who has been in Washington for two days. I explained to Long that the Department of Justice was unani-

41. Nussbaum oral history, July 30, 1958, Yad Vashem 01/222 (Collection Ball-Kaduri). We are grateful to David Bankier for a copy of this document.

42. Wise to McDonald, September 30, 1940, McDonald Papers, Columbia University, D361 (Stephen Wise Special File), Item 165.

43. Minutes of the Fortieth Meeting of the President's Advisory Committee on Political Refugees, September 12, 1940, Wise Papers, Box 65, Center for Jewish History.

mously in favor of the action Mr. Warren was urging. This seemed to carry weight with the Assistant Secretary. At any rate, he promised that he would himself call the Attorney General and implied that if the latter were as favorable as I believe he is, he (Mr. Long) would OK the visas.[44]

As McDonald had expected, Long approved the action, and on September 12 he explained in a letter of instruction to an official at the Department of Justice that the same principles used for assessing refugees in Europe should be applied to the passengers on the Quanza:

First, any persons aboard that ship recommended to us by the President's Advisory Committee as being political refugees in the sense that the committee has exercised discretion in defining that category would be accepted by the Department and they would be admitted on visitor or transit visas.

Second, any and all children on the boat recommended to us by Marshall Field's committee would be admitted, provided the Field committee would make the customary arrangements about support, etc.

Third, any persons on the vessel who had legitimate valid and existing visas to enter other countries would be admitted for transit purposes.[45]

In a confidential letter Stephen Wise explained what he viewed as some of the political background of the Quanza *case and refugee matters generally:*

There are certain things that we get done, other things cannot be done at all. One of the things that could be done could only be done because Eleanor R.[oosevelt] and Marshall Field appealed to the Skipper [FDR] for the liberation of the refugees on the *Quanza*. All of them were released. They were denied admission to Mexico, although every one of them had paid $100 for a transit visa and many of them, if not all, had paid $200 apiece for visas to Venezuela, etc., etc. They were shipped back, but after infinite effort on our part, both the President's [Advisory] Committee and the JDC, and [Cecilia] Razovsky and others, we were able to get them landed and now they are ashore. But of course it could not have been done unless the Skipper had taken the needful step.

With regard to the political refugees, we are in the midst of the most difficult situation, an almost unmanageable quandary. On the one hand, the State Department makes all sorts of promises and takes our lists and then we hear that the Consuls do nothing. A few people slip through, but we are afraid,—this in strictest confidence,—that the Consuls have private instructions from the Department to do nothing, which would be infamous beyond

44. McDonald to Wise, September 10, 1940, McDonald Papers, Columbia University, D361 (Stephen Wise Special File), Item 165.
45. Long Memo, September 12, 1940. Copy in FDRL, Official File 3186.

words. What I am afraid lies back of the whole thing is the fear of the Skipper's friends in the State Department that any large admission of radicals to the United States might be used effectively against him in the [presidential election] campaign. Cruel as I may seem, as I have said to you before, his re-election is much more important for everything that is worthwhile and that counts than the admission of a few people, however imminent be their peril. We are going to have it out in a few days. We are going to have a good and, I hope, understanding talk with Welles, whom we have reason to trust, as against Long, who is chiefly a friend of the Skipper, and Berle,[46] whom Felix calls a "Rosher."[47]

A representative of the President's Advisory Committee assisted immigration inspectors at Norfolk and helped to ensure that all 81 passengers on the Quanza *were allowed to land. He reported that Breckinridge Long objected at the last minute:*

Mr. Long informed me over the phone that he was displeased at the number of persons entering under the President's Advisory Committee procedure. When he told me that he felt he could not take responsibility for them, I informed him that they were already landing under the supervision of the immigration inspectors and he replied simply that he would not himself be responsible for it.[48]

Afterward, Long wrote in his diary:

The list of rabbis has been closed and the list of labor leaders has been closed. And now it remains for the President's Committee to be curbed in its activities so that the laws again can operate in their normal course.[49]

At the September 12 meeting of the President's Advisory Committee, McDonald called upon George Warren, who reviewed problems with the State Department:

Mr. Warren reported that some 567 names had been recommended to the Departments of State and Justice which had in turn approved them and that cables concerning them had been sent by the Department of State to the Consuls. He regretted to report, however, that up to date it appeared that only 15 visas had actually been issued. In light of this experience he had ceased send-

46. Adolf A. Berle, then assistant secretary of state for Latin American affairs.
47. "Roshe" is a Yiddish/Hebrew word for evil person. Wise was mistaken about Berle, who was a critic of State Department visa policies. George Warren also cited the influence of the United States Committee for the Care of European Children upon President and Mrs. Roosevelt as a reason for the likely positive decision (that day) on admitting the passengers from the *Quanza*. Wise to Otto Nathan, September 17, 1940; Minutes of the Meeting of the President's Advisory Committee, September 12, 1940, Wise Papers, Box 65, Center for Jewish History.
48. Malin to George Warren, September 17, 1940. Copy in FDRL, Official File 3186.
49. Long Diary, September 18, 1940, LC, Container 5.

ing further names to the Departments. . . . The Department of State had cabled the Consuls without informing the Department of Justice and the President's Advisory Committee that no visas should be issued until the applicants were in possession of French exit permits. This action virtually canceled the procedures with respect to those in unoccupied France. On protest by the Department of Justice and the President's Advisory Committee this action had been reversed a few days prior to this meeting. It was evident that instructions had also been cabled by the Department of State in similar manner to the effect that the arrangements applied only to prominent writers and labor leaders. This modification of the procedures had also seriously restricted their application.[50]

On September 19 Long issued a Circular Telegram to the Diplomatic and Consular Offices in Lisbon, Oporto, Marseille, Bordeaux, London, Zurich, Lyon, Nice, Casablanca, Moscow and Stockholm specifying again that

if any doubt exists regarding alien's activities in the past and possible activities in the United States . . . action in the case should be suspended and the alien should be requested to present clear evidence to establish essential facts. In considering lists of alien refugees transmitted by the Department with assurances of the sponsoring organization regarding support and arrangements to proceed to [a] third country, you should carefully examine cases as to the applicants' past and future activities and as to the aliens' status as refugee intellectuals or labor leaders or refugees in particular danger, and if any doubt exists action in the cases should be suspended.[51]

McDonald sought to enlist the help of members of the press sympathetic to the refugees' plight. In a letter to prominent journalist Dorothy Thompson he noted:

Sometime, at your convenience, I should like to bring Mr. George L. Warren, the very industrious and competent secretary of the President's Advisory Committee on Political Refugees, to tell you the full story of recent developments in the efforts to break down the resistance in certain quarters to the rescue of the sorely pressed political refugees.[52]

Long wrote to President Roosevelt to inform him that the State Department wished to modify the procedures that had been agreed upon on July 26, and asking him to approve a letter Hull planned to send to McDonald informing him of these

50. President's Advisory Committee minutes, September 12, 1940. Copy in Wise Papers, Box 65, Center for Jewish History.
51. Secretary of State to European Consulates, September 19, Circular Telegram, NA RG 59, 811.111/Refugees/260. Copy in McDonald Papers, USHMM.
52. McDonald to Dorothy Thompson, September 18, 1940, McDonald Papers, Columbia University, General Correspondence (Dorothy Thompson), Folder 383.

changes. Essentially, Long claimed that the Advisory Committee had expanded the boundaries of political and intellectual refugees and failed to do sufficient checking whether they might pose a risk to the United States if admitted. He also gave an inflated account of how many visas had actually been issued to refugees.

Under the circumstances we feel that in the interests of our national defense a more careful check should be made abroad by our officers in Europe of the persons whose names we send to them on the recommendation of the President's Advisory Committee. We feel that a more careful examination of the individuals abroad would contribute largely to closing the loopholes against the penetration of German agents or the use of the courtesy and hospitality of the United States for ulterior purposes.

. . . .

If you approve the proposal, I shall be very glad to advise the Secretary [of State Hull] so that he may sign the letter.[53]

McDonald responded to Hull, summarizing the real situation and detailing the complaints with the State Department:

We have received your letter of September 19 in which you suggest that no additional names of refugees be accepted by the President's Advisory Committee on Political Refugees for transmission to the Department of State and Justice except those of refugees in imminent danger who are intellectual leaders of the liberal movement in Europe.

. . . .

But of the 561 refugees whose names have been, on our recommendation, cabled by the Department of State, less than 15 visas have been issued to date according to the reports available to us.

This failure to ease the tragedy of those refugees in imminent danger is explained, in part at least, by the Department of State's action in modifying seriously the arrangements of July 26 without previous notice to the Department of Justice or to the President's Advisory Committee on Political Refugees.

. . . .

A relatively minor consequence of the changes made by the Department has been embarrassment caused to our committee—in its relations with the agencies and with the relatives and friends of refugees—through being encouraged to continue to act under an agreement which the Department had unilaterally and without notice to us fundamentally altered.

. . . .

53. Long to FDR, September 18, 1940, FDRL, Official File 3186.

We suggest that:

1. With respect to persons recommended the Department return to the basis for admission previously worked out. This would involve cancellation of instructions, among others, limiting the application of these emergency visas to leaders of the liberal movement in Europe and the issue of new instructions in closer conformity with the original arrangements.
2. That, in view of the fact that an erroneous impression may have been conveyed to the President as to the actions of this Committee, we have an opportunity to present the full circumstances to him.[54]

On September 24, McDonald, Welles, and Long met to discuss the points of disagreement between State and the President's Advisory Committee. Welles then cabled the overseas consulates to reconfirm the special arrangements agreed to in July, a cable that, as George Warren reported to the committee, had noticeably speeded up the process by which visas were issued. Long and Welles also agreed that McDonald and George Warren should meet with the president.[55]

In his diary Long wrote up his version of this meeting:

A long session this evening with James G. McDonald and his man Warren and Welles. McDonald is very wroth [*sic*] at the limitations upon the activities of his Committee, which were set out in a letter sent to him by the Secretary. He looks upon me as an obstructionist and was very bitter and somewhat denunciatory. There were a few warm words between us, but it straightened out. He said he wanted to see the President, and I said I hoped he would and would lay the whole matter before him.[56]

On September 28 the American Consulate General in Stockholm reported its visa situation, confirming that State Department instructions and Avra Warren's guidance had substantially slowed or blocked approvals.

German quota waiting list Stockholm 675 persons of whom 40 documentation previously approved; Czech waiting list 79, documentation approved 11; and Polish list 78, documentation approved 11; about 50 other refugees various quotas.

Delay issuance visaes [*sic*] occasioned principally by Department's increasingly strict instructions since June this year and Inspector Warren's explanation thereof necessitating changes in procedure and more investigations background documentation each case.

54. McDonald and Warren to Cordell Hull, September 23, 1940, McDonald Papers, Columbia University, D367 (PACPR), P21.

55. October 30, 1940, Minutes of the 41st Meeting of the President's Advisory Committee, Columbia University, D367 (PACPR), P64.

56. Long Diary, September 24, 1940, LC, Container 5.

Very difficult sometimes impossible refugees here satisfy us completely. . . .

Result has naturally been delay and drastic reduction issuance as envisaged Department's telegraphic instructions June 29.[57]

McDonald had to write a difficult letter to an old friend who had survived the German conquest of France and had sought John D. Rockefeller's aid to obtain a visa.

What an exciting and terrible experience you have had! It seems almost unbelievable that you could have escaped without serious injury. We are all delighted that you are safely out of the fighting.

Unfortunately, the prospect of anyone being admitted at the present time to this country, who cannot prove that he is an eminent scholar or distinguished labor leader and is in imminent danger, is very slight. In effect, our doors are hermetically sealed against newcomers, no matter how tragic their individual positions may be. Among the considerations which has led the government to adopt this restrictive policy is the feeling that[,] were the doors to be opened to all those who, through the pressure of economic circumstances, wished to immigrate here, there would be such a flood that public opinion would almost certainly demand changes in the law which would make exclusion a fixed policy for a long period. At the moment, the restrictive tendency is being enforced by administrative regulations and may, therefore, be modified in the same way. Unfortunate though this situation is, from the viewpoint of those who wish to come here, it is not as irretrievable as it would be were the Congress to cancel the quota system altogether.

Under these circumstances, I think John [D. Rockefeller III] was quite correct when he said to you that there is at present no possibility, irrespective of what he might do, which would hold out hope to you of early admission here. It grieves me sorely to have to confirm this bad news, but in truth I could not do otherwise.

Should the situation described above, change, in such a way as to make your admission possible, I shall be very happy to write you at once when I learn of such improvement. Meantime, Ruth and Barbara and Janet join in sending you their warmest greetings.[58]

McDonald was right to worry about Congress. Since May the State Department had been investigating the feasibility of tighter laws to control the admission of aliens.[59] By September 1940 the State Department and Justice Department were in discussions

57. Gray to Secretary of State, September 28, 1940, NA RG 59, 811.111 Refugees/376. Copy in McDonald Papers, USHMM.

58. McDonald to Adolphe Pervy, September 26, 1940, McDonald Papers, USHMM, Correspondence between McDonald family and Leland Robinson family. On Pervy, see chapter 3, p. 39.

59. Richard W. Flournoy [legal adviser at State] to Avra Warren, May 16, 1940: Memorandum: Legislative Authority for Denying Immigration Visas upon the Ground of Public Safety, NA RG 59, 150.01 BILLS/253. Copy in McDonald Papers, USHMM.

about introducing a bill into Congress designed to exclude "all aliens whose admission into the United States would be contrary to the public safety" whether or not they had been issued a visa.[60]

On September 27, 1940, Germany, Italy, and Japan signed the Tripartite Pact, formally tying the three "Axis" powers together and setting the basis for Germany to encourage Japan to attack the United States. Having been forced to postpone an invasion of Great Britain, Hitler had already decided that Germany's next big operation would come against the Soviet Union in the spring of 1941. (A formal military directive to this effect—Operation Barbarossa—was issued on December 18.)

On the same day George Warren met with Eleanor Roosevelt and then wrote to her, attaching relevant documents:

Thank you most kindly for listening to me at such length this morning.

. . . .

You will recall that we have two important concerns: (1) to correct the impression given the President by Mr. Long's letter [the September 18 letter to the president, excerpt above on pp. 211–212]; and (2) to have the President's comment on what is to be done about those refugees already recommended, and the future of the arrangements.

The Committee refuted Long's letter to the president point by point and summarized:

While it is true that names should not be submitted in unlimited numbers[,] experience with the arrangements to date clearly indicates the necessity of the following:

1. More liberal action on behalf of those already recommended.
2. A more concise statement of the qualifications of persons to be benefited.
3. Closer adherence to the arrangement when, such a statement is drafted, possibly in a second conference between the Department of State, the Department of Justice, and the President's Advisory Committee on Political Refugees.[61]

---

60. Hull to Harold D. Smith, Director, Bureau of the Budget, September 25, 1940, with enclosure, Draft of "A Bill to Provide for the Exclusion of All Aliens whose Admission into the United States would be Contrary to the Public Safety"; see also Record of Conference Between Justice and State regarding Proposed Legislation, September 25, 1940; Robert Jackson and Breckinridge Long, Memorandum of Conversation, October 1, 1940. All preceding documents located in NA RG 59, 150.01 BILLS/253. Copy in McDonald Papers, USHMM.

61. President's Advisory Committee on Political Refugees, "Memorandum on 'political, intellectual and other refugees' with particular references to the letter [from Long] to the President," no date, FDRL, Official File 3186.

*On September 28 Eleanor Roosevelt passed on all this documentation, and War-
ren's letter, to the president, along with her own comments:*

Mr. Welles promised to explain to you that Mr. Long's letter to you was
entirely erroneous regarding the situation. They now enclose these letters with
a refutation because they feel that this has not been presented correctly.

They handed 2,000 names to the State Department and the consuls abroad
have not certified more than 50 to come to his country.

If the consuls could be induced to make this agreement work, it might
come to an end, but as it is, it has not worked.

Mr. McDonald is so wrought up about it, he wants to talk to you for about
15 minutes. He would come to Washington, and I promised to help him. Because he feels that their good faith has been impugned and because he also feels
that there is something he ought to tell you which makes him extremely uncomfortable in relation to the whole situation, and about which he does not
wish to write, he is asking for an appointment.

I am thinking about these poor people who may die at any time and who
are asking only to come here on transit visas, and I do hope you can get this
cleared up quickly.

October 2, 1940.

MEMORANDUM FOR
THE UNDER-SECRETARY OF STATE
Please tell me about this. There does seem to be a mix-up. I think I must see
McDonald.

F. D. R. [62]

*On the evening on October 2, 1940, Ambassador Steinhardt in Moscow sent a
very long cable to the State Department that raised new fears about visa policy and
the role of the President's Advisory Committee. Whether or not Long solicited this
cable from the only sitting ambassador who was Jewish,[63] it certainly arrived at a
convenient moment when Long was locked in battle with McDonald and the President's Advisory Committee.*

*In Steinhardt's view, given the existing international situation, loosening visa
regulations for anyone was entirely inappropriate. And there was, he argued, a more
specific problem. Steinhardt charged that refugee assistance organizations had deliberately misrepresented the status of applicants to the State Department in order to gain
visa approvals. He also objected to what he saw as a policy which put the burden of*

62. Eleanor Roosevelt to FDR, September 28, 1940, and FDR to Under-Secretary of State,
October 2, 1940, FDRL, Official File 3186.

63. In mid-1941 Long wrote in his diary: "Steinhardt wrote me a very long letter in response to one of mine in which he went fully into the subject from the point of view of Russia."
See chapter 10, p. 249. It is not clear whether this comment refers specifically to Steinhardt's cable
of October 2, which was sent to Bern and picked up personally by Avra Warren there.

proof on consuls, rather than applicants, to show that they were (or were not) likely to engage in anti-American activities in the future.

I am persuaded that the best interests of the United States at this time will not be served by admitting individuals of this type in large groups, especially individuals who have coordinated with one another over a period of years and who might well transplant their entire political organization to the United States particularly, as I am not convinced that many of them intend to depart from the United States at the expiration of these so-called visits. Furthermore, I believe it is dangerous to allow groups to enter the United States indiscriminately merely because the members of these groups have been sponsored by organizations in the United States which have not hesitated to misrepresent to the Department and who are obviously more interested in finding a haven for these unfortunates than they are in safeguarding the welfare of the United States at the most critical period of its history. I still regard admission to the United States as a privilege, not a right.

. . . I have requested the Consular Section to suspend action in all doubtful cases pending the receipt of further instructions from the Department.

When the inevitable protest is made to the Department by the organizations which have misrepresented the status of many of these applicants in order to procure their admission to the United States by subterfuge[,] I have no objection to the Department's acquainting the sponsoring organizations with the contents of all or any part of this telegram as representing my personal views.[64]

Long quickly sent a note to the president, directing his attention to Steinhardt's telegram, so that FDR might read it before meeting with McDonald.[65] Some of the background to this action Long explained in his diary on October 3:

About noon I had a long satisfactory conversation with the President on the subject of refugees. McDonald, Chairman of the President's Advisory Committee on Refugees, has developed a very definite and violent antagonism to me. He thinks I have been non-cooperative and obstructive and has given evidence of his personal animosity. In a recent conversation in Mr. Welles' office he indicated that I had a superlative ego[,] and a vindicative [*sic*] mentality added to his disregard, to put it lightly, of me. During that conversation I responded enthusiastically to the thought that he lay the matter before the President. He did not do so at the time but apparently approached Mrs. Roosevelt and she got a wrong impression. As a matter of fact we had been more generous with the President's Advisory Committee

64. Steinhardt to Secretary of State, October 2, 1940, NA RG 59, 811.111 Refugees/397. Copy in McDonald Papers, USHMM.

65. Long to FDR, October 3, 1940, NA RG 59, 811.111 Refugees/397. Copy in McDonald Papers, USHMM.

than we had with any of the other groups which have been active in arranging for refugees to leave Europe, and that has been the case because he was Chairman of the President's Advisory Committee. Nevertheless, he presented the matter in a very sorry light and made several misstatements of fact in his conversation with Mrs. Roosevelt. She wrote the President; the President talked to Welles; and Welles suggested the President see me and talk it over.

So when I saw him this morning the whole subject of immigration, visas, safety of the United States, procedures to be followed; and all that sort of thing was on the table. I found that he was 100% in accord with my ideas. He said that when Myron Taylor had returned from Europe recently the only thing which they discussed outside of Vatican matters was the visa and refugee situation and the manner in which our Consulates were being deprived of a certain amount of discretion by the rulings of the Department.

Given what other evidence there is of Myron Taylor's views, it is likely that Long completely misinterpreted this comment. Taylor likely complained that the State Department had given the consuls such instructions to restrict visas that they had little discretion. Long, however, believed that Taylor had complained about the President's Advisory Committee's nomination of individuals for visas, complaining that the consuls felt bound when the State Department passed on these lists. Long continued:

It was these very things which created the most recent difficulty between McDonald and myself, because we had reinvested the Consuls with their legitimate authority after having noted from our experiences in the other and more lax administration that we were admitting persons who should not properly come into the United States. The President expressed himself as in entire accord with the policy which would exclude persons about whom there was any suspicion that they would be inimical to the welfare of the United States no matter who had vouchsafed for them and irrespective of their financial or other standing. I left him with the satisfactory thought that he was whole-heartedly in support of the policy which would resolve in favor of the United States any doubts about admissibility of any individual. I specifically presented to him the case Rabbi Wise had been urging upon me. They [*sic*] were a man and his wife who had represented the Rabbi's organization but who professed to a long series of political activities in Europe and an intention to follow a course in the United States irrespective of the desires of the American Government but to take orders from the World Jewish Congress. They professed to have been responsible for the overthrow of one Rumanian government and to have been very active in politics in Europe for years.

The President agreed that those persons ought not to be admitted to the United States in spite of the fact that Rabbi Wise in all sincerity desired them here. We discussed several other individual matters as illustrative of policy, and I found him in entire agreement in every single instance. He said he would call for Mr. McDonald and have a talk with him.[66]

On September 6 American Minister (in Lisbon) Herbert Pell had written the State Department about Wise's submission of the names of Dr. and Mrs. Ernest Knoepmacher as "outstanding intellectuals" and persons worthy of consideration as temporary visitors:

When their case was examined they openly stated that since 1932 they had been very active in political affairs in various countries on behalf of the World Jewish Congress and had been successful through their agitation in overthrowing one Rumanian cabinet, the policies of which they did not approve. They also stated that they were not certain what activities they would engage in in the United States but would act according to such instructions they might receive from the organization to which they belong.[67]

Rabbi Wise and other American Jewish officials sent many other visa recommendations to the President's Advisory Committee and to the State Department. These recommendations included rabbis and other individuals in territories taken over by the Soviet Union (Latvia and Lithuania) as well as by Germany. Although many of the original records were destroyed at the National Archives, even what survives is so voluminous that very little of it is reproduced here.

In early October McDonald told New York Times *publisher Arthur Sulzberger that he had heard a report about a Spanish government ban on Jewish refugees entering the country. Sulzberger checked with the State Department and with the* Times *correspondent in Madrid; then he responded:*

Washington advises that they have heard nothing about any Spanish action relative to Jews, and Mr. Hamilton replies:

> "Best information here there's no ban on Jews traversing Spain though it is more difficult for them to obtain visas and they like other refugees are liable to imprisonment unless they leave within a fixed time. Several Polish Jews arrived in Madrid only Friday."
> I hope they are right and that you are wrong![68]

McDonald's check produced a different finding:

66. *The War Diary of Breckinridge Long: Selections from the Years, 1939–1944*, ed. Fred Israel (Lincoln: University of Nebraska Press, 1966), October 3, 1940, 134–135.

67. Pell to Secretary of State, September 6, 1940, NA RG 59, 011.111 Refugees/239. Copy in McDonald Papers, USHMM.

68. Sulzberger to McDonald, October 7, 1940, New York Times Company Archive, AH Sulzberger Autograph File, McDonald.

It is true, as I reported to you last week, that the Spanish Government, I think it was Friday, announced that henceforth there were to be no more transit visas for persons from France who are Jewish under the Nuremberg laws. There was, perhaps, no public announcement to this effect but our government was notified.

Whether or not this regulation has been rigidly adhered to, my informants in Washington had no means of knowing. They did add, however, this very interesting information: the Gestapo has taken over control of the Spanish police in certain key cities, including Saragossa. The proof of this is that an order of the Spanish Foreign Minister for the release of Paderewski was negated by the local Saragossa police on orders from the Gestapo. Only after repeated interventions from Madrid, encouraged by a powerful voice from this side, was Paderewski permitted to go on to Lisbon.[69]

One case McDonald did not know of illustrated his point. On September 26 the German-Jewish writer Walter Benjamin, a mainstay of the Frankfurt School,[70] arrived at the French–Spanish border equipped with an American visa given to him in Marseilles. Spanish guards refused to recognize it and blocked him from entering Spain. Exhausted and ill, Benjamin committed suicide.[71]

On October 9 McDonald received a telegram from the Nobel Prize–winning German writer Thomas Mann, who was then in New York.

Remembering your understanding kindness on so many occasions I trust you may forgive me for appealing to you very urgently on behalf of my friend and publisher Fritz Landshoff now in London stop My daughter Erika cabled from Mayfair Hotel London quote Landshoff most acutely endangered consul ready for visa if advised by McDonald committee Please do utmost and more stop At least arrange McDonald cable me immediately that case pending and likely to come through stop Erhardt of American Consulate tells me that emergency visas here already granted in four other cases endquote I may add that Landshoff certainly deserves your friendly consideration being one of the finest men and best publisher I have ever known stop His state of health alarming after internment of several months stop Immediate action imperative stop Viking Press and myself granted financial moral affidavits stop With warmest thanks and regards Yours.[72]

69. McDonald to Sulzberger, October 10, 1940, New York Times Company Archive, Sulzberger Autograph File, McDonald. Ignaz Paderewski, noted pianist and former Foreign Minister of Poland.

70. A center of philosophy and leftist interdisciplinary research forced to leave Germany in 1933. See Martin Jay, *The Dialectical Imagination: A History of the Frankfurt School and the Institute for Social Research, 1925–1950* (Berkeley: University of California, 1996).

71. Saul Friedländer, *Nazi Germany and the Jews, 1939–1945: The Years of Extermination* (New York: HarperCollins, 2007), 127.

72. Mann to McDonald, October 9, 1940, Telegram, Columbia University, D367 (PACPR), P32.

On the same day, George Warren and McDonald, and Francis Biddle and Henry Hart of the Solicitor General's office in the Justice Department met with the president. FDR read aloud the telegram from Ambassador Steinhardt in Moscow. Warren and McDonald tried to counter Steinhardt's argument that the refugees denied visas were not really intellectuals, and instead stress the delay in issuance of approved visas, noting that "Dr. Alvin Johnson of the New School for Social Research had recommended some 40 outstanding intellectuals during the summer, only 2 of whom had actually received visas."[73] It appears that McDonald also directly criticized Assistant Secretary of State Long, who had in fact approved the visas for rabbis in Baltic countries taken over by the Soviet Union, and that the president cut off this line of discussion.[74] At the same time, he expressed concern about the visa delays that the committee reported and asked Justice and State to work on finding ways around the practical problems that were causing delays in helping those who did appear to be qualified.[75]

McDonald felt vindicated by this conference, as he reported in a letter the next day [October 10] to Felix Frankfurter, Justice of the Supreme Court,

[I]t [the conference with the president] helped to sharpen his perception of those points on which attempts had been made to mislead him. At the end, he must have known who are responsible for thwarting his will.[76]

McDonald wrote gratefully to Eleanor Roosevelt:

He [FDR] now knows the full story and where the responsibility lies for the breakdown of the arrangements between his Advisory Committee and the two departments. I trust that the arrangements to be worked out by Mr. Biddle and the State Department will offer a basis for the rescue of those in imminent peril.

73. October 30, 1940, Minutes of the 41st Meeting of the President's Advisory Committee, McDonald Papers, Columbia University, D367 (PACPR), P64.

74. Long was not present at this meeting. But FDR briefed him afterward in a way that gave Long some satisfaction. As Long recorded it:

> He said that he hadn't had time to listen to McDonald and when he started condemning and criticizing me the President told him not to 'pull any sob stuff' on him and said that he knew enough about the situation to know that the Consuls abroad were not in sympathy with the policy and that he as President could not agree with any plan which would allow any organization in this country . . . to recommend finally that any person abroad whom they had not seen be admitted to this country

Long Diary, October 10, 1940, LC, Container 5. The tone here is completely at odds with McDonald's letters excerpted in the text. Part of the difference probably lies in FDR's ability to say different things to different audiences, and part is Long's own habit of interpreting things the way he wanted to. Still, even in Long's own account, FDR wanted to give the Justice Department a role and a veto, and McDonald could deal with Attorney General Biddle, rather than Long, in the future.

75. October 30, 1940, Minutes of the 41st Meeting of the President's Advisory Committee, McDonald Papers, Columbia University, D367 (PACPR), P64.

76. McDonald to Felix Frankfurter, October 10, 1940, McDonald Papers, Columbia University, D367 (PACPR), P19.

It was a relief, though I was not surprised, to have the President indicate by his whole manner during the conference that he realizes that we, the members of this Advisory Committee, have throughout been motivated solely by two considerations, our obligations to our consciences and our loyalty to him.[77]

Despite McDonald's tone in these letters, he and the President's Advisory Committee recognized an increasingly difficult situation for those seeking to escape danger in Europe. Fewer and fewer refugees were able to find transportation across the Atlantic—so the quotas were no longer being filled. Breckinridge Long and Avra Warren had found ways to block visas to most of those who could qualify for immigration visas or visitor's visas. Only the opposition of the Justice Department to new immigration legislation and the unwillingness of Undersecretary Welles to back Long on all points gave the Advisory Committee leverage with regard to individual cases, but not much.[78]

Would the Justice Department remain firm in its support of the President's Advisory Committee? How would consuls interpret the range of formal and informal instructions they had received since June? Particularly in an election year, President Roosevelt did not want to look soft on national security. Consuls in Europe could insist on unreasonable financial guarantees or guarantees of security, and the State Department and the president would back them up.

In the late stages of the presidential campaign Republican candidate Willkie claimed that a Roosevelt victory would mean certain American entrance into the war. He denounced the deal FDR had made around Congress to trade "surplus" destroyers for British bases in the Western Hemisphere as "the most dictatorial act ever taken by an American President."[79]

On October 8 FDR had been accidentally tape-recorded while talking privately to associates:

[T]he time may be coming when the Germans and the Japs will do some fool thing that would put us in. That's the only real danger of our getting in.[80]

Advocates of assistance to refugees could not reach a consensus on how to deal with the complex political and bureaucratic situation in the weeks before the presidential election. McDonald's executive secretary commented at one informal meeting:

77. McDonald to Eleanor Roosevelt, October 10, 1940, McDonald Papers, Columbia University, D361 (Eleanor Roosevelt Special File).

78. The Justice Department was indeed arguing with State over the proposed legislation. However, the sticking point was not whether or not consuls overseas should have the legal right to deny visas to those deemed a threat to public safety (Justice agreed with that), but concerns about how changing this in law might affect deportation law relating to immigrants already in the United States. By the end of November these concerns appear to have been resolved. Jackson to Mr. Holtzhoff (cc. Hart and Welles), November 29, 1940. Long Papers, LC, Container 211, Visa Division file.

79. Morgan, *FDR,* 539.

80. Robert J. C. Butow, "The FDR Tapes," *American Heritage* 33 (February–March 1982), 16–17, quoted by Weinberg, *A World at Arms,* 241.

[H]e feels compelled to resist an effort of a group in the State Department in association with AW [Avra Warren] which of itself sets up new tests for immigration visas, a practice which apparently is growing to the point where no visas are being issued at all. If there is a danger of complete cessation of immigration, I believe it should be challenged in principle, even though I am prepared to recognize that in the practical situation in Europe today very few visas can be issued, or should be issued, unless transportation facilities are available and it is possible for the visas to be used.[81]

On October 18 Undersecretary Welles, Long, Attorney General Biddle, and Hart agreed that the President's Advisory Committee still had semi-official status and could submit names of those who needed rescue, but that visitors' visas would be restricted to intellectual and political refugees and those (and their families) in imminent danger. If State, Justice, and the President's Advisory Committee all agreed that an applicant should not be rejected for an immigration visa, that recommendation would bind the consul. At least, this was how the President's Advisory Committee interpreted the agreement. It was alleviation of a deteriorating situation, rather than progress, but it indicated that the meeting with FDR had not been in vain.[82]

All this wrangling took some toll on McDonald, who wrote to a friend:

The McDonalds too are anxious to see the Robinsons. The difficulty is that I am home from Washington so few days a week, sometimes as few as one, that it is not possible for us to be civilized in our relations with our friends. I am afraid, therefore, that we must postpone seeing you until I have finished this special assignment in Washington.[83]

On the evening of November 5, election day, FDR had a premonition that he would lose to Willkie.[84] But the returns were better than even Democratic optimists expected: a margin of nearly five million popular votes and an electoral college majority of 449 to 82. Secretary of the Interior Ickes wrote in his diary:

Toward the end of the campaign I was confident that the President would win, although I will admit that I was very anxious. I wanted the thing settled. There were too many elements of doubt and uncertainty in it to suit me. I realized that Willkie had to win every doubtful state in order to carry the election.

. . . .

81. Notes of PACPR Dinner Meeting, October 14, 1940, YIVO, RG 278, Joseph Chamberlain Papers, Folder 46.

82. October 30, 1940, Minutes of the 41st Meeting of the President's Advisory Committee, McDonald Papers, Columbia University, D367 (PACPR), P64.

83. McDonald to Leland Robinson, October 30, 1940, McDonald Papers, USHMM, Correspondence between the McDonald family and the Robinson family.

84. Morgan, *FDR*, 540.

I called Henry Wallace [newly elected as vice president] to congratulate him. Henry and I both see the danger of an attempted coup d'etat by the wealthy people of the country. We both suspect that there are some very bad spots in the Army and we both appreciate the necessity of the Government's being carefully on guard, prepared to put down with a prompt and vigorous hand any signs of trouble.[85]

On November 8 Long predicted that the Justice Department would soon agree to his suggestions (outlined in a memorandum he attached), and it could then go to the president for approval. According to Long's draft memorandum to Undersecretary Welles:

The President's Advisory Committee on Political Refugees is recognized as having a preferential standing in recommending the issuance of visas to political refugees who may happen to be in special peril. . . .

Political refugees are understood to be those persons of outstanding character and reputation with intellectual accomplishments in the learned professions, the sciences, the arts and in journalism who, by reason of their activities, have antagonized the authorities in control of the totalitarian governments and who for that reason are either in physical danger or in danger of being so circumscribed and hindered in the practice of their profession that it would be for the welfare of civilization that they be removed to the United States as a haven of safety.

The Advisory Committee on Political Refugees will submit only cases which, in the exercise of a high degree of selectivity, are considered to have meritorious qualifications such as to incorporate their names in the category above mentioned. . . .

The Advisory Committee will make a thorough investigation into the character of the individuals proposed for consideration and the purposes of their entry into the United States and will summarize the results . . . in biographical sketches somewhat more detailed than those heretofore submitted.

. . . .

It is understood that the cabling of an individual's name to the consul as one approved through the procedure of the Advisory Committee does not constitute a mandatory instruction to the consul to issue a visa to the individual in question. The consul will give consideration to additional evidence in his own possession or which he may procure. He will either report to the Department of State that a visa issued or inform the Department of the considerations which seem to him to make such action doubtful or improper.[86]

85. *Secret Diary of Harold L. Ickes,* III, November 9, 1940, 362–363.
86. Breckinridge Long Memo, November 8, 1940, LC, Long Papers, Container 211, Visa Division file.

This draft was not what the President's Advisory Committee had expected—eligibility for intellectual and political refugees and those in imminent danger. It would have excluded Jews threatened by Nazi policies or by those of Vichy France. And, of course, the consul had the final say on a visa, whatever advice State and Justice sent from Washington.[87]

On November 13 Long wrote about a battle on another front:

Yesterday was a tough day. Amongst the other difficulties it developed late in the afternoon that the Governor of the Virgin Islands, Cramer by name, under the guidance of the Solicitor in the Department of the Interior and a Mr. Hart in the Department of Justice, had issued a proclamation admitting refugees to the Virgin Islands on their appearance at the port of entry. After a short period of residence in the Virgin Islands and an affidavit that they are bona fide residents they may proceed without visas or other formalities to the United States. There is no consular investigation of the individuals prior to their arrival in the Virgin Islands. There are twelve thousand refugees in Portugal and the only practical limitation upon their proceeding to the Virgin Islands is that they have enough money so that they will not become public charges. Amongst the twelve thousand are many German agents. Avra Warren has just returned from an inspection of our missions and consulates in Europe and spent about two weeks in Lisbon. He knows the situation there very well. . . . It constituted a pipeline to siphon refugees out of Portugal into the United States without the precautionary steps of investigation and check and is part of a program which Mr. Hart has indulged in in connection with the President's Advisory Committee. Biddle, the Solicitor General, has been associated with him, but I think he has not quite understood the purposes and objectives.

As soon as I could see Hull I laid the matter before him. Prior to that I had tried to reach the President, but he was in his swimming pool. Hull authorized me to talk to the President, and I had the opportunity over the telephone at nine o'clock last night. When I explained the matter to him he was a little perturbed and asked me to talk to Ickes immediately and to call him back. I talked to Ickes and found that he knew of the order and had authorized it and that he was an advocate of the whole scheme. . . . I told him that our consular activities served as a sieve through which we could strain the applicants. His reply was that the holes in the sieve were too small and that they ought to be bigger and perhaps now we could negotiate and get them bigger. The inference was very plain that he was trying to take into the United States persons whom he thought the Department of State would not admit. He was rather obdurate and a little sarcastic.

At the end of the conversation I called the President again and told him the situation. He was still more provoked and said that he would send an order

87. All quotations here from October 30, 1940, Minutes of the 41st Meeting of the President's Advisory Committee, McDonald Papers, Columbia University, D367 (PACPR), P64.

over there suspending the proclamation and authorized me to proceed with the scheme within the lines of his policy, which he has laid down and which I think I thoroughly understand.[88]

The president subsequently sent a frank memo to Secretary of the Interior Ickes:

No other department of the Government and no Governor of an Insular Possession may make a decision or issue a proclamation which involves foreign policy without the approval of the State Department and the President.

I yield to no person in any department in my deep-seated desire to help the hundreds of thousands of foreign refugees in the present world situation. The Virgin Islands, however, present to this Government a very serious social and economic problem not yet solved. If the Interior Department could find some unoccupied place not now a social and economic problem where we could set up a refugee camp . . . , that would be treated with sympathy by the State Department and by me.

Tell Margold that I have every sympathy but that if he has some better plan[,] to come and tell me about it and I will give it really sympathetic consideration. I cannot, however, do anything which would conceivably hurt the future of present American citizens. The inhabitants of the Virgin Islands are American citizens.[89]

Secretary of the Interior Ickes thought that FDR had been misinformed, writing in his diary:

The President said that he had written me a memorandum on the subject [refugees to the Virgin Islands] which I found when I returned to my office. In his memorandum he rather slapped my ears back by telling me that refugee matters were for him and the State Department to decide. However, in our talk he seemed open to suggestions and we discussed the subject in a friendly manner. It was clear that he had not quite understood our proposition. He thought that the refugees would have to have work to support themselves in the Virgin Islands. He was impressed with the suggestion that they would have to have enough money either in hand or pledged to take care of them while they were in the Virgin Islands. He thought that if certain conditions were met, it might be all right to go ahead with our plan. . . . The President said that he saw no harm in putting the whole question before Justice and finding on the law.[90]

88. Breckinridge Long Diary, November 13, 1940, LC, Container 5.
89. FDR to the Secretary of the Interior, December 18, 1940, FDRL, Official File 3186. The Virgin Islands plan, written up by Solicitor Nathan Margold in Interior, would have given visitor's visas to the Virgin Islands to refugees waiting for their turn to come up under the German immigration quota.
90. *Secret Diary of Harold L. Ickes*, III, December 21, 1940, 398–399. The main problem was that State Department regulations prohibited giving a visitor's visa to anyone who had on file an application for an immigration visa. The State Department view, which had held up action, was

On November 16 Eleanor Roosevelt spoke to a dinner gathering of about 1,500 in Chicago celebrating the 60th anniversary of the ORT organization, which specialized in Jewish vocational training.

I wish so often that we could emphasize more than we do how much this country owes to minority groups since the very beginning of our nation's history. It so happened a short time ago that I was looking up some facts and I discovered some very interesting things which perhaps many of you know. As you may be aware, my husband knows a great deal about American history, and in the family we often try to find out some little thing that he doesn't know. And so when I happened to do this little bit of research and found a few of what to me were new facts, I told my husband about one or two of them. After I told him about the first one, he said, "Why, of course, I have always known that." I told him that I had not known that Robert Morris was not the only person who was responsible for helping the struggling government of revolutionary days to remain financially on its feet. I had learned that Mr. Haym Solomon of Philadelphia not only gave of his genius but all of his fortune, practically $650,000, which in those days was a sum of money that very few people had, and he died a poor man. . . .

. . . .

I think we also have just as much responsibility today for the people who need help in Europe of every nationality—it is not only the Jewish people, though they have suffered most; there are many others who are suffering today; and I think that we—all of us who are fortunate to live in a country where we are free, where we can meet as we please—all of us have an obligation to help this suffering world get back to a period where we can say again, "We live in a civilized world."[91]

By late November McDonald explained bureaucratic realities to Monroe Gold-water, who had written to request assistance in getting a visa for one Alfred Lentschner:

It would be creating false hopes, however, if I were to suggest that the prospects were favorable for prompt action in this case. More and more, it has been the policy of the Department of State to issue visas only to those persons who fall into the category of distinguished intellectuals or prominent labor leaders or who can prove that they are in imminent danger. It would be under

that this required new legislation. President Roosevelt did consult the attorney general—see Margold to Ickes, December 26, 1940, and FDR Memorandum, December 27, 1940, FDRL, Official File 3186. Nonetheless, the plan remained blocked.

91. ORT Economic Bulletin, November–December 1940. Copy in NA RG 59, Lot File 52D408, Intergovernmental Committee on Refugees, 1942–1947, Miscellaneous Subject File, Box 4.

this latter category that I assume Alfred Lentschner's appeal would normally fall. I have noted what you say about the special danger which he is in and hope that the Department will interpret those circumstances in such a way as to lead them to classify him as being "in imminent danger."[92]

On December 17, in a press conference, President Roosevelt laid the basis for a Lend–Lease program to extend military aid to Britain (and later, other countries):

It is possible—I will put it that way—for the United States to take over British orders, and, because they are essentially the same kind of munitions that we use ourselves, turn them into American orders. We have enough money to do it. And thereupon, as to such portion of them as the military events of the future determine to be right and proper for us to allow to go to the other side, either lease or sell the materials, subject to mortgage, to the people on the other side. That would be on the general theory that it may still prove true that the best defense of Great Britain is the best defense of the United States, and therefore that these materials would be more useful to the defense of the United States if they were used in Great Britain, than if they were kept in storage here.

Now, what I am trying to do is to eliminate the dollar sign. That is something brand new in the thoughts of practically everybody in this room, I think—get rid of the silly, foolish old dollar sign.

Well, let me give you an illustration: Suppose my neighbor's home catches fire, and I have a length of garden hose four or five hundred feet away. If he can take my garden hose and connect it up with his hydrant, I may help him to put out his fire. Now, what do I do? I don't say to him before that operation, "Neighbor, my garden hose cost me $15; you have to pay me $15 for it." What is the transaction that goes on? I don't want $15—I want my garden hose back after the fire is over. All right. If it goes through the fire all right, intact, without any damage to it, he gives it back to me and thanks me very much for the use of it. But suppose it gets smashed up—holes in it—during the fire; we don't have to have too much formality about it, but I say to him, "I was glad to lend you that hose; I see I can't use it any more, it's all smashed up." He says, "How many feet of it were there?" I tell him, "There were 150 feet of it." He says, "All right, I will replace it." Now, if I get a nice garden hose back, I am in pretty good shape.[93]

At the December 19, 1940, meeting of the President's Advisory Committee, George Warren reported that the October 9 meeting with the president had resulted in new arrangements for treatment of refugees, confirmed in a letter sent from State to the Attorney General on November 23. Warren believed it had language that pro-

92. McDonald to Monroe Goldwater, November 25, 1940, McDonald Papers, Columbia University, D367 (PACPR), P20.
93. http://www.fdrlibrary.marist.edu/odllpc2.html.

vided for "more liberal interpretations . . . of the term 'political refugee' with respect to those who had reached Lisbon."[94]

Warren went on to report that newspapers in Washington and New York had recently run articles critical of the State Department's handling of visas. Although the President's Advisory Committee had not been mentioned in these articles, according to the minutes, Warren and Pell had "reached a tentative conclusion that in view of the fact that the matter of visa issuance had become in effect a political football the primary work of the President's Advisory Committee on the general aspects of the problem of refugees might be jeopardized by the continuance of the activity of recommending individuals for emergency visas."[95] *The minutes record that after some discussion the members of the committee agreed, unanimously, to "discontinue the function of acting as a channel for recommendations for the issuance of emergency visas."*[96] *The committee may have felt frustrated that it had not even seen the State Department's letter of November 23 to Justice.*

The move to drop its role had some effect upon the State Department. The minutes of the January 3, 1941, meeting of the committee explain:

Later that afternoon [December 19] Mr. Sumner Welles, Under-Secretary of State, had telephoned to him [McDonald] expressing the concern of the President, Secretary Hull, and the Under-Secretary of State at the action taken. Mr. Welles assured McDonald that the President, the Secretary, and he himself did not desire the Committee to take such action and requested that the action be canceled.[97]

A later article in the liberal newspaper PM *gave some color on this move:*

[T]he President's Advisory Committee voted to withdraw from its agreement with the State Department. They were only dissuaded from doing so by Mr. Welles, who telegraphed the Committee to come to Washington, where he assured it that something would be done to straighten out the mess.[98]

On December 20, the State Department sent out a circular telegram, marked urgent, to consuls in Europe:

[T]elegraph prompt report regarding visa cases forwarded to your office with recommendation of President's Advisory Committee . . . if visa not

94. Minutes of the 42nd Meeting of the President's Advisory Committee on Political Refugees, December 19, 1940, Wise Papers, Box 65, Center for Jewish History.
95. Minutes of the 42nd Meeting of the President's Advisory Committee on Political Refugees, December 19, 1940, Wise Papers, Box 65, Center for Jewish History.
96. Minutes of the 42nd Meeting of the President's Advisory Committee on Political Refugees, December 19, 1940, Wise Papers, Box 65, Center for Jewish History.
97. Minutes of the 43rd Meeting of the President's Advisory Committee on Political Refugees, January 3, 1941, Wise Papers, Box 65, Center for Jewish History.
98. "Long is Responsible for Refugee Scandal," *PM,* February 11, 1941.

granted state status of case giving in each case reason for delay and specifically nature of any difficulty if visa refused give detailed reasons for refusal expedite report as information desired promptly.

．．．．．．．

. . . all President Advisory Committee cases to be expedited . . . exit permits need not repeat not be required before issuing visa and if no adequate reason appears for withholding visa expedite issuance . . . visa should not repeat not be delayed for specific evidence . . . recommendations of President's Advisory Committee covers assurance of support and ability to proceed to third country.[99]

A few days later Secretary of State Hull convened a conference to try to smooth matters.

Mr. Hull stated that the activities of the President's Advisory Committee in functioning as a channel for recommendations with respect to visas had been most helpful . . . and sincerely appreciated. He realized that on such a controversial matter differences of opinion would inevitably arise but expressed every confidence that these could be resolved and urged the Committee to continue its activities. Mr. McDonald stated . . . that the Committee had been requested by Under-Secretary of State Welles to perform this function in July and that the Committee was anxious at all times to meet the wishes of the Department of State in every respect. He requested that Mr. Hull explain to the personnel of the Department of State that the Committee has been . . . doing its level best to perform a useful service under many difficulties. Thereupon Mr. Welles had confirmed to Mr. Hull the original invitation . . . and expressed complete confidence in the work of the Committee, appreciation of its services, and the hope that it would continue in this capacity without interruption.[100]

McDonald then received a copy of the letter Sumner Welles had sent to the Attorney General on November 23.[101]

In the cover letter Secretary of State Hull wrote:

99. State Department Circular Telegram to Consuls, December 20, 1940. Quoted in James B. Stewart, American Consulate General, Zurich, Switzerland, to All American Consular Officers in Switzerland, December 23, 1940, NA RG 84, American Consulate Basel, General Records, 1936–46, 800–811.4, Box 23.

100. Minutes of the President's Advisory Committee, January 3, 1941. Copy in Wise Papers, Box 65, Center for Jewish History.

101. Warren had suggested that a copy of this letter be provided to the committee at a December 23 meeting between himself, McDonald, Hull, and Welles. Minutes of the 43rd Meeting of the President's Advisory Committee, January 3, 1941, Wise Papers, Box 65, Center for Jewish History.

I was glad of the opportunity to tell you how helpful you have been and the Department hopes that you will continue.

Not long ago representatives of the Departments of State and Justice agreed upon the procedure now in effect for dealing with the cases which your Committee submits to the two Departments. Special danger resulting from opposition to totalitarian governments abroad has been our criteria without regard for class or racial distinctions. I am advised that you are cognisant of the steps which led up to the agreement. . . . I told you that I would send a copy of that letter to you and I take pleasure in enclosing it herewith.[102]

102. Hull to McDonald, December 30, 1940, YIVO RG 278, Joseph Chamberlain Papers, Folder 69. The November 23 letter gave the Advisory Committee a preferential status in recommending visas for those in danger in specific locations. Key portions of the text follow:

> The President's Advisory Committee will submit to the Department of Justice and to the Department of State the names of aliens recommended by the Committee as coming within the above category. The immediate members of the families of the political refugees referred to may be included in the recommendation if residing with and desiring to accompany or follow them to the United States. Persons of the foregoing categories desiring to come to the United States may be recommended by the Committee for immigration visas, visitor's visas, or transit certificates.
>
> In view of the changed conditions in Europe and the practical difficulties of obtaining exit or transit permits to cross land borders in Europe, Africa, and Asia, and limited transportation facilities by land, sea, and air, the statutory immigration quotas will become current during the present quota year. Persons recommended by the President's Advisory Committee who do not desire to obtain immigration visas or who are unable to obtain such visas, due to the blocked status of any quota, may be considered for visitor's visas on the understanding that the President's Advisory Committee will assist such persons after arrival in the United States to proceed to a third country, and upon suitable undertakings by the persons themselves that they will attempt in good faith to proceed to a third country.
>
> Political refugees and members of their immediate families who are in possession of valid visas for entry into a country other than the United States may be recommended by the Committee for the issuance of transit certificates. Such persons will agree to remain at the immigration station at the port of entry until departure therefrom by vessel for the country of destination and agree to make no request for a change of immigration status or extension of stay in the United States. Friends and relatives will make similar commitments before submitting the names of such persons to the President's Advisory Committee.
>
> The President's Advisory Committee, before recommending the names of aliens for visas, will make as thorough an investigation as may be possible concerning the character of the individuals, the purpose of their entry into the United States, the responsibility of the sponsors, and the assurance of support for the applicants. The results of such investigations will be summarized in detailed biographical sketches. Assurances of support accepted by the President's Advisory Committee will, if jointly approved by representatives of the two Departments, be regarded as sufficient to meet the public charge provisions of the immigration law.
>
> The names of aliens recommended by the President's Advisory Committee for immigration visas, visitor's visas, or transit certificates will be considered by a committee composed of representatives of the Department of State, the Department of Justice, the Military Intelligence Division, and the Office of Naval Intelligence. This committee will be convened as frequently as the occasion warrants to consider the recommendations of the Advisory Committee, and to advise the Department of State and the Department of Justice with respect thereto.
>
> The Department of State, in agreement with the Department of Justice, will transmit the names of these aliens to the appropriate consular officer and will request the consul to report concerning the action taken. The names will be submitted and reports received by telegraph.

This adjustment of the visa process amounted to creation of a bureaucratic maze, not an adequate method for saving those whose lives were in danger. The President's Advisory Committee would continue to do a great deal of the work involved, and it could still provide assurances for refugees to replace otherwise required documents. But with all the committee's recommendations for visas going through the State Department before being sent to the consuls, there would be further delays. It was not a good way to close the year.

Consuls will give immediate consideration to the cases of aliens approved by the two Departments and will act favorably upon them unless information before the consul indicates some ground for the applicant's exclusion from the United States. Before refusing to issue a visa or transit certificate to a person recommended by the President's Advisory Committee on Political Refugees, the consul will suspend action and inform the Department of State fully with respect thereto by telegraph for the information of the inter-departmental committee which will be convened as frequently as practicable to consider all questions raised by the consul's reports.

10. Close Relatives as Hostages: 1941

In his annual message to Congress in January 1941, President Roosevelt called upon the world to recognize four essential freedoms:

The first is freedom of speech and expression—everywhere in the world.

The second is freedom of every person to worship God in his own way—everywhere in the world.

The third is freedom from want—which, translated into world terms, means economic understandings which will secure to every nation everywhere a healthy peacetime life for its inhabitants—everywhere in the world.

The fourth is freedom from fear—which, translated into international terms, means a world-wide reduction of armaments to such a point and in such a thorough fashion that no nation will be in a position to commit an act of physical aggression against any neighbor—anywhere in the world.

FDR's close adviser and speechwriter Harry Hopkins had warned that such language covered an awful lot of territory:

"I don't know how interested Americans are going to be in the people of Java."

"I'm afraid they'll have to be some day, Harry. The world is getting so small that even the people in Java are getting to be our neighbors now."[1]

This grand vision of the future clashed harshly with American political realities. Those who sought to insulate the United States from the war in Europe intensely resisted those who saw further American support of Britain in the war against the Axis powers as urgent. Having pledged to make the United States the arsenal of democracy and proposed a Lend-Lease program to aid Britain, President Roosevelt was in the second camp. He was, however, unwilling to bring the country into the war without overwhelming public support. Only the December 7, 1941, Japanese attack at Pearl Harbor and, several days later, Germany's declaration of war against the United States reduced American opposition to going to war to politically negligible proportions.

---

1. Quoted (and adapted slightly) from Elizabeth Borgwardt, *A New Deal for the World: America's Vision for Human Rights* (Cambridge: Belknap, 2005), 20–21.

Refugees seeking entry to the United States represented a danger for many interventionists and isolationists. On January 11 the New York Herald Tribune *published an article alleging that American consuls abroad had been careless in scrutinizing visa applications, allowing Nazi agents to enter the United States. The article was enough to draw the attention of Secretary of State Hull.[2] Worries about potential American involvement in the war and fears of spies and saboteurs made the political climate difficult for those who favored humanitarian action in 1941.*

McDonald and the President's Advisory Committee still had some allies in Washington. The Justice Department, particularly Solicitor (and then Attorney General) Francis Biddle often challenged the State Department's efforts to tighten restrictions and cut back visas for refugees. Eleanor Roosevelt was willing to listen sympathetically and to intercede either with her husband or with Undersecretary Welles. And Welles himself often wanted at least a compromise, rather than unilateral State Department action. Moreover, he seemed to be aware that the lives of people were at stake, even if many could not be saved.

In spite of the fact that Welles was FDR's favorite in the State Department, his position there was not at all secure. His relations with Secretary of State Hull were bad.[3] It seems likely that Assistant Secretary of State Breckinridge Long, for reasons of ambition as well as because of policy disagreements, intrigued against Welles. Long also had a personal relationship with the president, and Visa Division chief Avra Warren had direct contacts with most of the consuls in Europe. In addition, much of the State Department was more conservative than Welles.

On January 2, 1941, Secretary of the Interior Ickes wrote in his diary about a conversation with columnist Drew Pearson.

Welles also told Pearson that he had never been castigated by anyone in his life as he had been by Hull. According to Pearson, most, if not all, of the principal men in the Department of State are now lining up against Welles, and Welles fears that Hull will try to get rid of him by forcing him to take an ambassadorship. . . .

Pearson also told me that Judge Moore, the counselor of the Department of State, is in bad health and that, even if he recovers, he will resign shortly. He suspects that, in the event of a vacancy there, Hull will want to put in Breckinridge Long, which will increase the power of the anti-Welles people in the Department.[4]

Who among the many refugees and victims of persecution was considered suitable for American visas—outstanding figures, or those in danger of their lives and with American supporters? The question directly affected the fate of many central

2. Coulter to Long, January 13, 1941, NA RG 59, 811.111 W.R./336. Copy in Long Papers, LC, Container 211, Visa Division file.
3. Irwin Gellman, *Secret Affairs: FDR, Cordell Hull, and Sumner Welles* (New York: Enigma Books, 2003), 243–246.
4. *Secret Diary of Harold L. Ickes*, III, 401–402.

European Jews applying to enter the United States. During 1940 State Department officials and the President's Advisory Committee had fought over the issue without clear resolution. In early January 1941 the American consul in Marseilles had to inquire:

Are persons approved by Department of State and Justice supposed to be eminent intellectuals? And if so, does Department desire to be informed when it appears from investigation that individuals are not intellectuals?[5]

The State Department response showed that the President's Advisory Committee had not yet lost all leverage to protect and assist Jews:

Persons recommended to and approved by Departments State and Justice do not repeat *not* necessarily have to be intellectuals but rather individuals who are in danger of apprehension due to their past activities [emphasis added].[6]

The process of getting together enough information and paperwork to qualify for an American visa was extremely complicated. Assistant Secretary of State Adolf Berle himself complained about the maze of State Department visa regulations and the inconsistency of applying them, particularly regarding the financial assurances required.

Some consulates ask . . . for a trust fund. Others ask for affidavits. One particularly shocking case stated that nothing would be accepted save from a relative in the United States under a legal obligation to support the applicant. . . .

It does seem to me that this Department could pull itself together sufficiently to get out a general instruction which would be complete enough and simple enough so that the procedure could be standardized.[7]

American Consul (in Marseilles) Hugh S. Fullerton sent out a memorandum that he regarded as reflecting the consuls' attitude toward immigration. Its author, Consul William L. Peck, was in charge of issuing visas in Marseilles:

I do not subscribe to the school of thought which advocates refusing visas to all persons whose faces we do not like, on some flimsy pretext or by invoking the technicalities of the immigration law to extreme limits. I deplore as much as anyone else the influx into the United States of certain refugee elements, but I do not believe that we can set ourselves up as supreme judges of

5. Fullerton to Secretary of State, January 3, 1941, 811.111 Refugees/787. Copy in USHMM, Accession 1994.A.0342, Roll 44.
6. Secretary of State to American Consul, Marseille, January 11, 1941, 811.111 Refugees/787. Copy in USHMM, 1994.A.0342, Roll 44.
7. Adolf Berle to Eliot B. Coulter, January 23, 1941, NA RG 59, 150.062 Public Charge/1352. Copy in McDonald Papers, USHMM.

general immigration policy. The immigration law gives us the authority and the responsibility for proper administration of the visa regulations and gives us a legal basis for refusing visas even in opposition to the Department's instructions. When I am convinced that there is a sound legal basis for refusal of a visa I am prepared to fight the Department to the limit, because we are often in a better position to judge the facts. But in matters of general policy I consider that we are agents of the Department and should carry out its policy. . . .

I am convinced from the tone of the Department's individual and general instructions over a period of months that the Department does desire that visas be issued, when quota numbers are available, to persons legally qualified for admission to the United States. . . . I further think that the Department wishes us to give considerable weight to humanitarian considerations and would approve the policy I am trying to follow of facilitating as much as possible the issuance of visas to aged people, especially those in the camps. These are the real sufferers and ones who are dying off. The young ones may be suffering, but the history of their race shows that suffering does not kill many of them. Furthermore, the old people will not reproduce and can do our country no harm, provided there is adequate evidence of support.

Some offices make a practice of refusing visas to applicants who cannot produce all their . . . documents. . . . Others go to extreme technical limits in throwing out support evidence. . . . Here we maintain a strict . . . standard, but avoid exaggeration. . . .

Another arbitrary method of refusal is to say that any applicant is "inimical to our best interests" unless he can prove the contrary (an almost impossible task). In cases of old, broken-down people going to their relatives for a few years of peace before they die, this is a manifest absurdity. In cases of younger people, naturally everyone is prima facie open to suspicion. . . . All we can do is to talk to the applicant and use whatever judgment God has endowed us with in determining whether or not he is suspicious. Any refugee, for instance, who has arrived recently from the occupied zone, or a German Jew without the "J" on his passport, or a Jew who is known to have consorted with Germans locally, is likely to be refused entirely on suspicion. . . .

The question of ability to travel has always been a difficult one, as so many factors are involved. . . . I think it best to continue issuing visas as long as we have numbers. . . .

As regards the cases approved by the President's Advisory Committee, I don't like them in general and think it is regrettable that the thing was ever started. However, there is nothing we can do about it and I think it is now useless to contest these cases unless we have some evidence against them morally or politically. Whenever quota numbers are available within a reasonable time, we are now making them wait for numbers rather than give them visitor's visas, as in most cases they are not in a position to depart immediately anyway. We always notify them as soon as authorization is received, which is what the

Department wants. Some of our young colleagues think it is smart to refuse to tell them their visas are authorized unless they actually come in and inquire.[8]

Sometimes, however, a consul was more liberal than State Department officials in Washington. On January 22 the American consul in Luxemburg cabled:

Several Jewish refugees in Luxemburg of German origin are unable [to] comply instructions . . . regarding character affidavits two responsible persons and are under urgent pressure immediate departure from Luxemburg. Will Department waive this requirement in otherwise acceptable cases?

An official in the Visa Division wrote:

It is somewhat surprising that such a message as the attached should be received from Luxemburg. It seems quite likely that there may be some effort behind it, on the part of the German authorities, to find a loophole in our procedure established as a result of the action of the Germans in issuing "whitewashed" police certificates to criminals in order that they might emigrate from Germany and German-occupied territory.

It seems doubtful whether the United States is so badly in need of immigrants that we can afford to accept, under the present international conditions, aliens who do not know at least two people who can vouch for their moral character and fitness to enter the United States.[9]

The visa practices of the Soviet Union—until June 22, 1941, an ally of Nazi Germany—and the ability of some Jews to get permits to leave or travel through the USSR continued to receive special scrutiny in Washington. Ray Atherton of the State Department's European Division wrote to Assistant Secretary of State Breckinridge Long about how to deal with some of those who had sponsored visa applicants there:

Mr. Bloom,[10] Mr. Green,[11] and Mr. Hillman[12] should . . . be told orally that the Department, basing itself upon information received from a number of reliable sources,[13] is convinced that the Soviet Government is granting permission

8. Fullerton to Hull, April 11, 1941, NA RG 59, VD 811.111 France/26. Copy in McDonald Papers, USHMM.

9. Waller to Secretary of State and Alexander Memorandum for the Files, January 22, 1941, NA RG 59, 811.111 Germany/21. Copy in McDonald Papers, USHMM.

10. Representative Sol Bloom, Democrat of New York.

11. William Green, president of the American Federation of Labor 1924–1952.

12. Sidney Hillman, founder of the Amalgamated Clothing Workers of America, and its president, 1914–1946.

13. Ambassador Steinhardt in Moscow loudly and frequently pushed this view. For example,

Individuals who departed from the Soviet Union or Soviet occupied territory since the outbreak of the war and apply in neutral or unoccupied countries for American visas should be regarded by the Department as even more likely to have agreed to act on

to many persons in Soviet-controlled territory to leave the country for the United States only on condition that they agree to act as Soviet agents, and that furthermore the Soviet authorities have given these persons to understand that their relatives remaining in the Soviet Union will suffer if the agreements are not lived up to.

I also consider that the matter is sufficiently important to be brought to the attention of the President by personal letter.[14]

Long was just as worried about Nazi Germany, writing in his diary:

For a week I have been trying to talk to the Secretary on the general [refugee] situation. I talked to Welles, and he thought we ought to talk to the President and lay the situation before him. The situation is just this, briefly: Our quota with Germany is 37,000 a year. That many emigrants can leave Germany. That many can be given visas.

Under our law the Consul gives visas to persons who are not excludable under the law. One of our regulations is that they must have exit permits before they get the visas. The exit permit and the police character record are furnished by the Gestapo. Germany is now sending two trainloads a week, 500 on each train, out of Germany, through France and Spain to Portugal. Passage for these persons is paid by Jewish aid societies and friends in the United States. The cost is $485 per person. Of this sum Germany gets $325 for railroad fare and expenses[,] and the balance goes to the steamship company from Portugal to the United States. That means that Germany is getting $235,000 foreign exchange a week, there being two trains with 500 persons on each train each week. A travel agency run by a man named Tausig in New York is acting for the Hebrew societies and sympathetic persons on this side. The payments are made in this country. The United States Lines is contemplating running the *Manhattan* and the *Washington* between New York and Vigo. They came to discuss the matter with me last week in company with Truitt of the Maritime Commission. I tried to discourage it but could not be specific . . . [15]

While no arrangement exists between the two Governments, there is no doubt in operation a systematic traffic in private hands with the connivance of the German Government. It is sinister, because the German Government only

behalf of the GPU in the United States than those who apply within the Soviet Union. . . . A considerable percentage of those who receive such exit visas have agreed to cooperate with GPU agents in the United States.

Steinhardt to Secretary of State, May 30, 1941, NA RG 59, 811.111 Refugees/1456. Copy in McDonald Papers, USHMM.

14. Atherton to Long, January 17, 1941, NA RG 59, 811.111 Refugees/820. Copy in McDonald Papers, USHMM. In a handwritten memo attached to this file, Sumner Welles agreed.

15. The U.S. Maritime Commission soon refused them permission to send these two ships to Lisbon to pick up waiting refugees. Minutes of the 46th Meeting of the President's Advisory Committee on Political Refugees, March 18, 1941, McDonald Papers, Columbia University, D367 (PACPR), P65.

gives permits to persons they want to come to the United States. It is a perfect opening for Germany to load the United States with agents.[16]

Long's diary entry gives the impression that Germany was flooding the United States with tens of thousands of Jewish refugees. According to Visa Division records, in the period from July 1, 1940, to March 31, 1941, a total of 2,126 immigration visas were issued by American consulates in Greater Germany. Far more visas—10,020— were issued under the German quota—by American consulates in other countries (e.g., Great Britain, Cuba), where Germany had no leverage.[17] The full immigration quota for Germany (actually 27,370 for the fiscal year) was not being used.

In early February Eleanor Roosevelt's private secretary Malvina Thompson wrote to McDonald, drawing upon a phone conversation with Undersecretary Welles. Her information contradicted Long's version in several respects.

In regard to the question of expediting the getting out of the refugees who have visas for this country, the number of consuls have been increased and Mr. Welles feels that this should expedite the issuing of exit visas.[18] However the great difficulty is getting them out. They do not want them to go through Spain to Portugal because the Germans force the Spaniards to hold them up and not allow them to get to Portugal. The State Department is trying to get the French government to make it possible for ships to get them at Marseilles and take them to Casa Blanca [Casablanca]. They are also trying to get the United States Lines to send a ship to Casa Blanca when there are a sufficient number of refugees. Mr. Welles talked this over with the President, who is in full accord.[19]

This was not a picture of Germany seeking to flood the United States with refugees.

At the cabinet meeting of February 14, according to Secretary Ickes,

The President is wondering about the possibility of making the Azores available for refugees. He thought that these islands would be capable of taking care of a good many refugees and that then the United States would be justified in protecting them there. I think that what is running in the President's mind all the time is some formula that would justify sending American ships further east in the Atlantic.[20]

---

16. Long Diary, January 28, 1941, LC, Container 5.

17. Visas issued at German issuing offices by months from July 1, 1940, to March 31, 1941, USHMM, 1994.A.0342, Roll 48.

18. On December 30, 1940, Eleanor Roosevelt had written Welles about the problem of individuals who received American visas but were unable to use them: "one fact is that they cannot get visas to go through Spain." Roosevelt to Welles, December 30, 1940, 811.111 Refugees/773. Copy in USHMM, Accession 1994.A.0342, Roll 44.

19. Malvina C. Thompson, Secretary to Eleanor Roosevelt, to McDonald, February 3, 1941, McDonald Papers, Columbia University, D367 (PACPR), P43.

20. *Secret Diary of Harold L. Ickes*, III, February 16, 1941, 434.

On February 11 the liberal newspaper PM *published a scathing feature on Assistant Secretary of State Long, who was accused of lack of support for President Roosevelt's foreign policy, sabotaging the work of the President's Advisory Committee, and permitting anti-Semitic consuls to remain in Berlin and Zurich:*

If Mr. Long is to continue in his present position, most refugees in unoccupied France might as well give up hope of ever obtaining U.S. visas. Mr. Long says the U.S.A. can't grant visas unless the applicant has an exit permit from the country in which he is at present resident. The Vichy Government, before it will grant exit permits, requires that refugees have all their papers in order, including transit visas and visas of entry.

In other words, the Vichy Government will not grant exit permits until the applicant has a visa and the U.S.A. will not grant a visa until the applicant has an exit permit. Mr. Long simply denied that the Vichy Government required a visa to give an exit permit.[21]

On February 27 the American consul in Basel, Switzerland telegraphed the State Department:

Have learned from confidential but thoroughly dependable source that German Consulate here received instructions about three weeks ago to approach carefully selected German Jewish refugees, either already endeavoring to emigrate to the United States or who would like to emigrate and who have families or close relatives still in Germany, with offers of whatever financial assistance may be necessary to enable them to qualify for American visas, assistance in obtaining the necessary transit certificates, et cetera, provided they agree to work secretly for the German Government in the United States. . . .

It is stated that the same offers are being made in the Netherlands but have no definite information as to any other countries.[22]

This cable gave restrictionists in the State Department the evidence and the occasion they had been looking for. Even Assistant Secretary of State Berle, who had criticized the Visa Division previously, was alarmed by the cable from Basel:

For some time we have known that certain refugees were being approached by foreign governments and being asked to act as spies in the United States. The Russian Government was the greatest sinner in this respect, particularly with reference to refugees from the Baltic republics.

It is now established that Germany is doing the same thing (see telegram . . . from Basel). It must be assumed that the same process is going on in Portugal.

21. "Long is Responsible for Refugee Scandal," *PM*, February 11, 1941.
22. Blake to Secretary of State, February 27, 1941, 811.111 Refugees/1048, USHMM, Accession 1994.A.0342, Roll 46.

It seems to me that from now on every visa application will have to be referred to Washington . . . [which can give lists of these people to the FBI and otherwise have them checked].[23]

Robert Pell, the longtime State Department liaison with the Intergovernmental Committee on Refugees, who had been actively involved with resettlement efforts in the Dominican Republic,[24] was a victim of a sudden shift within the State Department. After he returned from a trip to Ciudad Trujillo in late February, he found complete upheaval. McDonald apparently was among the first who gave him the bad news, sending him a telegram and arranging a phone conversation:

Grateful if you would telegraph collect Care Henry Ittleson Pal[m]Beach, telephone number where I could reach you this evening about seven o'clock.[25]

There is no other record of their phone conversation, but Pell soon recounted developments to a friend:

I have not been as good a correspondent as I might because events were moving so rapidly here that I hardly had time to catch my breath. The sad fact is that while I was away a staggering blow was dealt to my bureau and my work. Mr. Wagg[26] was obliged to resign yesterday. No new Secretary of the Intergovernmental Committee has been appointed and there does not seem to be any prospect of appointing one. I have been instructed not to intervene further in any individual immigration cases, and to discontinue my liaison with the President's Advisory Committee, et cetera, et cetera. I can find very little trace of the machinery which I built up so laboriously during the last three years. . . . I cannot even send you the paper of the Intergovernmental Committee because it has been purloined.[27]

Pell's letters to his former boss Myron Taylor gave more details:

Henceforth I was [told] not to have any part in or knowledge of any individual cases of immigration, or cases including those of the President's Advisory Committee and the Dominican Republic Settlement Association; and . . . from that time on I was to discontinue my liaison with organizations in New

23. Berle to Hull, Welles, and Long, February 28, 1941, NA RG 59, 811.111 Refugees/1883. Copy in McDonald Papers, USHMM.

24. See chapter 11 for more details.

25. McDonald to Pell, telegram, February 27, 1941, NA RG 59, Lot File 52D408, Intergovernmental Committee on Refugees, 1942–47, Miscellaneous Subject File, Box 4.

26. Alfred Wagg, State Department official who acted as secretary for the Intergovernmental Committee on Refugees. Wagg had been heavily involved with the resettlement effort in the Dominican Republic.

27. Robert Pell to Georges Coulon, February 28, 1941, NA RG 59, Lot File 52D408, Intergovernmental Committee, 1942–47, Miscellaneous Subject File, Box 4.

York, including the President's Advisory Committee, Dominican Republic Settlement Association and the Coordinating Foundation. . . .[28]

The fact is that Mr. Long apparently made up his mind some months ago that he was not going to have any Intergovernmental Committee around this Department. He has since that time indulged in an unrelenting attack on the work and the officers who had the misfortune, not of their own choice, to be connected with it. There is just no use going on. I did not tell you in the letter but it is unfortunately a fact, Mr. Long tried to make personal charges against Mr. Wagg which had to be withdrawn after I put up a fight.[29]

I hate to bother you with these matters and don't wish you to do anything but reply formally to my formal letter that you regret that I can no longer continue in this work. That will complete the record. I do not know what the reason for it is but Mr. Long seems to have some special spite for anything with which you are associated. As you will recall he was the author of measures restricting the mechanical aspects of your office at the Vatican[30] and there is no doubt that he has made up his mind to put an end to the Intergovernmental Committee as well.

. . . .

I am sorry that all of our good work of the past three years has ended this way, but there it is.[31]

McDonald then questioned whether it was worthwhile to continue the existence of the President's Advisory Committee. He turned to Eleanor Roosevelt, who replied:

I spoke to the President and he says he certainly does not believe that the people in the State Department thought that he wanted the committee's work to come to an end, or that he does not want to get proper refugees over here.

The President thinks you are doing a very remarkable piece of work and he wants you to continue, and he wants the skeleton committee held together, because of the future.

He feels that if a few of the people are turned down you should not become discouraged, because sometimes things are discovered in an investigation which make it necessary to refuse, and these investigations have to be made.[32]

28. Pell to Taylor, March 7, 1941, FDRL, Myron Taylor Papers, Box 5, Folder Intergovernmental Committee on Political Refugees, Correspondence, October 1939–1941.

29. In an April 28, 1941, article published in the *New Republic*, Wagg charged that the American "refugee effort has been at best a stepchild in Washington, to be beaten and buffeted, and at worst a football for anti-Semitism and for petty bureaucrats, including those who take delight in sabotaging the President's program just because it is his." Quoted by Wyman, *Paper Walls*, 163.

30. In 1940 President Roosevelt had appointed Taylor as special envoy to the Vatican.

31. Pell to Taylor, March 3, 1941, FDRL, Taylor Papers, Box 5, Intergovernmental Committee on Political Refugees, Correspondence, October 1939–1941.

32. Eleanor Roosevelt to McDonald, March 2, 1941, Eleanor Roosevelt Papers, Box 1612, FDRL.

On March 5 Assistant Secretary of State Adolf Berle wrote in his diary:

[T]hen to a meeting in the Secretary's office, where we decided to elaborate some machinery to tighten up a little on the supervision of some of the refugees coming here in large numbers. This is an unhappy job, but it is necessary. We have evidence that both Russia and Germany are not allowing many of these refugees to get out unless they first sign agreements that they will act as spies for the government.[33]

The next day, Visa Division chief Avra Warren, expressing much the same view to the President's Advisory Committee, spelled out some of the bureaucratic details of a new plan.

[A] number of Interdepartmental Committees might be set up composed of representatives of the Departments of State and Justice, the F.B.I. and the Military and Naval Intelligence Services. The representatives of these Departments would devote full time to their tasks and the clerical staff of the State Department would be increased by 200 to 300 persons through a deficiency appropriation to be secured in Congress.

The plan also envisaged the submission of recommendations for visas to the Department of State by the President's Advisory Committee after preparation and approval in the manner already in operation. Documents in support of applicants would naturally also be presented directly to the Department of State but these latter would require more careful scrutiny and investigation by the Departments than those submitted by the President's Advisory Committee following its present practice.[34]

On March 13 FBI director J. Edgar Hoover sent a personal and confidential letter to Assistant Secretary of State Berle:

From a confidential source I have received information to the effect that Germans desiring to enter the United States for subversive purposes are able to obtain quota visas quite readily at the consulates. It is reported that Germans on the West Coast have remarked that it is very easy to obtain quota visas now since there are so many quota visas available.[35]

33. Berle Diary, March 5, 1941, Berle Papers, Box 212, Diary, January–April 1941, FDRL.

34. Minutes of the 45th Meeting of the President's Advisory Committee on Political Refugees, March 6, 1941, Wise Papers, Box 65, Center for Jewish History.

35. Hoover to Berle, March 13, 1941, NA RG 59, 811.111 Quota 62/995. Copy in McDonald Papers, USHMM.

Given the increased difficulties of getting a visa, McDonald took an initiative on behalf of those who had managed to get visas but were still stranded because of lack of transportation. He and George Warren cabled the president:[36]

At a meeting today of your Advisory Committee on Political Refugees the members voted to bring to your attention the desperate plight of refugees caught in southwestern Europe many of whom have American visas in hand but are unable to leave because of lack of shipping from Lisbon. The recent denial by the Maritime Commission of permits for the steamships *Washington* and *Manhattan* to call at Lisbon removes their last hope of escape for indefinite months to come when it may be too late. We respectfully urge you to ask the Maritime Commission to reconsider its decision.[37]

The committee's telegram to the president did little good. The president referred the issue to the State Department. On April 4, 1941, Breckinridge Long wrote to McDonald:

I have discussed this matter with Admiral Land of the Maritime Commission and understand that the *Manhattan* will be in dry dock until about the end of June and that the *Washington* has been chartered to the Army.

. . . Admiral Land indicated that consideration was being given to the question of chartering the *Siboney* for use in evacuating refugees. . . .

We have been very much interested in the Department in the problem of the evacuation to the United States of refugees who have obtained visas from our consuls in Europe, and this matter will continue to have our particular attention.[38]

Lisbon was crowded, and life for refugees there extremely difficult. The Portuguese government tolerated only limited numbers of refugees, who could not work to support themselves. Who knew whether the Germans would move in? On May 30 Secretary of the Interior Ickes wrote:

With Crete in the hands of the Germans as it now is, according to this morning's papers, all of the eastern Mediterranean may be closed to the British. There may follow the capture of all of North Africa by the Germans. Then Hitler will be ready to tackle Gibraltar, but before doing this he will probably

36. Original telegraph in capitals.

37. McDonald and Warren, on behalf of President's Advisory Committee, to President Roosevelt, March 18, 1941, Wire. Copy in McDonald Papers, Columbia University, D367 (PACPR), P65.

38. Long to McDonald, April 4, 1941, McDonald Papers, Columbia University, D367 (PACPR), P28. In May, George Warren reported to the committee that the U.S. Army had requisitioned the *Manhattan*. Minutes of the 48th Meeting of the President's Advisory Committee on Political Refugees, May 21, 1941, McDonald Papers, Columbia University, D367 (PACPR), P65.

Plate 20. Members of the President's Advisory Committee after calling at the White House on September 4, 1941, *left to right:* Paul Baerwald, Monsignor Michael J. Ready, J. P. Chamberlain, James G. McDonald, Hamilton Fish Armstrong, Archbishop Joseph F. Rummel, George L. Warren, and Rabbi Stephen S. Wise.

Photo by Harris & Ewing, *PM* newspaper, Joseph Chamberlain papers, YIVO Archive.

Plate 22. Jewish refugees building the road to Buena Tierra, Bolivia, a colony on the slopes of the Andes Mountains, established by Mauricio Hochschild with aid from the Joint Distribution Committee, ca. December 1941.

USHMM, courtesy of the American Jewish Joint Distribution Committee.

Plate 23. Approximately 20,000 German, Austrian, and Czech Jews were transported to the Łódź ghetto in the autumn of 1941 and deported to the Chełmno death camp in early 1942. Here a German Jew, laden with his belongings, waits at an assembly point for deportation to Chełmno, ca. January–April 1942.   USHMM, courtesy of YIVO.

Plate 31. Mauricio Hochschild *(center)* at the Exhibition of Industrial and Handicrafts Products by Jewish Immigrants, La Paz, Bolivia, October 1943.
American Jewish Joint Distribution Committee.

Plate 32: In both German and Latvian, the sign warns that anyone attempting to cross the fence or to contact inhabitants of the Riga ghetto will be shot. 1941–1943. USHMM, courtesy of Joseph Levy.

Plate 33. Third meeting of the Board of Directors of the War Refugee Board, in the office of Secretary of State Cordell Hull, March 21, 1944. *Left to right:* Hull, Treasury Secretary Henry Morgenthau, Jr., Secretary of War Henry Stimson, and Executive Director John Pehle.   USHMM, courtesy of Franklin D. Roosevelt Library.

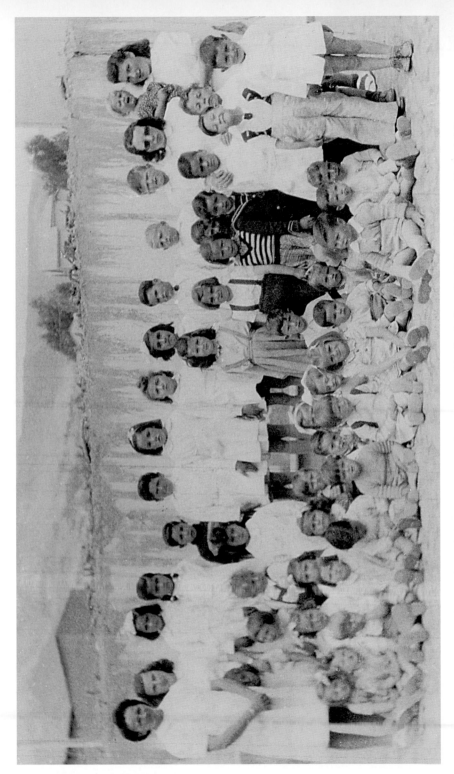

Plate 32. Kindergarten class at the Jewish Kinderheim in La Paz, Bolivia, supported by funds from the JDC and Mauricio Hochschild's Sociedad de protección inmigrantes, 1944–1945.   USHMM, courtesy of Leo Spitzer.

Plate 35. Under the supervision of an American soldier, survivors move carts laden with corpses to a spot behind the Dachau crematorium, April 29–May 5, 1945. USHMM, courtesy of Colonel Samuel A. Custer.

take Portugal and require France to come in on his side. The German line is closing in, the British are falling back, although fighting desperately, and we are still talking.[39]

Transit through Spain and transportation across the Atlantic continued to be serious constraints during the first half of 1941. McDonald later wrote to the acting governor of the Virgin Islands, who was interested in the case of a refugee in France:

For your own information, I might add that today the problem for persons in France trying to come to this country is not so much that of securing a visa, though this is extremely difficult, but even more that of securing transportation. In fact, after an American visa has been granted, there will still be the more and more difficult problem of getting transit visas through Spain and Portugal. Then following that, the present facilities for transportation out of the Portuguese capital give no promise of facilities for newcomers within a year and a half or two years. Meanwhile, the boats which formerly cleared intermittently from Marseilles have, with very rare exceptions, discontinued service from that port.[40]

On April 25 Breckinridge Long wrote in his diary:

The President has approved the proposal to concentrate visa control in Washington and has directed the allocation of space near the Department for that purpose. . . .

Simultaneously with the President's approval there came a proposal from the Secretary of War transmitting a copy of recommendation to the President by the chiefs of M.I.D. [Military Intelligence Division], O.N.I. [Office of Naval Intelligence][,] and F.B.I. to control all immigration into the United States through visas, diplomatic as well as others, and to institute an exit permit system. I have gradually been moving in that direction for a year. . . . Now the Secretary has approved it, and I am hopeful that legislation has been passed to effectuate it.[41]

On the same day Long had a telephone conversation with Clarence Pickett, head of the American Friends Service Committee, who wrote a summary of it. Pickett was following up the case of rabbinical students from Warsaw who had, with Long's

---

39. *Secret Diary of Harold L. Ickes*, III, May 30, 1941, 527.
40. McDonald to Robert Lovett, May 27, 1941, McDonald Papers, Columbia University, D367 (PACPR), P38.
41. Long Diary, April 25, 1941, LC, Container 5. This recommendation, dated April 25, 1941, put virtually all the existing American intelligence agencies behind the proposal to establish centralized control of admission of aliens and sought their participation in it. It was signed by J. Edgar Hoover, FBI, Sherman Miles, Military Intelligence Division, War Department, and Alan Kirk, Office of Naval Intelligence. NA RG 59, 811.111 W.R. Committees/1. Copy in McDonald Papers, USHMM.

approval, received American visas earlier. They had made their way across the Soviet Union and into Japan, but were stuck there.[42]

I told him that there were 38 of them there [in Yokohama] whose [American] visas had been withdrawn and whose permission to remain [in Japan] expired April 30th. He said that this was the result of a general order recalling visas from people who had relatives in Poland, Russia, or Germany. They have discovered that German and Russian agents in this country are putting pressure on refugees from Germany, Poland, and Russia to undertake certain espionage acts under threat of having their relatives in their country of origin punished if they do not carry out the requirements of the agent. While there are only a very few cases where this has happened, Mr. Long felt there were enough to justify this general order. He said that it did not mean that visas would never be given to people who had relatives in their country of origin, but it did mean that a new examination for each individual had to be carried out. . . .

I told him that while I did not know these particular young men, I did know the religious organization with which they were affiliated and believed in their complete integrity. While he accepted this, he still felt that no exception could be made. He insisted that he was greatly distressed by the discomfort that had been caused by the order, but still felt that the order was wise and necessary.

The next day Secretary of the Interior Ickes wrote:

Bill Bullitt called me up and I asked him to lunch with me on Tuesday [April 21]. I had not seen him for some time. He continued to be pessimistic about the war—more pessimistic than anyone with whom I have come in contact. And the dreadful part of it is that I don't know but that he may be right. He said that the next few days would bring very bad news from Greece and this proved to be the fact. He seemed to doubt whether England would be able to withstand Germany and he said that within four years our Government would be something entirely different from what it is today. This, too, may be true.

. . . He keeps insisting that the President is too tired to do anywhere near what he undertakes to do.[43]

On May 2 State Department Legal Adviser Richard W. Flournoy commented on a proposed telegram to consuls abroad to deny visas to applicants who had close relatives living in totalitarian countries:

42. April 28 Memorandum giving the gist of the telephone conversation . . . at 3:45 P.M. April 25, 1941, American Friends Service Committee Archives, Refugee Service 1941, Polish Refugees.

43. *Secret Diary of Harold L. Ickes,* III, April 26, 1941, 486–487.

The expression "totalitarian countries" worried me at first, since it is a colloquial term rather than a term of art. However, I suppose it will be understood by the missions and consulates to refer to the five countries: Germany, Italy, Japan, Russia and Spain, as intended by those who prepared the telegram.

. . . .

The Supreme Court of the United States has repeatedly emphasized the broad principle that the entry of aliens into the United States is a privilege, rather than a right, and, at a time like this when the safety of the country is imperiled, it seems fully justifiable to resolve any possible doubts in favor of the country, rather than in favor of the aliens concerned. I may add that this telegram seems to involve to a considerable degree the exercise of administrative judgment and discretion within the limits of the law.[44]

Subsequent discussion within the State Department narrowed the field of totalitarian countries to just Germany, Italy, and the Soviet Union.

On May 8 Ambassador Steinhardt in Moscow wrote a long personal letter to Assistant Secretary of State Long in which he expressed the view that "when there is even the remote possibility of a conflict between humanitarianism and the welfare of the United States [I am of the view] that the former must give way to the latter."[45]

On May 20 Representative Lindley Beckworth, a Texas Democrat, introduced a bill to empower consuls to refuse visas to anyone whose admission they considered to be a danger. A new member of the House Committee on Immigration and Naturalization, Beckwith had been in touch with Breckinridge Long since January and had expressed fear that:

persons coming in large numbers from the countries from which they were now coming, many of them would not hold ideas that were consonant with our ideas here; that he was apprehensive as to what might happen; that he understood that they were largely intellectuals, gifted in writing and lecturing; that they would continue an activity in this country that might not be to the best interests of this country; that he just wanted to know about it all and be in a position before his committee to examine the whole picture.[46]

Beckworth also asked the State Department for a list of cases of visa applicants recommended by the President's Advisory Committee, and the Visa Division also gave him a statistical summary of the occupations of numbers 400 to 500 on the committee's recommended list.

---

44. Flournoy Memorandum, May 2, 1941, 811.111 Refugees/1507, USHMM, 1994.A.0342, Roll 45.

45. Steinhardt to Long, May 8, 1941, NA RG 59, 840.48 Refugees/5-841.

46. Long's Memorandum of Telephone Conversation with Beckworth, January 28, 1941, Long Papers, LC, Container 211, Visa Division file.

Members of families (includes children, mothers, students, and widows)	43
Jewish leaders and rabbis	34
Lawyers and attorneys	5
Editors and publishers	2
Authors and journalists	2
Artists, lecturers on art and art dealers	2
School officials	2
Labor leaders	1
Merchants, businessmen, traders, industrialists, manufacturers, bankers	1
Metallurgist-accounts	1
Diamond dealers	1
No occupation given by alien[47]	4

Beckworth's bill, H.R. 4817, was a direct slap at the President's Advisory Committee and its recommendations. The State Department had originally conceived of this bill in September 1940, but Justice Department opposition had held it up.[48]

On June 4 Congressman John Rankin, Democrat of Mississippi, told the House of Representatives:

Mr. Speaker, Wall Street and a little group of our international Jewish brethren are still attempting to harass the President . . . and the Congress of the United States into plunging us into the European war, unprepared. . . . These international bankers are so afraid that this peace movement . . . might take root . . . before they can get us into it [the war] that on yesterday they held a rally in Wall Street and . . . made a plea to that effect.[49]

In a June 5 speech in the Senate Robert Reynolds of North Carolina quoted from Ambassador Steinhardt's October 5, 1940, cable regarding the Soviet Union's issuance of visas to Jews who agreed to perform espionage. Reynolds concluded:

I wish to say—and I say it without the slightest hesitation—that if I had my way about it at this hour I would today build a wall about the United States so high and so secure that not a single alien or foreign refugee from any country upon the face of the earth could possibly scale or ascend it.[50]

47. Avra Warren to Beckworth, March 15, 1941, 811.111 Refugees/1146B, USHMM, 1994.A.0342, Roll 46.

48. See chapter 9, p. 212. Also, George Warren summary of a meeting, Oct. 14, 1940, YIVO, Joseph Chamberlain Papers, RG 278, Folder 46.

49. "The Last Gavel," *Time,* June 16, 1941.

50. *Congressional Record,* June 5, 1941. Reynolds was an extreme isolationist and Anglophobe who once compared Hitler's conquests to American expansion westward.

George L. Warren contacted the members of the President's Advisory Committee:

You will note that Senator Reynolds has quoted extensively from the cable sent by Ambassador Steinhardt of Moscow last October. . . . You will recall that we were able to answer the charges of the cable very readily both directly to the President and to Mr. Sumner Welles and Mr. Breckinridge Long. Among other things we pointed out that the President's Advisory Committee had sent no recommendations to Moscow[,] as it was particularly restricted by the arrangements to the area of southwestern Europe. . . . [There is no justification for] the charges contained in the cable. How the copy of the cable came into the hands of Senator Reynolds is unknown. Such communications are in practice considered confidential and are not available to members of Congress.[51]

In early June the State Department released information about its plan to set up interdepartmental review committees to handle visa applications. The Visa Division, the Immigration Service (within the Justice Department), the FBI, the Military Intelligence Division, and the Office of Naval Intelligence would all send representatives to these committees, which would consider the cases of visa applicants "from the viewpoint of national defense." Their recommendations would be sent to consuls abroad, who had the right to make individual decisions. Nonetheless, the consuls were instructed to suspend action on doubtful cases and seek further guidance from the review committees in Washington.[52]

On June 17 Breckinridge Long wrote:

We are tightening up on our immigration and refugee problems. Steinhardt wrote me a very long letter in response to one of mine in which he went fully into the subject from the point of view of Russia. Other advices we have had from Berlin, Rome, Spain and other places together with Steinhardt's long letter serve as the basis for our decision to regulate the entry into the United States of persons with relatives in Germany, Russia or Italy or occupied territories. It has been well established that the practice of those Governments has been to use the relatives and their control over them as a means of directing the movements of those who have already reached the United States. It is an insidious practice and constitutes an effective control over many persons whom we have allowed to come to the

51. Francis Biddle, solicitor general in the Justice Department, also protested this use of Steinhardt's cable. Biddle to Welles, personal and confidential, June 27, 1941, NA RG 59, 811.111 Refugees/1613. Copy in McDonald Papers, USHMM. Long was known to have shown Steinhardt's cable around in order to muster support or defuse criticism. See Francis Pickett Journal, June 9, 1941, American Friends Service Committee Archive.

52. Proposed New Visa Regulations, June 3, 1941, NA RG 59, 811.111 Committees/3. Copy in McDonald Papers, USHMM.

United States to the end that they serve as agents of Germany or Italy or Russia. We have decided to prevent their coming to the United States.[53]

On June 18 the New York Times *published an article largely based on information in an announcement from the State Department:*

In view of the increasing number of instances known to the Department where persons leaving certain countries in Europe have been permitted to leave only after entering into an obligation to act as agent in the United States for the governments controlling the countries from which they desired to depart, the Department of State on June 5, 1941, telegraphing instructions to diplomatic and consular officers, directed the withholding of visas from aliens having close relatives still residing in certain countries and in territories held by these countries.

Although each individual applications for a visa is to be determined on its own merits, it was deemed advisable to withhold visas in all cases in which the visa applicant has children, parents, spouse, brothers or sisters still remaining in such territory.

In cases in which, in the consul's opinion, a visa may be granted without endangering the public safety of the United States to an alien who has some close relative residing in territory controlled by governments which have demonstrated that they have developed practices inimical to our national security, the consul is instructed to report the facts to the department for further consideration.[54]

That same afternoon, Reinhold Niebuhr, the chairman of the Union for Democratic Action, telegraphed Secretary of State Hull:

The effect of this ruling will be to discourage those courageous victims of Hitler who have been fighting our battles for many years and without whose active cooperation the struggle against totalitarianism cannot be successfully waged. We can imagine no justification for this ruling. Had the ruling been in effect in recent years, American asylum would have been refused to those great representatives of European culture whose contribution to American life and its defense has already been invaluable. We need only mention Albert Einstein,

53. Long Diary, June 17, 1941, LC, Container 5.
54. *New York Times*, Wednesday, June 18, 1941, "Instructions to Consuls." The *Times* clearly had access to the State Department circular telegram sent to consuls June 5, for the first three paragraphs of the newspaper article repeats its language almost word for word. It does not mention the circular's additional warning to consuls to watch out for applicants who try to conceal the existence of relatives in order to avoid being denied. See Cordell Hull's "Circular Telegram Sent to Certain Diplomatic Missions and to all consular offices except those in France, Belgium, the Netherlands, Germany and Italy." June 5, 1941. NA RG 59, 811.111 W. R./359 1/2. Copy in McDonald Papers, USHMM.

Thomas and Heinrich Mann, Franz Werfel and Conrad [Konrad] Heiden. So that American democracy, in its struggle to defend freedom, may have at its disposal the experience, the culture and the heroism of European democrats, we strongly urge that the State Department rescind its order made public this morning.[55]

The next day, June 19, 1941, the New York Times *published a long article headlined:*

U.S. RULING CUTS OFF MEANS OF ESCAPE FOR MANY
IN REICH
CURB ON REFUGEES WHO MIGHT BE SPIES HERE
TO SAVE KIN DRASTICALLY INTERPRETED
MANY VISAS TO BE VOIDED
THOUSANDS WHO HAVE BOOKED PASSAGE FROM LISBON
NOW FACE REJECTION[56]

Spurred by these press reports, Acting Attorney General Francis Biddle fired off an angry letter to Undersecretary of State Sumner Welles:

The Department of Justice had not been consulted at any time with reference to these instructions [regarding no visas for those with close relatives in totalitarian countries]. As far as I know, no regulations have been issued with respect to these "instructions," which radically change a long established immigration policy, and will practically result in the exclusion of most refugees from the United States. . . . I know of no law which could be construed to permit exclusion of aliens on the ground that they have relatives in the countries from which they came. . . .

On more than one occasion you have given me your assurance that no such steps [changes in what had previously been agreed to] would be taken without the approval of the Attorney General, as indeed is required by law, and under Reorganization Plan V, which provides that in case of any conflict, the Attorney General's views shall prevail.

You will remember that at a luncheon last autumn, at which Mr. Henry Hart, Mr. Breckinridge Long and I met with you to discuss differences of opinion which had arisen between the two Departments, you assured me of your complete cooperation, and in answer to my protests that the State Department

---

55. Niebuhr to Hull, June 18, 1941, NA RG 59, 811.111 Refugees/1539. Copy in McDonald Papers, USHMM.
56. *New York Times*, June 19, 1941. On June 30 the American Consulate General in Lisbon suspended action on the visa application of a couple there who had brothers and sisters remaining in Belgium, Germany, and the Netherlands. Wiley to Secretary of State, June 30, 1941, 811.111 Refugees/1617. Copy in USHMM, Accession 1994.A.0342 Roll 46.

had more than once taken action without consulting the Attorney General, you told me this would not occur again.

I do not express any opinion on the policy embodied in the "instructions" reported by the *Times*. I am not in a position to form such an opinion without knowledge of the facts, based on careful investigation and study. But I am compelled to point out to you that the issuance of these "instructions," without reference to this Department, was contrary to our understanding, and without authority under the law.[57]

On June 28 Secretary Ickes wrote about the latest turn in the war:

Last Sunday [June 21] we were stunned by the news that Hitler had declared war on Russia and that his troops were already on the run over the Russian border. . . . Probably he [Churchill] was taken as much by surprise as anyone, but he was ready to assume leadership and tell the British people that, while he had always been against communism, Great Britain would do everything in its power to help Russia against Hitler. He did not lose sight of the fact that it is Hitler who is the main threat to the civilization of the world and that our primary purpose must be to defeat him, even if we have to make common cause with Stalin and communism for the time being.

It seems to me that in boldly announcing this policy, Churchill did much to direct our own public opinion and policy so far as Russia is concerned.

. . . .

. . . Our more slowly moving President caught up with him by Tuesday, when, at a press conference, he let it be known, without any eloquent outburst on the subject, that we would aid Russia under the Lend-Lease Act, as we are aiding Great Britain. . . .

The isolationists lost no time in attempting to tie the Administration up with communistic Russia. [Montana Senator Burton] Wheeler was particularly nasty about it in referring to Churchill and Roosevelt sleeping in the same bed with Stalin. However, owing to Churchill's statesmanship and our own quick follow-up, mainly on the part of the newspapers, we have saved a situation that might have been very difficult indeed.[58]

The Soviet Union was now an ally of Britain and would carry the main burden of the war against Germany. But the vast clash in the east did not erase security fears in Washington. At a meeting in Welles's office on July 3, McDonald said that he understood that "the distinction of especially endangered persons was probably no longer valid" and stated that the committee would thus only submit names for visas

57. Biddle to Welles, June 20, 1941, NA RG 59, 811.111 W.R./359 1 /2. Copy in McDonald Papers, USHMM.
58. *Secret Diary of Harold L. Ickes,* III, June 28, 1941, 549–550.

in *"cases presenting exceptional circumstances."*[59] *The committee also agreed to take on a new role as liaison between the State Department and agencies serving immigrants.*

But both Warren and McDonald argued strongly against the close relatives provision, citing its potential to create undue hardship for refugees. Avra Warren and Welles gave no ground, with Welles only expressing his hope that the Visa Division would exercise judgment and discretion in its application of the new rule.[60]

Frank Kingdon, head of the Emergency Rescue Committee, asked McDonald to sign a letter of protest against the State Department's unjust move.[61] *McDonald responded:*

I am in complete sympathy with the admirable statement which you enclosed in your letter of July 8, but I, as chairman of the President's Advisory Committee on Political Refugees, must decline to be one of the signatories. You will, I know, understand my reasons for this. . . . .

You may rest assured that my colleagues and I on the President's Advisory Committee are doing everything we can by direct contact with government authorities to achieve the end you have in view.[62]

On August 8, at the suggestion of the President's Advisory Committee, McDonald requested a meeting with the president to discuss the close relatives rule.[63] *Historian Haim Genizi pointed out that McDonald did not initiate the request for a direct meeting with FDR, and that he apologized to Undersecretary Welles afterward.*

McDonald was deeply troubled by the behavior of Long and the Visa Division—he said so in his letter to Welles.[64] *The most likely explanation for this apology was that he recognized how busy FDR was with matters related to the war.*[65]

The president, was then en route to a secret shipboard meeting—his first—with Winston Churchill as prime minister. This meeting off the coast of Newfoundland produced a joint statement of common purpose by one country fighting a war desperately, and the other still not a belligerent. The eight-point Atlantic Charter was not

59. Probably because there was now room under most quotas, and because everyone— immigrant or visitor—had to undergo careful scrutiny in Washington.

60. Minutes of the 49th Meeting of the President's Advisory Committee on Refugees, August 7, 1941, McDonald Papers, Columbia University, D367 (PACPR), P65.

61. Frank Kingdon Statement, Undated, McDonald Papers, Columbia University, D367 (PACPR) P26.

62. James G. McDonald to Frank Kingdon, July 9, 1941, McDonald Papers, Columbia University, D367 (PACPR), P26.

63. Minutes of the 49th Meeting of the President's Advisory Committee on Political Refugees, August 7, 1941, McDonald Papers, Columbia University, D367 (PACPR), P65. McDonald to FDR, August 8, 1941, McDonald Papers, Columbia University, D361 (Franklin D. Roosevelt Special File).

64. Haim Genizi, *American Apathy: The Plight of Christian Refugees from Nazism* (Ramat-Gan: Bar-Ilan University Press, 1983), 90–91.

65. Genizi also criticized McDonald's attempt to flatter Welles and Secretary of State Hull just before August 8 and his general tendency to play the role of insider. Welles and Hull could, of course, overrule Long.

*only a democratic alternative to Nazi Germany's goal of a "new Europe" under Ger-
man domination, but a document with universal appeal, encompassing both the hope
for improved relations among nations and better protection of individual rights in the
postwar period. Elaborating on FDR's "Four Freedoms," it committed the United
States to active involvement in shaping the aims of the war and the postwar order.
Immediately after the closing luncheon of this summit conference, the president received word that the House of Representatives had voted to extend the Selective Service Act—the draft—by a margin of 203 to 202.*[66]

On August 19 Breckinridge Long wrote:

Very long day. [Secretary of State] Hull somewhat uneasy about policy
which puts through a careful scrutiny [of] all prospective immigrants who have
close relatives in Germany or Russia. There is a recrudescence of criticism from
radical elements and organizations interested in getting persons into the United
States from the doubtful territory. McDonald and his committee have telegraphed the President in protest and written Welles. "P.M." and "New Republic" have written highly critical articles. The President sent his telegram over.
Welles thought I should see the President and present him with the whole
picture.

*Long then briefed Hull, Welles, Atherton, and Duggan on the history of the close
relatives provision.*

Hull was afraid the opposition might carry some political embarrassment
but did not feel it necessary to trouble the President to see McDonald but
thought he ought [to] see me because there had been a dispute between two of
his important Departments. Welles thought I should see the President and he
should then see McDonald's Committee because we had to work with them
and the President could set them straight.[67]

*On August 20 Long wrote a Memorandum for the president on the subject of
aliens with close relatives in Germany and the Soviet Union.*

On June 5 the Department sent a telegram to its agents abroad directing
them to submit to the Department of State for final review the applications of
any persons for an American visa if these persons had close relatives remaining
behind in German or Russian controlled territory. . . . Persons have not been
excluded from the United States simply because they had relatives in occupied
territory. However, the telegram was sent after the Department had been thoroughly convinced that the German and Russian Governments were indulging
in the practice of holding as hostages for the performance of services in the

66. Borgwardt, *A New Deal for the World*, 21–35.
67. Long Diary, August 19, 1941, LC, Container 5.

United States close relatives of persons to whom they gave permission to leave occupied territory to proceed to the United States. This definite conclusion of the Department was arrived at after various communications from its representatives abroad.

. . . .

About half of the persons under the category (having near relatives in occupied territory) who have applied for admission to the United States were granted visas. The rest were not.

. . . .

The [June 5] telegram was intended as a "hold" order until the pending legislation [the Bloom Bill signed by President on June 21, 1941[,] giving government control over aliens coming in and going out] should become law. . . .

Mr. McDonald and his committee, as is probably quite natural, and also a number of other individuals and groups, have taken some exception to the procedure of the Department. . . . [But] uncontrolled acquiescence . . . might easily have resulted in the infiltration into the United States of a great number of foreign agents posing as refugees.

Long added that, unbeknownst to the President's Advisory Committee, some spies had been apprehended posing as immigrants.[68]

On September 4 McDonald and the members of the President's Advisory Committee[69] *met at the White House with President Roosevelt, Long, former Ambassador Joseph E. Davies (both representing the State Department), and Acting Attorney General Francis Biddle. McDonald opened the meeting with this statement prepared at a breakfast meeting earlier that morning:*

Assuring you [FDR] of our deep concern for the public interest and national safety shared in common with you and the Departments of State and Justice, we beg leave to make the following recommendations with respect to current practices in the issuance of visas:

(1) The so-called relative rule should be cancelled or substantially modified. Our experience with refugees has convinced us that it is unnecessary, illogical, ill adapted to the purposes claimed for it, and cruelly burdensome on the refugees affected by it.

(2) Existing procedures should be simplified. The information and advice of the War and Navy Intelligence Services and of the F.B.I. should be made

68. Long to FDR, August 20, 1941, FDRL, Official File 3186, Box 3, 1941.
69. Committee members present at this meeting were McDonald, Reverend Joseph F. Rummel, Right Reverend Michael J. Ready, Joseph P. Chamberlain, Paul Baerwald, Hamilton Fish Armstrong, Dr. Stephen S. Wise, and George Warren.

available to the officers of the Departments of State and Justice, who alone should decide on visa cases as competent under the law and familiar with the problem.

(3) A Board of Review should be established immediately to consider cases brought to it on appeal from the reconstituted Inter-Departmental Committees.

(4) Sponsors of applicants for visas, or their representatives, should be given opportunity to be heard by the Board of Review.[70]

After McDonald read this statement, Archbishop Rummel and Rabbi Wise briefed the president on the hardships faced by those affected by the "relative clause." In the discussion that followed members of the committee questioned Long as to why some visas that had been approved had not actually been issued. Long claimed that the quotas for the refugee countries were full, a statement that McDonald and Warren challenged, noting that the German and Polish cases approved for July and August (1,126) would certainly not have filled the quotas.[71] (As of May 1941, the immigration quotas for Bulgaria, China, Hungary, Latvia, Luxemburg, Rumania, Spain, Australia, and the Philippines were filled for the fiscal year that ended on June 30; for all other countries, including Germany and Poland, quota numbers were available.)[72]

The next day McDonald wrote to Eleanor Roosevelt:

The conference of the President's Advisory Committee on Political Refugees at the White House yesterday was very satisfactory. In addition to a nearly complete representation of our Committee, which yesterday included Archbishop Rummel of New Orleans, there were present at the conference Mr. Biddle, Ambassador Davies and Mr. Long. The latter's contribution was limited to a weird attempt to prove that the relatives clause and other restrictions were not in fact reducing immigration!

. . . Though he [FDR] did not commit himself definitely, we received the impression that all of the points we had urged, with the possible exception of the second, would be adopted and put into practice.

I am most grateful to you for your continued helpfulness.[73]

70. President's Advisory Committee on Political Refugees to President Roosevelt. Statement read at September 4, 1941, meeting at the White House, YIVO RG 278, Joseph Chamberlain Papers, Folder 70.

71. Minutes of the 50th Meeting of the President's Advisory Committee on Political Refugees, September 4, 1941, McDonald Papers, Columbia University, D367 (PACPR), P65.

72. Meeting of the Interdepartmental Committee on Political Refugees, May 9, 1941, NA RG 59, 811.111 Refugees/1422. Copy in McDonald Papers, USHMM.

73. McDonald to Eleanor Roosevelt, September 5, 1941, McDonald Papers, Columbia University, D361 (Eleanor Roosevelt Special File), Item 324. McDonald also expressed his thanks to journalist Dorothy Thompson, who earlier that week had written a column on the subject. McDonald to Thompson, September 5, 1941, McDonald Papers, Columbia University, D367 (PACPR), P65.

Unhappy with this meeting, Breckinridge Long took it personally:

At the request of the President [I] attended a conference with him, McDonald's Refugee Committee and Attorney General Biddle. They are critical of the Department's policy—consequently of me. Biddle is their advocate. Rabbi Wise and the Archbishop of New Orleans were their principal spokesmen. . . . Rabbi Wise always assumes such a sanctimonious air and pleads for the "intellectuals and brave spirits, refugees from the tortures of the dictators" or words to that effect. Of course only an infinitesimal fraction of the immigrants are of that category—and some are certainly German agents and others are sympathizers, the last named coming here because it is away from the scene of combat and looks like a safe place. I got a little mad and fear I betrayed it.

. . . .

Each of these men hates me. I am to them the embodiment of a nemesis. They each and all believe every person, everywhere, has a <u>right</u> to come to the United States. I believe <u>nobody</u>, anywhere has a <u>right</u> to enter the United States unless the United States desires. . . . They would throw me to the wolves in their eagerness to destroy me—and will try in the future as they have in the past to ruin my political status.[74]

On September 16, 1941, George Warren met with Avra Warren in New York, of which he said, in a letter to the committee marked "Strictly Confidential":

I came away from the conference with the distinct impression, shared by others present, that our recent conference with the President had produced useful results. Very definite efforts are being made by the Visa Division to improve administrative procedures and it is now hoped that delays in consideration of visa applications will be overcome within the next three weeks.

The following points have been accepted in principle:

(1) There must be other evidence than the mere existence of relatives to warrant the withholding of visas on the grounds of public safety.
(2) Other agencies than the Department of State will supply information and advice pertinent to visa applications to the Department of State, which recognizes its responsibility for making recommendations to the Consulates.

. . . .

74. Long Diary, September 4, 1941, LC, Container 5.

Mr. [Avra] Warren also reported that a Board of Review would be set up as soon as the proclamation and regulations are issued by the President.[75]

This was an extended bureaucratic battle in which every inch was contested. Two weeks later Breckinridge Long wrote:

Conference again with Secretary [Hull]. . . . Also I brought him up to date with our controversy with Justice—before my conference with [Attorney General] Biddle this afternoon. When Warren and I met Biddle and his immigration advisor we talked for two hours. I stated . . . the Secretary of State must maintain his historic function in charge of visas. That was agreed. Biddle then wanted a committee of review divorced from the "intelligence" members—without MID, ONI, FBI—with Justice and State only represented. I withheld agreement to consider the effect. He has been talking to the President today and tried to convey the impression he has Presidential approval but did not actually say so. I am not committed to any particular formula to operate the visa procedure but I do have two definite convictions—(1) The Secretary of State shall continue as final authority and (2) the public safety of the U.S. shall be safeguarded against the entry of undesirables and 5th Columnists. So we came to no conclusive agreement but the conversation had some advantage in closer understanding.[76]

On October 25 George Warren received a disquieting diplomatic report about early deportations of Jews from Germany proper to the east.

[W]ord has come through from Berlin to the effect that before the end of this month about 20,000 Jews are to be deported from German cities to German-occupied Poland, principally to the ghetto of Lodz. The first group of 1,000 reportedly left Berlin on October 18 last, and another group was scheduled to leave Berlin on October 24. A group comprising approximately 2,000 Jews reportedly left Frankfort on the Main on October 20 and a further 2,000 from Cologne on October 21.[77]

On November 28 Breckinridge Long wrote in his diary about Ambassador Steinhardt in Moscow:

Steinhardt is an able man and has decisiveness and courage. He took a very definite stand on the immigration and refugee question and opposed the im-

75. George L. Warren to Members of the President's Advisory Committee on Political Refugees, September 16, 1941, McDonald Papers, Columbia University, D367 (PACPR), P65.
76. Long Diary, October 1, 1941, LC, Container 5. Later entries indicated that discussions continued without agreement through October.
77. Maney to George Warren, October 25, 1941, NA RG 59, Lot File 52D408, IGCR, Alphabetical Subject File 1938–41, Box 14, Warren Memoranda.

migration in large numbers from Russia and Poland of the Eastern Europeans whom he characterizes as entirely unfit to become citizens of this country.[78] He says they are lawless, scheming, defiant—and in many ways unassibilible [*sic*]. He said the general type of intending immigrant was just the same as the criminal Jews who crowd our police court dockets in New York and with whom he is acquainted and whom he feels are never to become moderately decent American citizens.[79]

Eight days after the Japanese attacked Pearl Harbor, McDonald telegraphed Eleanor Roosevelt:

I am delighted you were photographed with children of Japanese parents STOP You can be of incalculable aid in forestalling move by super patriots to terrorize loyal "enemy aliens" and our foreign born citizens STOP The morale of all these millions will be undergirded by your attitude STOP I hope that there is under way in Washington a nation-wide program to reassure our German and Italian speaking citizens that their loyalty is not questioned and that their whole-hearted aid in the war effort is confidently counted upon STOP Only thus can we forestall the work of saboteurs who would undermine the morale of these millions.[80]

On December 23 McDonald accepted an unsalaried appointment to the second alien enemy hearing board for the eastern district of New York.[81] *These boards reviewed the cases of individuals categorized as enemy aliens and determined whether each person should be interned, paroled, or released unconditionally. This was an issue that had concerned McDonald for some time.*

On August 15, 1941, he had written to Arthur Sulzberger:

Those of us on the President's Advisory Committee on Political Refugees who have been closely in touch with developments in Washington on all phases of the refugee matter are beginning to fear lest, in the event of a declaration of war by our government, Congress be stampeded into hasty and ill-advised legislation affecting "enemy aliens" in this country, which might repeat the grave mistakes which Great Britain made at the beginning of the war. The fact that the British Government subsequently admitted that it had acted hastily and in such a way as to jeopardize its own best interests is no guarantee that Congress would profit by their experience.[82]

78. See Steinhardt's cable of October 6, 1940, excerpted in chapter 9.
79. Long Diary, November 28, 1941, LC, Container 5.
80. McDonald to Eleanor Roosevelt, December 15, 1941, McDonald Papers, Columbia University, D361 (Eleanor Roosevelt Special File), Item 324.
81. McDonald to Biddle, December 23, 1941, McDonald Papers, Columbia University, D367 (PACPR), P6.
82. McDonald to Arthur H. Sulzberger, August 15, 1941, Personal and Confidential, McDonald Papers, Columbia University, D367 (PACPR), P53. Britain had interned enemy aliens.

McDonald's subsequent work on the alien review board made a real difference in the lives of individuals. But acceptance of this position also signaled that the role of the President's Advisory Committee had been so reduced that it would no longer consume most of McDonald's spare time.

Visa Cutbacks in 1941: One Case

The bureaucratic and political battles between the State Department and the President's Advisory Committee directly affected the prospects of hundreds of thousands of people seeking to escape Nazi-dominated Europe.[83] One such case is now well documented. It illustrates McDonald's view that one should not try to circumscribe narrowly who was likely to be a good addition to the United States.

In late April 1941 Otto Frank, since 1933 a resident of Amsterdam, sought to revive his application for American visas for himself and his family, which included his wife Edith and his two daughters, Margot and Annaliese. The last has become known as Anne Frank.

In the German-occupied Netherlands Frank had to negotiate various difficulties, including finding American sponsors with sufficiently close connection to the family that an American consul would accept their assurances of support. Edith Frank's brothers Julius and Walter Holländer, who had already emigrated to the U.S., were willing to supply affidavits of support, but Otto Frank justifiably feared that their limited working-class incomes would not convince an American consul that they could also support a family of four. So on April 30 Otto Frank turned to his old college friend Nathan Straus, Jr. Grandson of the founder of Macy's, Straus was now head of the Federal Housing Authority in Washington.

I used to write to you for your birthday[,] wishing you the best[,] and this letter probably shall arrive about that time[,] bringing over my best wishes this year. But to be honest, this is not the only reason I am writing for this time.

. . . .

One says that no special difficulties shall be made from the part of the German Authorities [to prevent the Franks from leaving]. But in the case that an affidavit [of financial support] from family members is not available or is not sufficient the [American] consul asks a bank deposit. How much he would ask in my case I don't know. I am not allowed to go to Rotterdam[,] and without an introduction the consul would not even accept me. As far as I here [*sic*] from other people it might be about $5,000—for us four. You are the only person I know that I can ask: Would it be possible for you to give a deposit in my favor?[84]

---

83. Portions of this section are drawn from a report Richard Breitman prepared for the YIVO Institute for Jewish Research and are reprinted here with the permission of YIVO. We are grateful to YIVO director Carl Rheins.

84. Otto Frank to Nathan Straus, April 30, 1941, YIVO, RG 246, USNA/HIAS case file A-23007 (Frank, Otto).

In mid-June 1941 the United States required Germany to close its consulates in the U.S. because they supplied cover for German espionage activities. Germany retaliated, demanding the closure of American consulates in Germany and German-occupied territories. By July American consulates there either had closed or were closing.

From Amsterdam, Otto Frank now had to reach an American consulate in a neutral country before he could have any chance of getting visas for the Frank family.[85] American consuls there were not issuing visas unless prospective immigrants could show that they also had booked transportation to the United States.[86]

Nathan Straus wrote to Otto Frank:

I have taken up the matter of your immigration to this country with the National Refugee Service. I have also discussed it with the State Department officials as I would very much like to help you. I am afraid, however, the news is not good news.

Unless you can get to a place where there is an American Consul, there does not seem to be any way of arranging for you to come over. I am informed that there are still American Consuls in Portugal, Spain, Free France, and Switzerland. Those are the only countries in which a visa can be arranged.[87]

Otto Frank needed to leave the Netherlands and reach Spain or Portugal legally—he had to show an exit permit from the Netherlands and transit visas through the countries he would pass through.[88] If he had gone to Lisbon without all immediate family members, he would have been rejected for an American visa on the grounds that he had close relatives in Nazi territory. Finally, as of July 1, his supporters in the United States would have had to fill out new affidavits of support and send them to Washington for the scrutiny of the Visa Division and the interdepartmental review committee.

On September 8 Otto Frank wrote to Nathan Straus:

Many thanks for your kind letter of July 1st. I waited with my answer as I wanted to get more information here. Of course I heard in the meantime that visas for the U.S.A. cannot be obtained here but there is no chance to leave the country without a visa. The only way to get to a neutral country are visas of others States such as Cuba . . . and many of my acquaintances got visas for Cuba. Visitors Visas to Cuba seemed to be the only way and as the Cuba Consulate is closed too people do not know what is going to be done. Some pretend that visas will be given at Berlin[,] others were informed that there are negociations [*sic*]

85. Wyman, *Paper Walls*, 197. Augusta Meyerson to E. M. Rogan June 16, 1941, YIVO, RG 246, USNA/HIAS case file A-23007 (Frank, Otto).

86. Augusta Meyerson to Maurice Krinsky, June 9, 1941, YIVO, RG 246, USNA/HIAS case file A-23007 (Frank, Otto).

87. Nathan Straus to Otto Frank, July 1, 1941, YIVO, RG 246, USNA/HIAS case file A-23007 (Frank, Otto).

88. Nathan Straus to Otto Frank, September 11, 1941, YIVO, RG 246, USNA/HIAS case file A-23007 (Frank, Otto).

pending in order to have the Consul at Bilbao authorized to give visas and to inform the Spanish Consul here who would grant the departure to Spain then.

. . . .

I know that it will be impossible for us all to leave even if most of the money is refundable, but Edith urges me to leave alone or with the children. I hate this idea but it has to be considered. There might be situations in which one tries everything. If I have to leave alone there will be another difficulty as I had to stay at Cuba for some while. I was informed that nobody could enter the U.S.A. if he leaves family back in occupied countries. I do not know if that is true but it is pretended to be so here.

I am sure that you are better informed as I am here and in the case that there might be a chance to act and to get somewhere I kindly ask you to take the matter up with my brothers-in-law. I know that they would do everything they can to have us come and both are very straight reliable fellows.[89]

By the time Nathan Straus accumulated more information, Otto Frank had already concluded that the prospect of getting into the U.S. directly was dim. So he turned to Cuba as a possible refuge. Just where he could find a Cuban consul willing and able to issue visas was unclear.[90]

Tourist visas and visitor's visas to Cuba were extremely expensive, requiring, among other things, direct payment of about $250 per visa and bonds totaling $2,500 per person, refunded when the person left Cuba. A number of travel agencies in New York enjoying good connections with the Cuban government handled such bonding arrangements if American sponsors wanted to pay the fees. Julius Holländer, Nathan Straus, and the National Refugee Service all investigated this risky and expensive option.

State Department officials and various other government officials were highly suspicious of the Cuban government's willingness to sell visas dearly, believing that this was a corrupt device to circumvent American immigration restrictions and a means for unsavory elements to enter the Western Hemisphere. After the United States tightened its own visa procedure effective July 1, 1941, the American ambassador to Cuba informed the Cuban government that, under the new regulations, many of those Europeans coming to Cuba as "tourists" might no longer qualify for U.S. visas. So Cuba might be stuck with these people. Cuban government officials said that they might need to tighten their own immigration regulations.[91]

Still, some people did manage to get temporary haven in Cuba through payments to travel agencies in New York. One long American government report included a

89. Otto Frank to Nathan Straus, September 8, 1941, YIVO, RG 246, USNA/HIAS case file A-23007 (Frank, Otto).

90. Otto Frank to Nathan Straus, September 8, 1941, YIVO, RG 246, USNA/HIAS case file A-23007 (Frank, Otto).

91. Messersmith to Secretary of State, June 28, 1941, and July 2, 1941, NA RG 59, 837.55/208 and 811.111 W.R./428.

severe and, in retrospect, highly improbable indictment of the directors of the Compass Resettlement Service (and Compass Travel Bureau)—one of three options for Cuban visa bonds mentioned by the National Refugee Service.[92]

Herman Segall, president of this company, was born in Russia and is believed to be at present a citizen of Cuba and to have applied for his first United States naturalization papers. A definitely reliable source reports that Segall, together with his uncle, David Segall, was at one time active in Danzig under the notorious Nazi leader Forster. Segall is said to have smuggled men and money into Poland from Germany before the war and is described as definitely a Nazi agent and a member of the Gestapo.[93]

Otto Frank's efforts to move his family to the United States and Cuba mirrored the experience of many thousands of German Jews. Frank's case was unusual only in that he tried hard very late—and enjoyed particularly good or fortunate American connections. Still, he failed. The fact that Anne Frank was one of those who did not make it is a poignant reminder of what was lost.

92. Meyerson to Nathan Straus, October 2, 1941, YIVO, RG 246, USNA/HIAS case file A-23007 (Frank, Otto).

93. Confidential Report on Various Organizations and Individuals Engaged in Refugee Migration Activities. Copy in NA RG 59, 840.48 Refugees/3489. This 1942 report by the chief cable censor was judged to be of particular value in the State Department. See Shaw to DCR, December 16, 1942, NA RG 59, 840.48 Refugees/3489.

11. Refuge in Latin America

Looking for openings for refugees from Europe, McDonald and the President's Advisory Committee on Political Refugees often considered sites in Latin America. Most Latin American countries represented at the Evian Conference in July 1938 were not open to formal agreements to take in Jewish refugees, and their attitudes against Jewish immigration only stiffened during the war. Bolivia turned out to be the biggest exception.

In 1935 McDonald had encouraged Mauricio Hochschild, the Bolivian businessman who became the key figure in arranging for Bolivia to take in thousands of Jews from Europe in 1938–1940. The events described here revolve around Hochschild, not McDonald. Hochschild received assistance from the President's Advisory Committee at a critical moment in 1938.

Bolivia

Mauricio (Moritz) Hochschild was born in Biblis, a small town near Frankfurt, in 1881, into a family prominent in the mining and metallurgy business. In 1919 he moved to South America, acquired Argentine citizenship, and developed extensive mining companies in Bolivia. By the late 1930s Hochschild's firm[1] controlled one-third of Bolivia's mineral production. His vast business empire extended to Chile, Peru, Argentina, and Brazil. His companies were the biggest exporters of tin to the United States before and during World War II.

In the spring of 1935, in the midst of frenetic efforts to open Argentina to refugees, McDonald recorded in his diary that Hochschild was thinking of bringing large numbers of German Jews to South America, and that he hoped to avoid immigration restrictions by transporting them first-class.[2] Many countries with immigration laws and regulations restricting admission on economic grounds assumed that those who could pay for first-class shipping were not going to be an economic burden, whether they came as visitors or immigrants. Hochschild anticipated placing many in industry, commerce, and agriculture. He could do some of the hiring himself.

Following Hochschild's 1935 meetings with McDonald, he made efforts to bring refugees to Argentina. Then in 1936 he established links with the American Jewish Joint Distribution Committee (JDC), hoping to obtain money and expertise for set-

---

1. Hochschild's Bolivian entity was called "Mauricio Hochschild Sociedad Anónima Minera Industrial" and was part of his Latin American–wide company "Grupo Hochschild."
2. *Advocate for the Doomed,* diary entries for May 3, May 7, 1935, 715, 723–724.

tlement. That same year a JDC report noted that Hochschild had helped to bring over a thousand Jewish immigrants into Chile:

The persons who have done the most for them are Hochschild Brothers, who not only contribute a monthly amount of 5,000 Chilean pesos, but employ many of them in their mining concerns.[3]

Hochschild realized that Chile and Peru would not tolerate large numbers of Jewish refugees for long. He believed that there was, however, a solid long-term opportunity in Bolivia, where his political allies had come to power. The new president of Bolivia, German Busch, led a reformist, "military socialist" regime. Busch and his supporters hoped to regenerate the country following its disastrous Chaco War with Paraguay (1932–1935), a conflict that devastated the Bolivian economy and cost 65,000 Bolivian lives.

This war made the Bolivian government eager to settle people on the border with Paraguay and to offer them land. In July 1938—only weeks after the Evian Conference—the Bolivian Ministry of Agriculture and Colonization declared that the country was open to healthy persons everywhere willing to colonize in the eastern regions of the country. Although Agriculture Minister Julio Salmon soon excluded blacks, he explicitly included Jews suffering persecution.[4]

Hochschild had considerable influence with Foreign Minister Eduardo Diez de Medina, who was in charge of immigration, as well as several other members of Busch's cabinet. Hochschild served on a Jewish committee advising the Bolivian government on immigration policy. Possibly as a result, Bolivian immigration regulations placed no limit on those willing to seek employment in agriculture or industry and welcomed all who could bring $5,000 capital into the country.[5] Hochschild and Busch met several times and reached agreement on a grandiose scheme aimed at settling 20,000–50,000 German and Austrian Jews in the Chaco region, where they would farm as well as engage in industry and handicrafts.

At Hochschild's request, in 1938 the President's Advisory Committee asked Dr. Isaiah Bowman, president of Johns Hopkins University, to undertake a survey of Bolivia as part of a larger study of settlement possibilities in Latin America. Bowman reported to President Roosevelt in November 1938:

There is room for perhaps 50,000 people along the mountain border of Bolivia facing the Gran Chaco. This would require a brief field survey. Now that the boundary line has been settled, development will proceed rapidly. Capital is greatly wanted in Bolivia. The government would probably welcome

3. S. Weill to JDC Mission to Chile, September 12, 1936. JDC Archives, AR 33–44 (Refugees), Chile, Folder 1103.

4. Haim Avni, "Perú y Bolivia—dos naciones andinas—y los refugiados judíos durante la era nazi," *El Genocidio ante la Historia y la Naturaleza Humana*, ed. Beatriz Gurevich and Carlos Escudé (Buenos Aires: Universidad Torcuato Di Tella: Grupo Editor Latinoamericano, 1994), 335, 346.

5. Avni, "Perú y Bolivia," 347–348.

such a settlement. While the region is within the tropics, its latitude is about 18 to 22 degrees and the elevation is sufficient to make it tolerable. No doubt there will soon be a good outlet to the projected new port on the Paraguay River. The greater part of the Gran Chaco is not suited for settlement under present conditions. It is either too dry or flooded, very much as in the case of the Ilanos of Venezuela.[6]

A few months later, Bowman was a little less optimistic in a letter to Charles Liebman of the Refugee Economic Corporation:

No one can find in this world a paradise for the refugees. Indeed one can make a case against any area that is proposed. There is always a choice of evils. On the other hand, the situation is desperate and where we find a country admitting people we must make sure not to overlook any possibilities.[7]

Almar Hammerschlag, a German Jewish refugee who arrived in Bolivia in 1938, gave his impressions of life in La Paz in a pungent letter, full of irony, which he wrote to friends in England:

Bolivia is, as you know, a socialistic republic. Its president is a young colonel and even for a soldier a damned silly ass, but his ministers are soldiers too and about just as daft, and the minister of finances used to be a schoolteacher and knows about finances about as much as I about repairing a motorcycle. . . . On the other hand, Bolivia is not a bad country to live in. Foreigners are highly respected, and if one has a decent job one is all right. There are no restrictions of any kind, you can piss on the main street, you can beat a policeman up if you feel like it . . . you can drive your car without lights at night . . . personally I am doing quite well. I am a sort of manager and salesman of the most modern shop for imported sweets, wines, frocks, and parfums in La Paz and in about three quarters of a year I shall become a partner of the owner. . . . Of course, there are countries much more beautiful and civilized than Bolivia, but it is difficult to get permission to stay in those countries, and on the other hand there is much more competition in those countries. We for instance have a shop of no considerable size in the main street and we employ one girl to attend to customers and one Red Indian to keep everything clean, and because we have the right stuff the shop keeps the owner, his wife, two kids, one mother-in-law, a nice little house with a cook and a maid and me. . . . Naturally, we can only do that in a town in which you are the only one selling certain articles. . . . Besides, of course, we have all the Germans and English people as they like to be attended in their own language. Naturally, those relationships with the Germans

6. Isaiah Bowman to Franklin Roosevelt, November 21, 1938, FDRL, President's Secretary's File, Box 177, Refugees.
7. Bowman to Charles J. Liebman, January 9, 1939, NA RG 59, Lot File 52D408, Country Files, Box 1, Bolivia.

have their drawbacks, too. Last night I had to chuck a Nazi out of the shop because he made insulting remarks about my prices but, to be honest, I did not mind, in the contrary, I spent with him some of the most delightful moments I have had in Bolivia up to now. I fear I have lost him for a customer but he has lost one of his front teeth, which he left in the shop.[8]

In late 1938 the American minister to Bolivia, Robert Caldwell, noted the increased flow of Jewish refugees into the country.

The policy of the Bolivian government with regard to the admission of these people appears to be at present one of extreme liberality. Most of the immigrants arrive in Bolivia via the Chilean port of Arica and come directly to La Paz, the weekly train on which they arrive being colloquially known as the "Expreso Judío." Some of them are of the student class and appear to be quite well educated, while a few are qualified as teachers, scientists, doctors and lawyers. Others are carpenters, plumbers, domestic servants, restaurateurs, barkeepers or artisans of various kinds. In most cases they have been able to bring only a small amount of capital, estimated to average something less than $100 a piece. At any rate, their financial condition is such that they would not be admitted to many countries in the absence of special provisions. I have also been informed that there are thousands of Jews in Europe who have obtained visas to come to Bolivia. There are rumors to the effect that many of these emigrants in their panic to escape are paying high sums for visas which entitle them to remain in this country only a few months. Concern is felt for their fate when their temporary permits shall have expired.[9]

Six weeks later Caldwell added:

The [Bolivian] Foreign Minister has informed me that within the past six or eight months some 7,000 foreigners have entered Bolivia. Five thousand of these have since left. Of the remaining 2,000 somewhat more than half may be called refugees. This figure tallies with that received from well informed private sources. The average amount of money brought by each refugee stated to be about $50. Refugees coming through Arica [Chile] are understood to have had no difficulty so far with transit visas. There is an increasing newspaper campaign for the restriction of immigration but a continued liberal policy is advocated by the Foreign Minister.[10]

8. Tony Kushner, "The Bolivian Jewish Connection: Germany to South America via a Southampton Pig Farm," in *Jewish Culture and History* 1, no. 1 (Summer 1998): 91–93. Hammerschlag, the son of a banker, was hardly "typical."

9. Robert G. Caldwell to Secretary of State, 5 December 1938, NA RG 59, Lot File 52D408, Country Files, Box 1, Bolivia. At the beginning of 1938 there were only about one hundred Jewish families in Bolivia.

10. Caldwell to Secretary of State, January 20, 1939, NA RG 59, Lot File 52D408, Country Files, Box 1, Bolivia.

Assistant Secretary of State George Messersmith expressed concern that some of the thousands of refugees who had entered and then left Bolivia might try to enter the United States.

It is assumed that the figures of seven thousand entries and five thousand departures are general figures covering the admission of persons visiting Bolivia temporarily and departing in due course. It appears possible, however, that these large figures might include refugees who have gone to Bolivia and subsequently moved on to other countries. The Department would appreciate further information on the matter, which would indicate more clearly what the actual situation is with regard to the entry into and departure from Bolivia of refugees, and as to whether there is any reason to believe that refugees have been making their way to the United States from Bolivia through other than the established channels.[11]

In January 1939 Hochschild created a permanent organization to manage the flow of refugees. The Sociedad de Protección a los Inmigrantes Israelitas (SOPRO) was financed by Hochschild in partnership with the JDC. It established offices in La Paz and five other Bolivian towns (Cochabamba, Sucre, Potosi, Oruro, and Tarija). In each town, this society provided loans and temporary accommodation and in La Paz, a hospital, children's home, a home for the aged, and employment assistance. One source estimated that 90 percent of the immigrants to Bolivia received some form of financial assistance from SOPRO.[12]

There were reports that five Bolivian consulates in Europe were issuing (or selling for profit) increasing numbers of visas to Jews desperate to leave Europe. The visas were issued under the authorization of Bolivian Immigration Ministry Edict 1444; these visas duly (and fictitiously) attested to the fact that the immigrant was an "agriculturist" by profession.[13]

Caldwell reported that Bolivian opposition to Jewish immigration was growing:

. . . I have the honor to report that a campaign has been initiated in the local press, emphasizing economic and social difficulties which are involved and demanding some form of limitation of further immigration to the cities and especially La Paz. All the newspapers agree that Bolivia stands in great need of increased population in the country districts and of larger supplies of

11. Messersmith to Caldwell, February 1, 1939, NA RG 59, Lot File 52D408, Country Files, Box 1, Bolivia. Caldwell informed Messersmith that he had been told by Foreign Minister Medina that those who left Bolivia went to Chile and Uruguay. Messersmith to Caldwell, February 1, 1939; Caldwell to Hull, February 13, 1939, NA RG 59, Lot File 52D408, Country Files, Box 1, Bolivia.

12. Leon E. Bieber, "La Sociedad de Protección a los Inmigrantes Israelitas: Su aporte a la integración económica de judíos en Bolivia, 1939–1945" in *Latin American Research Review* 34, no. 2 (1999): 152–178.

13. Bieber, "La Sociedad de Protección," 155–156.

common labor. They all seem to favor the continuation of a liberal policy, without regard to race or creed. The editors are however at the same time insistent that increased immigration into the cities has already tended to displace Bolivians previously employed by local firms, and that this problem unless promptly resolved must necessarily cause an increasing amount of discontent.[14]

Opponents of the Busch regime helped launch a harsh press campaign against Jewish immigration in the La Paz newspapers. Much of the criticism was aimed personally at Hochschild. His ally, Foreign Minister Medina, who had been accused of profiting from the sale of visas, was ousted.

Feeling that his political base and his immigration scheme were in danger, Hochschild lashed out. He accused HICEM, the European Jewish emigration agency, of sending too many immigrants to Bolivia. In a letter to the JDC, he also vented some of his own prejudice against Eastern European Jews.

As Messers. Borchardt and Glick[15] probably will have reported to you, the President of Bolivia has on various occasions told me that he is quite willing to take up 20,000 Jews for settlement on the land and that his government will give us every reasonable support to carry out that scheme, and I feel quite confident that this will be done. As you know, I have taken the two gentlemen together with Mr. Saphir to the President and the Minister of Agriculture, and no doubt Mr. Borchardt has written to you direct about those visits. . . .

Meanwhile between 2700 and 2800 Jews have already arrived, of which at least 1,000 have not found any work as yet, since there is no room for them in the country outside agriculture. Of those out of work we have naturally sent some to the other cities in the country, but most of them are in La Paz, where they fill the streets, the coffee-houses, and the few hotels which there are, and naturally create anti-Semitism.

As soon as I returned from my trip, we asked HICEM not to send any more, until we had organized a colonization; but, of course, they hardly took any notice of that and not only sent us German Jews, but about 40% of Polish Jews, for which there was no necessity whatsoever. They also sent us some thieves and other crooks.

In order not to endanger the big scheme, I had asked the government to suspend all immigration for 6 months, and a decree in that direction had come out last week. However, we have naturally been able to arrange with the government that the people, who are already en route and swimming, will be allowed to enter the country. But should HICEM, in spite of our informing them of the above decree, continue to send men, I shall myself ask the President

14. Caldwell to Hull, January 13, 1939, NA RG 59, Lot File 52D408, Country Files, Box 1, Bolivia.

15. Friedrich Borchardt and David Glick (the same David Glick who had met with Himmler and Heydrich in 1936—see chapter 6) had undertaken a trip to Bolivia and Chile to check out conditions there for the JDC.

of Bolivia to let them return on the same steamer, since I see no reason whatsoever, why HICEM should undo what we are trying to do in Bolivia for the German Jews. We also do not wish any further Polish Jews and shall insist upon, in [the] future, that the Jews for colonization will be chosen by the proper organization in Germany and Austria.[16]

In June 1939 McDonald wrote to Paul Baerwald of the JDC about State Department views of Bolivia:

As to Bolivia, Mr. Duggan, the head of the American Republics Division and his colleague, Mr. Butler, were both more than skeptical about the possibility of that country's offering refuge for any considerable number of immigrants. On the contrary, they thought that the condition there is no different from that in most of the other Latin American countries. They emphasized the point that Bolivian officials, as others in South and Central America, have been disillusioned by the unwillingness of so many of the refugees to stay on the land. The governments, therefore, are loath to accept any more immigrants who are nominally agriculturists unless effective assurance can be given that the newcomers will remain on the soil.[17]

In July 1939 Busch ordered Hochschild's arrest and execution.[18] But Hochschild was spared and released through the intervention of the United States and several other countries.

In spite of Hochschild's narrow escape and Busch's death—an apparent suicide—in August, the flow of Jewish refugees to Bolivia continued. Decrees aimed at stopping immigration were ineffective. Hochschild reported at this time that there were 8,000 Jewish refugees in Bolivia, 1,500 of them Polish Jews.[19] In August the American chargé d'affaires reported that immigration into La Paz continued, and that many refugees were illegally crossing into Argentina:

STRICTLY CONFIDENTIAL. The German Chargé d'Affaires informally estimates the number of German Jews now in Bolivia at about 15,000. Representatives of the Jewish community in charge of distributing relief from New York sources insist that the figure is only 5,000 to 6,000. From personal observation, my estimate would be that there are at least 5,000 in La Paz alone.

The Argentine Minister has informed me that his Government has had considerable difficulty during recent months with illegal immigration into Ar-

16. Hochschild to Baerwald, May 10, 1939, JDC AR 33/44, Bolivia, Folder 1075.
17. McDonald to Baerwald, June 6, 1939, McDonald Papers, Columbia University, D361 (Baerwald Special File).
18. Hochschild was accused of flouting Busch's June 7, 1939, decree ordering tin companies to turn over foreign earnings, by circulating a petition against the decree.
19. Hochschild to Baerwald, August 11, 1939, JDC, AR 33/44 (Refugees), Bolivia, Folder 1077.

gentina of refugees admitted into Bolivia. He estimates that such illegal entries have averaged as high as 300 a month, although this estimate seems exaggerated to me. He states that most of the persons have been smuggled into Argentina through the border towns of Villazón and La Quiaca for $20 a head by a Bolivian ring headed at one time by Dr. Eduardo Díez de Medina, ex-minister of Foreign Affairs, and that he is by no means convinced that Don Eduardo's connection with the ring has been severed despite the investigation now being conducted by the Bolivian government into immigration irregularities during his incumbency.

The Argentine Minister states that the difficulty in controlling illegal entries into Argentina lies in the fact that, once past the border, there is no proper passport inspection. He claims that the cédula system for residents of Argentina is not effective in this respect inasmuch as residents do not have to show proof of legal entry.

The Chilean Ambassador, on the other hand, asserts that his government has managed to hold illegal immigration from Bolivia down to a minimum because of a provision that the national police (Carabineros) may demand a foreigner's passport at any time. He says that they have instructions to hold for deportation any foreigner not in possession of a valid passport and visa granted by a duly authorized Chilean consul. The Argentine Minister has suggested to his government that similar measures be put into effect in the northern provinces of Argentina but so far without success.[20]

Hochschild labored to raise large sums of money for his refugee settlement scheme, lobbying the JDC, the President's Advisory Commission, and the State Department. State Department official Robert Pell wrote:

At the request of Mr. Herbert Feis I discussed with Mr. Hochschild, who has tin interests in the country, a scheme for settling large numbers of refugees in Bolivia. I ascertained from Mr. Hochschild that he had previously discussed this project, which he has had investigated by experts, with Mr. Baerwald and Mr. [George] Warren. Mr. Hochschild said that his scheme involved the settlement of as many as 20,000 refugees, who should be partly Jewish and partly Catholic, in a very rich district of Bolivia. Mr. Hochschild said that the Bolivian government was agreeable to the project and would facilitate it in every way. Mr. Hochschild was now attempting to raise a minimum of $2,000,000 in order to get the scheme started. He figured that ultimately it would require the expenditure of approximately $7,000,000. Mr. Warren, who called later, confirmed that this project had been discussed in New York. He said that Mr. Hochschild enjoyed a high reputation for reliability and judgment with the JDC and HICEM people. Mr. Baerwald was

20. Allan Dawson to Secretary of State, August 16, 1939, NA RG 59, Lot File 52D408, Country Files, Box 1, Bolivia.

very favorably impressed with his project, but again the question was, who would put up the money.[21]

In March 1940 Hochschild, in partnership with JDC, founded the Sociedad Colonizadora de Bolivia (SOCOBO) for the "settlement, training, oversight, and management of refugees in agricultural colonies." They established a settlement called "Buena Tierra" in the sub-tropical area of North Yungas in Chapare province northeast of La Paz. The site was a virtual jungle, and it never attracted many immigrants. At its peak, in 1943, the population was made up of 180 adult Jews, who attempted to grow bananas, vegetables, and coffee on 1,000 hectares of difficult terrain.

The settlement's physician, Dr. Blumberg, recalled Hochschild's visit to Buena Tierra toward the end of 1943:

He brought along an entire entourage of high-ranking Bolivians, including government ministers, as well as diplomats like the American ambassador and the papal nuncio. An impressive personality with great charm, Hochschild delivered an enthusiastic speech to the assembled colonists . . . he asked the children what it was they most wished for, and they responded "a swimming pool"—which he immediately approved for construction . . . but I had the impression that Hochschild failed to recognize the difficulty of the problems we were facing. He offered to purchase a motorcycle for my medical rounds. This was, of course, senseless (given the terrain and lack of adequate roads). I would have been much happier if, in its stead, he had authorized a good riding mule for my use.[22]

Despite Hochschild's continuing enthusiasm and financial support, the site was abandoned in 1945. In a letter to Charles Liebman in 1943, Hochschild hinted at the real significance of "Buena Tierra": he believed that the promise represented by the settlement had facilitated large-scale immigration to Bolivia and would continue to do so after the war.[23]

Immigration into Bolivia continued throughout 1940 insofar as the wartime shipping situation allowed. "Eight months ago legislation stopped immigration, but it did not work," reported the American consul in La Paz on April 23, 1940. A grace period before the cutoff was extended, family members of those who had already settled were excluded, and some illicit sales of visas continued.[24]

An anonymous letter from a refugee in La Paz which reached James Rosenberg of the Joint Distribution Committee, painted a bleak picture of life there:

21. Memorandum of a conversation between Hochschild and Pell, October 25, 1939, NA RG 59, Lot File 52D408, ICGR, Country Files, Box 1, Bolivia.

22. Leo Spitzer, *Hotel Bolivia: The Culture of Memory in a Refuge from Nazism* (New York, Hill & Wang, 1998), 136.

23. Hochschild to Liebman, February 2, 1943, cited in Leo Spitzer, *Hotel Bolivia*, 135–136.

24. Jenkins to Secretary of State, April 23, 1940, NA RG 59, Lot File, 52D408, Country Files, Box 1, Bolivia. Also Avni, "Perú y Bolivia," 351.

[L]ife here has become very difficult. Every day there are articles against the Jews in the papers, which apparently originate with the German Embassy. The embassy gives food to 50 Indios every day, and incites those people so much that it is hardly safe for us to appear on the streets. They call out after Jews, and we are jostled and spat on, in the street, and we cannot defend ourselves. It is almost the way it was in Germany. The Hilfsverein says that it will not end until there have been a few murders, and then the government will finally do something. That is a nice prospect. We only go out of the house now when it is absolutely necessary. These Indios are a dirty, uncultivated mob, who does not know what it is that they call out. We hope that this state of affairs will end soon. These articles appeared first only a few weeks ago, but they worked fast. Many hotelkeepers have announced that they will not accept "dirty" Jews in their hotels. If it were not so sad, it would be funny.

Otherwise, our health and business are both good. We have a satisfactory number of orders, but do not know what will happen if this anti-Semitism continues.[25]

Contacted about the letter, Hochschild responded to Rosenberg, revealing that in April 1940 there were at least 9,000 Jews in La Paz:

Thanks for the extract from a letter received from a refugee living in La Paz, dated April 1940.

I naturally do know and have been informed all along from La Paz that anti-Semitism has not only developed up there, where it never existed before, but that it is also increasing rapidly. The reason is obvious. We have brought in, mostly into that city, between 9,000 and 10,000 Jews against the promise to the government that they would be colonized on the land and that the funds necessary here for would be put at our disposal by the Jews of the United States.

Unfortunately, we have not been put in a position to comply with that promise, with the result that the 9,000 to 10,000 Jews now in La Paz are filling the coffee houses, the few available dwellings and, in order to make some sort of living, are doing some peddling. Besides, quite a number of them have proved to be of a pretty bad character and some of them are crooks.

When I arranged with the government that we could bring in a total of 30,000 Jews for colonization, I fully realized that we would have some anti-Semitism in Bolivia, but I never dreamt of what has come since. However, we cannot only blame the Bolivians for this state of affairs. It is not for nothing that I have begged all along my friends here to cooperate and build up that colonization project. You know that we have studied it and that the Joint [Distribution Committee] has spent quite a lot of money on that study and that the

25. "Recent letter from a refugee, settled in La Paz, Bolivia," April, 1940, NA RG 59, Lot File 52D408, Box 1, Bolivia.

two agronomists have stated that colonization in Bolivia would even be a splendid business and that there was no doubt but that the capital invested could and would be refunded plus a reasonable rate of interest. But all of that was of no avail[,] and hitherto only the insignificant amount of $100,000.00 has been placed at my disposal, and with that we can but colonize about 100 to 150 families or perhaps 400 people out of 9,000 to 10,000 who are already there.

Thanks to our influence in Bolivia, that country has not yet closed its doors entirely, in spite of the anti-Semitism that has been growing, and a few hundred immigrants are still coming in every month. I am worried not only because of the growing anti-Semitism in Bolivia, but I am afraid that it will spread from there all over South America.

Where I formerly had expected that we would make a real big colonization in Bolivia, in which country, according to Mr. Bowman, President of John[s] Hopkins University, conditions are most favorable of all of the South American countries, and where we thus expected to set an example to the surrounding countries that would induce them to also take each tens of thousands of Jews, we are now, due to our being unable to keep our promises and due to the lack of money for colonization, breeding anti-Semitism in South America. If I could only get even now about one million dollars put at our disposal, to be spent over the course of two years, to start a big colonization scheme, I feel quite sure that we could even at this late moment at least stop the development of further anti-Semitism, if not reduce it again.

Toward the middle of last year we placed about 100 people on a small farm in Miraflores. Those people have already become practically self-supporting and only require, for the time being, an additional assistance of $1.00 US per month and per head, which certainly is a remarkable result over such a short time.

I wish to God our friends here would realize that danger of anti-Semitism in South America and would invest some of their money in an enterprise that would not only help the poor Jews from Europe, and give them a new existence, but which would also guarantee them the return of their capital and safeguard them against anti-Semitism in South America.

I am returning the copy you sent me. I should not be surprised if in the future you receive more letters of this kind, but let us be honest with ourselves and let us not blame the Bolivians for that anti-Semitism.[26]

In the spring of 1943, Paul Baerwald of the JDC wrote to another JDC official about the possibility of continued financial assistance to Hochschild in Bolivia:

We need to go further than we have now with the Bolivia enterprise in order to establish it as a success. We must take a chance. There are no guarantees that it will be the success that Hochschild envisages. Hochschild has done

---

26. Hochschild to James Rosenberg, April 30, 1940. Leo Baeck Institute Archives, Papers of Moritz Hochschild, AR 25048, Series 1/3, Box 1, Folder 22.

much. Early in the refugee movement it was his effort which kept the doors open. He is a very influential man as you know. It is wrong to put difficulties in his way. We can be grateful that he has done what he did.[27]

In October 1943 Hochschild sponsored an Exhibition of Industrial and Handi-craft Products in La Paz, highlighting the achievements of Jewish immigrants and their positive contributions to Bolivian society. In December military officers led by Gualberto Villarroel and with the backing of Victor Paz Estenssoro, leader of a na-tionalist organization called the MNR, carried out a coup. The provisional govern-ment was suspected of being pro-Axis. Hochschild was arrested, imprisoned in a mili-tary barracks, and again threatened with execution. Released through American diplomatic pressure, he was subsequently kidnapped and held for sixteen days. He left Bolivia on August 2, 1944, never to return.[28]

In May 1944 Avra Warren, American ambassador to the Dominican Republic, visited Bolivia to get a sense of the various forces in the new Bolivian government and to press for Bolivian cooperation with the United Nations, particularly with re-gard to turning over Axis nationals to the United States and to keeping Bolivia's distance from pro-Axis Argentina. In the process, Warren picked up a certain amount of information about Jewish refugees who had come to Bolivia. An American diplo-mat prepared a detailed summary of Warren's discussions, from which the following segments (from May 15 and 16) are drawn:

[Victor Paz Estenssoro] admitted agitation against Jewish immigrants on the part of the MNR at one time but declared that feeling against Jews locally was not a racial matter but an economic one—caused by the entry into Bolivia of Jewish refugees who came as agriculturists [*sic*] but who promptly began competition in small shops, who aggravated the housing and food situations and who were ostentatious in their amusements. Both Paz and Lavadenz [man-ager of the government petroleum monopoly and another leader of the MNR] asserted that the Jewish immigration has now been assimilated and that there is no particular feeling against them at the present.

. . . .

This morning two leaders of the La Paz Jewish community, Israel Kleinman of the Circulo Israelito, and Dr. Guillermo Mueller (M.D.) of the Communi-dad Israelito, came in. During their conversation they revealed that one of the chief reasons for the successful entry into Bolivian commerce by Jewish refugees was their subsidization by the Joint Relief Distribution Agency [Joint Distribu-tion Committee] of New York until they became sufficient well established to become financially independent. Their activities in the small shopkeeping field,

27. Baerwald to George Backer, May 6, 1943, JDC AR 33/44, Bolivia, Folder 1084.
28. *New York Times*, August 2, 1944, p. 5; September 6, 1944, p. 11. Hochschild died in Paris in 1965.

and the dislodgment of Bolivians through their competition appears to be the basic cause of anti-Jewish feeling here (one sees anti-Jewish slogans on walls about the town, although not to any great extent). The fact that the refugees came to Bolivia with agricultural visas and then straightway were assisted by a relief organization to establish themselves in business is judged by Bolivians as a breach of faith. Mr. Kleinman and Dr. Mueller reported, for instance, that the long-time resident Jews will have little to do with the refugee group.[29]

How many Jewish refugees entered Bolivia between 1938 and 1944? The number 20,000 used by historians Spitzer and Avni is based on the mid-1940 Bolivian Ministry of Agriculture census. The census, the first of its kind, does not include children under sixteen, nor can it include those who entered Bolivia briefly before undertaking "backdoor" immigration to Argentina and other countries. Nor does it count the smaller number who managed to reach Bolivia later in 1940 or afterward. Therefore, 20,000 is the minimum number, with the real total likely considerably higher.[30] Whatever the exact number, the evidence sustains Avni's assessment that Bolivia saved more Jews than any other Indo-American nation and, in proportion to its size, more than any American nation.[31]

The documents reprinted here do not gloss over the mixed motives of some of those involved in bringing Jews to Bolivia and then to other South American countries just before and during the Holocaust. Nor do they contradict claims here and elsewhere that those who came to Bolivia had to struggle dearly. Still, it is not an exaggeration to say that, lacking this option, many of these more than twenty thousand Jews would have died during the Holocaust. Mauricio Hochschild was a very important and little-known rescuer of Jews.

Dominican Republic

McDonald had been present at the Evian Conference in July 1938 when the representative of the Dominican Republic offered to take in up to 100,000 refugees. But American diplomats in Santo Domingo soon discounted the sincerity and feasibility of the invitation from dictator General Rafael Trujillo. Some of their information came from Dominican sources:

It will be recalled that the question of the relief of political refugees was brought to the attention of the Dominican Government by this legation under the department's instruction and that the Dominican government joined in the work of the Inter-Governmental Committee on Political Refugees largely with the feeling that it was safe policy to follow the lead of the United States in this endeavor. From frank conversations with persons in the Dominican govern-

29. W. Tappley Bennett, Jr., Resumé of Conversations Held by Ambassador Warren in La Paz, May 7–20, 1944, in Duggan to Lyon, June 16, 1944, NA RG 59, 824.00/3298.

30. Spitzer, *Hotel Bolivia*, 203–204, n2; Avni, "Perú y Bolivia," 345.

31. Avni, "Perú y Bolivia," 345.

ment who are particularly interested in immigrants for whom relief is now sought (namely, Jewish refugees mostly from urban centers) is almost precisely the type of immigrant not desired by the Dominican government. The Dominican Republic is keenly anxious to secure "neo-white" agricultural colonists and looks to Puerto Rico with the hope that the United States government, anxious to relieve the pressure of population in the neighboring island, would be willing to defray the cost of transferring Puerto Ricans of the agricultural class to this country where they would be sent to the frontier provinces to form a bulwark against Haitian infiltrations.

The primary desiderata in the eyes of the Dominican government are assimilable agricultural immigrants of near white race, obtainable at minimum expense.

I feel, therefore, that Mr. Myron Taylor may be informed that the Dominican offer is simply a gesture on the international stage, and that it is not to be taken at its face value.[32]

Dominican Law #48 of December 23, 1938, called for an "entrance tax" of 500 pesos for each Jew admitted into the Republic temporarily or permanently.[33] The American minister noted, quite early on, that many of those wishing to enter the country were primarily interested in escaping from the Reich and, if possible, entering the United States, not settling permanently in the Dominican Republic.[34]

Undersecretary of State Sumner Welles sent a formal endorsement for an envoy sent by the President's Advisory Committee to the Dominican Republic.

It is a pleasure to introduce to you Mr. Alfred Houston, who is visiting the Dominican Republic at the request of the President's Advisory Committee on Political Refugees to investigate the possibilities of settlement there.

You are aware of the deep interest of the President in the plight of these unfortunate people and of the efforts which this government is making to bring about a practical solution of the problem through the settlement of political refugees from Germany in other parts of the world. The Dominican Republic has, as you know, very generously offered to admit large numbers of refugees and the purpose of Mr. Houston's trip is to make a thorough study of the possibilities of settlement along the lines of that offer.

He will no doubt wish to discuss the matter with General Trujillo and other officials of the Dominican government. I know that you will be happy to show him every courtesy and to facilitate his mission so far as may be possible.[35]

32. R. Henry Norweb to Secretary of State, August 20, 1938, NA RG 59 Lot File 52D408, Country File, Box 3, Dominican Republic, vol. 1.
33. Simone Gigliotti, "'Acapulco in the Atlantic': Revisiting Sosua, a Jewish Refugee Colony in the Caribbean," *Immigrants & Minorities* 24, no. 1 (March 2006): 29.
34. Norweb to Secretary of State, November 7, 1938, NA RG 59, Lot File 52D408, Country File, Box 3, Dominican Republic, vol. 1.
35. Welles to Eugene M. Hinkle, November 30, 1938, NA RG 59, Lot File 52D408, Country File, Box 3, Dominican Republic, vol. 1.

The American legation, basing its evaluation on talks with Dominican officials, continued to play down possibilities, while noting an increase in the number of applicants for visas.

The legation had already intimated that it is unlikely that this government [the Dominican Republic] will be in a position to accept large members of such involuntary immigrants.

Recent conversations with the local immigration authorities and other officials here indicate that this is still the case. They have stressed the desirability of this country taking only those immigrants whose services would be particularly needful. These officials do not hope to be able to secure the type of agriculturists needed for this country and expect to confine their acceptance of immigrants largely to skilled artisans, technicians, teachers, and professors. Doctors and lawyers are apparently not desired. Therefore, from present indications it would seem that this country will be willing to take in only a handful of carefully selected immigrants whose services will be of particular value.

In this connection the Director of Immigration states that the number of political refugees who have made applications to enter this republic have increased from 2,000, as already reported, to 2,800.[36]

High officials in Washington put pressure on American diplomats in Santo Domingo to do more.

To go back to the beginning, you may or may not realize how deeply this government is committed to finding a solution of the problem of German refugees and how strong an interest in it the President and Mr. Welles have. I can assure you that the interest of the department and the administration in this matter is very great.

As you, of course, know, the problem of finding actual opportunities for the settlement of these refugees in other countries is exceedingly difficult. The universal view is "we don't want any more Jews," but a solution of the problem requires that we start at that point rather than end with it.

The Dominican government is almost the only government which has expressed a willingness to take very substantial numbers. We are of course aware of the possible difficulties involved in mass colonization of Jewish refugees in the Dominican Republic and are inclined to share your feeling that the offer of the Dominican government is so large as to strain credulity, at least as to settlement of the specific numbers mentioned. It may nevertheless prove feasible to settle very substantial numbers there and we are anxious that every possibility of doing so be pushed to the utmost.[37]

36. Hinkle to Secretary of State, December 5, 1938, NA RG 59, Lot File 52D408, Country File, Box 3, Dominican Republic, vol. 1.

37. Sheldon Chapin to Hinkle, December 7, 1938, NA RG 59, Lot File 52D408, Country File, Box 3, Dominican Republic, vol. 1. Chapin headed the U.S. Foreign Service.

Following negotiations with Trujillo, Undersecretary Welles informed President Roosevelt that a mission of technical experts was being sent to the Dominican Republic.

Your Advisory Committee on Political Refugees is sending a mission of technical experts to study the possibilities of refugee colonization in the Dominican republic, in view of the Dominican Government's offer to the Intergovernmental Committee on Political Refugees to admit from fifty thousand to a hundred thousand involuntary emigrants from Germany.[38]

Rumors about large-scale corruption in the sale of visas, involving the Trujillo family, were frequent during this period. Robert Pell, State Department official attached to the Intergovernmental Committee on Refugees, wrote:

We have convincing proof that the Dominican offices in Europe have broken out in a smallpox of corruption in view of the word that their country is opening its doors to the settlement of refugees. The Paris and Vienna offices are the worst, but those in other capitals are not without blemish.[39]

Some Jews reached the Dominican Republic by March 1939, despite the steep tax. An American consul in Santo Domingo expressed concern about the possibility of their subsequent emigration to the United States:

Jews, at least some, will continue to come for a while longer to the Dominican Republic in spite of the $500 tax. There will also be in all probability a number of them who in paying that tax will exhaust what little means they have, and thus will add their number to those who are already destitute. The Dominican government obviously does not intend to provide relief, and it follows that the only hope for these people, at least until the other more fortunate Jews get on their feet, will be contributions from Jewish organizations or committees in other countries, principally the United States.

The indication are that ultimately few refugees will come to the Dominican Republic unless especially provided for by some such plan as that of the refugee Committee which sponsored the group of technical experts who are now in the country. In the event that such a large scale settlement is agreed upon, special provision will have to be made in the Immigration Law as it now stands.

The present set up, moreover, will act as a definite curb upon those Jews who desire to come to the Dominican Republic solely for the purpose of applying for immigration visas for the United States. The reason for this is that the

---

38. Welles to Roosevelt, February 27, 1939, NA RG 59, Lot File 52D408, Country File, Box 3, Dominican Republic, vol. 1.

39. Pell to Theodore Achilles, March 23, 1939, NA RG 59, Lot File 52D408, Country File, Box 3, Dominican Republic, vol. 1.

two amendments to the Immigration Law are being construed as applying to entrance into the country for whatever purpose, and regardless of whether or not the ultimate intent is for permanent residence.[40]

In early June 1939 the Dominican Republic made an offer to admit the SS Saint Louis *passengers, an offer that the foreign minister conveyed to American diplomats.*[41]

The Foreign Minister informed me that in response to a cabled inquiry from the Dominican Consul in Habana he had replied that the refugees aboard the SAINT LOUIS would be admitted here provided they could pay the $500 head tax levied on persons of Semitic race and meet medical requirement.[42]

This offer was discussed by the JDC executive committee and rejected. The President's Advisory Committee soon became concerned that, whether out of pursuit of financial gain or for other reasons, the Dominican government was considering so many different offers that it made feasible planning and real settlement extremely difficult or even impossible. State Department official Stephen Morris wrote:

This morning Mr. [George] Warren expressed to me his perturbation over a press report that General Trujillo is anxious to take in five hundred Jewish refugees at once. Mr. Warren gave me the following background of this report: Mr. Arthur Lamport, Treasurer of the United Jewish Appeal and a Zionist belonging to the Rabbi Silver group, was introduced to General Trujillo by Carlos Davila, former Ambassador to the United States from Chile and for a brief period President of Chile. To Mr. Lamport, General Trujillo made the following statements:

(1) He is upset by the report of the commission which was sent under the auspices of the President's Advisory Committee to investigate possibilities for refugee settlement in the Dominican Republic and he believes it to be more political than economic.
(2) He does not understand why something isn't being done immediately to settle the refugees in the Dominican Republic, for he feels that he has made all sorts of offers (at Evian, etc.) and that nobody has taken him seriously.
(3) Trujillo does not want to deal through official channels (probably because he wants to be relieved of any official responsibility).
(4) He really wants refugees.

40. Report from the American Consulate at Ciudad Trujillo, Dominican Republic, March 25, 1939, NA RG 59, Lot File 52D408, Country File, Box 3, Dominican Republic, vol. 1.
41. On the *St. Louis* story, see chapter 8, p. 175.
42. Telegram from Norweb to Hull, June 3, 1939, NA RG 59, Lot File 52D408, Country File, Box 3, Dominican Republic, vol. 1.

The General said to Mr. Lamport that the Dominican Republic would accept several thousand refugee families, but Lamport, realizing the impracticability of this offer, cut it down to five hundred. Under the Lamport plan, some refugees would be agriculturists, some intellectuals and some would develop small industries (a complete reversal of Trujillo's former policy that refugees must under no circumstances enter business). Trujillo then put forth a pet idea of his own which is to take in fifty to sixty refugee children between the ages of thirteen and fifteen and to make them wards of the state for a two-year period.

Mr. Warren asked Lamport to do all he could to keep the General from making this scheme public. However, in spite of this request, the General gave the report to the ship's reporters before sailing yesterday.[43]

Warren and Lamport joined forces and came to a preliminary agreement with the Dominican Minister to Washington, Andres Pastoriza, who played a crucial role throughout the negotiations. A Dominican Republic Settlement Corporation— DORSA—was to be established. It was headed by James N. Rosenberg and linked to the JDC. George Warren described the outlines of the proposal.

1. With the understanding that the $500 entrance fee will be removed, the proposed Dominican Republic Settlement Corporation will settle an indefinite number of refugees, to be made up of professional men, technicians, and agriculturists. It is proposed that the number of agriculturists be controlled by dividing the number of acres available by twenty-five.
2. The proposed corporation to take over the care of refugees already in the Dominican Republic, provided their number not be increased.
3. That all German, Austrian, and Czech refugees enter only through the corporation.
4. That the corporation set up receiving barracks, agricultural training stations, and locate farm areas for refugees.[44]

The funding soon took shape, with the JDC playing a major role. McDonald later indicated that the President's Advisory Committee had managed to spark Rosenberg's interest in the Dominican Republic and get him directly involved.[45] Rosenberg was among the initial donors, and his activity helped to convey the strength and seriousness of American support.

43. Memorandum of conversation between Warren and Morris, August 3, 1939, NA RG 59, Lot File 52D408, Country File, Box 3, Dominican Republic, untitled folder.
44. Memorandum of conversation between Warren and Morris, August 24, 1939, NA RG 59, Lot File 52D408, Country File, Box 3, Dominican Republic, vol. 1.
45. McDonald's comments, February 15, 1940, at a Town Hall Meeting "Concerning Refugee Settlement in the Dominican Republic," YIVO, RG 278, Joseph Chamberlain Papers, Folder 77.

[George] Warren said that on the basis of Mr. Berle's[46] letter steps were being taken to set up the Dominican Corporation, with an initial capital of $200,000, at once. Mr. Lessing Rosenwald[47] had donated $50,000 in cash immediately upon the receipt of our letter; Mr. [James] Rosenberg had given another $50,000; the Joint Distribution Committee would make up the rest out of its funds. The corporation when formed would notify the President's Advisory Committee of its establishment and there would then take place an exchange of letters with Señor Pastoriza, the Dominican Minister. It was hoped that the corporation would be actually functioning by the time of the President's meeting and it was felt that that would be a suitable occasion in which to announce its establishment.[48]

On a number of occasions General Trujillo had promised to find and donate land for this settlement, but it had never been formally ceded. Trujillo's brutal dictatorship was not popular in the United States. These problems were taken up at a meeting sponsored by the President's Advisory Committee and attended by Rosenberg, Pastoriza, and others.

After these points had been reviewed and clarified with the Dominican Minister, Mr. Rosenberg said that he was going to be quite frank. He said that the Minister was probably aware of the fact that there was a considerable hostility, but he was frank to say that it included a number of potential Jewish subscribers. Mr. Rosenberg believed that if General Trujillo would prove his good faith by making a free grant of a substantial amount of land settlement, it would dispose of the criticisms and convince some people who were doubters of the sincerity of the Dominican authorities in opening up this opportunity for settlement. Mr. Rosenberg made it clear that no one present at the meeting had any doubt of the good intentions of the Dominican government but there were others not present who hesitated to take part in this enterprise because of uncertainty in their minds as to the intentions of the Dominican government.

Señor Pastoriza said that he was fully aware of the criticisms that were directed against his country in certain quarters and of the suspicions which had been aroused by ill-intentioned persons. He said that he was certain that General Trujillo would wish to make a grant of the kind indicated by Mr. Rosenberg and he would consult the General immediately.

Mr. Rosenberg then inquired as to the manner in which the Dominican government would legalize the contract with the corporation.

46. Adolf A. Berle, assistant secretary of state.
47. Lessing Rosenwald, prominent member of the family that owned Sears Roebuck.
48. The allusion was to the October 17, 1939, meeting of the Intergovernmental Committee on Refugees in Washington. Memorandum of conversation between Warren and Pell, October 4, 1939, NA RG 59, Lot File 52D408, Country File, Box 6, Philippines.

Señor Pastoriza said that the President would issue a decree covering the contract and the General Trujillo would make the announcement of his contribution at the same time.

Monsieur van Zeeland, who had not taken part in this discussion, here said that he was greatly impressed by the businesslike manner in which this project was undertaken and assured the meeting that it would have his full support. He said that he was prepared to write a letter to Mr. Rosenberg to that effect.

Privately, after the meeting, Mr. Rosenberg said that he could raise another $500,000 tomorrow if he could have some further affirmation from Washington that the President thought well of the project.[49]

Almost one and a half years after the Evian Conference, and after the war in Europe began, the following press release was issued:

Mr. James G. McDonald, Chairman of the President's Advisory Committee on Political Refugees, upon his return form Washington today emphasized President Roosevelt's satisfaction that actual steps can now be taken to begin settlement of European refugees in the Dominican Republic, following the official announcement made by General Rafael Leonidas Trujillo, former President, that his country will immediately admit 500 selected refugee families without the payment of the usual $500 immigration fee.

McDonald said:

"The Dominican Republic offers the first immediate concrete step toward clarifying many of the problems inherent in settling mass populations anywhere in the world other than Palestine. The Dominican government has just made a written, precise proposal of terms of settlement which look toward the ultimate absorption of 100,000 people.

. . . .

The President's Advisory Committee has had the Dominican experiment under careful and constant consideration since the Intergovernmental Committee's Conference in Evian in July 1938.

Preliminary studies made by a Commission of experts selected by Dr. Isaiah Bowman, President of Johns Hopkins University, leading authority on resettlement, recommend settlement in the Dominican Republic, pointing to the necessity of soundly worked out long-term plans which must however begin on a small, modest scale.

Conditions of life for the refugees are reported favorable. Plans provide agricultural settlement of a non-sectarian nature with full guarantee for free

---

49. Memorandum of a meeting of the President's Advisory Committee, October 1939, NA RG 59, Lot File 52D408, Country File, Box 2, Dominican Republic, vol. 2.

exercise of religion and all rights and privileges enjoyed by citizens of the republic. Full citizenship is granted in two years.

Settlement will take place under the auspices of a non-profit corporation financed by interested groups under the leadership of Mr. James N. Rosenberg, Chairman of the American Jewish Joint Agricultural Corporation. Within the next month it is expected that specialists in settlement projects will leave for the Dominican Republic to lay the foundation for future work.

Since the future success of the project depends largely on the human material involved, the refugees themselves, careful steps are being taken in selecting men and women who can settle successfully in the Dominican Republic."[50]

The American legation in Santo Domingo focused on the corruption and duplicity of the Trujillo regime:

Recapitulation of Incidents of 1939

(a) While the Dominican government was agreeing in principle to the settlement plan of the President's Committee after discussions with Mr. Houston in December 1938, Trujillo was at that the same time negotiating through his brother, Virgilio, the Dominican Minister in Paris, for a "private" settlement of 3,000 Czechs under the Kulka Action which was to be financed by subscriptions collected in Czechoslovakia. If this plan had succeeded, it would have given Trujillo over a million dollars in taxes, fees, et cetera. No preliminary survey or preparation was made in connection with the establishment of these refugees. . . .

(b) Trujillo has been reluctant up until only recently to give normal publicity to Dominican government's agreement "in principle," badly as he has desired a "good press" in the United States. The honorary Dominican Consul General in London was "sacked" for issuing a statement to the press early in January 1939 regarding the acceptance of the plan. What is more, Trujillo took great pains to keep from knowledge of the President's Advisory Committee the fact that he was negotiating with Kulka Action for a "private" settlement at considerable profit.

(c) The negotiations with Kulka Action apparently reached the point where the Czech government was about to permit the transfer of funds to a bank in Paris (in General Trujillo's name, see Ciudad Trujillo dispatch no. 800) through a treaty which was to be concluded by March 20, 1939. These negotiations, however, were terminated, of course, when Germany established the protectorate over Czechoslovakia on March 15, 1939. Hopes for this settlement nevertheless continued, as witnessed by the attached copy of a letter appealing to the Carnegie Foundation for International Peace,

---

50. "Re: Dominican Refugee Settlement Project," PACPR Release, November 6, 1939, Wise Papers, Box 107, Roll 71, Center for Jewish History.

West 117th Street, New York, dated Prague, August 14, 1939, with which was enclosed a scheme for colonization. . . .

(d) When the report of the Technical Commission, headed by Dr. Barker, was sent to the Dominican government through the American Legation at Ciudad Trujillo for approval at the end of May, its immediate publication was desired by the Advisory Committee, which action again would have given Trujillo the whole-hearted support of the American press. Instead, the Dominican government "stalled" for nearly two months on the pretext that certain statements in the report should be changed. These corrections could have been made in as many days or a week at most. When finally approved, the psychological time for publication had passed.

(e) As late as October 1939, a Czech Jew by the name of Phillip, formerly a banker and apparently having access to means, was in Cuidad Trujillo and talking a refugee settlement project. It is not known whether any agreement had been reached but there was a rumor in Ciudad Trujillo that fifteen hundred refugees (not substantiated) were supposed to embark in November from Amsterdam.

(f) Trujillo's apparent whole-hearted support of the Agro-Joint settlement project, and for the first time actually taking the initiative, was made known only after his return to the United States from Europe by Pastoriza's letter to Mr. James N. Rosenberg, dated October 19, 1939, two days after President Roosevelt's welcoming address to the Chairman of the Intergovernmental Committee.

(g) The ostensible reasons for Trujillo's support are the following:
　(i) White immigration.
　(ii) Settlement of the land.
　(iii) Introduction of new capital.
　(iv) Possibility of favorable trade agreement with United States at some future date.
　(v) Anticipated increase in revenue from taxes.
　(vi) Humanitarian (to be discounted, but which is hoped will help his American press).

Conclusions

From the very first Trujillo has had in the fire (several irons) which he intended ultimately to play off one against the other. With a record like this, there is little doubt that Trujillo's personal profit was the primary motive at the beginning for his "humanitarian" gesture and might yet have to be carefully watched in order not to permit it to endanger the success of the plan. The other motives were rationalizing considerations, increased government revenue, for example, being secondary. Nevertheless, if the situation is thoroughly understood and the necessary safeguards are provided, there seems now to be an excellent chance to achieve practical results by acting upon Trujillo's present offer. The establishment of a single successful refugee project such as this one would go a long way toward finding an ultimate solution of the problem.[51]

In a January 1940 letter to Rosenberg, Trujillo offered land on the northern coast for the use of the Jewish colonists.

My country property located in Sosua, province of Puerto Plata, has, as you have informed me, been selected by Dr. Joseph A. Rosen as an appropriate place for settlement.

This property of about 26,685 acres, contains twenty-four dwellings, reservoir and other installations for the accommodation of settlers. The property has 4,950 acres of cultivated pasture, and large extent virgin forest, with an abundance of valuable timber, which represents for me an actual investment of not less than $100,000.

I am deeply interested to cooperate in a practical way with the humanitarian plans of President Roosevelt. I hope the immigration of European refugees, to the Dominican Republic, will stimulate the progress of our country, and will intensify the development of our natural resources, as well as industries.

As I mentioned to you in personal conversation, it is indispensable to create an agricultural bank in Santo Domingo, to aid the work of these immigrants, by helping the marketing of their crops. Such a bank will also be in a position in this country to secure favorable agreements, which will benefit our entire farming population, by offering them short-term crop loans at moderate interest.

To repeat, I am deeply interested in the realization of this settlement enterprise, because I am convinced that we must cooperate within our possibilities for the success of this humanitarian and noble effort. It is, therefore, my dear Mr. Rosenberg, my pleasure to offer to the Refugee Association, of which you are the esteemed President, my Sosua property, as my personal contribution for the establishment, there, of the first refugee settlement in the Dominican Republic.[52]

DORSA publicized the establishment of a settlement in the Dominican Republic. The Dominican legation in Washington received many inquiries about Dominican visas for relatives in Europe whose ultimate destination was the United States. Two examples are reprinted here:

My parents, Leopold & Alice Klein, as well as my grandmother, Amelie Rothschild, all residing at Cologne-Germany, being German Jews, are planning to emigrate for a long time already. They are registered at for a United

51. Memorandum prepared by Edward Anderson, November 25, 1939, NA RG 59, Lot File 52D408, Country File, Box 3, Dominican Republic, vol. 2.

52. Rafael Trujillo to Rosenberg, January 20, 1940. Copy in minutes of the meeting of the President's Advisory Committee on Political Refugees, February 1940, YIVO, RG 278, Joseph Chamberlain Papers, Folder 77.

States immigration visa (on German quota) under No. 19402 and 19403. It is expected that they will get their visas in a few months, in any case some time this year. They have been asked in January this year, to send the necessary papers, and all the guarantees required (affidavits) for their support after arrival in this country have been furnished.

On account of the latest developments, I am most anxious to arrange their emigration and to find a refuge for them as fast as possible.

I understand that the Dominican Republic has signed a contract recently which was made official only about two weeks ago, providing for the immigration and settlement of a considerable number of refugees and I would appreciate if you would be kind enough to let me have your information and further details in this regard.

As you may understand, the above mentioned relatives of mine have the chance to enter the United States and to be united with me within a rather short while and thus, their stay in the Dominican Republic would be of only temporary nature. Guarantees for their maintenance, so that they never could become a burden to anybody, could be furnished without any difficulty.

Any information and advice from you in this regard, especially about possibilities, regulations and requirements, will be highly appreciated.[53]

Erwin Klein

I shall appreciate if you will kindly let me know the conditions necessary for immigration into the Dominican Republic. My parents are living in Germany, and according to the quota system I can't bring them into the U.S.A. at present. If they could enter the Dominican Republic for the time waiting for their U.S.A. visa, they wouldn't become any public burden as I'll provide them with money for their livelihood. Thanking you in advance for your kind reply I am respectfully yours,

Magdalene Bernstein[54]

There were also inquiries from several American politicians on behalf of relatives of people close to them. The letter below was from U.S. Senator Clyde M. Reed, Republican from Kansas (1939–1949) and former governor of the state (1929–1931).

My office has been working for some time on the case of an elderly Jewish gentleman, now in Berlin, Germany for whom we have been trying to secure some visitors visa or transit visa to some place of haven until his quota number for entrance to the United States is called sometime this fall.

53. Erwin Klein to Dominican Legation, March 11, 1940, USHMM Archives, RG 63, Selected Records from the Legation of the Dominican Republic in Washington, 1940 roll, part 1.
54. Magdalene Bernstein to Dominican Legation, March 26, 1940, USHMM Archives, RG 63, Selected Records from the Dominican Legation in Washington, 1940 roll, part 1.

This gentleman, Mr. Joseph Lowenstein, is the stepfather of my personal physician, who is a resident of Johnson County, Kansas and has been citizen of this country for a number of years.[55]

And another request from Cornelius Vanderbilt, Jr., was on behalf of a young artist, soon to become famous.

I have been interested for some time in assisting a young artist, now resident in Genoa, Italy, with a view to assisting him to establish himself in this hemisphere.

He is Saul Steinberg, a Rumanian citizen holding a passport signed by the Rumanian legation to Rome, No. 279160, issued on November 29, 1939. Young Steinberg, who is 26 years old, has been studying in Milan and is a graduate architect as well as a talented artist. During the past months samples of this work have appeared in such leading American publications as Harper's Bazaar and Life. The May 27th issue of Life Magazine devotes three pages to his cartoons.

Although there is every prospect that Mr. Steinberg will be able to make an excellent living in this country, our immigration policy, as you must know, makes it impossible for him to settle here. However, he has several friends in your country, and has applied to the Minister from the Dominican Republic in Genoa, Italy, amply insured by friends in this country, details of which I would be glad to supply you.

I am applying to you because the Minister of your country in Genoa has told Mr. Steinberg that if you would cable him wither a suggestion or an authorization that a visa be granted for Mr. Steinberg, he would do so. Since the war situation in Europe, and especially in Italy, is so precarious, I am most anxious to expedite this matter just as much as possible. I should be very happy to pay for the expense of any cables or investigations and inquires necessary for you, of you are willing to assist me in this matter.

I feel that your country would be the gainer of a very talented and worthwhile resident, if you were to open the doors for editors that he will be able to earn a considerable amount of money in the United States, which he will, naturally, spend in the Dominican Republic.

If it is possible for you to do so, I cannot urge upon you strongly enough, that you cable the minister or consul in Genoa, Italy, requesting that he consider Mr. Steinberg's application favorably.[56]

---

55. Clyde M. Reed to Pastoriza, August 20, 1940, USHMM Archives, RG 63, selected Records from the Dominican Legation in Washington, 1940 roll, part 1.

56. Cornelius Vanderbilt to the Minister of the Dominican Republic, June 1, 1940. USHMM Archives, RG 63, Selected Records from the Dominican Republic Legation in Washington, 1940 roll, part 1.

Pastoriza contacted James Rosenberg, and Saul Steinberg received his visa. He spent two years in the Dominican Republic and immigrated to the United States in 1942.

On January 30, 1940, the Dominican Republic Settlement Association (DORSA) signed an agreement with the Dominican Government which was endorsed by the country's legislative assembly. It guaranteed freedom of religion, expedited immigration procedures, and granted various other concessions. DORSA owned and governed the settlement of Sosua and represented it before the Dominican government. Former General Electric executive Solomon Trone was appointed by DORSA to travel around Europe recruiting refugees for Sosua. He went to Britain, Switzerland, Spain and Portugal but found few with agricultural experience. One review of an accepted applicant read:

Good impression, agricultural experience of about three months in Germany and one year in England. Simple boy who will certainly make good under strong direction. . . . Medically examined by Dr. Monson-Bahr and found fit for residence in Santo Domingo.[57]

Although the Dominican Republic granted 5,000 visas between 1940 and 1944, only 645 Jews actually reached the country. The population of the colony on June 30, 1942, consisted of 472 persons, with 104 married couples, 158 single men, 38 single women, and 68 children under 15. The peak population of 476 was reached in 1943.[58]

The isolated settlement on the northern coast was built on the site of a former United Fruit Company banana plantation which had been abandoned. The land was not very fertile. The settlers, mostly German Jews, at first farmed communally, growing tomatoes and raising lemongrass (used in perfume). DORSA brought experts from Palestinian kibbutzim to teach the settlers communal agriculture. Eventually, a meat-packing plant and a dairy factory were established. DORSA invested about one million dollars in the project, which was an expensive one, judging by the itemized cost of a single homestead:

A house on one hectare of land: $800
One additional hectare of garden land: $35
Furniture, fixtures, and garden tools: $120
Small livestock: $25
One horse, one mule: $45
One saddle: $15
Two cows: $45
Miscellaneous equipment: $15

57. Nicholas Ross, "Sosua: A Colony of Hope," *American Jewish History* 82, no. 1–4 (1994): 241.
58. Gigliotti, "Acapulco . . . ," 34.

Credit per family for DORSA approved undertaking: $500
Total: $1,600[59]

In 1944 communal life was abandoned, and the settlers obtained private plots. Most settlers left for the United States and Israel after the war, although a small number remained. Today (2007) 25 families remain in Sosua.

Many settlers left family behind in Europe. One such settler, a former passenger on the SS Saint Louis, *contacted State Department official Robert Pell:*

I am a settler at the Dominican Republic Settlement Association in Sosua. My wife and my boy are now stranded in Amsterdam since they were forced to sail back with the S.S. "St. Louis" from Havana because, as you know, the government of Cuba did not allow the disembarkation of all passengers who were on board the ship.

At the 15th November 1940 the Department of State of the Dominican Republic cabled the visas for my family to the Consul General at Amsterdam.

There is now no prospect that the whole group of settlers can leave Holland. I have no doubt that my wife together with my 5 year's old son is able to reached Lisbon, but it is impossible for her to do so without the American transit visa which would help her to overcome all the many difficulties.

I therefore ask you very instantly for your help in recommending my wife to the American Consul general in Amsterdam asking him for securing the American transit visas for my wife, Else Blumenstein, Amsterdam, Hemonystraat 52, HOLLAND, and my son, Heinz Georg Blumenstein, above address.

It was nearly two years ago that I have been dismissed from the concentration camp in Dachau and since this time I have been separated from my dear family. I sincerely hope and do pray that you will make it possible to help me, so that we can all be reunited after two years of sorrows and worries.

I take the liberty in enclosing as reference a list of American citizens who I personally know and who are fully prepared to give you any required information about my person.

I want to thank you very much in advance for all the troubles which I hereby caused to you and remain as
Your obedient servant,
Franz Blumenstein[60]

59. Ross, "Sosua . . . ," 242.
60. Franz Blumenstein to Robert Pell, December 13, 1940, NA RG 59, Lot File 52D408, 1942–47, Box 4, Miscellaneous Subject file. Blumenstein was eventually reunited with his wife and son.

Ironically, Avra Warren, former head of the State Department Visa Division and staunch restrictionist, was appointed American minister to the Dominican Republic in 1942. This appointment was a symbol of a once-promising resettlement venture gone off course, with great effort needed to overcome problems and skeptics in order to save modest numbers of people.

In general, during the war the State Department consistently discouraged Latin American countries from granting visas to refugees because many of them were "secret agents or sympathizers of the totalitarian countries."[61] Historians have uncovered one case of a German military intelligence (Abwehr) agent who posed as a Jewish refugee on a ship to Cuba before the war. This man was arrested and eventually executed.[62]

61. Max Paul Friedman, "The U.S. State Department and the Failure to Rescue: New Evidence on the Missed Opportunity at Bergen-Belsen," *Holocaust and Genocide Studies* 19:1 (Spring 2005), 37–38.

62. Thomas D. Schoonover, *Hitler's Man in Havana: Heinz Lüning and Nazi Espionage in Latin America* (Lexington: University of Kentucky Press, 2008).

12. The War and the Holocaust: 1942–1945

After the Japanese attack on Pearl Harbor, Germany declared war on the United States, and Americans found themselves at war on two fronts. The government rushed to mobilize more troops and expand production of weapons, ammunition, planes, and ships. Americans followed the course of the battles in Europe and the fate of American troops in the Pacific and, by late in 1942, those who had landed in North Africa.

Reports of Nazi atrocities during the war provoked anger, horror, or indifference across the country. Average Americans did not grasp the scope, pace, or significance of what we have come to call the Holocaust, in part because it was not highlighted or particularly well reported in the mainstream media. But even some who paid considerable attention to the situation of Jews in Europe could not quite grasp what was taking place. It was literally incredible.

McDonald was an exception. He knew that Nazi leaders and ideologues regarded Jews as vermin, and so they might well view extermination of Jews as entirely appropriate. Lacking a diary for this period, however, we do not know exactly when McDonald recognized that Nazi mass murder had become an industrialized process using extermination camps and poison gases, and that all Jews in Nazi territories or in areas under Nazi influence faced the prospect of murder on the spot or deportation and death.

In January (effective March 1, 1942) McDonald resigned as president of the Brooklyn Institute of Arts and Sciences. His move to Brooklyn had probably been a mistake in the first place. Though he had a great love for music and the arts, administration was not his strong point, and the job had been a complete break with his life career path and his interest in foreign affairs. At the time he said he had resigned because of "the exigencies of the war and my desire to have the opportunity to work more directly in the national defense effort." What plans he had, if any, he said were "too secret for a public announcement at present."[1] But if he was contacted about working for the new American intelligence agency, the Office of Strategic Services, he did not reach agreement with OSS. We found no written record of a direct OSS contact.

McDonald pursued some new activities in 1942, serving on an enemy alien clearing board. In a February 1942 letter to his former deputy Norman Bentwich, McDonald had commented on some of this work:

1. "McDonald Quits Post," *New York Times,* January 9, 1942.

As to enemy aliens, we have, I think, made a good beginning. Contrary to the desires of some groups in this country, the numbers of enemy aliens arrested thus far have been relatively few, perhaps not more than 4,000 (this, of course, does not include those considerable numbers of Japanese who have been required to move from the West Coast defense industry areas to the interior). I have been sitting as one member of one of the so-called Enemy Alien Hearing Boards, the task of which is to examine the enemy alien in informal procedure. . . . The cases against the aliens are presented by the Federal Bureau of Investigation and by the Immigration Authority. It has interested me to see how in nearly every instance the three members of our Board have been unanimous an[d] almost invariably we have been able to agree on a decision satisfactory to the FBI. It begins to look as if—provided, of course, there are no great outbursts of public passion because of expensive sabotage—our Government would be able to manage the Enemy Alien matter with a minimum of injustice to individuals.[2]

In February 1942 Joseph Chamberlain prepared a memo regarding enemy aliens who might be exempted from security restrictions. The President's Advisory Committee sent it to the president and to the State Department and Justice Department. Shortly afterward, the government exempted Austro-Hungarians, Austrians, those former enemy nationals who had acquired new citizenship elsewhere, and those who had enlisted in the U.S. armed forces. The committee also pressed for exempting those whom Germany and expelled and those who could prove that they left their country of origin because of racial, religious, or political persecution.[3]

McDonald also wrote a letter to the New York Times *urging the expansion of these clearing boards so that aliens of enemy nationalities could clear their names of any suspicion and contribute to the war effort. This initiative was part of a broader effort to reverse the categorization of German Jews as enemy aliens. The* Times *wrote a supporting editorial.[4] Wendell Willkie commented to McDonald:*

I have been hoping that someone would open a discussion of that question [unfair treatment of enemy aliens]. I think that some of the things that have been done by the government in that regard are almost sickening.[5]

2. McDonald to Bentwich, February 20, 1942, McDonald Papers, Columbia University, General Correspondence (Bentwich), Folder 38a.

3. Fifty-Third Meeting of the President's Advisory Committee on Political Refugees, March 2, 1942, YIVO RG 278, Joseph Chamberlain Papers, Folder 63.

4. *New York Times*, April 6, 1942, p. 32. McDonald was responding in part to lobbying by officials of Agudath Israel, with whom he was on good terms. See Confidential Report for the Chawerim Nichbodim of the Agudath Israel World Organization, January 1–June 30, 1942, and July 1–December 31, 1942, Archives of Agudath Israel, Michal Tress Papers, two-way F 3–5. McDonald was said to be strongly in favor of early classification of German Jews as friendly aliens.

5. Willkie to McDonald, April 6, 1942, McDonald Papers, Columbia University, D361 (Willkie Special File).

On March 24, 1942, President Roosevelt sent a memo to Sumner Welles, then Acting Secretary of State, asking "What do you think [about a government post for McDonald]?" Welles replied:

[C]oncerning the invitation extended by the Federal Communications Commission to Mr. James G. McDonald to accept the directorship of the Foreign Broadcast Monitoring Service, I think, of course, that Mr. McDonald could undertake this work usefully and effectively.

I wonder, though, if he would not be of more use to the Government at this time if he were to obtain that opportunity for radio broadcasting which he has been trying to get for the last two or three months. He has, as you know, great knowledge of our foreign policy and of world affairs in general, and I believe regular national broadcasts by him would be of more value at this time than his service in the position proposed.

Jesse Jones[6] told me the other day that he was optimistic as to the possibility of his securing some broadcasting opportunity for Mr. McDonald, and if such an opportunity can be found for him, that would seem to be the better solution.[7]

Possibly, this was a tactful way of indicating that McDonald had created too many problems in the recent past on the President's Advisory Committee to be placed in a high government post. But Welles's suggestion of broadcasting was reasonable and appropriate—McDonald had considerable broadcasting experience. Starting in 1928, when he headed the Foreign Policy Association, he had done regular or annual series of broadcasts about foreign affairs, and he liked doing them.

On July 25, 1942, McDonald resigned as the Brooklyn member of the New York City Board of Education to devote more time to speeches and to his radio broadcasts. He started a broadcast series on foreign affairs on the National Broadcasting Company's Blue Network. It ran Monday through Friday for fifteen minutes. His program was unusual in that it engaged the audience in a dialogue. At the end of his prepared broadcast he posed a question and asked for responses. In the next broadcast he discussed the better comments from the audience. Responses came from across the country and showed real interest. If appropriate, McDonald sent a postcard in reply to a question.

Meanwhile, he continued to chair the President's Advisory Committee on Political Refugees. But the committee met less frequently and was less active after its bruising defeats in 1941. It was, however, able to intervene in a number of special situations.

---

6. Probably Jesse H. Jones, prominent Houston businessman, whose various holdings included radio and media outlets. Secretary of Commerce, 1940–1945.
7. Welles to FDR, March 25, 1942, NA RG 59, 800.76 Monitoring/59 1/2 (Box 3311).

The Caribbean

On April 18, 1942, the Cuban government prohibited all nationals of Axis and Axis-occupied countries, including all those who had already received Cuban visas, from entering the country. The Cuban decree created an emergency for 257 passengers on the Portuguese ship San Thome, *who had received visas three weeks earlier and who had sailed initially to the Mexican harbor of Veracruz. It seemed to be a repeat of the May 1939 case of the SS* St. Louis, *whose passengers Cuba had refused to take in.*

George Warren reported to the President's Advisory Committee:

On Sunday, April 19th, in the absence of Mr. McDonald, Mr. Baerwald and I wired a report of the plight of these passengers to Under Secretary of State Welles. Mr. McDonald on his return the next day wired Mr. Welles requesting his good offices in suggesting to the Cuban Government that the degree should not be applied to refugees already on the water when the decree was issued. The same day Messrs. Baerwald, Chamberlain, and Warren met with members of the Joint Distribution Committee to consider the situation[,] and later Mr. Warren telephoned Archbishop Rummel in New Orleans[,] who agreed readily to send cables both to President Batista of Cuba and to the Papal Nuncio at Havana.

. . . .

In the meantime representatives of the British, Portuguese, Czechoslovak, Polish, and United States Governments were intervening at Havana. The representatives of the American Jewish Joint Distribution Committee were also pressing the matter[,] and Archbishop Rummel reported that Archbishop Caruana in Havana had intervened and had enlisted other support. As a result of all of these efforts all of the passengers were finally admitted under surveillance to the immigration station at Tiscornia in Havana on Monday, May 4th.[8]

The President's Advisory Committee helped rescue the passengers of another ship, the Cabo de Hornos, *excluded from Brazil in November 1941 despite their possession of Brazilian visas. Pressed by Britain and the United States, the Dutch island of Curaçao agreed to take the passengers temporarily provided that the Joint Distribution Committee guarantee their support. Of the roughly eighty passengers nineteen were found eligible to be admitted to the United States during 1942, and an additional group was sent to the Dominican Republic.[9]*

8. Warren to Members of the President's Advisory Committee, May 2, 1942, YIVO, RG 278, Joseph Chamberlain Papers, Folder 71.

9. Warren to President's Advisory Committee, May 2, 1942, YIVO, RG 278, Joseph Chamberlain Papers, Folder 71. On the Jewish settlement in the Dominican Republic, see chapter 11.

France

The best chance of saving some of the Jews within the reach of the Nazis was in France. The Vichy government controlled nearly half of the country—the rest was under German occupation—and the United States still had diplomatic representation at Vichy during most of 1942.

On March 27, 1942, a train took about one thousand Jews from France to Auschwitz—the first deportation to a destination that remained obscure to much of the world. In June Adolf Eichmann and his subordinates speeded up the schedule, and five more trainloads of approximately the same size were sent in June and July. German authorities in France and Vichy French officials publicly claimed that those transported were to be laborers in the East in a Jewish colony. Reich Führer SS Heinrich Himmler wanted to limit the transports at first to those Jews between ages 16 and 40 to maintain this cover story.

At this time Vichy's Prime Minister Pierre Laval and his subordinates refused to agree to deport French Jews from the unoccupied zone, but Laval actually volunteered to send Jewish children with their parents. Eichmann agreed to take them. His superiors in Berlin wanted to avoid having trains with only children whose parents had been deported previously. Those children had to be mixed with adult deportees to avoid the "wrong" image.[10]

The YMCA's representative in France, Donald Lowrie,[11] deduced that Nazi Germany was going ahead with its threatened purge of "undesirable elements" from Europe.[12] French and foreign relief agencies in unoccupied France managed to place groups of foreign Jewish children in summer camps, private centers, religious institutions, or in the care of non-Jewish families in various locations to avoid having them rounded up and deported by French authorities.

Learning that more deportations of Jews were imminent, a coordinating committee of various American-based relief agencies met with Laval on August 6. Laval declared that France was glad to be rid of foreign Jews. He rejected the charge that Germany's real purpose was extermination, calling this claim preposterous and questioning why the United States and Britain did not take these Jews in if these governments were so concerned.

Laval agreed to consider exempting from the deportations foreign Jews who held immigration visas to the United States and were scheduled to leave within six weeks. American Chargé d'Affaires S. Pinkney Tuck quickly asked French authorities to suspend deportation of those with immigration visas as well as three hundred children.[13]

---

10. Susan Zuccotti, *The Holocaust, the French, and the Jews* (New York: Basic Books, 1993), 96–99. Renée Poznanski, *Jews in France during World War II*, tr. Nathan Bracher (Hanover: Brandeis University Press in Association with the United States Holocaust Memorial Museum, 2001), 255, 264–265. Laval was eager to get rid of non-French Jews.

11. Donald A. Lowrie and his wife Helen O. Lowrie served the YMCA in Eastern Europe and Russia during World War I and the Russian revolutions. During World War II he labored to save Jewish children in France.

12. Poznanski, *Jews in France*, 289–290.

13. Breitman and Kraut, *American Refugee Policy*, 161–162.

McDonald may have gathered that Jews deported from France were being sent to their deaths in the East. He had experienced enough of Laval's ire and hostility toward aliens in the past to regard the French leader as capable of any kind of collaboration with the Nazis, and he had sensed from his meeting with Hitler in April 1933 where the Nazi regime was heading.[14]

The President's Advisory Committee took up the matter. George Warren later reported:

On August 13 Messrs. McDonald, Baerwald and Warren sent a wire to Under Secretary of State Sumner Welles requesting the intervention of the Department of State in an effort to halt the deportations[,] and another wire to Archbishop Rummel requesting that he consider the practicability of requesting similar intervention by the Vatican. In response to these requests the Department of State had reported that our Chargé d'Affaires in Vichy had been instructed to intervene vigorously.[15]

Welles replied that the American chargé at Vichy had already been instructed to support the appeal . . . for the suspension of deportation proceedings though he did not hold out much hope.[16] Subsequent American meetings with both Laval and Petain produced the impression that deportations of Jews from France could not be halted; on the other hand, more exceptions might be made. Chargé Tuck made it as clear as possible to State Department officials in Washington that those deported to the East would not survive.[17]

George Warren told the President's Advisory Committee that anywhere from a thousand to thirty-five hundred children were under immediate threat of deportation.

The United States Committee for the Care of European Children, in collaboration with the American Jewish Joint Distribution Committee, had virtually completed arrangements for the admission of 1,000 of these children to the United States. After full discussion it was moved, seconded, and voted that the project for securing the admission of 1,000 children to the United States be approved and supported by the President's Advisory Committee. . . . It was suggested that McDonald communicate with Mrs. Franklin D. Roosevelt.[18]

By late August 1942 much more specific information about Nazi death factories then reached the United States through different sources and channels. The best-known

14. On this background, see *Advocate for the Doomed*, 47–48.
15. Fifty-Fifth Meeting of the President's Advisory Committee on Political Refugees, September 9, 1942, YIVO RG 278, Joseph Chamberlain Papers, Folder 63.
16. Welles to McDonald, August 19, 1942, McDonald Papers, Columbia University, D367 (PACPR), P70.
17. Breitman and Kraut, *American Refugee Policy*, 161–162.
18. Fifty-Fifth Meeting of the President's Advisory Committee on Political Refugees, September 9, 1942, YIVO RG 278, Joseph Chamberlain Papers, Folder 63.

is a telegram sent by Gerhart M. Riegner[19] from Geneva to Rabbi Stephen Wise in New York (received on August 28) about a Nazi plan under consideration at Hitler's headquarters to exterminate three and a half to four million Jews at one blow through the use of poison gas based on prussic acid, thereby resolving the Jewish question in Europe once and for all.[20] Wise immediately consulted Undersecretary Welles, who urged caution and asked Wise not to publicize this report until it had been confirmed. Wise, however, also discussed this telegram with a number of his contacts, including the President's Advisory Committee.[21]

McDonald was also involved in discussions of another shattering report from Switzerland that the Nazis had already murdered one hundred thousand Jews from the Warsaw ghetto. A similar fate awaited those deported to the East, according to the telegram from the Agudath Israel representative in Bern to Dr. Jacob Rosenheim in New York. (It also stated inaccurately that the Nazis were using Jewish corpses to make soap.) McDonald's secretary sent a copy of this telegram from Switzerland to Supreme Court Justice Felix Frankfurter, noting that on September 4 McDonald was in conference with representatives of Orthodox Jewry about this matter.[22]

As American Jewish leaders conferred hurriedly on September 8 to consider some kind of general response to the horrific news, the President's Advisory Committee went into action on behalf of Jewish children in France. Seeing an advantage in using established contacts, the President's Advisory Committee met on September 9 with Myron Taylor, who was now President Roosevelt's special envoy to the Vatican.

Immediately following the meeting Mr. McDonald telephoned Mrs. Roosevelt[,] and I [George Warren] went that evening to Washington. Conferences with the State and Justice Departments during the following two days finally resulted in the approval in principle to admit 1,000 children from unoccupied France to the United States. This message was transmitted to Dr. Cavert, who left on the Clipper [by air] for Europe on Saturday morning, September 12th. Details of the project remain to be worked out and in the meantime the reports from France present no basis for any hope of an immediate amelioration of the situation.[23]

19. A German Jew who had left Germany in May 1933 and become a representative of the World Jewish Congress in Switzerland. See Gerhart M. Riegner, *Never Despair: Sixty Years in the Service of the Jewish People and the Cause of Human Rights* (Chicago: Ivan Dee in Association with the United States Holocaust Memorial Museum, 2006).

20. For the background to this telegram, Walter Laqueur and Richard Breitman, *Breaking the Silence: The German Who Exposed the Final Solution* (Hanover: University Press of New England, 1994); Riegner, *Never Despair*, 35–54.

21. Breitman and Kraut, *American Refugee Policy*, 152–53, 280n28 and n29.

22. Secretary to McDonald to Frankfurter, September 4, 1942, McDonald Papers, Columbia University, D361 (Frankfurter Special File).

23. Warren to the Members of the President's Advisory Committee enclosed with a copy of the minutes of the September 9, 1942, meeting, McDonald Papers, Columbia University, D367 (PACPR), P66.

In the meantime I have accepted a proposal to facilitate the reception here of 1,000 Jewish children from France. Another effort will be made to move 5,000 to 8,000 to this hemisphere. They are derelicts. Their elders are being herded like cattle and ordered deported to Poland or to German work-shops. The appeal for asylum is irresistable [*sic*] to any human instinct and the fact of barbarity just as repulsive as the result is appalling. But we can not receive into our own midst all—or even a large fraction of the oppressed—and no other country will receive them or even a few thousand, except that the gov't of San Domingo [*sic*] offered to receive and care for 3,500 children. Even Myron Taylor, with whom I discussed it on the telephone just before his departure, was doubtful of the bona-fides of the offer of Trujillo. My personal reaction is that Trujillo was trying to embarrass [Avra] Warren.[24]

McDonald reported to Welles:

Acting immediately on the basis of early reports of the deportations of children from France, the United States Committee for the Care of European Children,[25] with the backing of the President's Advisory Committee on Political Refugees, presented guarantees of support for 1,000 children to the Department of Justice. Thereafter the Department of State generously concurred in the decision to admit that number of children to the United States. Instructions to issue visas were cabled to the consuls on Friday, September 18, 1942.

Later cables disclosed that all foreign Jews, including children in unoccupied France, irrespective of the date of entry, were under order of arrest; that a minimum of 6,000 children were under threat of deportation with or without their parents, and that no French exit visas were being granted.

Because the numbers of children affected are much larger than originally estimated, the interested private agencies desire to rescue as many children as possible within the limits of U.S. immigration laws and available financial resources. They are confident that they can raise $4,500,000 to cover all costs and guarantees to the government for a total of 5,000 children. The total of funds to be raised by the private agencies cannot be determined until the government indicates the maximum number of children which may be admitted.

1. The private agencies therefore respectfully request a decision by the government that, on the presentation of the required financial guarantees, a

24. Long Diary, September 13, 1942, LC, Container 5. Avra Warren had recently been appointed American minister to the Dominican Republic. See chapter 11, p. 291.

25. Eleanor Roosevelt was honorary chair of this organization, established in 1940, and department store owner Marshall Field III was its president. See Judith Tydor Baumel, *Unfulfilled Promise*, 56–60.

total of 5,000 children may be admitted on a temporary basis from unoccupied France under the provisions of the present immigration laws.

2. It is also respectfully requested that the Department of State consider the feasibility of an announcement of its decision to grant asylum to children in unoccupied France.

. . . .

The announcement of asylum granted by the United States would add to the list of these humanitarian projects [in other countries] and might produce constructive results in the situation in France. It would give notice to the American public that every effort to rescue children was being made within the limits of the immigration laws.[26]

Assistant Secretary of State Breckinridge Long regarded Eleanor Roosevelt as responsible for this effort to expand the number of visas for children, and he tried to make sure that President Roosevelt was aware of the situation before anything further was approved.[27] But on October 2 Welles was able to report back to McDonald:

The President authorizes me to inform you that he approves the decision to grant visas to five thousand instead of one thousand destitute children now in France. He does not believe it desirable however, that any public statement be made concerning his decision on the part of this government.[28]

That same day McDonald gave Justice Felix Frankfurter the good news, adding:

Though the financing of their movement and care here will be a heavy task, there has been such a spontaneous response to the first quiet solicitation that those in charge of the undertaking are confident that the approximately $5,000,000 which will be necessary will be raised promptly.[29]

Rescue efforts in France had been organized with speed and with political skill. But for most, it came too late. On November 9, 1942, Allied troops landed in French North Africa. In response, on November 11 the Germans sent troops into the unoccupied zone of France. No longer were French authorities willing to grant exit permits to any Jews seeking to leave.

26. McDonald to Welles, September 24, 1942, YIVO, RG 278, Joseph P. Chamberlain Papers, Folder 71. Also, Warren to the Members of the President's Advisory Committee, October 16, 1942, Wise Papers, Box 65, Center for Jewish History.

27. Long Diary, September 26, 1942, LC, Container 5.

28. Welles to McDonald, October 2, 1942, McDonald Papers, Columbia University, D361 (Sumner Welles Special File).

29. McDonald to Frankfurter, October 2, 1942, McDonald Papers, Columbia University, D361 (Frankfurter Special File).

On December 1 McDonald, reporting to Sumner Welles on what had happened in France, requested help for other children:

Effort to rescue children in southwestern Europe
Children in France

The Vichy Government restricted the granting of exit visas in the first instance to an original group of 500 children whose parents had already been deported from France. 98 exit visas were issued prior to November 7, 1942. No children actually left France prior to the [German] occupation of southern France. The Swiss and French Red Cross organizations are now prepared to offer their services in convoying children to the French border. The interested agencies will appreciate being advised:

1. Whether the Department of State will undertake through the medium of the Government of Switzerland to determine if children will now be permitted to depart from France as originally planned, to Spain or Portugal where United States consular services are available.
2. Whether such negotiations offer sufficient promise of a successful outcome to warrant the holding of the American escorts at Lisbon for an indefinite period pending their conclusion.

Children in Spain

When the possibility of rescuing children from southern France was greatly reduced by the German occupation, the attention of the interested agencies was directed to the possibility of rescuing refugee children in Spain of the same nationalities as those originally the subject of concern in southern France. It is estimated that between 2,000 and 2,500 individuals, including about 500 children, managed to cross the border into Spain between July 15, 1942, when the deportations began in France, and November 11, 1942, when southern France was occupied by Germany.

The Visa Division has indicated a willingness to accept children in Spain for admission to the United States, but has restricted the choice of such children to those whose parents have been deported. In the early days of the recent exodus into Spain the Spanish authorities deported a limited number to France. These deportations ceased within a few days. The number of children in Spain whose parents have been deported is therefore small and insufficient to justify special efforts to rescue them.

Of the estimated 500 children in Spain, 200 are reported to be interned in prisons and jails with their parents. The remainder are children whose fathers and/or mothers have been interned, or children who are residing with their parents in the community under the threat of internment.

The interested agencies believe that the lives of the latter two groups of children are in jeopardy and that these children should be accepted for admission. The Visa Division has indicated a preference to expedite the examination of the applications of all the members of the family rather than to accept children only as an emergency procedure. The interested agencies believe that the examination of the entire family and the organization of its immigration will inevitably be delayed for many valid reasons here and abroad and that if this procedure is followed[,] few if any children will be rescued. The Visa Division has also commented that admission of the children in these families may later condition the examination of the parents whose admission may be urged on the grounds that the parents should join their children in the United States. . . .

The interested agencies therefore request that children whose fathers and/or mothers are interned, children who are themselves interned, and children who are living in the community in Spain with their parents under threat of internment be included among those to be admitted to the United States.

Escorts

18 American citizen escorts selected by the United States Committee for the Care of European Children left Baltimore on Saturday evening, November 7, 1942, and have arrived safely in Lisbon. They are awaiting instructions there. The decision to have all or some of them return on a Portuguese boat leaving Lisbon about December 20, 1942, will be based on the advice of the Department of State in the foregoing matters.

If the negotiations with the Vichy Government through the medium of the Swiss Government offer promise of successful results all of the escorts should be held for a reasonable time at Lisbon, otherwise those should be recalled on the first boat which may not be needed for the selection and escort of children from Spain.

If, with respect to the children in Spain, the final decision of the Department of State is that only those children may be selected whose parents have already been deported, all the escorts should be recalled by the first boat because the number of such children is insufficient to warrant the entry of any of the escorts into Spain for selection and escort.[30]

After McDonald and George Warren met with Welles on December 2, Warren reported to the members of the President's Advisory Committee:

Children in France

The American Embassy at Bern has been asked to inquire of the Swiss Government if it can determine from the Vichy Government whether the 500 children to whom exit visas were promised prior to the severance of relations between the United States Government and the Vichy Government may now be permitted to leave France for Lisbon.

---

30. McDonald to Welles, December 1, 1942, McDonald Papers, Columbia University, D367 (PACPR), P66.

Children in Spain

1. The American Consuls in Spain have been authorized to issue visas to children without the restrictions formerly imposed.
2. Ambassador Hayes in Madrid has been asked to confer with the Spanish authorities with a view to making arrangements under which applicants for United States visas who are interned may visit the Consulates for the purpose of advancing their visa status.
3. Ambassador Hayes has been requested to consider the wisdom of applying for Spanish visas for such American escorts now in Lisbon as may be required to select and escort the children who may be granted American visas.[31]

Portugal

On December 10 George Warren wrote that the State Department had authorized consuls in Portugal to issue visas to between 75 and 100 children under age sixteen.[32]

In a short account written many years later Howard Wriggins, a relief worker for the American Friends Service Committee, explained the desperate situation of Jewish families in Lisbon and the process of getting some children into the United States, even if few of them were the children in France originally envisioned.

I was in Lisbon from May 1942 to August 1943 with AFSC. Thinking back to that awful period, I was what you might call a young, twenty-four-year-old refugee social service caseworker. Every day perhaps a dozen or more destitute, pursued, confused, and lonely people came into our small two-person office. They had fled originally from Germany, Austria, Poland, Hungary, and who knows where, but most recently from France.

They often came to Portugal without documents. In those days documents were almost as important as food to eat, shelter over your head, and clothes to wear. Many had fled from France, crossed Spain, and entered Portugal illegally. If they didn't have documents, these people could be jailed, and the jails were quite medieval institutions.

⫶⫶⫶⫶⫶

I am not sure when we first heard about the large number of children's visas somehow pried out of the United States government in response to the awful deportations from France that had begun in the summer of 1942.

The United States Committee for the Care of European Children, supported by the JDC, the French, and others somehow worked wonders. . . .

31. Warren to President's Advisory Committee, December 8, 1942, McDonald Papers, Columbia University, D367 (PACPR), P66.
32. Warren to President's Advisory Committee, December 10, 1942, McDonald Papers, Columbia University, D367 (PACPR), P66.

A group of some 150 children gathered in Marseilles to get their papers together for the U.S. consulate. But they couldn't be moved, because the French had closed the frontier with Spain. During this period illegal crossings into Spain greatly increased. I don't know how many came through Spain and stayed in the Spanish refugee camps, but a lot were able to get that far.

. . . [But after the German occupation of the rest of France] all previous agreements regarding sending children abroad were cancelled. No more children would be authorized to leave France. French border controls became more severe.

. . . .

It was finally decided that we in Lisbon could do nothing for the children in France.

After some negotiations in Washington, it was agreed that available visas could be used by children in Casablanca, Spain, and Portugal. There were children whose families were stuck in Casablanca and so [were] still under the Vichy regime and in internment camps in Spain under Franco. . . .

Some families were enthusiastic about the possibility of seeing at least one member of the next generation get a foothold in America and quickly identified the oldest as the one to go. Others were more deeply ambivalent or were not interested unless brothers and sisters could go and be placed together.

In the end, I think some 30 children left from Portugal at that time [on the *Serpa Pinto,* along with 27 escorts and 300 other children from Casablanca and Spain].

Those were a hectic, uplifting, and distressing three months—thinking about, getting discouraged about, and in the end sending at least some of the thousand children. We reminded ourselves that over three hundred had been given opportunities for new lives away from what was then an accursed continent.[33]

Orthodox Rabbis

McDonald's warm contacts with Orthodox rabbis stemmed from his partly successful efforts in 1940–41 to include rabbis and rabbinical students from Eastern Europe among those endorsed by the President's Advisory Committee for visas to the United States.[34] A 1943 report of the Agudath Israel explained:

It was one of the few real achievements of Jewish rescue work during the last years, that in the early months of 1941, our American friends—principally

33. J. Howard Wriggins, "My Time as a Rescue Volunteer," reprinted in *Don't Wave Goodbye: The Children's Flight from Nazi Persecution to American Freedom*, ed. Philip K. Jason and Iris Posner (Westport, Conn.: Praeger, 2004), 116–122.

34. For example, McDonald to Long, August 30, 1940, McDonald Papers, Columbia University, D367, PACPR), P28. Hull to Schenkolewski, September 23, 1940, 811.111 Refugees/325. Copy in USHMM, Accession 1994.A0342, Roll 44.

through the energetical efforts of Messrs. Schenkolewski[35] and Tress—succeeded in obtaining from the State Department so-called Political Emergency Visas to the United States of America for about 400 leading Rabbinical personalities and Agudist leaders with their families and partly with their pupils in Eastern Europe (Lithuania, Poland, etc.) based on specific lists submitted by the Agudas Israel to the State Department.[36]

Agudath Israel consulted McDonald about the horrific 1942 reports from Switzerland about Nazi massacres of Jews. (Meier Schenkolewski was the contact between the Agudath Israel and its president, Jacob Rosenheim,[37] and McDonald and the President's Advisory Committee.) In a December 1942 letter to Rosenheim, Schenkolewski passed along McDonald's assessment of his most recent dealings with the State Department:

I had quite a long conversation with Mr. Macdonald [*sic*] today concerning the question *what else could be done*, to save at least the children in the countries that are still free, such as Switzerland, Spain and Portugal. In strict confidence he told me that he—as chairman of the President's Advisory Committee for Refugees—had another fight with the Department of State. The "Anti-immigrants" (Long, as a leader, is definitely one of them) still prevail in the Department of State and it is impossible to achieve an easing of the immigration laws, not even for children. Thereupon Macdonald [*sic*] contacted Mrs. Roosevelt and had a private discussion with her last week. Until today it seems that Mrs. Roosevelt's efforts have been just as unsuccessful and that the same faction of the Department of State would interfere with her efforts. Also, it seems to be this group of people together with like-minded persons in Congress that prohibited the rights, which the President had stated in his new immigration-bill.[38]

This last sentence is a quite garbled version of what McDonald must have told Schenkolewski. In November 1942 President Roosevelt had asked Congress to approve a Third War Powers Act that included a provision about immigration. The administration's draft allowed the president to suspend laws hampering "the free movement of persons, property, and information into and out of the United States." In late November the president had met with Vice President Henry Wallace and Sam

35. Meier Schenkolewski was executive director of the Beth Jacob World Organization, a group that maintained religious schools for Jewish girls. Schenkolewski referred to McDonald as "my best connection I have in this country." Schenkolewski to Michael G. Tress, December 9, 1942, Archives of Agudath Israel, Rosenheim papers, M. Schenkolewski two-way F 3–5.

36. Fifth Confidential Report to the Chawerim Nichbodim of the Agudas Israel World Organization, July 1 December 31, 1943, Archives of Agudath Israel, Tress papers, F 3–5.

37. Jacob Rosenheim (1870–1965) served as president of Agudath Israël from 1912 to 1965. He was originally anti-Zionist, but the Holocaust brought him to change his views.

38. Schenkolewski to Tress, December 9, 1942, Archives of Agudath Israel, Rosenheim Papers, M. Schenkolewski two-way F 3–5.

Rayburn, speaker of the House of Representatives, to speak chiefly about the need to loosen restrictions on immigration and imports.

Congressman Rayburn pointed out that there was great congressional opposition to this move, particularly in the Ways and Means Committee. Roosevelt then retreated, saying that this was Congress's responsibility to decide. Conservative members of the Ways and Means Committee first deleted the word "persons" from the provision and then held up passage of the War Powers Bill until the whole provision died.[39] *Schenkolewski's comments suggest that McDonald believed FDR would have used the provision about immigration, had it survived, to bring in more children.*

Schenkolewski continued:

According to Macdonald [*sic*]—he himself is more than willing to do so—the only remaining option is (a) to bombard Long with Committees and statements until he surrenders; eventually with the help of influential Congress-people etc. (b) once/if we really have a practicable NEW plan to save children, to forward it to Mrs. Roosevelt in written form. However, overall Macdonald [*sic*] is more than pessimistic; we have simply got to do [these things] to carry out our duty and to be able to have the certainty of not having missed anything.[40]

The History of the Vaad ha-Hatzalah in America written in 1957 summarized:

When the Second World War broke out . . . our colleagues were preoccupied with the possibility of rescuing the Torah Sages from the valley of tears in Europe, and we resolved to appeal to the government in Washington with this in mind. The door to Washington was opened for us by James McDonald, the same one who later became the first American representative in the State of Israel. He (McDonald) should be regarded as one of the Righteous from Among the Nations. He once declared: "if I were a Jew, I would be an observant one, a member of Agudath Israel." He put us in contact with one of the highest government officials, Mr. Breckinridge Long, who demonstrated a highly positive attitude to the problem and who asked us to prepare a list of rabbis whom we might want to bring to America.[41]

---

39. See Breitman and Kraut, *American Refugee Policy,* 158–159.

40. Schenkolewski to Rosenheim, December 9, 1942, Archives of Agudath Israel, Rosenheim Papers, M. Schenkolewski two-way F 3–5. Throughout 1943 Schenkolewski continued his close contacts with McDonald and George Warren, bringing suggestions about food for Polish Jews, pamphlets to drop over Germany, help for Jews in Nazi satellite countries, always with a sense of urgency. Even on the rare occasion when someone was saved, he urged Jacob Rosenheim: "We must press on. . . . If not now when? All other work must be put aside. We do not do our duty when we just sit here. It matters not how slim the chances of success are" (translation). Schenkolewski to Rosenheim, July 19, 1943, Archives of Agudath Israel, Rosenheim Papers, M. Schenkolewski, two-way F 3–5.

41. *Hurbn und Retung (Disaster and Salvation): The History of the Vaad ha-Hatzalah in America* (New York: Vaad Hatzala Book Committee, 1957), 204. (No author or editor given.) Translation.

What an irony that the unidentified author should later credit McDonald with giving Agudath Israel entrée to a supportive Breckinridge Long. Schenkolewski had known better at the time.

Recognition of the Holocaust and Responses to It

On November 25 the New York Herald Tribune *published a story under the headline "Wise Says Hitler Has Ordered 4,000,000 Jews Slain in 1942." A State Department investigation of Gerhart Riegner's telegram about the Nazi Final Solution had turned up enough confirmation, and Undersecretary Welles passed on the results to Rabbi Stephen Wise, who immediately held a press conference.[42] Other similar information came to London around the same time in the person of Polish underground courier Jan Karski. Suddenly, media coverage of what we now call the Holocaust increased. Jewish organizations in Britain and the United States, as well as the Polish government-in-exile, lobbied for a substantive response.[43]*

On December 17, 1942, many Allied governments and governments-in-exile issued a joint statement denouncing Nazi Germany's implementation of Hitler's frequently repeated threat to annihilate the Jewish people of Europe. This statement minced no words. It did not use the term holocaust (uncommon at the time), but it suggested what we have come to understand as the Holocaust. The only remedy mentioned was the threat to punish those responsible at the end of the war.

This official statement by Allied governments contributed to wider public awareness of what was taking place in Nazi territories. It led in 1943 to growing pressure from Jewish and liberal circles in Britain and the United States for Allied responses designed to save lives.

The American Jewish Congress, the AFL, the CIO, the Church Peace Union, and the Free World Association organized a mass meeting at Madison Square Garden on March 1. The participants adopted a resolution to stop Hitler now, which contained eleven recommendations for rescue or relief. Rabbi Wise sent these materials to President Roosevelt.[44]

Some of Wise's suggestions were drawn from his experience on the President's Advisory Committee. Yet McDonald was reluctant to play a prominent role in this rally or subsequent acts of public protest. His semi-official status on the President's Advisory Committee (and perhaps also his broadcasting job) led him to leave this route for others. A comment he had made earlier about a different controversy gives some insight about his attitude toward involving himself in public disputes:

I have not been active in the questions growing out of Palestine and the proposal of a Jewish Army here. Just at the moment I am being forced to make

---

42. Breitman and Kraut, *American Refugee Policy*, 157. Wyman, *Abandonment of the Jews*, 151, 161.

43. On the sequence of events, see Breitman, *Official Secrets*, 142–154.

44. Wise to FDR, March 4, 1943, FDRL, President's Personal File 5029.

up my mind whether or not to be a member of a delegation of which the Zionists are sending to Lord Halifax[45] next Tuesday.

After thinking about it a good deal I am inclined to beg off, first, because I do not like to be responsible for what a delegation may say at the conference and even more for what they may say to the press afterward; and second, my own plans are still so uncertain that I think it would be unwise for me to be prominently associated at this moment with such a highly controversial issue.[46]

On the other hand, McDonald expressed his own views when he had the opportunity. In an early 1943 article he wrote that, for the large mass of Jews in Europe, the alternative to Palestine was death. Although the British had committed themselves to upholding limits on Jewish immigration, he continued, White Papers[47] were not immutable, and the difficulties of absorbing large numbers in Palestine were not insuperable. Chaim Weizmann thought enough of this article to want to have it reprinted.[48]

McDonald recommended other shelters besides Palestine too. With the support of the President's Advisory Committee, he suggested removal of refugees already in the neutral countries Spain, Sweden, Switzerland, and Turkey to sites in the Western Hemisphere—Canada, the United States, Mexico, British Honduras, Jamaica, Cuba, and other Latin American countries—where they would receive temporary asylum. Western Hemisphere concerns about Nazi sabotage and espionage had proved highly exaggerated, and security screening mechanisms were already in place. He noted that Portuguese ships were available to move refugees across the Atlantic.

The purpose of this transfer was to benefit others in greater peril. Once their existing refugees were gone, the neutral countries in Europe might be willing to shelter new refugees escaping from Axis territories or Vichy France.[49] These were modest, but realistic, notions, some of which surfaced again later in the war.

In March 1943 a wide range of American Jewish organizations set up a Joint Emergency Committee to influence public opinion and lobby for stronger Allied action to rescue those in peril. One of the subcommittees conferred with McDonald, who apparently played the role of a background adviser:

45. Edward Frederick Lindley Wood, 1st Earl of Halifax, British ambassador to the United States, 1941–1946.

46. McDonald to Bentwich, February 20, 1942, McDonald Papers, Columbia University, General Correspondence (Bentwich), Folder 38a.

47. Successive British governments had outlined their policies toward Palestine in official reports called White Papers; the May 1939 White Paper cut Jewish immigration off after 75,000 were taken in.

48. The article appeared in *New Palestine*. Weizmann to Louis Levinthal, March 23, 1943, *The Letters and Papers of Chaim Weizmann*, vol. XXI, Series A, *January 1943–May 1945*, ed. Michael J. Cohen (New Brunswick, N.J.: Transaction Books, 1979), 15.

49. McDonald and Warren to Welles (draft) and Warren to McDonald, Armstrong, Baerwald, Cavert, and Chamberlain, March 11, 1943, YIVO, RG 278, Chamberlain Papers, Folder 72.

The drafting committee is drawing up a statement of demands for action similar to that adopted at the [American Jewish] Congress mass meeting, which Wise and Proskauer will discuss with Myron Taylor, Paul Van Zeeland and James G. McDonald this week, prior to taking it up with Sumner Welles and through him with the President.[50]

By this time the British and American governments had committed themselves to meet to consider steps to ameliorate refugee problems. The President's Advisory Committee drafted its own memo on what a British-American refugee conference could accomplish.[51] On March 23 McDonald and George Warren presented it to Undersecretary Welles.

With respect to the problem of offering assurance to neutral countries that stateless refugees would be removed from their territories after the war, Mr. Warren reported that the suggestion had been made to Mr. Welles that the United Nations might give assurance to neutral countries that the removal of such stateless refugees from their territories would be given a high priority by such United Nations authority as may be created after the war to plan for the repatriation or placement of dislocated groups in Europe. Mr. Welles responded that this suggestion was quite practical and would receive further consideration.

In further discussion of the Committee's memorandum Mr. Welles explained that the serious lack of shipping facilities available to the United Nations greatly restricted capacity to take helpful action and that specifically the suggestions of the Committee with respect to the placement of refugees in Jamaica and British Honduras would not prove practical on that account. It was implied that the same considerations would apply to any area in the Western Hemisphere.

Mr. Welles suggested that Turkey seemed to be the one neutral country through which relief might be sought since refugees might be admitted to Turkey from the Balkan countries and removed from Turkey to areas in the Near East without the requirement of shipping.[52]

Orthodox Jewish representatives hoped that McDonald would play an important role at—and would allow them access to—the joint British-American refugee conference initially slated for Ottawa, and then switched to the more secluded island of Bermuda.[53] McDonald, however, could not exploit his position as insider as

50. David Rosenblum to Frank N. Trager and Richard C. Rothschild, March 17, 1943, Archives of the American Jewish Committee, ajcarchives.org/ajcarchive/digitalarchive.

51. Warren to McDonald, Armstrong, Baerwald, Cavert and Chamberlain, March 11, 1943, McDonald Papers, Columbia University, D367 (PACPR), P67.

52. Fifty-Seventh Meeting of the President's Advisory Committee on Political Refugees, March 30, 1943, McDonald Papers, Columbia University, D367 (PACPR), P67.

53. It seems that McDonald is again becoming very active and if he really becomes the leading personality in Ottawa and also later in dealing with the refugee problems,

effectively as he had earlier in the war. Breckinridge Long controlled most of the preparations for the April 1943 Bermuda Conference.

Long's friend Harold Dodds, a conservative Republican who was president of Princeton University, ended up as chair of the American delegation, which also included Democratic Senator Scott Lucas of Illinois and Representative Sol Bloom of Brooklyn. McDonald's icy relationship with Long explains why neither he nor any member of the President's Advisory Committee was involved.

As the Bermuda Conference began, Breckinridge Long reviewed some of the background in his diary, in the process revealing why the meeting was not likely to take major initiatives.

One Jewish faction under the leadership of Rabbi Stephen Wise has been so assiduous in pushing their particular cause—in letters and telegrams to the President, the Secretary [of State Hull], and Welles—in public meetings to arouse emotions—in full-page newspaper advertisements—in resolutions to be presented to the conference—that they are apt to produce a reaction against their interest. . . . One danger in it all is that their activities may lend color to the charges of Hitler that we are fighting this war on account of and at the instigation and direction of our Jewish citizens. . . . In Turkey the impression grows and in Spain it is being circulated—and in Palestine's hinterland and in North Africa the Moslem population will be easy believers in such charges. It might easily be a definite detriment to our war effort.[54]

George Warren attended the Bermuda Conference in the capacity of technical adviser to the American delegation. Plagued by disagreements between the British and Americans (and by differences within the American delegation), the Bermuda Conference agreed upon only minor steps that were kept confidential.[55] Warren felt bound by his pledge of confidentiality and was only willing to make two comments to the President's Advisory Committee after his return:

It had appeared to him that the private organizations and individuals interested in the problem[,] in making recommendations to the Conference[,] had failed to give sufficient consideration to the exigencies of the war and the limitations imposed upon both Governments by the shortage of shipping and military considerations. . . .

then we can count on McDonald giving the Orthodox representatives their rightful and important place at the table. For, if this were not the case, McDonald wouldn't have needed to recommend to Mr. [Myron] Taylor that he meet with us. It can't be just politeness since we didn't ask for the appointment.

Schenkolewski to Jacob Rosenheim, March 8, 1943, Archives of Agudath Israel, Rosenheim Papers, M. Schenkolewski two-way F 3–5 (trans.).

54. Long Diary, April 20, 1943, LC, Container 5. Cited by Feingold, *Politics of Rescue,* 197.
55. For a short assessment, see Feingold, *Politics of Rescue,* 197–207.

The recommendations which the President's Advisory Committee had made to Mr. Welles prior to the Conference contained suggestions with respect to the recognition and special treatment of the stateless among the refugees. Mr. Warren stated that his impression was that Governments would be unwilling to recognize the special position of the stateless . . . and would insist on treating them as nationals of the Governments which had expatriated them or failed to extend protection to them. However sympathetically Governments may treat refugees within their territories[,] they will always reserve the right for security reasons to preserve the legal status of refugees as alien enemies.[56]

Perhaps influenced by his antipathy for Long, McDonald (after the fact) was very critical:

As the war entered its fifth year and the plight of millions of Jewish and other displaced persons in Europe became more and more acute the British and American Governments convened the Bermuda Conference in April, 1943, to consider possible new steps of rescue. But Bermuda was from the beginning condemned to futility. On the eve of its opening and as if in competition, the two governments in an exchange of correspondence made untenable claims about their past performances on behalf of refugees. Those apologies were disconcerting but accurate auguries of failure.

On nearly every proposition brought forward, the attitude of those at the conference was half-hearted or negative. Large scale movements of people from Nazi controlled Europe were, it was decided, impossible under the war conditions then existing. Earlier proposals to attempt to rescue Jewish children from Axis controlled territories were said to be impracticable. As to finding places of permanent refuge for those of Hitler's victims who had escaped to neutral countries, the experts at the conference pleaded that the lack of shipping precluded effective action. In answer to suggestions of possible places of permanent refuge, the British representatives insisted that Palestine could not be considered as the maintenance unchanged of the White Paper of 1939 was "essential from the point of view of stability in the Middle East." They also objected to the further entry of Jewish refugees into Cyprus and British East Africa. As to opening wider the doors of the United States, Secretary Hull reminded the conference—which could scarcely have needed the reminder—that Congressional action determines this country's immigration policy.

Thus having reached negative conclusions on most of the issues raised, the Bermuda Conference made the unoriginal and not very helpful suggestion that additional wartime refugee problems be handled by a revived and strengthened Intergovernmental Committee.

56. Fifty-Ninth Meeting of the President's Advisory Committee on Political Refugees, May 17, 1943, YIVO, Joseph Chamberlain Papers, Folder 64.

This objective summary only deepens the mystery: why was the Bermuda Conference held when it was so obvious that neither the American nor the British Government had any plan for the meeting which held the slightest prospect of success?[57]

In late June 1943 Breckinridge Long reported to Secretary of State Hull on difficulties that had arisen in an effort to move some 4,500 Jewish children and 500 adults out of Bulgaria and then summarized his view of the fundamental problem:

All the other Jews who need help are within the confines of Germany or occupied territory but there is no help that we can give them short of military destruction of German armies and the liberation of all the oppressed peoples under its jurisdiction.[58]

In June 1943 McDonald was offered the post of vice director of the Intergovernmental Committee on Refugees. He said he turned it down in order to continue his radio broadcasts.[59] But one may surmise that either he did not think the organization could be effective under the leadership of Sir Herbert Emerson, or that the Bermuda Conference had given it too limited a range of options.

One of the few positive decisions for refugees in the last half of 1943 related to emergency visas for rabbis. The State Department renewed the expired visas of Orthodox rabbis and rabbinical students who had been unable to use them earlier:

Of these 400 Jewish families, unfortunately only about 40 could then escape the hell of Eastern Europe and, passing Siberia, succeeded to come to the hospitable shores of America. Many of them are now the spiritual leaders in this country, the founders of Yeshivoth and the creative forces, who have assisted in the establishment and development of the "Vaad Hahatzala."

Now, during the period under report, one of our collaborators had the good idea to approach the State Department again and ask for the RENEWAL OF THESE IMMIGRATION-PERMITS OF 1941 for those, who were then unable to make use of them. After some conversations with the competent officials in the State Department, the request was granted, and consequently, complete lists of those approximately 350 families were officially transmitted to the United States Embassies in Iran, Turkey, Spain and Portugal and also to the Agudist representatives in England, Palestine and some neutral countries, informing them of this next possibility of rescue for the remnant of our spiritual leaders. The Consulates of the United States have been instructed to grant

---

57. McDonald's Address Before the National Conference for Palestine, Chicago, November 19, 1944, McDonald Papers, Columbia University, D355, Manuscripts and Speeches, MS27 (1944).

58. Long to Hull, June 29, 1943, NA RG 59, 840.48 Refugees/4009.

59. McDonald to Taylor, June 3, 1943, McDonald Papers, Columbia University, D367 (PACPR), P55.

visa on desire, to all the persons mentioned on the lists, for the event of their succeeding to escape to a neutral country. How far it will be actually possible to get in touch with the favored persons and, if this can be done, how far they will be able to escape, remains to be seen in the near future.[60]

By the second half of 1943 many Jews in Europe who had managed to escape deportation and death were still threatened with serious privation and disease. One of many rescue and relief proposals offered during 1943 was to arrange for food and medicine to Jews in hiding in France and to what was left of Jewish communities in eastern European countries allied with Germany. To avoid economic warfare restrictions, the World Jewish Congress recommended borrowing money from wealthy sources within these countries, with repayments placed in escrow in accounts in other countries that could not be accessed until the end of the war so that there was no way the escrowed funds could be drawn from to aid the German war effort.

After President Roosevelt gave an encouraging signal, the Treasury Department got to work on the plan, only to run into opposition. The British were ardent defenders of economic warfare and also concerned about measures to rescue Jews in eastern Europe who might put pressure on their immigration limit on Palestine. But the State Department was equally opposed, for reasons that seemed less obvious. Aided by a source within State, Treasury officials began to look at the pattern of State Department behavior. When they found that the State Department had tried to prevent Gerhart Riegner's August 1942 telegram about the Final Solution from reaching Rabbi Wise, they reacted vehemently. Although Long was not solely responsible for all of the State Department opposition to rescue and relief, he was in charge of refugee policy and was an obvious target.[61]

Meanwhile, Representative Will Rogers, Jr.,[62] of California introduced a resolution urging the president to create a commission of experts to formulate a plan of immediate action "designed to save the surviving Jewish people of Europe from extinction at the hands of Nazi Germany."[63] It was referred to the House Foreign Affairs Committee, which began to hear testimony. Oscar Cox, the influential general counsel of the Foreign Economic Administration, warned Edward Stettinius, the new undersecretary of state, that it was important politically for the administration to move quickly to create a rescue agency: otherwise, Congress might seize the initiative, might not choose the most feasible course, and might gain the credit for something the government should do anyway and "should have done a long time ago."[64]

60. Fifth Confidential Report to the Chawerim Nichbodim of the Agudas Israel World Organization, July 1–December 31, 1943, Archives of Agudath Israel, Tress papers, F 3–5.

61. All of the major works on American government responses to the Holocaust cover these events in some detail: for example, Breitman and Kraut, *American Refugee Policy*, 182–190. Because this complex episode has been covered extensively in previous scholarly works, and because McDonald entered into it only toward the end, we will summarize only the basic features here.

62. Will Rogers, Jr., son of the famous comic, served in Congress in 1943–1944, before resigning to join the army.

63. Senator Guy M. Gillette (Democrat, Iowa) introduced the same resolution into the Senate.

64. Cox to Stettinius, November 20, 1943, Stettinius Papers, University of Virginia, Box 727, Refugees.

Invited to testify to express his opposition to Rogers's resolution, Long insisted upon appearing in executive session of the House Foreign Affairs Committee. On November 26 he enumerated all the positive steps the State Department had taken since 1933.

Long claimed that the United States had accepted approximately 580,000 refugees.[65]

It was not a momentary slip. In the discussions leading to the Bermuda Conference earlier in the year, the United States had informed the British government that, since the start of the Hitler regime (until June 30, 1942) nearly 548,000 visas had been issued to natives or nationals of various countries dominated by the Axis and "practically all of the (228,964) aliens who received them during the war years 1939–1942 have actually arrived in the United States and have remained here, many of them having entered in a temporary status and not yet having departed."[66] By November 1942 the total had supposedly risen to 580,000.

Long's tendency to see only the evidence that fit his preconceptions and his inability to grasp details accurately finally caught up with him here because numbers of this magnitude were hard to miss. After Congressman Emmanuel Celler circulated Long's testimony, McDonald was among the experts who pounced upon the discrepancies. He wrote to Long:

It has proven difficult to reconcile this estimate [580,000 refugees taken in] with the statistics of the Immigration and Naturalization Service. More specifically, questions have arisen as to whether the estimate of 580,000 is one of visas issued or of persons actually admitted to the United States, as to possible duplication of persons in the figures and as to whether there are included as refugees natives or nationals of western and southeastern European countries resident in countries of the Western Hemisphere or who were admitted to the United States prior to the time when their countries of origin or of nationality were affected by the war in 1939 or 1940.

There is doubt with respect to the 135,000 refugees coming in one year as to whether the year was 1941, as stated on page 19, or 1942 as stated on page 41 of the testimony. The question has arisen also as to whether the figure of 135,000 refers to visas issued or to persons actually admitted. Again it has been difficult to reconcile the figure with the statistics of persons actually admitted of the Immigration and Naturalization Service for either year.

The President's Advisory Committee on Political Refugees believes that confusion will result from failure to clarify the existing record and, therefore, will welcome such explanation or elaboration of your statement before the House Committee as you are in a position to make.[67]

65. Feingold, *Politics of Rescue*, 230–237.

66. Hull to British Ambassador, February 25, 1943, *Foreign Relations of the United States: Diplomatic Papers, 1943, General*, vol. 1, 141–142.

67. McDonald to Long, December 31, 1943, McDonald Papers, Columbia University, D367 (PACPR), P67.

In reply, Long quoted from a letter he had written to Congressman Sol Bloom, chairman of the House Foreign Affairs Committee, on the same question:

Recently when I was before your Committee I gave a running account of the activities of the Department of State in connection with the refugee problem and tried to present the picture of what this Government had done to save the people who were suffering from Nazi oppression. In the course of my long statement at one point I used the words 'We have taken into this country since the beginning of the Hitler regime . . .' approximately 580,000 refugees. More properly I should have said 'We have authorized visas to come to this country. . . .' The Department of State does not keep a record of persons who enter the United States. We do keep a record of visas authorized and issued.

The whole tenor of my remarks was to show what we had done to help. This is indicated by other statements I made in the course of my remarks both before and after the sentence in question and is further indicated by the documents that were part of the Committee's record and were on the table at the time of my appearance. Of course one sentence taken out of its context and separated from the other statements which had a bearing on the general subject is susceptible of being given an entirely different meaning. The point is that we tried to give them an opportunity to escape from their oppressors and to come to the United States.

Since that time I have had made a careful study of the visas authorized and issued during the period under discussion. It shows that during that period and to persons in or coming from enemy and enemy occupied countries 568,556 visas were authorized, of which 544,999 were actually issued.

With reference to the statement . . . to the effect that a sufficient number of visas were issued during the year ending June 30, 1941, to save approximately 135,000 refugees, the [State] Department does not have the consular records showing the details of these cases. However, the number of persons mentioned is substantially correct.[68]

Long's defense was wildly inaccurate. He continued to ignore the fundamental difference between visa applicants of all types from all countries throughout the world and the far smaller number of refugees from Europe. He also overlooked distinctions between the number of visas granted and the much smaller number of people actually admitted to the United States. Not all those who received visas could get transportation, and the more extensive paperwork required during the war, security screenings, and visa review boards meant that Nazis had already deported a good many whose visas were granted. A reasonable estimate of the number of European refugees taken into the United States since 1933 was about 200,000 of whom perhaps 140,000 were Jews.[69]

68. Long to McDonald, January 2, 1944, McDonald Papers, Columbia University, D367 (PACPR), P67.

69. See Breitman and Kraut, *American Refugee Policy*, 144.

After a discussion with members of the President's Advisory Committee, Mc-Donald, George Warren, and Joseph Chamberlain made every effort to correct the impression that so many refugees had come in. George Warren dispelled any illusions about current State Department practices and attitudes with regard to visas. In late December he told an official of the American Friends Service Committee "that visa issuance is being conducted solely from the political angle and all appeals from the humanitarian aspects no longer avail. . . ."[70]

Meanwhile, the Treasury Department group was working at full tilt to expose State Department malfeasance. This was an extended effort aimed at the creation of a new government organization designed to save the lives of at least some of the remaining Jews and others threatened by the Nazis. One of Secretary Henry Morgenthau's associates, Josiah DuBois,[71] spent Christmas Day 1943 drafting a report that Morgenthau could use with Secretary of State Hull and with the president. He entitled it "Report to the Secretary on the Acquiescence of this Government in the Murder of the Jews." He laid the blame for inaction squarely on the State Department and cited Breckinridge Long as responsible for the bottleneck in the granting of visas.[72]

On January 16, 1944, Morgenthau and his subordinates John Pehle and Randolph Paul met with the president at the White House to discuss the scathing report DuBois had drafted, now possessing a less jarring title. They observed that a number of people saw anti-Semitism as the motivation of certain State Department officials and warned of a potential nasty political scandal. FDR was disinclined to believe that Long wanted to block action to save refugees. Long supposedly had soured on refugees because some had turned out to be undesirable. Morgenthau pointed out that Attorney General Biddle had stated in the cabinet that only three Jews admitted during the war fell into this category. On January 22 FDR issued an executive order establishing a War Refugee Board.[73]

The War Refugee Board

McDonald later commented approvingly on the War Refugee Board:

Its terms of reference are broad: "to take action for the immediate rescue from the Nazis of as many as possible of the persecuted minorities of Europe, racial, religious, or political and all civilian victims of enemy savagery . . . to take all measures within the Government's power to rescue the victims of enemy persecution who are in imminent danger of death and otherwise to assist such victims with all possible relief and assistance consistent with the success-

70. Schauffler Confidential Memo re visa policy, December 21, 1943, American Friends Service Committee, Refugee Service 1943, Committees and Organizations, U.S. State Department.

71. As assistant general counsel for the Treasury Department, DuBois (1913–1983) worked with Foreign Funds Control, a joint committee with the State Department, to freeze German assets abroad.

72. Breitman and Kraut, *American Refugee Policy,* 189.

73. Breitman and Kraut, *American Refugee Policy,* 190.

ful prosecution of the war." Its organization is admirable for effective action in wartime. The Board is made up of the Secretaries of States, War and the Treasury. It thus has direct access to the highest authority.

The Board is fortunate in its chief executive officer, John W. Pehle.[74] Young, energetic, experienced in governmental mechanism, and yet always ready to cut red tape, he has never hesitated to move wherever he thought there was any prospect of being helpful. Moreover, Mr. Pehle has surrounded himself with able colleagues chosen from the Treasury and other governmental departments and from the outside . . .

The importance of the War Refugee Board lies partially in the fact that it enables all organizations engaged in refugee rescue and relief work to deal with a single Government agency. More significant, perhaps, is the Board's moral implication. During the first few months of its existence it was possible to employ a kind of psychological warfare in order to stimulate those willing to help the Jewish refugees in the occupied and satellite countries, and to warn those who persisted in persecuting them.[75]

Pehle asked his subordinate James H. Mann[76] for information about the President's Advisory Committee. Mann listed its members and explained:

It appears that the Committee is not active now. Its first activity was assisting Myron Taylor at the Evian Conference. Apparently the Committee's function, in the early days of its existence, was attempting to resettle refugees with such projects as the Dominican Republic resettlement. It helped Taylor set up the coordinating foundation which was intended to finance refugees from Germany and which never amounted to much. It has been instrumental in obtaining about 2,500 American visas which helped many people get out of Germany. Of these 2,500, 2,000 landed in the Western Hemisphere or in England. However, in July of 1941 the nature of the refugee problem changed and the work stopped.

The President's Advisory Committee had slowed down. It met less often during 1943 in the face of the many obstacles discussed here and in the previous chapter. It was not true that its work had stopped. During 1944 George Warren was offered and took a job at the State Department, probably in connection with Breckinridge Long's loss of responsibility for refugee problems. Warren had been more than McDonald's

---

74. Pehle was director of foreign funds control and assistant to the secretary of the treasury. He became executive director of the War Refugee Board at its creation and served there until early 1945.

75. McDonald's Address to the National Conference for Palestine, Chicago, November 19, 1944, McDonald Papers, Columbia University, D355, Manuscripts and Speeches, MS27 (1944).

76. As a representative of the War Refugee Board, Mann worked on the evacuation of refugees through Switzerland and the funding of relief issues. In August 1944 he traveled to Spain to assess the refugee situation there.

right-hand man—he ran things day-to-day. His move must have seriously depleted the committee.

Mann concluded:

The Committee seems to be a well informed group and should be of some assistance to the War Refugee Board.[77]

The Board decided to try to make use of McDonald to help deal with a thorny situation in Spain. Pehle appointed McDonald as special representative to Spain after getting approval from Undersecretary Stettinius[78] and Secretary Hull.[79] Hull sent the following telegram to Carleton Hayes,[80] the U.S. ambassador in Madrid:

In order to review the refugee situation in Spain with you and to report to the War Refugee Board and the Department the Board desires to send a representative to Spain. The services of James G. McDonald, who it is understood is well known to you, have been secured for this mission. It is a matter of personal interest to me that Mr. McDonald be accorded every facility by the Embassy in order that he may carry out this assignment. Mr. McDonald is to have diplomatic status for the time that he is in Spain on this particular mission and will be attached to the Embassy with the title of Special Attaché. It is assumed that there will be no objection on the part of the Spanish Government although in your discretion if you consider it necessary or advisable to do so you may approach the Spanish authorities informally. You will of course be advised in advance of the date of Mr. McDonald's departure. Kindly advise immediately if there is any reason why this designation should not be made.[81]

Pehle wrote to McDonald:

It is the Board's desire that you proceed to Spain at the earliest possible moment to review with Ambassador Hayes the refugee situation there and to report your findings to the Board and to the State Department. I understand that you are making arrangements for an early departure to Spain.[82]

77. Mann to Pehle, March 22, 1944, FDRL, War Refugee Board Records, Box 19, Folder PACPR.

78. Welles resigned in September 1943 following accusations that he was involved in a homosexual incident and threats of a Senate investigation. Edward R. Stettinius (1900–1949) succeeded him, later serving as secretary of state and as U.S. ambassador to the United Nations.

79. Memorandum of Conversation Pehle and Stettinius, May 17, 1944, University of Virginia, Collection 2723, Box 745, Folder War Refugee Board.

80. Professor of European history at Columbia University, Hayes, appointed ambassador to Spain in 1942, later wrote *The United States and Spain: An Interpretation* (1951).

81. Hull to Hayes, May 18, 1944, NA RG 59, 095–101.502/7, Box 47.

82. Pehle to McDonald, May 30, 1944, McDonald Papers, Columbia University, D367 (PACPR), P68.

McDonald never went. Part of the problem was that he had to get a number of inoculations to travel safely, and the Board wanted someone who could go quickly. But there was also some resistance in Madrid. Ambassador Hayes had been on the defensive because of criticism that he was not making every effort to be helpful to the War Refugee Board. He felt as if he were being pushed aside. In April Pehle explained to Leonard Ackerman, one of the Board's special representatives:

I think you are probably familiar with the situation in Spain. A number of requests have been made by the War Refugee Board and the State Department that Ambassador Hayes approach the Spanish Government or otherwise take steps in accordance with our objectives. To date the Ambassador has not seen fit to comply with our requests. In addition, he appears quite opposed to the assignment of a full time representative of the War Refugee Board in Madrid. You will recall that we first proposed Blickenstaff as our representative. Ambassador Hayes, before discussing the matter with Blickenstaff, cabled that, by reason of the excellent work which Blickenstaff was already doing in heading up the relief organizations in Spain, he did not feel Blickenstaff could devote his full time to WRB activities. In view of this, and in view of certain other information which we had indicating that Blickenstaff might not be the type of person who would adopt an aggressive approach to the refugee problem, we proposed Jim Saxon. Ambassador Hayes then came back objecting to this on the ground that he was not convinced of the necessity of appointing a full time WRB representative. He said that if any appointment were necessary, he preferred Blickenstaff. This, I think, indicates what we are up against in Spain.[83]

McDonald had spent his honeymoon in Spain and must have had fond memories of the country. But he was not eager for a junket.[84] Meanwhile, he found other ways to help the War Refugee Board.

He arranged for Pehle and Myron Taylor to meet with the President's Advisory Committee at an April 10 luncheon. Although we lack detailed information about what occurred at this meeting, it was likely an opportunity for the "old guard" to pass on their experience and their judgment as to what would work to a new group of activists.

One of the results was committee support of the War Refugee Board's plan for "free ports." On May 12 McDonald wrote to President Roosevelt:

The President's Advisory Committee on Political Refugees has noted with great interest the recent discussions of the so called "Free Port Plan" for the relief of refugees. It is the Committee's understanding that under this plan relief centers would be established in the United States for the maintenance and

---

83. Pehle to Leonard E. Ackerman, April 5, 1944, FDRL, War Refugee Board Records, Box 1, Ackerman.

84. McDonald to Warren, May 12, 1944, McDonald Papers, Columbia University, D367 (PACPR), P68.

care, under proper safeguards, for the duration of the war of persons in danger of extermination by Hitler and who may be able to reach this country.

The Committee recently met with John W. Pehle, Executive Director of the War Refugee Board, and reviewed with him current efforts to rescue refugees from Axis-occupied Europe.

It is the considered judgment of the Committee that this Government would make an important contribution by announcing to the world at this time that it will receive into the United States, on a temporary basis, Hitler's intended victims. In our view, not only would this constitute a great forward step in our Government's program of giving aid to refugees, but would be likely to stimulate other countries to expand their efforts in similar directions. It would, moreover, demonstrate to our people and to all peoples, that even in a period of war crisis, a democracy is prepared to adopt concrete and effective measures to aid the victims of the ruthless dictatorship which it is fighting.[85]

In a June 12 message to Congress President Roosevelt explained the reasons for taking in a small number of refugees.

To us the unprovoked murder of innocent people simply because of race, religion or political creed is the blackest of all possible crimes." . . . [The War Refugee Board was] entrusted with the solemn duty of translating this Government's humanitarian policy into prompt action."

The president explained that the facilities for refugees in southern Italy had become so overcrowded that temporary provisions were being made in other countries and that he felt the United States should share this task.

Accordingly, arrangements have been made to bring immediately to this country approximately 1,000 refugees who had fled from their homelands to southern Italy. Upon the termination of the war they will be sent back to their homelands. These refugees are predominantly women and children. They will be placed on their arrival in a vacated Army camp on the Atlantic Coast where they will remain under appropriate security restrictions.[86]

Because of strong political opposition to anything involving bringing people into the country outside the immigration quotas and regulations, the Roosevelt administration insisted on sharp restrictions and tight confinement of these refugees at a camp in Oswego, in upstate New York. Nor was this camp the beginning of a trend to take in those who had escaped the death camps: Oswego was an isolated experiment. (The

85. McDonald to FDR, May 12, 1944, McDonald Papers, Columbia University, D367 (PACPR), P68.

86. President Roosevelt's message to Congress, reprinted in *New York Times,* June 13, 1944, p. 8.

story of how nearly one thousand refugees, more than 90 percent Jews, finally man-
aged to reach Oswego and later avoid being sent back to Europe after the war has now
been told in two books.)[87]

There were constant reminders that it was easier for the Nazis to slaughter Jews
than it was for the outside world to save them. In the summer of 1944 additional
information reached the West about the deportation and murder of hundreds of thou-
sands of Hungarian Jews and about the Nazi use of gas chambers and crematoria at
Auschwitz-Birkenau. The New York Times *received information along these lines*
from its correspondents in Jerusalem and Bern. After some delay it published a story
originating from Reverend Paul Voght in Switzerland that confirmed the existence of
two extermination camps and estimated that 1,715,000 Jews had been exterminated
there between April 15, 1942, and April 15, 1944.[88]

On July 6 the Times *published an editorial entitled "No Peace with Butchers," in*
which it said that it was "impossible for a civilized mind to grasp the reality of figures
given out [last] week as to the fate of Europe's Jews." It mentioned the claim by repre-
sentatives of the World Jewish Congress that four million Jews had now died at the
hands of the Nazis.[89]

This editorial induced McDonald to add his voice in an effort to convince the
public of what was happening and just how far back its roots lay. Perhaps he thought
that the better the American public understood the situation, the greater would be the
support for actions by the War Refugee Board. On July 14 he wrote a long letter to the
editor, which the Times *published three days later.*

Referring back to his visit to Germany in the spring of 1933, McDonald wrote
without consulting his diary and jumbled a number of details. But his memory sup-
plied more details of Hitler's words than he had been willing to include in his diary at
the time.[90]

A statement made to me by Adolf Hitler within three months of his becoming Chancellor will perhaps help to make more real to your readers the
Nazis' persistent policy of exterminating Jewish men, women and children who
are directly or indirectly within Nazi power. It was in the course of my first and
only private interview with Hitler, on March 31, 1933, the very eve of the notorious Boycott Day, April 1, when the Nazi gangsters were first authorized to
make an open demonstration of their sadistic brutalities.

87. Sharon Lowenstein, *Token Refuge: The Story of the Jewish Refugee Shelter at Oswego*
(Bloomington: Indiana University Press, 1986); Ruth Gruber, *Haven: The Dramatic Story of
1,000 World War II Refugees and How They Came to America* (New York: Three Rivers Press,
2000).
88. See the discussion in Leff, *Buried by the Times*, 275–277. The story appeared on page 3.
The information stemmed from a detailed report by two escapees from Auschwitz, Rudolf Vrba
and Alfred Wetzler, which is now well known. See Rudolf Vrba, *I Escaped from Auschwitz* (London: Robson Books, 2006).
89. Leff, *Buried by the Times*, 277.
90. Cf. *Advocate for the Doomed, 1932–1935*, 47–48, 796–797.

Hitler Revealed Aim

As an American who had a long and consistent record of friendship toward Germany—I was then still chairman of the Foreign Policy Association—I was given an opportunity to tell Hitler frankly that his anti-Jewish statements and policies were injuring Germany. Immediately Hitler retorted in words which I shall never forget: "Even if Germany must draw its belt very much tighter, that will be a small price to pay for ridding itself of the menace of the Jew."

Then he added words which fully disclosed his foul purpose: "The world will yet thank us for teaching it how to deal with the Jews." Obviously he then was confident his unspeakable example would be followed everywhere until one of the world's great peoples had ceased to exist.

The following day one of Hitler's closest confidants,[91] who had arranged my interview with the Fuehrer, dined with me. Before the meal was finished— perhaps under the influence of his favorite wine—he became loquacious and indiscreet. . . .

"Do you know that we have arranged to wipe out the entire Jewish population in the Reich? Each Jew has a Storm Trooper assigned to him. Everything is ready and can be done in a single night."

. . . .

Wherever the swastika has gone, even in Italy, this spoliation and murder of the Jews have been enforced. This part of his awful program Hitler has largely achieved.

This terrible fact, so illustrative of the true Nazi spirit, and the failure of the German people—save a few exceptional leaders and a small minority of the masses—to make any effective protest against Hitler's murder of millions of innocent men, women, and children should not be forgotten as the day for a reckoning with the enemy approaches. Their slaughter of the Jews shows what the Nazis really are.

The Times *published this letter under the headline*: HITLER FORETOLD SLAUGHTER: REVEALED PURPOSE TO EXTERMINATE JEWS IN PRIVATE TALK IN 1933.[92]

The Last Phase and the Future

By the fall of 1944 the Allied armies were making such rapid progress that it seemed victory might come in a few months. What impending defeat meant for Nazi Germany and those whom it had declared its racial enemies was the subject of widespread rumors. On October 8, 1944, McDonald received a telegram from one of his

---

91. The allusion was to Ernst Hanfstaengl. Again, the sequence of events is inaccurate. See *Advocate for the Doomed*, 26.

92. *New York Times*, July 17, 1944, p. 14.

Orthodox Jewish contacts, Meier Schenkolewski, indicating that the extermination policy of the Nazis would continue to the very end.

We received today from our representatives in Switzerland following authentic message: "The Germans intend in the last moment to exterminate all internees in concentration camps. These plans were worked out by Himmler and chief officers of the camps in Oswiecim [Oswieciem] and Birkenau. There are about 120,000 Jews in these camps. The order is to start the extermination in the next three days. It is of urgent necessity for the American Government to give immediate warnings to the Germans." Mr. Jacob Rosenheim who is out of town asks me to go immediately to see you. We need your advice in this tragic hour. Through your advice we were able to save the lives of many Jews from death in the past. Mr. Rosenheim appeals to you not to let us alone in this moment. Monday is a Jewish holiday. I will come to see you and will call your secretary this morning about ten o'clock to ask at what time you will see me for a short while. I will bring you some suggestions from Mr. Rosenheim.[93]

McDonald sent the following express letter to Eleanor Roosevelt:

I am informed by reliable orthodox Jewish representatives that "the Germans intend in the last moment to exterminate all internees in concentration camps. These plans were worked out by Gestapo Chief Himmler and chief officers of camps in Oswiciem, Birkenau, and Nauss and affect over 100,000 Jews." These orthodox representatives are most anxious explain tragic situation to you personally and would fly to meet you at any time or place you might designate, for they are certain the matter is of the utmost urgency. Their spokesman is Meier Schenkolewski.[94]

The War Refugee Board had already inquired whether General Dwight Eisenhower, the Supreme Allied commander in Europe, would be willing to issue a statement warning Germans not to exterminate those held in forced-labor battalions and concentration camps. President Roosevelt approved a draft statement that warned Germans not to harm citizens of the United Nations and stateless persons, "whether they are Jewish or otherwise." Eisenhower asked for and got a change in the warning to "stateless persons without regard to their nationality or religious faith" and then released the statement on October 30.[95]

Whether McDonald and Eleanor Roosevelt had any influence on the release of this statement cannot be determined. But in general, McDonald must have understood that the War Refugee Board was now in charge of such matters, and there was

93. Schenkolewski to McDonald, October 8, 1944, McDonald Papers, Columbia University, D367 (PACPR), P49.

94. McDonald to Eleanor Roosevelt, October 8, 1944, McDonald Papers, Columbia University, D367 (PACPR), P49.

95. Breitman and Kraut, *American Refugee Policy*, 201.

neither a point nor a need for involvement by the President's Advisory Committee. McDonald turned his thoughts to the future, hoping that the War Refugee Board would be able to deal with what would soon be called displaced persons:

Admirable though the purposes and work of the War Refugee Board are, it is drastically limited in time. It is a war agency and will logically come to an end when the fighting in Europe ceases. It, therefore, has no mandate to deal with the vast problem of postwar refugees. However, it is to be hoped that its able and farsighted executive will climax its work by preparing and presenting to the President a comprehensive plan to deal with those hundreds of thousands of refugees who will be left stranded when the European war is over. Such a plan with the backing of the three Secretaries who make up the Board would surely have great weight with the President.[96]

In an address entitled "Lessons of Twenty-Five Years" McDonald set out some of his thoughts about refugees in a postwar world. He cited estimates of thirty million refugees and displaced persons in Europe at the end of the war, and he noted that a million or more Jews might survive. They posed special problems, because it was unlikely that they would be able or willing to return to countries such as Germany, Poland, Hungary, Romania, Bulgaria, or Czechoslovakia.

In reaching this pessimistic conclusion, I have not been unmindful of the probability that the treaties at the end of the war will contain special provisions requiring the governments of the former enemy states to guarantee equality of rights and opportunities to their citizens without discrimination on the basis of race or religion. I cannot have confidence, however, that these treaties will be effective.

. . . .

Twenty-five years of governmental and intergovernmental activities on behalf of refugees drive home these truths:

(I) The shortsightedness of the great powers and their unwillingness to act in time to check the Hitler program of destruction of racial and religious minorities (when this could have been done without the least risk of war) helped to make the war inevitable and was, therefore, a direct cause of the more than ten million casualties to date among the fighting men and the death of millions of European civilians including three or four million Jews and of the displacement of other tens of millions of civilians of which one to two million are Jews.

---

96. McDonald's Address, "The Record of a Quarter Century of Intergovernmental Efforts on Behalf of Refugees . . ." delivered to the National Conference for Palestine, Chicago, November 19, 1944, McDonald Papers, Columbia University, D355, MS27 (1944).

(II) The League of Nations' traditional approach was inadequate primarily because the States Members of the League never made the solution of the refugee problem a major objective.

(III) For precisely the same reason the Intergovernmental Committee for Refugees and its plans (so far as these are known) are of necessity inadequate; the leading governments represented on the Intergovernmental Committee have yet to demonstrate that they are seriously determined to use the Committee to carry out a comprehensive program.

(IV) On the record Palestine offers incontestably the primary hope for the solution of the problem of Jewish refugees. The conclusion which emerges inescapably from a realistic resume of twenty-five years of intergovernmental dealings with refugees and from a realistic appraisal of the world situation is that in Palestine and only there can the mass of Jewish refugees hope to be welcome and be assisted to integrate themselves in the life of the community. Only in Palestine will most of them feel that they have returned home.

A SUGGESTED PROGRAM OF ACTION

(I) The Great Powers, particularly the United States, Great Britain and Soviet Russia, must be made to understand that the tragedy of refugees constitutes a major problem the solution of which is urgent in the interests of common humanity and vital in the making of a durable peace.

(II) The Intergovernmental Committee for Refugees must be radically strengthened and provided with the funds essential to enable it to carry on its vast task of aiding and resettlement overseas of many hundreds of thousands of refugees who cannot return home.

(III) Palestine, including Transjordania, should be opened to Jewish immigration limited only by the absorptive capacity of the area. The 1939 White Paper closing the door to Jewish immigrants was a surrender to Arab pressure sharpened by years of Arab terrorism. It was but the latest of Britain's interpretations of its obligation under the Mandate; it is not sacrosanct. Neither in law nor in equity is Britain the sole judge of the future of Palestine.

(IV) Specifically, President Roosevelt, Prime Minister Churchill, Marshal Stalin[,] and General de Gaulle (if he should also be present), should be urged to place the future of Palestine on the agenda of their projected forthcoming meeting. Nothing less than an agreement among the four Great Powers interested in the Middle East can lay the basis for a real Palestine settlement.

(V) Enlightened governmental cooperation is vital, but Jewish self-help on a scale not yet achieved is also vital. Much larger sums than previously must be raised if the minimum necessities of the refugees are to be answered. The greater the generosity of the Jewish people in the rescue of their own, the better the prospects that governments can be persuaded to advance the major funds necessary for large scale migration and settlement.

. . . .

Beyond this call for action, I venture in closing to suggest an idea about the role of Palestine in the longer future, an idea which may seem to some of you remote or mystical. It is that Palestine offers hope beyond its role as the place of refuge of the oppressed and the homeless.

Were I a Jew, I should be, I think, Orthodox with a sense of Messianic mission for my people. As I have met and come to know Jewish leaders and men and women among the Jewish masses throughout the world, as I have studied the words of the Zionist leaders, for example, those of Rabbis Wise, Goldstein, Heller and Silver, and I add, Magnes, and as I have learned more of Jewish History, of the tragedies of the Jewish people and of their triumphs in the moral and spiritual realms and of their incalculable contributions to the world's storehouse of philosophy and religion, I seem to glimpse a transcendent role for Palestine.

What I am groping for was expressed powerfully the other day by the President of the Jewish Theological Seminary of America, Rabbi Finkelstein,[97] when he wrote: "We have failed to make the world understand that we Zionists consider the establishment of a Jewish Palestine indispensable to a reformation of world culture as well as one of the major expressions of that reformation itself. . . .

"The very suffering through which we are passing may be the means necessary to re-open our minds and hearts to the Prophetic vision so that we can the better understand it and help interpret it to the world. The Jewish homeland can become in our day what all the Jewish seers since Moses conceived it to be, an instrument for the ennoblement of Israel, and an inspiration for all men."[98]

In January 1945 Rabbi Stephen Wise wrote to McDonald, saying that he and a number of others

felt very strongly that you ought to have some important post in the State Department. There is the possibility of suggesting, unless it has already been done, that you become the Ambassador to Turkey. Better still from our point of view it would be if [Wallace] Murray[99] were to be promoted to Ankara or kicked upstairs (and the harder the kick, the better we would be suited), and you enter the State Department as Special Adviser on the Near East and Pales-

---

97. Rabbi Louis Finkelstein (1895–1991), chancellor of the Jewish Theological Seminary 1940–1972.

98. McDonald's address to the National Conference for Palestine, November 19, 1944, McDonald Papers, Columbia University, D355, Manuscripts and Speeches, MS27 (1944).

99. Wallace Murray (1887–1965), key State Department official in the Division of Near Eastern Affairs, ambassador to Iran, 1945–1946. Murray was considered pro-Arab.

tine. . . . I'd like to talk to you about this for I shall be going to Washington rather soon and it is possible, and only possible, that I shall see the President. I count upon Mrs. Roosevelt's friendship if I decide to go forward in the matter of ascertaining what can be done with respect to the possibility of your taking one of these important posts to which I have alluded.[100]

McDonald was quite interested in a high-level State Department post,[101] but it never came about in 1945. He had worked with State Department officials since the 1920s. He felt free to ask for appointments, to consult or to report on his trips. He rarely criticized them publicly and was circumspect about what he told others of his conversations at the State Department. However, he was not part of the "old boy network" despite his years at Harvard. More important, he had often advocated policies diametrically opposed to the State Department's views—particularly during the time he had served as chair of the President's Advisory Committee. His support of Zionism, increasingly obvious by late 1944, also could not have endeared him to quite a number in the State Department.

The death of President Roosevelt in April 1945 and the end of the war in Europe in May led McDonald and the President's Advisory Committee to volunteer to serve President Truman if he thought they could be of use. But Truman did not respond, and the President's Advisory Committee quietly went out of existence.[102] McDonald, however, had already begun to shore up links with those who focused on postwar problems.

In the late summer of 1942 Myron Taylor had proposed the creation of a single international agency to deal with the problems of those displaced by the war. On December 1, 1942, McDonald discussed post-war refugee problems with former Governor Herbert Lehman of New York following Lehman's appointment as American director of the Office of Foreign Relief and Rehabilitation.[103] In June 1943 George Warren (executive secretary of the President's Advisory Committee) also joined the staff of the newly created United Nations Relief & Rehabilitation Administration (UNRRA) at Lehman's request.[104] Warren subsequently kept McDonald fully informed of the progress of UNRRA. At the last meeting of the President's Advisory Committee in June 1945 McDonald passed along a report from the Vatican that there

100. Wise to McDonald, Wise Papers, Box 65, Folder 11, Roll 74–46, Center for Jewish History.

101. See, for instance, McDonald to Edward J. Flynn, July 30, 1945, McDonald Papers, Columbia University, General Correspondence (Edward J. Flynn), Folder 134.

102. On May 24, 1945, McDonald met with Undersecretary Joseph Grew to ask whether he and President Truman thought the committee should continue. Grew said that he had not yet had a chance to consult the president on the matter, but that he hoped the committee would continue, and that it might play a more active role. McDonald to Baerwald, May 31, 1945, McDonald Papers, Columbia University, D361 (Baerwald Special File). See also Genizi, *American Apathy*, 94.

103. McDonald to Lehman, December 1, 1942, McDonald Papers, Columbia University, D367 (PACPR), P66.

104. Warren to PACPR members, June 25, 1943, McDonald Papers, Columbia University, D367 (PACPR), P67.

were "a surprisingly large number of Catholic prospective refugees—the figure is several hundred thousand."[105]

McDonald may also have had a small role in a sharp turnabout—an improvement—in the treatment of Jewish displaced persons in the American occupied zone of Germany. And he was soon led into a new thicket of controversy regarding Jewish emigration to Palestine. But that is a story for volume 3 of this series.

105. McDonald to Chamberlain, May 31, 1945, YIVO, RG 278, Joseph Chamberlain Papers, Folder 73.

Conclusion

Richard Breitman

Could anyone have substantially mitigated or prevented the Holocaust? Hindsight does not have 20/20 vision if it overlooks or ignores the obstacles that would-be rescuers encountered as they tried to save lives. Diaries and other contemporary records help us guard against simplistic or unfair judgments long after events.

This volume and its predecessor offer the unique perspective of a well-informed observer of politics in Nazi Germany and the United States who recorded many of his immediate reactions at the time and added his reflections at later moments. McDonald's record keeping is valuable in showing not only what he knew but what he did: in revealing what worked and what did not. It changes traditional views of a number of subjects ranging from the attitudes of the German Jewish elite toward emigration during the 1930s, to the consistency of anti-Jewish policies in Nazi Germany, to the role of the State Department in reducing German Jewish immigration to the United States, to the attitudes of President Franklin D. Roosevelt. And it changes some previous views of McDonald himself.

In a 1985 discussion of the High Commission for Refugees from Germany, historian Michael R. Marrus stated that James G. McDonald "issued no ringing call to open the gates of immigration," but even in his letter of resignation, he "could not say everything that was on his mind. . . . Certainly there was no sense of imminent catastrophe."[1] Marrus did not have access to McDonald's diary. Now we know much more of what was on his mind, and he did have a sense of impending catastrophe.

Among the many fascinating subjects covered by McDonald is the reaction of German Jewry to Nazi persecution during the 1930s. The number of German Jews who kept frank private diaries and ran the risk of having them seized by the police was very small. Officials of the central Jewish organization, the Reichsvertretung der deutschen Juden, and the Hilfsverein, specifically involved in emigration efforts, knew that they were subject to close

---

1. Michael R. Marrus, *The Unwanted: European Refugees in the Twentieth Century* (New York: Oxford, 1985), 162–163.

surveillance by police authorities; what they put on paper could be quite misleading.

McDonald had frank conversations with Max Warburg, Wilfrid Israel, Mark Wischnitzer, and a number of other members of the German Jewish elite, and he was able to record at the time their gloomy appraisals of the future of German Jewry. They did not know exactly what would happen, but they sensed that it would be very bad—that many German Jews would not survive if the Nazi regime lasted. On the other hand, they could not do anything publicly without bringing severe punishment on themselves and others. They had to work indirectly through people like McDonald, and even such outsiders could help only limited numbers at particularly fortunate moments.

How much time and opportunity did they have? Most scholars have reconstructed the flow of political events in Nazi Germany from government documents, surviving records of the Nazi Party and its various organizations, or letters or other records kept by perpetrators at various levels. The search for ever more primary sources kept by perpetrators, hardly at an end, is both necessary and commendable. Yet many such primary sources also have limitations.

Government bureaucrats observed conventions and traditions in what they did or did not record. They did tend to write up points of disagreement, but they often did not spell out shared understandings.[2] They rarely recorded the political climate within which they worked. Within the Nazi Party or the SS other forms of discretion prevailed. Some issues were too sensitive to be written frankly, and other sensitive matters made their way onto paper but were destroyed before the end of the war. Hitler personally kept few records.[3] All of these practices make it risky—or unsound—to draw conclusions based on the absence of certain kinds of evidence in official Nazi records. These considerations also make it difficult to reconstruct the dynamics among those who made key decisions, and they leave room for wide variations of interpretations among scholars about whether Hitler and Nazi Germany followed a consistent course of action toward war and genocide.

McDonald's direct talks with Nazi officials, including one with Hitler himself, and his frequent conversations with journalists and diplomats (who had their own direct links with the government and party) enabled him to triangulate the regime's course at the time. Simply put, he recognized that racial anti-Semitism was at the heart of the Nazi movement, and Hitler, in personal control of German foreign policy, was bent on war and vast expansion almost

2. Raul Hilberg, *Sources of Holocaust Research: An Analysis* (Chicago: Ivan R. Dee, 2001), 54–59, 142–160.

3. See my detailed discussion of these points in Richard Breitman, *The Architect of Genocide: Himmler and the Final Solution* (Hanover, N.H.: University Press of New England, 1994), 26–32. Hilberg, in *Sources of Holocaust Research*, gives a more detailed and technical analysis of a wide range of Holocaust sources, but from a different perspective. He agreed, however (pp. 34–35), that Hitler relied on oral orders and instructions.

from the beginning. On October 18, 1935, McDonald forecast a European war involving most of the continent.[4]

His diary comments and subsequent reflections bear a remarkable similarity to the interpretation in Gerhard L. Weinberg's prize-winning 1970 work *The Foreign Policy of Hitler's Germany: Diplomatic Revolution in Europe, 1933–1936*. Weinberg showed that Nazi ideology based on notions of German ("Aryan") racial superiority and Nazi paranoia about Jews as a corrupting force permeated not just domestic policy, but foreign policy. Beliefs that Germans lacked sufficient living space and that conflict was inevitable and necessary suffused the Nazi elite and, despite apparent diversions or contradictions, Hitler set a course toward rearmament, diplomatic assertion, and eventual war. If McDonald had lived long enough to read Weinberg's book based on a vast range of primary and secondary sources (but not on McDonald's diary), he could well have declared, "yes, that was the Nazi regime I saw."

After 1935 McDonald did not visit Hitler's Germany, but he followed German events closely. Through his contacts with British Jewish leaders he came across traces of an early 1936 German conception, probably floated by Economics Minister Hjalmar Schacht and with the support of Max Warburg, for the mass emigration of a substantial proportion of German Jewry, financed with (or accompanied by) an increase in German exports and the expropriation of much German Jewish property.[5] Schacht tried to negotiate such an arrangement with the Intergovernmental Committee on Refugees in late 1938 and early 1939. This strategy indicated that some less extreme elements in Nazi Germany wanted to send Jews out of the country, but only in ways that extracted other benefits. Only occasionally did Nazi officials simply cooperate with orderly Jewish emigration.[6]

If economic stipulations and the Nazis' ideological battle against world Jewry ended up limiting the level of Jewish emigration, that result was quite acceptable to party officials, many of whom wanted to inflict punishment on Jews as much or more than they hoped to drive Jews elsewhere. At the end of the war Artur Prinz, a former German Jewish official with the Hilfsverein, wrote an article with the paradoxical, but true-to-the-facts, title "The Role of the Gestapo in Obstructing and Promoting Jewish Emigration." Prinz thought that a predominantly constructive attitude among Gestapo officials toward Jewish emigration prevailed only during the period between the September

---

4. McDonald to Leland Robinson, October 18, 1935. Copy in McDonald Papers, USHMM.

5. See chapter 3, pp.

6. Artur Prinz, "The Role of the Gestapo in Obstructing and Promoting Jewish Emigration" (September 1945), reprinted in *Jewish Immigrants of the Nazi Period*, vol. 4, *Jewish Emigration from Germany, 1933–1943; A Documentary History*, part 4/2, *Restrictions on Emigration and Deportation to Eastern Europe*, ed. Norbert Kampe (Munich and New York: K. G. Saur, 1992), 548. The Haavara (Transfer) agreement of August 1933 between Nazi Germany and the Jewish Agency put emigrants to Palestine in a favored category, because the agreement stimulated German exports.

1935 Nuremberg Laws and June 1938.[7] Working with McDonald's former deputy Norman Bentwich and with the Warburgs, American lawyer David Glick was able to sense and take advantage of the improved climate for emigration during 1936 after a personal meeting with Himmler.[8]

What were the Nazis' alternatives to the emigration and expulsion of Jews? McDonald was present, along with Myron Taylor, and a small group of American Jewish leaders, at the White House on May 4, 1939, when President Roosevelt warned that the situation of the Jews in Germany was not a matter of money but of lives, and that the warnings from the American Embassy in Berlin were sound, not exaggerated. Consul General Raymond Geist, who was also first secretary in the Embassy, had been telling Assistant Secretary George Messersmith for some time that Jews left in the country when war broke out were doomed. McDonald knew Geist well and respected his judgment.

Scholars have spent considerable time over the last quarter century investigating and debating the question of when the Nazi regime formally or informally adopted a policy of genocide. Most of the experts agree that critical decisions were made during 1941—precisely when during that year is still at issue. At a time when Nazi control of the continent was likely, racial fanatics from Hitler on down could think and plan big. As German military control expanded, those who enforced German racial policies accompanied the troops or followed closely behind. So it is not surprising that there was a fundamental and decisive escalation of murderous racial policy in 1941, connected with German invasion of the Soviet Union. It is unfortunate that McDonald did not keep a diary for this period, and we cannot tell just when he noticed the escalation.

Was the road from the beginning of the Nazi regime to Auschwitz twisted?[9] From 1933 on the Nazi regime pursued various and contradictory policies toward Jews, some of which bore no connection with a future policy of genocide. But even in the spring of 1933 McDonald was able to pick up the consistency and the intensity of Nazi anti-Semitic ideology and the powerful emotions fueling it. He also sensed then and later that Hitler held a supreme, unchallengeable authority, and he knew from direct observation what Hitler wished. The road from the wishes of Hitler's inner circle to fulfillment in Auschwitz was not nearly so twisted, except in a different sense of the word.

When, in July 1944, the *New York Times* published reports about mass extermination at Auschwitz-Birkenau, McDonald reminisced in print about his visit to Berlin in March and April 1933. He had heard and seen enough even at that time to forecast what was likely to happen to German Jews when war broke out. He knew that Hitler and others close to him were willing to make

---

7. Prinz, "The Role of the Gestapo," 547–553.
8. See chapter 6, pp. 116–118.
9. In the sense suggested originally by Karl A. Schleunes, *The Twisted Road to Auschwitz: Nazi Policy toward German Jews 1933–1939* (Urbana: University of Illinois Press, 1970). Schleunes, however, disagreed with some later functionalists in that he noted that anti-Semitism was at the heart of the Nazi movement and that the SS gained control of Jewish policy by late 1938 (260–261).

sacrifices to remove German Jewry, and that mass murder was a likely option. Indeed, McDonald had warned some others about this upon his return to the United States in 1933. The *New York Times* published McDonald's 1944 letter to the editor under the headline "Hitler Foretold Slaughter."

The question about the timing of Nazi decisions regarding genocide is very important, but it is not the only very important question. In some ways Nazi Germany crossed the moral divide when it began to think seriously about mass murder of a substantial portion of German Jews. The fate of German Jews was more sensitive politically in Germany than that of foreign Jews: German Jews had non-Jewish friends, neighbors, and even relatives. If the Nazis could seriously conceive of murdering hundreds of thousands of German Jews, why would they not carry out such policies as they moved into what they regarded as a battle against international Jewry?

The evidence in McDonald's diary and the related materials in these two volumes indicate that murderous Nazi intentions toward German Jews preceded World War II and that perceptive observers could discern the direction of future policies. If he had lived long enough to follow the debate between those scholars who believed that the Nazis planned the Holocaust (the intentionalists) and those who saw it as improvised after a period of trial and error (the functionalists), McDonald would readily have chosen sides. He had a sense of the broad thrust of Nazi policies from the beginning.

McDonald's diaries, papers, and related materials in this volume are an even more detailed source about American government (and some private) responses to Nazi persecution and genocide. This subject, too, has generated intense interest, a great deal of research, and passionate debate.[10] Not all of it is grounded in political realities.

Suppose that the only way to save half a million people in Darfur in 2009 were to evacuate them, suspend American immigration laws, and bring them to the United States as immigrants or as visitors of indefinite duration. What kind of political strategy would maximize the numbers admitted to the United States? There is no simple answer. How could the American public and Congress be persuaded to support such a course in light of current attitudes toward illegal immigration?

---

10. Among treatments by those outside the academy, Arthur Morse, *While Six Million Died: A Chronicle of American Apathy* (New York: Random House, 1968); and the WGBH video production, *America and the Holocaust: Deceit and Indifference.* On the opposite side: Robert N. Rosen, *Saving the Jews: Franklin D. Roosevelt and the Holocaust* (New York: Thunder's Mouth Press, 2006); and Robert Beir and Brian Josepher, *Roosevelt and the Holocaust* (New York: Barricade Books, 2006). Among academics, contrast David S. Wyman, *The Abandonment of the Jews: America and the Holocaust, 1941–1945* (New York: Pantheon, 1984) with William D. Rubinstein, *The Myth of Rescue: Why the Democracies Could Not Have Saved More Jews from the Nazis* (London: Routledge, 1997). These authors clash over what was feasible in the way of saving victims of the Nazis and over the morality of American policies. *Roosevelt and the Holocaust*, ed. Verne W. Newton (New York: St. Martin's, 1996), edited by the former director of the Franklin D. Roosevelt Library, contains a summary of a conference on the topic and some pro-Roosevelt essays and others that are critical, but not extreme.

Some factors in this crude analogy are faulty. Darfur lacks extermination camps (though Nazi Germany did not create them until late 1941), and it suffers from domestic strife. Media coverage of Darfur has been good, and it has affected American public opinion. The educated public is quite conscious of the fact that genocide is possible. And a Darfur evacuation would pose fewer logistical and financial problems than extracting hundreds of thousands of Jews from Nazi territories in the late 1930s. By late 1941 that simply could not have been done.

Leaving such differences aside, in our hypothetical example it is likely that substantial numbers of Americans and American politicians would complain that the United States should not and could not bear the entire burden of saving Darfur. If the United States took in only a small portion of Darfurians, who would be to blame for those left behind to die? Unfortunately, there are various political constraints in such circumstances.

The level of anti-foreign and anti-Semitic attitudes among ordinary Americans during the 1930s and 1940s was much higher than today. Good politicians were aware of such attitudes. When they on occasion ventured well beyond them, as Franklin Roosevelt started to do in March 1938, other people and events had a way of reining in their initiatives. We have tried here to give a realistic sample of diplomatic, political, and bureaucratic forces affecting refugee policies from 1935 to 1945 in irregular fashion and to show the mixed results. Sweeping moral judgments about the nature of the Roosevelt administration's policies obscure significant changes over time.

Cold War historian John Lewis Gaddis has established broad categories of historical interpretation based on notions of "disposition" and "situation." Dispositional interpretations are based on the mentality or character of key decision makers: for example, Stalin reacted with hostility to each American move with regard to Eastern Europe, because he could not bear to share influence with anyone, let alone a capitalist power. Situational interpretations involve decisions based on maximizing advantages or minimizing risks to the nation. But situational explanations also allow for considerable shifts as decision makers react to changes in circumstances and the moves of their adversaries. Also, there is the role of imperfect understanding, perception, and anticipation of future events.

Examining the Holocaust and Western reactions to it requires attention to both dispositions and situations. Hitler's disposition explains a good deal, though not all, of Nazi Germany's Jewish policies. It certainly explains why the Holocaust continued until Nazi Germany collapsed from military failure. Roosevelt, however, was, above all, a master politician who tried to carry out some humanitarian steps while juggling political and military constraints. One needs to weigh situational factors heavily for FDR.

McDonald did not have an easy time working with President Roosevelt, but he got a hearing in the Oval Office on a number of occasions. Unfortunately, Assistant Secretary of State Breckinridge Long was better positioned to influence the president. Some historians have used Long's disposition to explain State Department policies. This may be too simple, but it is not off the mark. McDonald's interactions with Long lay out more clearly some of Long's strategy and maneuvers to restrict immigration sharply.

By following McDonald closely, we have uncovered some key episodes in changing American refugee policies previously overlooked. One of McDonald's associates, Arthur Sweetser, got a very good sense of just how broad FDR's hopes were in the spring of 1938 to remove millions of Jews from central and eastern Europe to settlements abroad, predominately in the Western Hemisphere. This information must have empowered McDonald to ask for action to match words. In mid-November 1938 President Roosevelt promised McDonald and George Warren, under the right circumstances, to ask Congress to appropriate $150 million to help resettle refugees in various parts of the world. This pledge was the reverse side of FDR's subsequent unwillingness to endorse the Wagner-Rogers Bill to bring 20,000 German Jewish children into the United States outside the immigration quota. At a time of great foreign policy clashes with Congress over the degree of American involvement in Europe, the President did not want to add a pitched battle with Congress over a measure that could only chip away at a big refugee problem. He saw that bill as a gesture—not a solution. He was a man of grand vision who wanted to resettle a much larger number of refugees from Germany. Thinking politically, he believed that after the American immigration quotas were filled—and they were quickly filled as a result of 1938 decisions—the others had to go elsewhere. If he got similar financial support from Britain and private Jewish contributions on a large scale, Roosevelt believed that major settlements in underdeveloped parts of the world ranging from Angola to British Guiana were feasible.

In July 1939 Myron Taylor told the Intergovernmental Committee on Refugees that Congress might appropriate funds to help an international effort to extract Jews and others suffering persecution in Germany. This volume contains much additional evidence of Roosevelt's serious interest in resettling refugees during 1938 and 1939. The problem was that most of the initiatives to resettle refugees in underdeveloped areas proved impossible, met substantial resistance abroad, or developed very slowly—because of resistance by the Department of State, difficulties with Germany, and divisions among American Jewish leaders. The outbreak of war destroyed most of what opportunities remained. McDonald recognized this fact before President Roosevelt did, but the two had very different reactions to changed circumstances.

In 1940 President Roosevelt moved away from humanitarian action. The war changed his views as to how much humanitarian spirit the United States could afford at a time of grave dangers abroad and perceived foreign dangers to national security. State Department officials, most of whom dragged their feet during earlier refugee initiatives, quickly found evidence and ways to sharply reduce immigration and admission of visitors to the United States as well as refugee resettlement efforts abroad. Congress was at least as suspicious of foreigners coming in as was Assistant Secretary of State Long. The State Department was hardly the only restrictionist force in government, but it occupied many of the key pressure points and used them to considerable effect. It had a clear edge in terms of public opinion, something that McDonald and his allies recognized.

The most restrictionist phase of American refugee policy—from mid-1941 to mid-1943—overlapped with the first two years of the Holocaust. After October 1941 Jews could no longer leave most German territories. Yet escape for substantial numbers elsewhere in Europe was possible. Jews in unoccupied France, if they obtained American visas and had money for transportation across the Atlantic, could often get permission to go to Spain and Portugal. Some Jews also got out of the Netherlands during the second half of 1941 and were able to get papers to enter various countries in the Western Hemisphere. Otto Frank and his family were just a little too late in their effort to leave Amsterdam. McDonald and the President's Advisory Committee continued to work on small numbers of individual cases—and to save some lives. But over time, they lost more and more of the battles over visas, even when they appealed to Undersecretary Welles or the president.

A combination of pressures, along with mistakes by Breckinridge Long, but above all, an offensive by a group of Treasury Department officials against State Department policies brought about another reversal in American policy toward the end of 1943. Starting so late (January 1944) and with limited authority, there was much that the War Refugee Board could not do, but its efforts during the last seventeen months of World War II stand up well to the light of history. Raul Wallenberg, posthumously made an honorary American citizen, went to Hungary to save lives with the support of the War Refugee Board.[11]

The Holocaust was such a catastrophe—a rupture in Western civilization—that there is a tendency to unleash blame upon almost everyone—except those willing to become martyrs or risk their lives in protest—as accomplices to genocide. James G. McDonald was not a martyr, and he did not want to give up a career or sacrifice himself and his family for a noble cause. Yet he managed to do some good.

According to its own data, during 1940–1942 the President's Advisory Committee submitted the names of 2,975 visa applicants either to American consuls abroad or to the State Department itself. Of that total, 2,133 received visas and made it either to the United States or to other places of safety in the

11. A monograph on the War Refugee Board remains to be written. A long institutional history was written shortly after the war and is available at the FDRL. For a condensed account of some of the board's activities, see Breitman and Kraut, *American Refugee Policy*, 182–221.

Western Hemisphere.[12] Given entrenched attitudes in the State Department, few of these individuals would likely have received visas without the committee's lobbying. McDonald and the committee were also instrumental in arranging for more than one hundred Orthodox rabbis and rabbinical students to obtain visas. McDonald played a major role in inducing the president and the State Department, in October 1942, to authorize visas for 5,000 Jewish children in Vichy France; although few of the original group could benefit, some hundred other children did make it from Portugal or North Africa to the United States. A little more than a year later, McDonald added his voice to those who pressed for the ouster of Breckinridge Long and brought about the establishment of the War Refugee Board.

One can judge humanitarian efforts by intentions and by results. From a humanitarian perspective, the intentions of the President's Advisory Committee look very good, and American government policies look somewhat better than those of other governments at the time. The results, of course, fell far short of the intentions.

Would a more confrontational strategy by humanitarian activists have yielded better results? The answer depends on assessing political calculations. Congress and the American public were less tolerant than the Roosevelt administration on issues involving Jews and on immigration and refugees generally. McDonald and others on the President's Advisory Committee judged that it was better to save a limited number of people than protest openly or resign and save none.

Results often depended on indirect or even unexpected, serendipitous factors. Unsuccessful conferences like the Evian Conference and unrealistic resettlement possibilities that never materialized—such as the settlement of Jews in Alaska—alerted those threatened to look at feasible options for emigration. It was sometimes a matter of chance what worked out.

Two countries—the Dominican Republic and Bolivia—responded positively to Roosevelt's Evian initiative. Dominican Republic dictator Rafael Trujillo was more interested in publicity and financial benefits than Jewish settlers, so it was not surprising that the results proved disappointing—some five hundred people, some of whom thought of the Sosua settlement on the island as a way station. But the behavior of some State Department officials and diplomats did not help send larger numbers there.

While McDonald was directly involved in the Sosua settlement, he never went to Bolivia—a sign of the difficulty determining which situations held most promise. But he contributed something to the determination of South American business magnate Mauricio Hochschild to save German Jews, and the President's Advisory Committee (and its allies in the Joint Distribution Committee) helped Hochschild in Bolivia in 1938. At least twenty thousand

12. Fifty-Sixth Meeting of PACPR, December 1, 1942, McDonald Papers, Columbia University, D367 (PACPR), P66.

Jews made it to or through Bolivia. That is no small feat in the context of rescue efforts before and during the Holocaust.

McDonald's efforts from 1933 on to rescue a large portion of those threatened in Germany and by Germany were mostly unsuccessful. He and his allies achieved limited successes—nothing so dramatic as rescuing millions before the Holocaust or snatching hundreds from the gates of Auschwitz during the Holocaust. Yet he certainly made a difference. We can still learn from the record of his successes and failures.

INDEX

Bolivia: Buena Tierra settlement, 272; Evian appeal and, 337; Exhibition of Industrial and Handicraft Products, 275; immigration considerations, 264–266; MNR coup, 275–276; opposition to immigration in, 269–270; refugee population in, 267, 270–271, 276, 337; social life of refugees, 266–268, 272–273. *See also* Hochschild, Moritz "Mauricio"

Bolshevik Revolution, 1

Bonnet, Henri, 30, 30n43

Borchardt, Friedrich, 269, 269n15

Borchardt, Lucy, 34

Bowman, Isaiah, 148, 148n63, 152, 155–156, 265–266, 283

boycott (international boycott of German goods), 26

Brandeis, Louis D., 131, 153–154

Brazil, 35, 63, 76, 295

Brett, Homer, 119

British East Africa, 311

British Guiana, 148, 153, 168, 172–173, 173n36, 176, 181, 184, 186–187, 188, 335

British Honduras, 309

Brodetsky, Selig, 6, 6n4

Bru, Laredo, 175

Buena Tierra (Bolivia), 272

Buerkel, Gauleiter, 182

Bulgaria, 312

Bulkeley-Johnson, Mr., 59–60

Bullitt, William C., 15–16, 15n50, 18–19, 182–183, 183n59, 246

Bülow, Bernhard Wilhelm von, 8, 8n24

Burgess, Anthony, 17n1

Burgin, Edward Leslie, 32, 32n53

Busch, German, 265, 269–270

Butzel, Leo, 113

Caldwell, Robert, 267–268

Cameroons, 148, 154

Cantor, Eddie, 113, 141, 160

capital export tax, 66, 152

Carnegie Foundation, 152

Carnegie Foundation for International Peace, 284–285

Caruana, Giorgio, 295

Catholics: Austrian Catholic refugees, 132, 138; German government relations with, 20, 84, 98; immigra-

tion policy and, 131; Italo-Abyssinian dispute and, 69; Nazi agreement of 1933, 39; postwar refugee relief initiative for, 327–328; support for non-Jewish refugees, 69, 158; Vatican support for resettlement initiatives, 140, 203. *See also* non-Jewish refugees

Cavert, Samuel McCrae, 127–129, 130

Cecil, Lord Robert, Viscount of Chelwood: on Bérenger, 30n44, 46; biographical sketch, 32n52; on British-German relations, 58–59; discussion of JGM resignation, 80; High Commission funding and, 32; on the League reorganization plan, 42, 49–50; mentioned, 70

Celler, Emmanuel, 314

Central British Fund, 106–107

Chamberlain, Joseph P.: biographical sketch, 124n7; on Cuban visa revocations, 295; enemy alien exemption memo, 293; President's Advisory Committee on Political Refugees and, 130n22, 131–132, 136, 156n83; response to Long's immigration testimony, 316; on U.S. immigration policy, 124; White House conference on refugees and, 128

Chamberlain, Neville, 127n15, 147n58, 189

Chase National Bank, 144

Children's Committee, 57

Chile, 63, 265, 267, 271

Christians: Anglican Church refugee initiative, 56; Anglican position on the Anschluss, 127; Christian colonization project, 96; Evangelical Church, 84, 96n3; Free Churches, 68–69; German government relations with, 20; immigration policy and, 131; refugee initiatives and, 64–65, 83–84. *See also* Catholics; Evangelical Church; non-Jewish refugees

Church Peace Union, 307

Churchill, Winston: Atlantic Charter, 253–254; biographical sketch, 58n46; on the invasion of Russia, 251; as League supporter, 58

France (*continued*)
France, 61, 75; use of protectorates
for refugees, 201–202. *See also* Vichy
French territory
Franco, Francisco, 203
Frank, Anne, 260
Frank, Otto, 260–263, 336
Frankfurter, Felix, 138, 298, 300
Free Churches, 68–69
Free Port Plan, 319–320
Free World Association, 307
French Guiana, 148, 156n83
Fullerton, Hugh S., 235

Gaddis, John Lewis, 334
Galeazzi, Enrico, 140
Gascoyne-Cecil, James E. H., Fourth
Marquess of Salisbury, 70, 70n1
Gascoyne-Cecil, Robert Arthur James,
Viscount Cranborne, 25, 25n25
Geist, Raymond: account of German
Jewish emigration difficulties, 143;
biographical sketch, 10n32; David
Glick initiative and, 117; on Nazi
brutality, 10; on Nazi foreign
affairs, 21; report on impending
danger to Jews, 173, 332; Rublee
agreement and, 168–169
Genizi, Haim, 253
George V, King of England, 109–110,
109n12
Gerig, Ben, 35, 37, 37n4
German Jews
—general: diaries kept by German Jews,
329–330; necessity of full-scale
emigration, 75n15; need for identity
papers, 86; non-Jewish German
friends/relations, 333; population
estimates, 8; prewar emigration
efforts, 61–62, 119–120, 143;
proposed Nansen passports for, 41;
views of Polish Jews, 57
—living conditions: food and medical
shortages, 44; schools for Jewish
children, 43; Sholem Asch publications, 26
—Nazi actions against: capital export
tax, 66, 152; denationalization, 35;
deportation to Lodz ghetto, 258;
discriminatory taxation, 142;
economic isolation, 9; exclusion
from war dead memorials, 58, 63;

historic significance of, 52; Jews as
scapegoats for economic decline,
10; Kristallnacht, 146–148,
151–152; possibility of negotiation,
100n9; prohibited contact with
foreign Jews, 116, 116n29, 142;
Schacht's Königsberg speech and,
10, 21, 24; seizure of personal
diaries, 329–330; SS opposition to
negotiations, 166, 169; work/
business prohibition, 142
See also Germany; Jews; Nuremberg
Laws; refugees
Germany: German loyalist immigrants
in U.S., 197; Protestant/Catholic
religious relations, 20; Tripartite
Pact, 215; Tyrell "antithesis of
civilization" theory of, 70. *Assessment of conditions in:* Dodd, 20;
Ebbutt, 20–21; Geist, 10; Hahn,
63; Israel, 47–48, 330; JGM, 24, 52;
Rothbarth, 39; Erich Warburg, 44;
Max Warburg, 330; Wischnitzer,
330. *See also* German Jews; Hitler,
Adolf; Nazi Regime; World War II
Gilbert, Prentiss, 37, 37n2
Gilchrist, Thomas, 35, 35n62
Ginsberg, Marie, 38, 38n5, 86, 93
Glick, David, 116–118, 269, 269n15, 332
Goebbels, Paul Joseph: exclusion of Jews
from war dead memorials by, 58, 63;
Father Coughlin as supporter of,
158; Göring conflicts with, 20;
Hanfstaengl firing and, 11; as
instigator of brutality, 9, 10; lavish
lifestyle of, 11; on property
confiscation laws, 20; Schacht
dispute with, 20–21; on the U.S. as
Nazi war target, 182
Goldmann, Nahum, 26, 26n32, 51,
84–85, 93–94
Goldwater, Monroe, 227–228
Göring, Hermann, 20, 143, 164, 167, 169
Gottschalk, Max, 47
Great Britain: colonization negotiations
with Germany, 63; Committee of
Five membership, 94n2; declaration
of war, 181; "enemy alien" initiatives
in, 259; fascist ideology in, 59;
Hoare-Laval agreement, 100–101;
Intergovernmental Committee
participation, 131; invasion of

Holländer, Julius, 260, 262
Holländer, Nathan, 260
Holocaust: early Swiss reports of, 298, 305; effect of Allied victories on, 322–323; first Auschwitz deportations, 295; historical views of, 329–330; "Holocaust" term, 307; internationalist vs. functionalist theories of, 333; *New York Times* articles of 1944, 321–322, 332–333; public recognition of, 307–316; Riegner telegram, 298, 298n19, 307, 313; Wannsee Conference, 84n30; wartime U.S. perception of, 292
Honduras, 139
Hoover, Herbert: on African settlements, 150; immigration policy and, 129, 157–158, 161; on the likelihood of European war, 127; opposition to Rublee proposal and, 167
Hoover, J. Edgar, 243
Hopkins, Harry, 233
Horace, Sir. *See* Rumbold, Sir Horace George Montagu
Houston, Alfred, 156n83, 277
Houstoun-Boswall, Lady, 14n49
Huddle, Jerome Klahr, 118–119
Hull, Cordell: discussion of protectorates as settlement sites, 152; Evian Conference proposal and, 122; immigration policy and, 123–124, 211–212, 225, 229–232, 231n102, 234; on the interdepartmental visa review directive, 254, 258; War Refugee Board and, 318; White House conference on refugees and, 129
Hungary, 183
Hyman, Joseph C., 22, 22n16, 103, 119, 121, 156n83

ICA. *See* Jewish Colonization Association
Ickes, Harold L.: as Alaskan initiative supporter, 181; Cleveland Zionist Society speech, 156–157, 156n85; Intergovernmental Committee Conference and, 191–192; on the invasion of Russia, 251; on Nazi war intentions, 182, 183n59; on the U.S. refugee initiative of 1938, 125–126,

125n14; wartime immigration policy and, 225–226, 234
Idelson, Vladimir Robert, 51, 51n34, 74, 78
immigration. *See* refugees—travel and immigration; United States—immigration
Inman, Samuel Guy, 34–35
intellectual/professional refugees: Biro-Bidjan (Soviet Union), 16, 24; Bohemian manufacturers' settlement, 67; Dominican Republic settlements and, 278; "eminent intellectuals" qualification, 234–235; wartime dangers to, 202, 224–225. *See also* refugees
Intergovernmental Committee on Refugees: Advisory Committee discussion of, 130–135; Bermuda Conference and, 311–312; Coordinating Foundation and, 175, 177; creation at Evian, 138; development of passport system, 142; JGM assessment of, 325; policy on wartime refugees within Germany, 188, 191; proposed U.S. withdrawal from, 195–196; Roosevelt Conference of 1939, 179, 186–188, 190–191; Rublee agreement and, 164–171; Rublee-Warburg (Max) meeting, 141–143; Spanish Civil War refugees and, 162; Wagg resignation and, 241; wartime functions of, 185, 188. *See also* Evian Conference
International Refugee Commission, 147
Iraq, 78, 156n83
Iredale, Elenora, 56, 64–65
isolationism (U.S.). *See* United States—isolationism
Israel. *See* Palestine
Israel, Wilfrid, 47–48, 47n26, 172–173
Italy: as buffer to German power, 53; Hoare-Laval agreement, 100–101; Italian loyalist immigrants in U.S., 197; League relationship with, 27–28; League reorganization report of 1935, 97; occupation of Abyssinia, 10, 37, 52–53; refugee emigration to, 62, 64, 288, 320; Tripartite Pact, 215; White House conference on refugees and, 126.

Pool, David de Sola, 109
Popkin, Louis, 103
Portugal, 148, 148n62, 206, 225, 239, 240–241, 244, 261–262, 295, 302–305, 336
Potocki, Jerzy, 134
President's Advisory Committee on Political Refugees: Bermuda Conference and, 310–311; Bolivian settlement study and, 265–266; discussion of U.S. immigration quota, 161; Dominican Republic settlements and, 277, 280–281, 284–285; enemy alien exemption memo, 293; first meeting of, 130; formation of, 3; interdepartmental visa review directive and, 243, 245, 249–259; membership, 129, 130n22; pragmatic strategy of, 337; *Quanza* incident and, 209; response to Holocaust, 309; response to Kristallnacht, 151–152; response to Long's immigration testimony, 316; Riegner telegram and, 298; State Department immigration policy and, 210–213, 215–219, 222–226, 228–232, 234–237; State Department memo, 180–181; Steinhardt cable and, 249; transportation for visa holders and, 244–245; Truman administration discontinuance of, 327; U.S. admission of refugee children and, 297–301; Wagg resignation and, 241–242; War Refugee Board and, 317–320; wartime refugee strategy of, 184–186, 201–202, 206. *See also* Roosevelt, Franklin D.
Prinz, Artur, 331–332
Proskauer, Joseph M., 170–171, 170n25, 176, 309
Prudential Insurance Company, 66
Pye, Edith M., 51, 87

quotas (immigration). *See* refugees—travel and immigration; United States—immigration

race theory of Nazis, 121, 121n1, 141, 292, 330–331. *See also* Hitler, Adolf; Nazi Regime
Raffalovich, Isiah, 76

Railroad Administration, 19
Rauschning, Hermann, 189, 189n72
Rayburn, Sam, 305–306
Razovsky, Cecilia, 124, 124n8, 195, 209
Ready, Michael J., 128–129, 132, 141, 156n83
Reconstruction Finance Corporation (U.S.), 180
Reed, Clyde M., 287–288
Refugee Economic Corporation, 61, 181
Refugee Foundation. *See* Coordinating Foundation
refugees
—financial concerns: British fundraising initiatives, 68, 75n15, 160; church support, 64–65, 83–84; Coordinating Foundation, 166, 169–177, 171n32; earmarking, 176–177; entrance taxes in settlement states, 277, 279–280; first-class shipping exception, 264; JGM Experts' Committee presentation and, 83; Nazi exploitation of emigration, 238–239; Refugee Economic Corporation, 61; resettlement services, 262–263, 281; Rublee agreement trust fund, 165, 170, 179, 183; selling of visas, 268; united Jewish plan and, 80–81, 83; U.S. proposals, 152, 154; war debt as leverage, 148–149; wartime financial concerns, 184–185
—general, 207, 304–305; Anglican Church initiative for, 56, 64–65; children of refugees, 57, 161, 201–202; children's escorts in U.S., 302; "eminent intellectuals" qualification, 234–235; "involuntary emigrants" term, 139; Jewish nationals' view of settlers, 276; as Jewish vs. general issue, 107n8, 122, 128, 149, 185; "non-Aryans" term, 134; "political refugee" term, 128, 136, 207, 224–225, 228–229, 231n102; protectorates as settlement sites, 148–150, 148n62, 152–153, 173, 188, 201–202, 335; *Quanza* incident, 208–210; rabbinical refugees, 207, 304–307, 312–313, 337; recognition of German Jewish residents as, 139; Spanish Civil War refugees, 162; status of wartime

refugees within Germany, 188, 191; wartime conditions and, 183, 190, 193, 201–202

—settlements: Africa, 132, 150; Alaska, 181, 188n69, 191–192; Angola, 148n62, 150, 160, 172, 180, 335; Argentina, 61, 63, 75, 203; Asia Minor, 138; Australia, 119; Azores, 239; Bohemia, 67; Bolivia, 264–276; Brazil, 35, 63, 76; British East Africa, 311; British Guiana, 148, 153, 168, 172–173, 173n36, 176, 181, 184, 187, 188, 335; British Honduras, 309; Cameroons, 148, 154; Caribbean protectorates, 201–202; Central America, 12; Chile, 63, 267, 271; Colombia, 34–35, 84; Cuba, 132, 175, 195, 195n4, 239, 261–263; Cyprus, 9, 9n28, 63, 65, 311; Czechoslovakia, 31, 67, 81; Dominican Republic, 139, 156n83, 172, 173n36, 181, 184, 190–191, 241–242, 276–291, 299; Dutch Guiana, 148; Ecuador, 62, 62n56; France, 41, 61, 75; French Guiana, 148, 156n83; Greece, 133; Guatemala, 61; Italy, 62, 64, 288, 320; Jamaica, 309; Latin America, 122, 133, 152, 162; Madagascar, 207–208; Mindanao, 172, 173n36; for non-Jewish refugees, 68; Northern Rhodesia, 181; Peru, 84; Philippines, 168, 172, 173n36, 181, 191; Santo Domingo, 181, 299; South Africa, 63, 67; Soviet Union, 18, 27, 90; Spain, 203; Turkey, 309; United States, 43, 119

—travel and immigration: extension of temporary U.S. visitor visas, 150–151, family connections and, 62–63; German emigration efforts, 61–62; German emigration proposal of 1936, 106–107; granting of U.S. visas, 61, 78, 110; individual discretion in awarding visas, 136, 138; League emigration support, 46n25; Nansen passports for, 41; passport renewals, 12, 33; property contingencies, 145; Rublee agreement and, 164–171; Schacht emigration plan, 21–22; substitute documentation and, 136; U.S. immigration policy and, 61, 72, 72n10, 118–119, 143–144, 161–162, 161n6

See also German Jews; intellectual/professional refugees; non-Jewish refugees; Palestine; *permits de séjour* (residency permits); *permits de travail* (work permits); Refugee Economic Corporation; United States—refugee initiatives

Reich Citizenship Law. *See* Nuremberg Laws

Reichsbank, 8–9, 63. *See also* banking

Reichsvertretung der Juden in Deutschland, 119–120, 139, 329–330

Reichswehr, 10, 12, 21, 24

retraining (of refugees), 7, 7n9

Reynolds, Robert, 118, 248–249

Rhodesia, 150

Ribbentrop, Joachim von, 11, 11n39, 12, 84n30

Riegelman, Carol, 35, 35n61

Riegner, Gerhart M., 298, 298n19, 307, 313

Robinson, Leland, 52–53, 223

Rockefeller, John D., Jr., 79, 89

Rockefeller, John D., III, 39n15, 40, 102, 214

Rockefeller Foundation, 152, 156. *See also* Fosdick, Raymond D.

Rogers, Edith Nourse, 161

Rogers, Will, Jr., 313–315

Roland-Marcel, P., 82, 92–93

Romania, 183, 218–219, 288

Roosevelt, Eleanor: Eisenhower statement on harming stateless persons and, 323–324; JGM White House dinner with, 111; ORT address, 227; *Quanza* incident and, 209; response to Wagg resignation, 242; Slattery Report and, 188, 188n69; U.S. admission of refugee children and, 297–298, 300, 305–306; wartime immigration policy and, 215–216, 221, 234, 256, 259

Roosevelt, Franklin D.: acknowledgment of impending danger to Jews, 173–174, 332; on Angola as settlement site, 160, 335; appeals to, on behalf of German Jews, 105;

Roosevelt, Franklin D. (*continued*)
approval of visa control consolidation, 245; Atlantic Charter, 253–254;
on the Azores as settlement site, 239;
Coordinating Foundation and, 178;
death of, 327; dispositional vs.
situational interpretation and, 334;
Eisenhower statement on harming
stateless persons and, 323–324;
Evian Conference proposal,
122–123; "Four Freedoms" address
(1941), 233, 254; immigration policy
(pre-war) and, 71–72, 72n10,
122–129, 129n20, 154–155;
immigration policy (wartime) and,
191–192, 203–206, 209–213,
215–232, 231n102; Intergovernmental Committee Conference proposal,
179, 186–188, 190–192; on the
invasion of Russia, 251; JGM
meetings with, 111, 127–129,
151–152, 187–188, 221–222,
255–256; on JGM position at FCC,
294; on Palestine, 118, 153; press
conferences following Kristallnacht,
146–148, 150–151; refugee initiative
of 1938, 3, 122–129, 129n20,
133–134; refugee policy of, 4–5;
Rublee agreement and, 170–172;
Herbert Samuel meeting with,
109n11, 110; Wagg resignation and,
242; War Refugee Board formation,
316. *See also* President's Advisory
Committee on Political Refugees
Roosevelt, John, 111
Rosen, Joseph A., 16n53, 156, 156n83,
286
Rosenberg, Alfred, 11, 11n40, 84
Rosenberg, James N.: aide-mémoire
supporting Rublee agreement and,
169–172; biographical sketch,
32n51; Bolivia settlements and,
272–274; Coordinating Foundation
and, 169–170, 177; Dominican
Republic settlements and, 281–286,
289; draft of final report and, 74; on
Experts' Committee funding, 32;
JGM correspondence with, 29, 77;
on non-Jewish refugees, 101;
President's Advisory Committee on
Political Refugees and, 156n83;
Temple Emanu-el address, 108–110

Rosenberg, Marcel, 89–90, 89n1, 95
Rosenblut, Martin, 85, 93
Rosenheim, Jacob, 298, 305, 306n40,
323
Rosenman, Samuel I., 169–172, 171n30
Rosenwald, Lessing, 282
Rothbarth, Margarete, 39, 41
Rothenberg, Morris, 7n14
Rothmund, Heinrich, 97, 97n5
Rothschild family, 59–60, 160
Rothschild, Amelie, 286–287
Rothschild, Anthony de, 45, 72–73, 98,
141, 172–173
Rothschild, Baron Robert de, 39, 39n10
Rothschild, James A. de, 55n40, 99,
99n8
Rothschild, Lionel de, 68, 75, 98
Rublee, George, 138, 141–143, 151–152.
See also Rublee agreement
Rublee agreement, 164–165, 166–171,
177. *See also* Rublee, George
Rumania. *See* Romania
Rumbold, Sir Horace George Montagu,
59, 59n48, 75–76, 83, 93, 94
Rummel, Joseph (archbishop of New
Orleans), 140–141, 158–159,
256–257, 295, 297
Ruppin, Arthur, 84, 84n31, 87
Russia. *See* Soviet Union

Sacher, Harry, 54, 54n37, 60–61, 67, 73
Salisbury, Lord. *See* Gascoyne-Cecil,
James E. H., Fourth Marquess of
Salisbury
Salmon, Julio, 265
Samuel, Herbert, 98, 100, 106, 109,
109n11
Samuel, Walter Horace, Second Viscount
Bearsted, 79, 79n24, 99–100,
106–107, 109, 109n11, 172–173
San Francisco Chronicle, 103
Sandler, Rickard, 13, 32
Santo Domingo, 168, 181, 299
Sargent, Sir Orme G., 63, 99
Sawyer, Olive, 23, 23n22, 116
Saxon, Jim, 319
Schacht, Hjalmar: biographical sketch,
8n26; disregard for Jewish financial
agreements, 39; emigration plan of,
21–22, 331; Königsberg speech, 10,
21, 24; opposition to Nazi radicals,
20–21; settlement negotiations of

130–132, 130n22, 135; on the
Quanza incident, 207–208; Riegner
telegram and, 298, 307, 309, 313; on
the U.S. refugee approach, 105, 124,
184–185; visa nominations by,
218–219; White House conference
on refugees and, 129n20
Wohlthat, Helmut, 164, 173, 176,
177–178
Wood, Edward Frederick, 1st Earl of
Halifax, 308
work permits. *See permits de travail* (work
permits)
World Alliance, 65, 69
World Jewish Congress, 218–219, 313,
321
World War II: Allied North Africa
campaign, 300; Atlantic Charter,
253–254; "Blitz" Nazi bombing
campaign, 208; closing of U.S. and
German consulates, 261; invasion of
Poland, 181; JGM premonitions of,
53, 330; Munich Agreement effect
on, 189; Nazi conquest of eastern
Mediterranean, 244–245; Nazi
conquest of Greece, 246; Nazi
invasion of Denmark, Norway,
Belgium, and the Netherlands, 196;

Nazi invasion of France, 150n68,
196–197; Nazi invasion of Russia,
251, 332; Nazi invasion of Vichy
France, 300–301; Nazi-Soviet Pact,
179, 201; Pearl Harbor attack, 233,
292; Soviet invasion of Estonia,
Latvia, and Lithuania, 200;
Sweetser predictions on, 127;
Tripartite Pact, 215; U.S. neutrality,
189–190, 198, 222, 233
World Zionist Organization, 6, 7
Wriggins, Howard, 303
Wurfbain, André, 27, 27n34, 68, 77, 78

Youth Aliyah, 141
Yugoslavia, 183

Zemurray, Samuel, 61, 61n53
Zionism: Coordinating Foundation and,
176–177; JGM tribute to, 326–327;
political vs. religious Zionism,
54–55, 58, 60–61; President's
Advisory Committee consideration
of Palestine and, 135. *See also* Jews;
Palestine; World Zionist Organization
Zionist Organization, 6, 7
Zionist Organization of America, 177

Richard Breitman is professor of history at American University. He is author of *The Architect of Genocide: Himmler and the Final Solution* and *Official Secrets: What the Nazis Planned, What the British and Americans Knew*, among other works. He is author (with Alan Kraut) of *American Refugee Policy and European Jewry, 1933–1945* (Indiana University Press, 1988) and editor-in-chief of the United States Holocaust Memorial Museum's journal *Holocaust and Genocide Studies*. He served as director of historical research for the Nazi War Criminal Records and Imperial Japanese Records Interagency Working Group, which helped to bring about declassification of more than eight million pages of U.S. government records.

Barbara McDonald Stewart, a daughter of James G. McDonald, received a Ph.D. in history from Columbia University and has taught at George Mason University, Pace University, and Northern Virginia Community College. She is author of *United States Government Policy on Refugees from Nazism, 1933–1940*.

Severin Hochberg teaches at George Washington University. He previously taught at Sarah Lawrence College and is a historian, formerly at the Center for Advanced Holocaust Studies of the United States Holocaust Memorial Museum, where he specialized in refugee and displaced persons issues.